Roswitha Sieper

W0045171

The Student's Companion to Britain

British History, Geography,
Life, Institutions, Arts and Thought

Max Hueber Verlag

Acknowledgements

Acknowledgement is made to the following for permission to reproduce the photographs contained in this book:
Reproduced by courtesy of the Trustees, *The National Gallery*, London: Gainsborough, Mrs. Siddons; Constable, Weymouth Bay; Reynolds, Anne, Countess of Albermarle.

The National Portrait Gallery, London: Kneller, Sir Isaac Newton; Richard II (after a portrait in Westminster Abbey); Walker, Oliver Cromwell; Hilliard, Sir Walter Raleigh; Millais, Disraeli, Earl of Beaconsfield; Millais, William Gladstone; Watts, John Stuart Mill.

By courtesy of the Trustees of *The Tate Gallery*, London: Gainsborough, The Market Cart; Rossetti, Ecce ancilla domini; Palmer, A Hilly Scene; Millais, Christ in the House of His Parents; Crome, Moonlight on the Yare; Blake, Satan Smiting Job With Sore Boils.

Mrs. Harold Gilman: Mrs. Mounter at the Breakfast Table.

Mr. Henry Moore: The Family Group.

British Features, Bonn: 12 photographs on various items.

British Travel Association, London: eight photographs on British architecture.

Mr. Eric Kay, B.A., F.R.G.S., Fareham, Hampshire: three photographs on various items.

Reproduced from "The British Isles" (Global Geographies) Pub'd. *George Philip and Son Limited*, London: reproduction of four maps.

Süddeutscher Verlag: Cover photo

6. 5. 4. | Die letzten Ziffern
2006 05 04 03 02 | bezeichnen Zahl und Jahr des Druckes.
Alle Drucke dieser Auflage können, da unverändert,
nebeneinander benutzt werden.
8. neubearbeitete Auflage 1993
© 1967 Max Hueber Verlag, D-85737 Ismaning
Druck und Bindung: Ludwig Auer GmbH, Donauwörth
Printed in Germany
ISBN 3-19-002104-X

CONTENTS

PREFACE

This book, which is intended as an aid to students of British life and institutions at universities and language schools, attempts to present in a fairly systematic form a subject, which, like the English language itself, does not readily lend itself to systematization. Brevity always involves the risk of over-simplification. The aim of the book—on the one hand to do justice to the complexity of the subject, on the other to draw the student's attention to the more essential facts—has necessitated presentation in the form of a reference book rather than a textbook: Facts are given in a clipped style, important points are spaced, titles and catchwords printed in italics.

However, this book should not go into print without the author expressing her sincere gratitude and thanks to all those who have contributed to it by means of helpful suggestions and kind assistance. To Mr. D. J. Davis, M. A., lately Principal Lecturer, Newmann College, Birmingham, who has contributed his comprehensive knowledge of political, economic, social and cultural conditions in Britain, and to Mr. James Taylor, B. A., who was helpful as an expert on politics. Thanks are also due to Mrs. Valda Sauter, who helped with her mastery of the English language and her profound knowledge of English life and institutions; to Mr. Stephen Dye, Mr. Timothy Wilson and Mrs. Michaelis, lately Lecturer at the Munich School of Languages, who assisted with their knowledge as native speakers of English; to Fräulein Erika Niggel, who typed the manuscript and in so doing did not spare the critical comment of the student who tests the value of a textbook in view of future examinations. Above all, thanks are due to my mother, who contributed her rich experience of Britain gained in many visits to her English relatives and friends, for her untiring interest in a tiring work.

For the eighth edition 1993 the whole text has been revised and brought up to date.

Munich, March 1993

Roswitha Sieper

ENGLISH HISTORY

Early English History

Invasions

Invasions were encouraged by the natural conditions of Britain: proximity to the Continent, an easily accessible coast, fertile land in the southeast, a temperate climate and mineral treasures (the name *Tin-Islands* used by the ancient Greeks probably refers to the British Isles).

A. **EARLIEST POPULATION** (Neolithic Age, Bronze Age from c. 1500 B.C.): dark Mediterranean race probably coming from Spain, therefore referred to as I b e r i a n s.

1. Settlement: The most ancient centre of settlement was the grass hills in the south of Britain, which were suitable for grazing rather than farming. The population on the hills was not subject to the dangers of primeval forests and low-lying marshy land, which was flooded by the sea at high tide.

2. Subsistence consisted of hunting, fishing in marshes, stock raising on downs, primitive arable farming on the fertile soil of the southeast in places where the land was neither marshy nor wooded.

3. Cultural achievements included pottery, weaving, metal work, flint-stone quarrying, stone-circles (p. 223): *Stonehenge,* the most ancient monument in Europe (c. 1800 B.C.), stood in the centre of the most ancient settled region, where routes along the South and North Downs and Chiltern Hills converged.

B. **CELTIC PERIOD** (Iron Age), c. 600 B.C. to 450 A.D.

I. **Celtic Immigration** took place in two waves, each wave driving earlier settlers to the western and northern highlands.

Result:

1. G o i d e l s or G a e l s (the earliest Celtic invasion c. 600 B.C.) are found in Scotland and Ireland. Scotland, first inhabited by the Picts, was later named after the Gaelic tribe of the Scots, who immigrated from Ireland from about 600 A.D. onwards.

2. B r i t o n s, arriving c. 400 B.C. and settling in England, gave the whole island the name of Britain.

The Celts mixed with the dark-complexioned native inhabitants. Their descendants surviving only in the mountains of the *Celtic Fringe* (Gaels in the Scottish Highlands, Britons in Wales and Cornwall) were until the 20th century darker than the Anglo-Saxon population in England.

II. Celtic Civilization

1. Subsistence consisted of agriculture and fishing on plains, while the settlers in the mountains and in Ireland led a nomadic life as herdsmen (cf. the great ancient Irish legend of *Cuchulain* describing a cattle war). No draining of swamps or clearing of forests.

2. Settlements were hill forts (p. 224) or small villages ('trevs') as centres of small agricultural enclosures with round earth and stone huts or pile dwellings in marshes.

3. Religious life was ruled by the priest caste, or D r u i d s , who were also the highest authority on astrology and law.

4. Political organization was in c l a n s (small tribes) headed by chieftains and petty kings. In Ireland the names of the provinces of Ulster, Leinster, Munster and Connaught go back to ancient Celtic kingdoms. In the Scottish Highlands the clan system survived until the mid-eighteenth century.

C. ROMAN OCCUPATION, 43 A.D. to c. 400 A.D.

I. Conquests

1. Invasions by C a e s a r of south Britain 55 B.C. and 54 B.C. did not lead to permanent occupation, but prepared the Romanization of Britain through closer contact with Romanized Gaul. King Cymbeline, who ruled the tribe of the Catuvellauni 5–40 A.D. and held virtual suzerainty over southeastern Britain after conquering the tribe of the Trinovantes, introduced Roman culture and called himself 'Rex Britorum'. His new capital of Colchester in the land of the Trinovantes later became a major base of Roman rule in Britain.

2. Final conquest of the southeast under Emperor Claudius, 43 A.D., was extended by successive governors to Wales and Scotland:
a) W a l e s was subdued through a battle on the Isle of Anglesey 61 A.D. where the last resistance under the Druids was broken.
b) N o r t h e r n B r i t a i n was conquered by Governor Agricola (described by his son-in-law Tacitus) through a battle in the Scottish Highlands at Mons Graupius (cf. Grampian Mountains) 83 A.D. A first line of forts between Clyde and Forth had to be given up after

repeated setbacks in the north. The Roman Wall between Solway Firth and Tyne, which Emperor Hadrian had built in 123 A.D. (Hadrian's Wall), became the final frontier against the unsubdued Picts, and the northern limit of Roman rule.

3. Rising of the Iceni under their queen B o u d i c c a 61 A.D. during the conquest of Anglesey ravaged southeastern towns, but was cruelly put down, Boudicca committing suicide.

II. **Romanization of Britain** was thorough but not lasting because, apart from Roman soldiers, officials and merchants, there was no Roman immigration.

1. Military camps (cf. place-names ending in -chester, -cester, -caster) were built and connected by paved roads, the most important of which were *Watling Street* (Dover–London–Chester), *Ermine Street* (Portsmouth–London–Lincoln–York), and Fosse Way (Devon, Lincoln).

2. Roman civilization in the southeast: The Celtic population was Romanized and ruled by British chieftains acting as Roman officials. Five major towns (York, Lincoln, Colchester, Gloucester, St. Albans) became independent municipalities. London was already an important commercial centre (harbour and junction of *Ermine* and *Watling Streets*). Towns were built on the Roman pattern with fora, temples, market-halls, shops and amphitheatres (p. 224). Bath (Aquae Sulis), where the hot springs were utilized for medicinal baths, became a fashionable Roman spa. Agriculture was promoted by draining marshland. Rural economy centred around unfortified Roman villas. Roman finds include remains of Roman walls, mosaic floors (p. 224), 'Samian pottery' (p. 237), sculptures, coins.

3. Military occupation along the R o m a n W a l l in the north and the fortified Welsh border: Three legions were stationed in York, Chester and Caerleon ('castle of the legion' in South Wales, later legendary capital of King Arthur). The frontier lines were protected chiefly by native auxiliary troops. The Celtic clan system survived.

4. Christianity was brought to England by Roman soldiers and merchants, while it was still being officially persecuted by the Roman government. The first British martyr, S t. A l b a n , was put to death c. 303 in the town that bears his name.

5. Withdrawal of the Roman legions from c. 400 onwards became necessary when Germanic tribes invaded Italy. The Romans left Britain after having established a defence system against early Saxon raids along the east and south coast from the Wash to the Isle of Wight *(litus Saxonicus)*.

6. Result of the Roman occupation: In contrast to Gaul and Spain, Britain did not become a Latin country, the Roman culture being completely destroyed by later Teutonic invaders. But the Roman influence was, while it lasted, considerable, and survived in W e l s h C h r i s t i a n i t y. Ireland, which was introduced to Christianity by a Welshman, St. Patrick, in the 5th century, became a main influence in missionizing central Europe.

D. ANGLO-SAXON PERIOD c. 450–1066 A.D.

I. Anglo-Saxon Invasions (most important event in early English history).

1. ANGLO-SAXONS came from the Continent: A n g l e s from north of the Eider (Schleswig), S a x o n s * from northwest Germany, J u t e s came from Jutland or the Rhine. They were probably called over by the Britons to help them against invasions of Picts from Scotland and Scots from Ireland. However, the story of Hengist and Horsa, who are said to have sought the protection of the British king Vortigern as exiles and to have conquered the Britons after having called in large bodies of their countrymen, is chiefly legend: no historical documents of this period exist.

2. BRITONS withdrew to W a l e s ('Welsh' is a Germanic word also on the Continent, for foreign neighbours), C o r n w a l l ('Wales' inhabited by Cornish tribes), and 'B r i t t a n y' in France. The Celts' short and futile struggle against new invaders is immortalized in the legend of the Celtic hero King Arthur (presumably a historical figure), which originated in these three regions.

3. HEPTARCHY developed from seven Anglo-Saxon kingdoms, which soon began to be loosely connected by a common overlord, *Bretwalda* ('ruler of Britain'): Jutes in K e n t and the Isle of Wight, Saxons in S u s s e x, E s s e x, W e s s e x, Angles in E a s t A n g l i a (comprising the earlier divisions of Suffolk and Norfolk), M e r c i a and N o r t h u m b r i a.* Angles gave the land and language their name owing to their numerical and early literary predominance.

4. Crystallizing of three major kingdoms:
a) N o r t h u m b r i a stretching from the Humber to the northern limit of Germanic settlement, the Scottish Lowlands, comprised the two earlier kingdoms of Deira between Humber and Tyne, and Bernicia between Tyne and Forth. Under its powerful king Edwin, the probable founder of Edinburgh, Northumbria held political and

---

* The local distinction between Angles and Saxons in Britain derives from Bede's *Ecclesiastical History of England* and is doubted by some modern historians who believe that the Anglo-Saxons were one people.

cultural predominance in the 7th century. (Edwin was *Bretwalda* and introduced Christianity into Northumbria). The western highlands in Galloway and Cumbria (Strathclyde) remained Celtic.

b) M e r c i a , as 'mark'land bordering on Wales the most war-like kingdom, predominated in the 8th century by expansion to the north and east. King Penda (still a heathen) defeated and slew King Edwin in 633 and his successor Oswald in 642. The Mercian power reached its peak under King Offa (757–796), who achieved virtual over-lordship over the whole of England. Offa built ˙*Offa's Dyke*, the greatest earthwork in early English history, as a boundary against Wales.

c) W e s s e x , resisting conquest by Mercia, predominated from the 9th century onwards. King Egbert achieved a first union of England by annexing the southern kingdoms, by agreements with East Anglia and Northumbria, and by defeating Mercia in the battle of Ellan-dune, 825.

II. **Scandinavian and Danish Invasions** during the 9th c. via two routes:

1. V i k i n g s from Norway sailed via the Orkneys to the west of Scotland and Ireland. They were the first Germanic tribes to settle in southwest Scotland, Cumbria and Westmorland, where many Scandinavian place-names are found. They occupied the Isle of Man and Ireland where they founded Dublin and Waterford, but were finally defeated by the Irish in the battle of Clontarf, 1014.

2. D a n e s , using the eastern route, invaded east England from Thames to Tyne, looting coastal settlements and devastating the country. East Anglia, southern Northumbria and east Mercia were subdued, Wessex attacked. Finally defeated by Alfred, King of Wessex, the Danes became Christians according to the *Treaty of Wedmore*, 878.

They were confined to the Midland area north of Watling Street, henceforth called D a n e l a w , where they settled. In contrast to the Anglo-Saxons, they rebuilt Roman towns, e.g. Lincoln, Chester, Leicester (strong trading instinct of Vikings!) and administered the country from urban centres (in the area of the Danelaw counties are usually called after towns, e.g. Nottinghamshire, Leicestershire, Lincolnshire, while southern counties are called after tribes, e.g. Sussex or Dorsetshire after the Celtic Durotriges).

III. **Union of England Under the Kings of Wessex:**

1. A l f r e d t h e G r e a t , 849–900, equally remarkable as warrior, statesman, scholar and promoter of culture, saved England from complete subjection by the Danes. Driven into the swamps of Somerset, he gathered an army and defeated the Danes in the battle

13

of Ethandune (878). To protect the country from further invasions, he built a navy and forts with standing garrisons. Alfred established a court school for the sons of his nobles, and founded English prose literature through translations of Latin works. He encouraged scholars and craftsmen from other countries to come to Wessex, and issued a body of laws. His capital, Winchester (in legend also associated with *King Arthur's Round Table*), became England's cultural centre.

2. E d w a r d   t h e   E l d e r , Alfred's son, 900–924, united England through the annexation of the Danelaw. His son

3. A t h e l s t a n , 924–940, a shrewd statesman and administrator, first gained the overlordship over the whole of Britain, annexing Cornwall and receiving homage from the Welsh and Scottish kings. He defeated an allied Scandinavian-Scottish army under the kings of Ireland and Scotland in the battle of Brumanburh 937 (one of the few historical events surviving in early English poetry). He issued a body of laws and charters, which suggest that an efficient administration had already developed.

IV. Anglo-Saxon Civilization

1. Rural civilization, superior to that of the Celts, developed after the annihilation of Romano-Celtic urban culture (cf. Old English elegy on the ruins of Bath). Swamps were cultivated, forests cleared. Large villages, partly with well-built log-houses, and an open-field system with crop rotation (p. 134) replaced the primitive Celtic agriculture in enclosed trevs (small settlements).

2. CHRISTIANITY was introduced early in the 7th century:
a) R o m a n   m i s s i o n : The Roman monk Augustinus began to missionize in Kent (597), Paulinus in Northumbria (627), Canterbury and York later becoming archbishoprics.
b) I r i s h   m i s s i o n : After repercussions due to the military predominance of pagan Mercia, Northumbria was re-Christianized from the Irish monastery on the island of Iona (563) through the Scottish monk Aidan, who founded the monastery of Lindisfarne ('Holy Island').
c) S y n o d   o f   W h i t b y   (664) summoned by the Northumbrian king Oswy decided in favour of the Church of Rome.
d) The English church was organized into archbishoprics, bishoprics and county parishes by the Greek Archbishop of Canterbury T h e o d o r e   o f   T a r s u s   (669–690). Through land grants and bequests, the Church soon became a great feudal power and played an important part in administration and jurisdiction, family law and the administration of ordeals being its main provinces.

e) Christian culture: Since only the clergy were able to write, the Church became the main instrument of education and culture. Monasteries became centres of art, literature and scholarship, esp. N o r t h u m b r i a n m o n a s t e r i e s in the 7th c. The first English poem, Caedmon's hymn in praise of the Creator was written at Whitby. The V e n e r a b l e B e d e wrote his *Ecclesiastical History of England* in the monastery of Jarrow. In the 10th c. the centre of Christian culture shifted to W e s s e x , where the reform of Cluny was introduced by Dunstan, abbot of Glastonbury.

3. SOCIAL STRUCTURE: Community life in early Anglo-Saxon England was based on kinship (implying mutual responsibility before the law and duty of vengeance when a kinsman was slain), and on personal (not tribal) allegiance to a lord (from 'hlaford' = bread giver). This relationship together with land grants to the lord's followers (later also to the Church) led to feudalism: While the land-owning classes increasingly took over military, administrative and judicial functions, the peasant class was bound to feudal service on the lord's land in return for military protection. Peasants lost their freedom; the lord replaced the kindred as the peasant's legal representative. The population was divided into three main classes (legally distinguished by their wergild, i.e. the amount to be paid for having slain one of their members):
a) Landed aristocracy consisted of a t h e l i n g s (to which members of the royal family belonged), e a l d o r m e n (from the 11th c., under Scandinavian influence called e a r l s) and, later, t h a n e s (originally name for personal dependents of the king).
b) Peasants (c e o r l s) were originally freemen owning their land and not bound to the soil. Later in various grades of dependence, they were distinguished by different names: geneatas, gebur, cotsetlan (cottage-dweller). The Danelaw had the largest number of free peasants.
c) Slaves were penal slaves, prisoners of war, or people who had become unfree because of debt. They were chattels, not entitled to wergild; their offspring was also unfree.

4. GOVERNMENT was still largely decentralized owing to difficulties of communication. Earls, who ruled shires, had large powers (cf. German dukes).
a) Central government: The h e r e d i t a r y k i n g was chosen from the royal family by the Witan ('wise men'). He sometimes ruled with a number of underkings, who were usually his younger brothers. He was advised on legislation, land grants and matters of policy by the W i t a n , which consisted of bishops, ealdormen, royal officials, the more important abbots and king's thanes. The Witan met at

15

irregular intervals at the Witenagemot ('the wise men's meeting'), which took place at high festivals (Christmas, Easter).

b) Local government: Ealdormen ruled shires and led their forces in war. When ealdormen began to rule several shires, shire reeves (later 'sheriffs') ruled the single shires. Shire reeves were always appointed by the king, while the ealdorman's office became hereditary. Towns were in charge of wic or port reeves. As the king's representatives these officials collected the fines due to the king.

5. LAW was administered in f o l k m o o t s (meetings) in the open, which consisted of freemen and were presided over by thanes (ealdormen, reeves, local gentry). Later, courts were called after administrative divisions, the shire moot meeting twice a year, hundred moots (in the Danish north 'wapentakes') every month, borough moots in towns three times a year.

In lawsuits the accused was (in lieu of evidence) allowed to prove his innocence by an oath with the aid of compurgators. If he failed to find such oath-helpers, he had to undergo the ordeal. Practices of redress changed in course of time, the blood feud being replaced by wergild paid to the kindred of the man slain. As feudalism took the place of tribal organization and kinship as legal basis, the popular courts were gradually replaced by patrimonial courts.

V. England Under Cnut, 1016–35

The reign of the weak king Ethelred the Unready (978–1016) saw new Danish invasions. The Danegeld, an exorbitant tax paid to ward off further ravages, speeded the servitude of the peasantry. Finally the country was conquered by King Swen Forkbeard while Ethelred fled his kingdom. After Swen's death, his son Cnut, after a short struggle with Ethelred's son Edmund Ironside, became king.

Though England now formed part of a vast dominion including Denmark with overlordship over the Baltic countries and Norway, England, with Winchester as capital, remained the centre of administration. Cnut pursued a wise policy of peace and reconciliation and was a liberal patron of the Saxon Church, whose cultural importance he recognized. He issued a code of Anglo-Saxon laws and a first charter of liberties, which made him highly esteemed by his English subjects.

VI. E d w a r d t h e C o n f e s s o r, 1042–66

Edward, son of Ethelred, was recalled after the death of Cnut's son. A pious man who lived an ascetic life, he was later canonized. He built Westminster Abbey and moved the court from Winchester to Westminster, where it has remained ever since. The son of a Norman princess, who had spent his youth as an exile in Normandy, and a weak ruler, he was strongly influenced by Normans. He appointed Normans to important positions and exiled the powerful Earl of Wessex, Godwin, and his son Harold, who, however, soon regained power when their earldom rose to support them. When Edward died, 1066, leaving no heir, H a r o l d was crowned king. His election by the Witan, however, was contested by William, Duke of Normandy, who claimed succession on grounds of relationship and promise of the crown by Edward. Moreover, Harold had sworn the oath of allegiance to William during his exile in Normandy, renouncing the English succession.

E. NORMAN PERIOD, 1066–1154

W i l l i a m   t h e   C o n q u e r o r, 1066–87, an able statesman, efficient and ruthless.

1. B a t t l e   o f   H a s t i n g s : Sailing from Normandy, where Vikings (called Normans) had settled in 912, William conquered England by his victory at Hastings. The Saxons, exhausted from a battle against new Danish invaders in the north (battle of Stamford Bridge), were defeated, owing to the superiority of Norman chivalric tactics: The Norman archery charging from a distance, and the quickly-moving cavalry armed with spears and swords were superior to the Saxon warriors fighting on foot and armed only with battle-axes. Harold and most of his followers were slain. William was crowned King of England in Westminster Abbey (the famous *Bayeux Tapestry* in Normandy shows the complete history of the conquest).

2. A punitive expedition to the rebellious north led to the complete devastation of the north of England, which did not recover its importance until the Industrial Revolution (18th c.).

3. William strengthened his military power by building fortifications (Durham, York, Tower of London) and establishing military lordships along the Scottish and Welsh frontiers (Durham, Chester, Shrewsbury).

4. The land of hostile Saxons was granted to Normans, who built strong castles, from which they oppressed the subdued Saxons.

5. Establishment of a strong monarchy through c e n t r a l i z a t i o n   o f   t h e   g o v e r n m e n t.
a) The newly established Royal Council (C u r i a   R e g i s) was more dependent on the king than the Saxon Witan had been.
b) The six large earldoms were broken up. Wessex, Mercia, Northumbria disappeared. New land grants to individual Norman barons were scattered over the country to prevent an accumulation of power through consolidated landed property. The hereditary office

17

of the earl was abolished, the sheriff, who was appointed and could be discharged, becoming the chief county official.

c) The land was registered for taxing purposes in the *Domesday Book*, 1086 (one of the most important historical and topographical documents in medieval history).

d) Forests (one third of the entire land) became royal preserves, for which special courts were established to punish poaching. Saxon opposition to the cruel punishments (mutilation, death) later found expression in the legend of Robin Hood (p. 216).

e) The King demanded the oath of allegiance even of minor vassals to prevent their allegiance to their immediate feudal lords being used against him.

6. Results of Norman conquest:

a) Anglo-Saxon culture and literature were destroyed through adoption of the F r e n c h   l a n g u a g e in leading circles. The English language, however, finally prevailed, enriched by French terms chiefly pertaining to political and cultural life.

b) Division of the nation into privileged Normans and suppressed Saxons caused bitterness and hatred.

c) F r e n c h   c h i v a l r i c   f e u d a l i s m led to clearer class divisions: namely tenants-in-chief (barons), knights, as an intermediate class of subtenants receiving fiefs for the newly introduced equestrian military service, serfs (villeins) including the former peasants (ceorls) and slaves (p. 15).

d) Connection with France (Normandy now being ruled by England) brought political disadvantages (neglect of England through frequent absence of the king), but an immense enrichment of literature and art: Most of the principal English cathedrals were built in the Norman style within 30 years after the conquest.

W i l l i a m I I (Rufus), 1087–1100

Despotic and grasping, William precipitated a conflict with A n s e l m , Archbishop of Canterbury (greatest representative of early Scholasticism) concerning ecclesiastical appointments. William refused to fill vacant ecclesiastical offices in order to collect their incomes.

H e n r y I , 1100–35

Henry won the respect of his subjects through his rigorous justice (hence Lion of Justice) and his wide learning (hence the nickname Beauclerc). He was capable and shrewd.

1. Henry strengthened his position by seeking popularity among his English subjects:

a) He took as wife a descendant of the ancient line of Saxon kings.

b) He issued a charter of liberties, *Carta Libertatum*, 1110, based on the law of King Edward the Confessor, to be read in every shire court.

2. Henry restored order in the Church by recalling Anselm from his exile in Rome. A new conflict, however, arose over the i n v e s t i t u r e o f b i s h o p s by the king, which was now forbidden by the Pope. The *Treaty of Bec* (1106) provided a compromise (cf. *Wormser Konkordat* in Germany, 1122): The King renounced the investiture of bishops with ring and staff (in future to be conveyed by the Church authorities), but retained the right of homage before consecration. The right of nomination virtually remained in the King's hands, his nominee being normally elected by the cathedral chapter.

3. Henry reduced the baronial power by suppressing rebellions and further strengthening the central administration through royal officials and permanent courts:
a) Chief ministerial offices were the justiciar, the King's main representative and regent during his absence, the chancellor, who attended to the government's written work (records, charters, grants) and had charge of the King's seal, and the treasurer, who was responsible for financial matters.
b) C o u r t o f E x c h e q u e r (meeting round a table resembling a checkerboard for counting purposes) received payments from sheriffs and nobles and settled financial disputes.
c) Curia Regis now became a regular meeting of ministers apart from the barons' council, to carry out the King's business, local suits being decided, if necessary, by sending judges on circuit.

S t e p h e n o f B l o i s , 1135–54

As Henry's nephew and nearest male heir, Stephen was chosen and immediately crowned by the people of London and acknowledged by the Pope. The claims of Henry's daughter Matilda (Maud) to the throne led to c i v i l w a r and anarchy lasting fifteen years. The *Treaty of Wallingford*, 1153, between the contending parties, provided for the succession of Matilda's son Henry after Stephen's death.

Later Middle Ages

A. **PLANTAGENETS**, so called after their badge, a sprig of planta genista, ruled from 1154 to 1399.

H e n r y I I , 1154–89

Henry was one of the greatest English kings. Though passionate and undisciplined, he possessed determination and a genius for organization and statesmanship. The son of Geoffrey Plantagenet, Count of Anjou, Henry founded the dynasty of the Plantagenets (sometimes called Angevin kings). He united England with large possessions in France (one half of the country): from his mother (Normandy with overlordship over Brittany), from his father (Anjou, Maine, Touraine), and from his wife Eleanor of Aquitaine (Guienne, Gasconne, Poitou).

1. Henry restored peace by re-establishing a highly competent government, and freed England from feudal strife (disastrous on the Continent) by putting down baronial rebellions. Castles, now largely dismantled, began to be replaced by unfortified manor houses, feudal armies by a compulsory militia of all freemen and mercenary forces paid from the scutage (new tax levied upon barons in lieu of military service).

2. Henry and the Church:

   a) *Constitutions of Clarendon* attempted to restrict clerical jurisdiction by bringing more ecclesiastical cases before the King's courts. Delinquent clerics, tried and found guilty by ecclesiastical courts, were to be sentenced and punished by secular authorities.

   b) T h o m a s à B e c k e t : The restriction of clerical influence met with opposition from Thomas à Becket, who had been Henry's trusted friend and Chancellor until the King made him Archbishop of Canterbury. In the long ensuing struggle Thomas was finally murdered by the King's friends at the altar steps of Canterbury Cathedral and was later venerated as a martyr and saint, the King himself repenting barefoot at his grave. The reaction to Becket's murder strengthened the Church: The clergy gained new immunities, the Pope's influence on ecclesiastical jurisdiction increased.

3. C o n q u e s t o f I r e l a n d , 1170, authorized by the Papal *Bull Laudabiliter* was effected by Welsh feudal lords under Fitzgilbert, Earl of Pembroke ('Strongbow'). The kingdom of Dublin was annexed to the Crown and opened to settlement by the 'men of Bristol'. From this time this area, called the Pale, was strongly anglicized.

4. Uniform jurisdiction through royal courts and royal judges on circuit (Justices of Assize) developed the E n g l i's h C o m m o n L a w , today the legal basis of all English-speaking countries. Even civil suits came increasingly under royal jurisdiction, particularly where land tenure was concerned. This strengthened the royal authority as against feudal and clerical privileges. Henry established the j u r y s y s t e m : The accusation, which was formerly left to a private plaintiff, was made a public duty falling to twelve sworn men of each hundred—the jury of accusation (later called grand jury)—while the trial (petit) jury acted as witnesses as well as judges.

5. Repeated rebellions of Henry's sons, Richard and John, who were supported by the kings of France and Scotland, were put down, but darkened the closing years of the King's reign.

R i c h a r d I, 'the Lionhearted', 1189–99

Richard, one of the most chivalrous and popular English kings, spent most of his reign abroad: He took part in the T h i r d C r u s a d e (storming of Acre and siege of Jerusalem) and, en route to England, was shipwrecked near Aquileja and captured by his personal enemy, the Duke of Austria. He was held prisoner in Austria (Dürnstein) and Germany (Trifels). Finally released upon payment of a heavy ransom, he returned home, but soon left England again and was killed in a private feud.

J o h n, called L a c k l a n d, 1199–1216

John was one of the most unpopular English kings. Intriguing and cruel, he was soon hated as a tyrant and despised for his cowardice and sloth.

1. Loss of French possessions: After a conflict between John and his nephew Arthur of Brittany, which ended with Arthur's capture and murder, John lost his possessions in France. A later attempt to recapture them through an alliance with the Emperor Otto IV against the French King failed, John's and Otto's armies being defeated in the battle of Bouvines.

2. *M a g n a C a r t a*, 1215, basis of English liberty:
   a) Conflict with the Church: Since John refused to appoint to the Archbishopric of Canterbury the Pope's candidate Stephen Langton, the Pope laid an interdict on England. Only when France, at his instigation, threatened invasion, did John surrender. He paid tribute to the Pope, acknowledging him as feudal overlord.
   b) B a r o n s' C o n s p i r a c y: Supported by the clergy and merchants, who were equally embittered by John's misrule and dependence on the Pope, the barons tried in vain to force a charter on the King. When the Londoners opened their gates to the barons' army, John yielded and met the barons at Runnymede.
   c) Chief provisions of the charter:
   no taxation without consent of the Common Council (Parliament);
   no man may be imprisoned without fair trial by his equals;
   free election of bishops and abbots by the English clergy;
   the King subjected to the control of a council of 25 barons.

H e n r y I I I, 1216–72

1. B a r o n s' W a r:
   a) Henry's dependence on foreign influence and subservience to the Pope (appointment of Italians to ecclesiastical offices) resulted in

strong baronial opposition. This was aggravated by a papal bull, which absolved Henry from observing the *Provisions of Oxford,* 1258, which subjected the King to control of the barons.

b) The war was waged chiefly between Edward, the heir apparent, and the barons' leader S i m o n   d e   M o n t f o r t, who, himself a Frenchman, had inherited the title of Earl of Leicester. Defeated and captured in the battle of Lewes, 1264, Edward escaped and destroyed the baronial army in the battle of Evesham, 1265, in which Simon was killed. After the *Settlement of Kenilworth* Edward fully re-established the royal power.

2. Simon de Monfort's importance for the development of Parliament: for the Parliament of 1265 he summoned for the first time t w o b u r g h e r s   f r o m   e a c h   b o r o u g h, together with t w o k n i g h t s . f r o m   e a c h   s h i r e.

E d w a r d I, 1272–1307

Edward was the most successful king of medieval English history, strong-willed, popular because of his chivalry and military strength (participation in the Seventh Crusade). On account of his legislative genius he was called the English Justinian. He was the first king with purely British interests (annexation of Wales and Scotland).

1. Edward's M o d e l   P a r l i a m e n t, 1295, established permanently the representative system in the Great Council by admitting representatives of the commonalty (two knights elected from each shire and two burghers from each borough) to vote on taxation.

2. S t a t u t e   L a w (written laws adopted with the consent of Parliament) began to supersede royal instructions and the Common Law established by custom:
   a) *Quo Warranto,* 1290, withdrew special privileges from feudal lords unless confirmed by royal grant and long usage.
   b) *Quia Emptores* prohibited subinfeudation (granting away of land legally belonging to the feudal lord).
   c) *Statute of Mortmain* prohibited land-grants to the Church without financial compensation to the Crown.

3. Jurisdiction began to be divided from administration through the establishment of separate courts: Common Pleas for civil suits and King's Bench chiefly for criminal cases, both in Westminster Hall.

4. C o n q u e s t o f W a l e s, 1276–82:
   a) Before Edward, lords marcher (Anglo-Norman barons along the Welsh border endowed with special military rights for defence) made private expeditions across the border, building castles and establishing English feudalism in the eastern border country.

b) Edward conquered the pastoral population in the western part through an expedition against the Welsh prince Llewellyn, who, as a former ally of Simon de Montfort, had refused to pay homage to the King. After Llewellyn's defeat and death, Edward annexed his land as a separate principality to be ruled by his son Edward as 'Prince of Wales' (which became the permanent title of the heir-apparent even after the full union of Wales with England). Edward built strong castles (Conway, Caernavon, Harlech) to protect new towns built as centres of English trade and influence.

5. **Scotland in the Middle Ages:**
   a) After the decay of the Northumbrian kingdom 884, Picts and Scots were united under Scottish kings ruling in Scone and crowned on the Coronation *Stone of Scone.*
   b) First Anglo-Saxon influence under M a l c o l m I I I , who, on usurpation of the crown by M a c b e t h , lived as an exile at Edward the Confessor's court and married a Saxon princess. After regaining the Scottish crown through the defeat of Macbeth, Malcolm was slain in a battle against William Rufus in 1093.
   c) Under Malcolm's son David I, Anglo-Norman families such as the Baliols and the Bruces settled in Scotland.
   d) E n g l i s h i n v a s i o n under Edward I: In a Scottish succession dispute Edward intervened in favour of J o h n B a l i o l against the Bruces. On refusing to submit to Edward's overlordship Baliol was attacked and defeated by Edward at Dunbar, deposed and banished. Scotland was ruled by English officials, the Scottish crown and the Coronation Stone of Scone were taken to England, where the Stone of Scone was placed under the Coronation Throne in Westminster Abbey.
   e) N a t i o n a l r e s i s t a n c e aroused by the great patriot and daring warrior W i l l i a m W a l l a c e was broken when Wallace, after initial successes, was defeated at Falkirk and later captured and executed on Tower Hill (1305), living on as a national hero in Scottish legends (cf. Walter Scott's *Tales of a Grandfather*).
   f) R o b e r t B r u c e declared himself Scottish King in 1306 and, after Edward's death, gradually drove the English from most positions in Scotland. The devastating border-warfare, however, continued for centuries, destroying settlements and monasteries in the Scottish Uplands.

E d w a r d I I , 1307–27

Weak and incompetent, Edward was dominated by unworthy favourites.

1. Loss of Scotland through Bruce's victory at Bannockburn. Scots even invaded northern England.

23

2. A rising of discontented nobles, who were jealous of Edward's favourites, was led by Queen Isabella and her favourite Mortimer. Edward was deposed, imprisoned and murdered (cf. dramas *Edward II* by Christopher Marlowe and Bert Brecht).

Edward III, 1327–77

While Edward was a minor, his mother ruled as regent. The real power however, rested with Mortimer, who, three years later, was executed by the young king. Edward III was highly popular because of his national and chivalric tendencies (foundation of the Order of the Garter).

1. Outbreak of the H u n d r e d Y e a r s ' W a r , 1337: After the death of the last Capetian king in France, Charles IV (Edward's brother-in-law), Edward wished to assert English rights of succession and to secure the English wool trade with Flanders, which was endangered by the growing French nationalism. The English fleet defeated the French fleet at Sluys, while the army, landing in Normandy, defeated the French at C r é c y . The English victory demonstrated the superiority of the English archers, fighting with dismounted knights, over the French feudal cavalry. C a l a i s was captured after a long siege. Six burghers, who, in order to save their town, surrendered as hostages to be hanged, were pardoned.
   Edward's chivalrous eldest son, the Black Prince, won a brilliant victory in a battle at P o i t i e r s , in which the French king John II was captured. While John, as a captive, was receiving chivalric honours in England, southern France was devastated by raids of the Black Prince. In the Peace of Bretigny, 1360, Edward renounced succession but retained Calais and southern France from the Loire to the Pyrenees as the independent Dukedom of Aquitaine.

2. *Statute of Provisors* restricted papal influence on ecclesiastical appointments ('provisions').
   Statute of Praemunire restricted papal jurisdiction by prohibiting appeals to the papal court.

3. Development of self-government in shires through voluntary, unpaid, non-professional j u s t i c e s o f t h e p e a c e (J.P.s).

4. The English language was from now on used in courts and Parliament and studied in grammar schools instead of French.

5. The p l a g u e 1348–49 reduced the English population by one half, causing important social changes particularly in the working conditions of the rural population. The depopulation of the country forced landlords to give up tillage and to resort to highly unpopular e n c l o s u r e s of common land for sheep-raising.

6. Development of Parliament: Excessive taxation during the French war enhanced the importance of knights and burgesses, who began to meet separately for financial debates before voting taxes. This led to the division of the Great Council into the House of Lords (personally summoned barons and bishops) and the House of Commons (elected representatives of counties and boroughs). The two-chamber system, and the predominance of the Lower House, where the bourgeois element was strengthened through the landed gentry, have since constituted the two principal features of the English Parliament.

5. During the last years of Edward's reign, the government lay chiefly in the hands of his son John of Gaunt, who founded the House of Lancaster and continued the wasteful raids in France.

Richard II, 1377–99

The son of the Black Prince who had died before Edward III, Richard succeeded to the throne at the age of ten. Personally weak and inefficient, he remained a victim of intrigues and the influence which powerful subjects had exercised on him while he was a minor.

1. Peasants' Revolt, 1381: The decrease in population through the plague 1348–49 created a great demand for labour and thus a rise in wages, which the government under Edward III had tried to keep at pre-plague level by the *Statute of Labourers*. This and a poll tax caused discontent among peasants, increased by the agitation of the poorer clergy, especially the itinerant preacher John Ball. Under leadership of Wat Tyler and John Ball, thousands of insurgents marched to London to present their demands to the King. During riots in the city, the Archbishop of Canterbury, Sudbury, was executed, foreigners were killed. After the King had induced the rebels to leave the city by making promises, he met Wat Tyler before the city walls. Tyler was killed by the King's followers. Thereupon the revolt was put down, the leaders were executed and all relief hitherto granted was cancelled. Nevertheless serfdom came gradually to be replaced by free tenancies.

2. John Wycliffe, Master of Balliol College at Oxford and a powerful preacher, was the first religious reformer in Europe. He influenced Huss. He assailed the practices and doctrines of the Church, disputed the authority of the Pope and clergy, advocated a humble Christian life, and the English vernacular for divine service and prayers (first translation of the Bible). Censured by Rome, Wycliffe was protected by the University against the Church authorities. Finally forbidden to teach at Oxford, he withdrew to

his rectory of Lutterworth, where he died unmolested. Under a decree of the Council of Constance, his bones were exhumed and burned (1428).

3. King Richard, unpopular because of illegal taxation and attacks against nobles, was deposed by Act of Parliament at the instigation of his cousin Henry Bolingbroke of Lancaster (son of John of Gaunt), whom Richard had exiled and who returned to England with a military force to claim the crown.

B. HOUSE OF LANCASTER, 1399–1461

Henry IV, 1399–1413

1. Conspiracies of Welsh and Northumbrian nobles were vigorously crushed:
a) Henry Percy ('Harry Hotspur') and his father, the Earl of Northumberland, were slain in battle.
b) Welsh national rising under the Welsh chieftain Owen Glendower, inspired by Welsh bards, was put down by the King's eldest son Henry.

2. Cruel persecution of Lollards, Wycliffe's adherents: Under a statute against heretics, recusants were burned and hanged.

Henry V, 1413–22

As prince, Henry was in frequent conflict with his father owing to his dissolute habits and preference for low company (cf. Shakespeare, *Henry IV*). As King, he was strong, efficient, and highly popular because of his interest in art and sports. A brilliant military leader who had crushed a Welsh rising at sixteen, he revived enthusiasm for the French war.

1. Henry renewed the H u n d r e d Y e a r s ' W a r through a brilliant victory at A g i n c o u r t (1415) against fivefold odds, and conquered Normandy.

2. *Treaty of Troyes* provided for Henry's marriage with the French princess Catherine and succession to the French throne (cf. Shakespeare, *Henry V*). The early death of Henry two years after his marriage, however, thwarted the English claims.

3. Vigorous action against an attempted Lollard rising finally crushed Lollardism, which became an obscure sect.

Henry VI, 1422–61

Henry succeeded to the throne while an infant. Weak and later temporarily insane, he fell a victim to the contests of ambitious nobles.

Genealogical Table of the Houses of Lancaster, York and Tudor

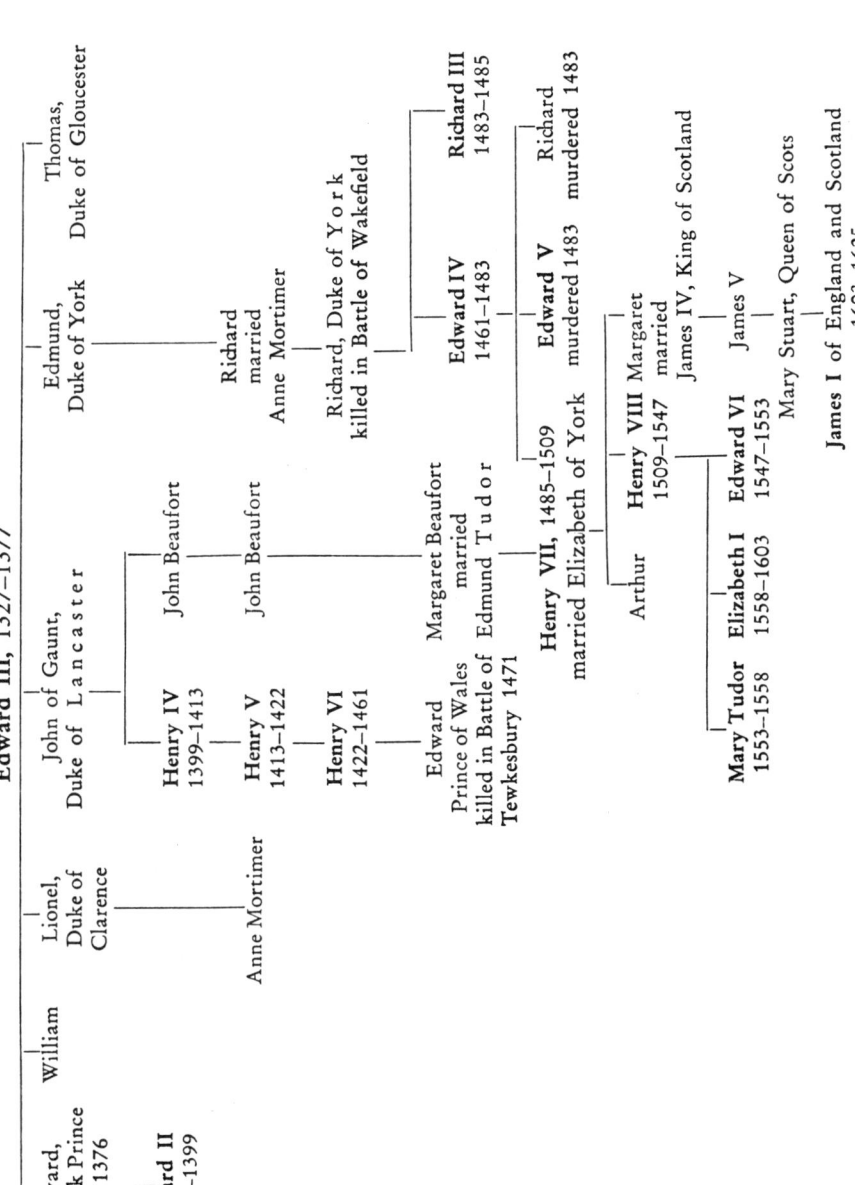

Edward III, 1327–1377

Edward, the Black Prince died 1376

William

Lionel, Duke of Clarence

John of Gaunt, Duke of Lancaster

Edmund, Duke of York

Thomas, Duke of Gloucester

Richard II 1377–1399

Anne Mortimer

John Beaufort

John Beaufort

Richard married Anne Mortimer

Henry IV 1399–1413

Henry V 1413–1422

Henry VI 1422–1461

Margaret Beaufort married Edmund Tudor

Richard, Duke of York killed in Battle of Wakefield

Edward Prince of Wales killed in Battle of Tewkesbury 1471

Henry VII, 1485–1509 married Elizabeth of York

Edward IV 1461–1483

Richard III 1483–1485

Edward V murdered 1483

Richard murdered 1483

Arthur

Henry VIII 1509–1547

Margaret married James IV, King of Scotland

Mary Tudor 1553–1558

Elizabeth I 1558–1603

Edward VI 1547–1553

James V

Mary Stuart, Queen of Scots

James I of England and Scotland 1603–1625

1. Loss of French conquests after the intervention of Jeanne d'Arc, who strengthened the French resistance by raising the siege of Orleans and conducting the Dauphin to Reims to be crowned King of France. Supported by England's former ally, the Duke of Burgundy, Charles VII drove the English from Paris, and in later fights from Gascony, Maine and Normandy.

2. **Wars of the Roses, 1455–85** between Houses of Lancaster (descended from the fourth son of Edward III) and York (descended from the third and fifth sons of Edward III): The Yorkist family emblem of the white rose induced the Lancastrians to adopt a red rose as the badge of their cause. The war, which plays a part in some of Shakespeare's plays, marked the climax of lawlessness and violence to which the English nobility had become used during the French wars. While the Lancastrian side was led by Henry's wife Margaret, the Yorkist leaders were Richard of York, and his son Edward, aided by the powerful Earl of Warwick:
   a) Brilliant Yorkist victory over the King's army at Northampton.
   b) In the battle of Wakefield, Richard of York was defeated and slain by Margaret's army.

C. HOUSE OF YORK, 1461–85

E d w a r d I V, 1461–83

The son of Richard of York, able and highly popular, Edward was proclaimed King by the Yorkists on the death of his father.

1. Continuation of Wars of the Roses:
   a) Edward defeated Margaret's army in the murderous battle at Towton, where most Lancastrians were slain. The royal family fled to Scotland where the King was captured, while Margaret escaped to France.
   b) Conflict between Edward and Warwick, 'the King Maker', whose power Edward began to fear, led to the last temporary victory of the Lancastrian cause. Warwick gathered an army with Margaret, forced Edward to flee, and restored Henry to power.
   c) Edward returned to England, recaptured Henry, slew Warwick at Barnet and crushed Margaret's army at Tewkesbury, where her son was slain and Margaret herself captured. Henry VI is said to have been murdered in the Tower.

2. The royal power was strengthened through the confiscation of estates of extinct noble families and 'benevolences' (loans forced from the merchant classes).

E d w a r d V , who succeeded his father in 1483 at twelve, was murdered
with his brother Richard in the Tower. His death is generally attributed to
his uncle and ruling protector, Richard of Gloucester, who succeeded as

R i c h a r d I I I , 1483–85
Richard's two years' reign was haunted by conspiracies put down by ruthless
force. Finally Richard was defeated and killed in the b a t t l e o f
B o s w o r t h , 1485, by the last male representative of the House of
Lancaster, Henry Tudor, who had landed from France with a strong force
of fellow-exiles.

D. DISINTEGRATION OF FEUDALISM

1. **Rise of towns** in the 13th and 14th centuries, when the growing need
   of rulers for money (feuds under Stephen, crusades, ransoms) caused
   feudal lords to grant charters against payment of fixed sums. Merchant
   and craft guilds held the right to assess taxes together with other
   privileges (e.g. regulation of trade, jurisdiction, election of mayor)
   and thus represented the municipal government ('corporation'). The
   guilds encouraged an intensive corporative life, their members often
   living in the same street and forming one parish. They provided
   social and moral security through the regulation of working
   conditions, training of apprentices, benefits in cases of sickness and
   death. From 1265 onwards boroughs (self-ruling towns) gained
   political influence through returning two burgesses (property-holding
   burghers) to Parliament. The 14th and 15th centuries saw the gradual
   decline of towns due to the growing centralization of government
   and the break-up of the guild system through division into distinct
   social groups: liveries (capitalist traders wearing liveries), master
   guilds, and yeoman guilds (employees). Moreover the competition of
   unauthorized industries in rural districts deprived the guilds of their
   monopolies in trades.

2. **Rise of yeomanry:** From the 14th century onwards decay of the
   manorial system through commutation of services (manumission):
   Numbers of former serfs freed themselves from feudal services by
   paying a fixed sum (firma), which made them 'farmers' (freeholders),
   while the rest became permanent paid land-labourers. Thus serfdom
   was abolished four hundred years earlier than on the Continent. The
   yeomanry were long one of the proudest classes in England. As
   archers, yeomen contributed to the military glory of England in the
   Hundred Years' War.

3. **Decline of nobility:** The Wars of the Roses, which were fought chiefly
   by barons, extinguished many noble families and encouraged

lawlessness and violence among nobles and their retainers (military employees used also in the Hundred Years' War). This led to the elimination of the old nobility from political influence and the creation of a new aristocracy of court officials under the Tudor kings.

The Tudors

Renaissance, Reformation

1485–1603

The Tudors were the most popular dynasty in English history, uniting absolutist tendencies with respect for Parliament and the interests of the powerful new middle classes through their keen instinct for England's commercial possibilities.

Henry VII, 1485–1509

Austere and sober, clear-sighted and economical, Henry was the first exponent of a modern conception of state based on a sound fiscal system and efficient centralized administration. Aided by able officials, he eliminated the influence of the feudal classes.

1. Termination of the Wars of the Roses: Henry, descended from the House of Lancaster (p. 27), defeated Richard III in the battle of Bosworth and strengthened his claims by marrying the Yorkist princess Elizabeth (daughter of Edward IV).

2. Suppression of revolts of the usurpers Lambert Simnel and Perkin Warbeck, who claimed relationship with the House of York.

3. Henry restored order and royal authority by r i g o r o u s t a x a - t i o n and suppression of the lawless nobility, who were forbidden to keep retainers. The former political influence of the nobility was now superseded by a n e w g e n t r y (reliable officials drawn from middle classes).

4. Revenues from heavy fines for lawlessness, from customs and feudal dues made the King largely independent of Parliament.

5. S t r e n g t h e n i n g o f c e n t r a l p o w e r by developing an efficient administration through a central council as distinct from parliamentary rule:
a) P r i v y C o u n c i l emerged as an inner council of efficient loyal officials. It executed royal directives in legislation through influence

on Parliament, in local administration through control of justices of the peace, in jurisdiction through membership in the new Court of b) S t a r   C h a m b e r, established to punish lawlessness. Not bound to strict rules of procedure like ordinary courts (indictment and trial by jury), the Star Chamber became a powerful instrument of absolutism, particularly under the Stuarts.

6. A skilful marriage policy helped to settle foreign controversies: Arthur, Prince of Wales, was married to Catherine of Aragon, who, after Arthur's death, married his younger brother Henry, later Henry VIII. The marriage of Henry's daughter Margaret to the Scottish king James IV later led to the union between England and Scotland.

7. Ireland: The *Poyning's Act* (1494) provided that laws passed by the Irish Parliament required the previous consent of the English government.

8. Henry encouraged f o r e i g n   t r a d e by legislation and monetary support:

a) Privileges granted to the association of M e r c h a n t   A d v e n - t u r e r s gave the company the virtual monopoly of the wool trade with the Netherlands and central Europe.

b) English shipping was favoured at the expense of the Hansa and other foreign traders; first restrictions on exports and imports (e.g. Gasconne wines) not carried on English ships.

c) Challenge to the Venetian monopoly of Italian trade by the establishment of a wool-staple at Pisa.

d) Royal grants for building merchant ships.

e) Support of the first overseas expedition from England by John Cabot, who discovered N e w f o u n d l a n d in an attempt to find the western route to Cathay (China).

f) Treaty with Denmark opened Iceland to English fishing and trade.

Henry VIII, 1509–47

A typical Renaissance prince, Henry was versatile, interested in music, art and letters and a brilliant sportsman. He promoted humanism despite his strong belief in Catholic doctrines (he received from the Pope the title of Fidei Defensor for a pamphlet against Luther, 1521). In the later part of his reign Henry became despotic, extravagant and violent.

1. C a r d i n a l   W o l s e y, of humble descent, rose to the highest offices in Church and State; he became Archbishop of York, papal legate and Lord Chancellor. In his personal life licentious and extravagant (he built the magnificent palace of Hampton Court),

Wolsey organized a highly efficient administration fully under his control, since the King was at first more interested in cultural affairs.

a) Wolsey's f o r e i g n p o l i c y largely strove to promote his personal profit and his ambition to become Pope. In the w a r s b e t w e e n S p a i n a n d F r a n c e, England changed sides three times. In a first campaign against the French, the English won a victory at the Battle of the Spurs, 1513. Despite a later alliance with France in the pageant-like encounter between Henry VIII and Francis I on the Field of the Cloth of Gold, England again joined Spain in 1522. New invasions of France, however, brought small territorial gain compared with the heavy war expenditures, while the growing power of Emperor Charles V, who had sacked Rome, caused Wolsey to form a new alliance with France to preserve the b a l a n c e o f p o w e r.

b) W o l s e y ' s f a l l was caused by general hostility engendered by his arrogance and rigorous taxation, and by his failure to secure a papal licence for Henry's divorce from Catherine of Aragon, whom Henry had married after his brother Arthur's death. Wolsey's property was seized, he himself removed from all his offices and tried for treason, the humiliation of which led to his death (1530). Wolsey was replaced as Chancellor by England's greatest humanist, Thomas More.

2. **The Reformation** in England had chiefly political causes, though ideas of the Reformation had already been voiced in England in the 14th century by Wycliffe (p. 25) and were now re-introduced through contact of the University of Cambridge with Continental reformers. With the support of Parliament, which represented the general a n t i - c l e r i c a l i s m a n d d e s i r e f o r n a t i o n a l i n - d e p e n d e n c e, Henry separated the Church of England from Rome, since the Pope had refused to license Henry's divorce from Catherine of Aragon, and Henry wished to secure male succession through a new marriage with Anne Boleyn. The Reformation was thus a matter of legislation.

REFORMATION STATUTES enacted by Parliament, 1529–36:

a) Abolition of papal jurisdiction, of Annates and the Peter's Pence hitherto paid to Rome.

b) Legislation of the Convocation (church assembly) was made dependent on royal license.

c) *Act of Supremacy* (1534) made the k i n g s u p r e m e h e a d o f t h e C h u r c h with the right to determine doctrinal questions and to nominate bishops. Thomas More and Bishop Fisher, who refused to take the oath of supremacy, were beheaded.

3. D i s s o l u t i o n o f m o n a s t e r i e s was effected by the rigorous methods of the newly-appointed vicar-general Thomas Cromwell: Relics, ornaments and shrines were destroyed, monastic lands ($^1/_3$ of the whole country) sold by the government to lay subjects. New landowners began to form a new gentry loyal to the government.

4. P i l g r i m a g e o f G r a c e : A rebellion against the Reformation in the conservative northern counties under the leadership of Robert Aske was put down and cruelly punished. Nevertheless the *Act of Six Articles* enjoined under penalty the return to Catholic doctrines and practices.

5. IRELAND: An Irish rebellion under the leadership of Fitzgerald, Earl of Kildare, was rigorously suppressed. Fitzgerald was hanged with his five uncles. The Anglican Church was established, but Ireland remained largely Catholic. The dissolution of the monasteries destroyed the few existing cultural centres.

6. SCOTLAND: The Scottish alliance with Henry's enemy, France, led to t w o S c o t t i s h i n v a s i o n s , which were subsequently repulsed. In the battle of Flodden King James IV was defeated and killed. His son, James V, was defeated at Solway Moss, 1542, and died in the same year. When the betrothal of his infant daughter Mary Stuart to Henry's infant son Edward was cancelled by the regent, the Earl of Arran, Henry sent a punitive expedition to Scotland, which was, however, repulsed.

7. The Chancellor was replaced by a 'secretary' as head of the Privy Council ('secretary' is still used for 'minister' in England and the U.S.A.). The Chancellor remained speaker of the House of Lords and retained his judicial functions.

8. A n a v y was built under Henry's personal control.

9. Succession: Out of six marriages Henry had three children:
Mary Tudor, daughter of Catherine of Aragon,
Elizabeth by his second wife Anne Boleyn, (who was beheaded),
Edward, son of Henry's third wife Jane Seymour, who was the first to succeed to the throne as his only male heir.

E d w a r d V I , 1547–53

Edward, who succeeded as a child of ten, was sickly but precocious.

1. Under the protectorship of the Duke of Somerset the Reformation was fully introduced by Archbishop Cranmer, who compiled the *Book of Common Prayer*, 1549, and the *Articles of Religion*. Somerset's rigorous religious measures (abolition of celibacy, chantries,

33

pilgrimages, vestments) led to rebellions among the peasantry in Cornwall and Devonshire, while opposition among the land-owning classes to his social laws against enclosures caused his fall and later execution.

2. Duke of Northumberland, who succeeded Somerset as protector, tried to secure the crown for his family by marrying his son to Henry's great-niece Lady Jane Grey (aged 16) and persuading Edward to acknowledge her as his successor.

Mary Tudor, 1553–58

Mary was the first woman to succeed to the English throne. As daughter of Henry's Spanish wife Catherine of Aragon, Mary was fanatically Catholic. She had no appreciation of national interests and made England subservient to Spain through her marriage with King Philip II.

1. Mary took a firm stand against attempts to prevent her succession:
   a) Her cousin Lady Jane Grey and Northumberland, who had proclaimed her Queen after Edward's death, were executed.
   b) A rebellion in Kent to depose Mary in favour of her sister Elizabeth was suppressed when the rebels marched on London. Their leader, Thomas Wyatt, was executed, Elizabeth imprisoned.

2. Ruthless restoration of Catholicism (hence 'Bloody Mary'): Cranmer and Latimer were burnt, as well as hundreds of Protestants, while others, including the Scottish reformer John Knox, went into exile on the Continent.

3. Loss of Calais, 1558, in the war of Philip II against France signified the end of English expansion in Europe.

Elizabeth I, 1558–1603

Elizabeth was open-minded and versatile. She spoke five languages, played several instruments and was proficient in riding, hunting and archery. She combined personal vanity and capriciousness with political prudence and deliberation. Her vitality and love of festivity, her appeal to national instincts and to the spirit of individual enterprise among her subjects made her highly popular.

I. Religious Development in England and Scotland:

Since the Roman Catholic Church did not acknowledge Elizabeth's right of succession, Elizabeth favoured the Reformation in England and Scotland. For political reasons, however, she persecuted free Protestant sects in order to preserve the unity of the English Church.

1. *Act of Uniformity*, 1559, re-established the Anglican Church with Protestant doctrines, but episcopacy and much of the

Catholic ritual were preserved. A Court of High Commission was instituted to punish violations of the Act as treason (no longer as heresy). Bishops and clergy who refused to acknowledge the Queen as 'Supreme Governor of the Church' under the *Act of Supremacy* were discharged.

2. REFORMATION IN SCOTLAND was introduced by the Scottish reformer J o h n K n o x , who had been a follower of Calvin in Geneva. Aided by Scottish nobles, who had joined in the 'Congregation of the Lord', Knox brought about a religious and national uprising against the Catholic rule of Mary Guise, who, as regent for her daughter Mary Stuart (after the Earl of Arran's death), had tried to uphold Catholicism with the help of the clergy and French troops. A military intervention from England saved the Scottish Reformation. The French troops withdrew. After the death of Mary Guise, the S c o t t i s h P r e s b y t e r i a n C h u r c h was organized, based on Calvinist doctrines and principles of church administration. Episcopacy was replaced by a centralized system of democratic church assemblies presided over by presbyters (p. 192).

3. PURITANISM IN ENGLAND: Strict Calvinists, disappointed by the compromise of the Anglican Church and failing to disestablish episcopacy by legislation, formed P u r i t a n c o n v e n t i c l e s (Presbyterians, Congregationalists, Baptists), which were suppressed by Elizabeth through the Court of High Commission.

4. Suppression of a p r o - C a t h o l i c r e b e l l i o n in the North (1569) under the Earls of Westmorland and Northumberland (who had hoped to restore Catholicism through establishing the succession of Mary Stuart), was answered by the Pope with the e x - c o m m u n i c a t i o n o f E l i z a b e t h under a Papal Bull proclaiming her deposition (1570).

5. C o u n t e r - R e f o r m a t i o n was promoted by priests (particularly Jesuits) specially trained on the Continent, who travelled in disguise through England trying to proselytize. Elizabeth answered with rigorous laws against Catholics imposing heavy fines for hearing and saying mass. Several priests were executed under the charge of treason.

II. Social Legislation

1. *Statute of Artificers* (also called *Statute of Apprentices*), 1563, regulated labour conditions:
   a) Wages to be settled annually by justices of the peace.
   b) Apprenticeships to last seven years (usually from 14 to 21).

c) Persons who had not served an apprenticeship to seek work as agricultural labourers on pain of stocks and flogging.
The main purpose of the Act was to e n c o u r a g e t r a d e s a n d a r a b l e f a r m i n g and to keep youth under discipline.

2. L e g i s l a t i o n a g a i n s t e n c l o s u r e of common land for sheep raising, 1563, sought to restore arable farming and to prevent the depopulation of villages.

3. F i r s t p o o r r e l i e f on a national basis to prevent beggary and vagrancy was established by a number of laws from 1563–1601 (in force until 1834).
a) A land tax to be raised by overseers of the poor.
b) Sale of goods and imprisonment of those who refused to pay.
c) Almshouses to be erected for the old and impotent.
d) 'A convenient stock of flax, hemp, wool, iron' to be supplied to set the able-bodied poor to work.
e) Pauper children to be apprenticed.
f) Vagrants and beggars to be taken and punished as rogues.

III. **Naval and Commercial Ascendancy:** After the discovery of the New World, England's possibilities of expansion, hitherto limited to the European continent, were immensely widened through command of the sea routes and her position in the centre of the land hemisphere.

1. G r e a t n a v i g a t o r s encouraged by Elizabeth and popular nationalism explored new countries, encroaching on Spanish preserves. Sir Walter R a l e i g h founded the first English colony, Virginia, and introduced tobacco into England. Martin Frobisher, William Baffin, John Davis and Henry H u d s o n tried to find the Northwest Passage to Cathay (China) via North American waters, preparing the way for the fur trade of the later Hudson Bay Company. Richard C h a n c e l l o r, in search of the Northeast Passage, opened Russia to English trade. Ralph Fitch sought the land route to India and the Far East (Malacca). Francis D r a k e sank Spanish ships, raided Spanish settlements in the West Indies and sailed round the world. Elizabeth's acknowledgement of his achievements by dubbing him knight on his return was the first official challenge to the Spanish dominance of the seas.

2. Commerce was encouraged through the founding of the Royal Exchange, 1567, and the chartering of c o m p a n i e s f o r o v e r - s e a s t r a d e (e.g. the Muscovy, Levant and East India Companies).

3. Trades developed through the importation of new raw materials (e.g. for dyeing) and through skilled craftsmen from the Continent.

F l e m i s h   i m m i g r a n t s   improved cloth-weaving and lace-making, H u g u e n o t   r e f u g e e s   introduced silk-weaving and improved the glass and paper trades.

IV. Foreign Relations and Mary Stuart

1. Era of neutrality: In order to gain time to consolidate her reign in the face of the Catholic reaction (claims of Mary Stuart to the English throne, Counter-Reformation), Elizabeth pursued a shrewd policy of appeasing and playing off against each other the Catholic countries Spain and France by interminable marriage negotiations with both.

2. The D u t c h   s t r u g g l e   f o r   i n d e p e n d e n c e   against Spain was nevertheless supported in 1585 to retain trade with the Dutch.

3. M a r y   S t u a r t , Queen of Scots, was, as an infant, betrothed to Henry VIII's son Edward. The cancellation of the marriage treaty by the Scots led to two expeditions to Scotland under Henry VIII and the Duke of Somerset to take Mary to England by force. This induced her mother Mary Guise to take her to France. At sixteen Mary was married to the French Dauphin, later King Francis II. She called herself 'Queen of Scotland and England' despite the official Scottish renunciation of the Stuart succession in England through the *Treaty of Edinburgh*. After Francis' death she returned to Scotland at 19 and married her cousin Darnley. Alarmed at Mary's attempts to reintroduce Catholicism and scandalized by her third marriage to the Earl of Bothwell, who had murdered her husband, the Scots rose against her and forced her to abdicate in favour of her son James. Mary sought refuge in England, where she was held in confinement for 19 years in castles which became centres of Catholic conspiracies against Elizabeth. Plots of the Dukes of Northumberland and Norfolk and of courtiers under the leadership of Babington were punished with execution. In 1587 Mary herself was brought to trial and beheaded in the Castle of Fotheringay.

4. W a r   w i t h   S p a i n   was finally brought about by colonial rivalry, by the English support of the Dutch rebellion against Spain and the execution of Mary Stuart. Philip II prepared the conquest of England by sending an immense fleet, but the Spanish A r m a d a   w a s   d e s t r o y e d   in 1588 through the brilliant cooperation of the English fleet (Navy and merchant vessels) under Lord Howard and Drake. The war with Spain continued with varying success. In 1596 Drake sacked Cadiz, but English attacks on Lisbon and the Azores failed. D r a k e   revolutionized naval strategy by destroying ships with his b r o a d s i d e s   (guns on the ship's broadsides), which

37

proved superior to the Spanish method of boarding the enemy's ship and fighting on deck (custom since Roman times).

V. R e b e l l i o n in I r e l a n d under the Earl of Tyrone was cruelly suppressed. The devastation of the land and starvation of the population are described in a report of the poet Edmund Spenser, who acted as secretary to the Viceroy of Ireland.

VI. Elizabeth's favourites fall into two groups:

1. Cool and able political advisers: William Cecil (L o r d B u r g h l e y), his son Robert Cecil (Lord Salisbury), and Sir Francis Walsingham acting as Secretaries of State.

2. Personal attachments:
Robert Dudley, E a r l o f L e i c e s t e r , was imprisoned during Mary Tudor's reign after the execution of his father, the Duke of Northumberland. He won Elizabeth's favour by intrigue, was nevertheless involved in Norfolk's plot in favour of Mary Stuart, whom he later betrayed. He commanded troops sent in aid of the Dutch rebels against Spain without success and was recalled.
S i r W a l t e r R a l e i g h gained the Queen's favour by his chivalry and daring voyages of exploration. He served in campaigns in France and Flanders, against Spain and Ireland and was generously rewarded for his services with land grants in Ireland.
Robert Devereux, E a r l o f E s s e x , served in his stepfather's (Leicester's) campaign in the Netherlands, held commands in expeditions against Spain and against Tyrone's rebellion in Ireland. Losing the Queen's favour through concluding a premature truce in Ireland, he tried to raise a riot in London, was brought up for trial (conducted by the lawyer and philosopher Bacon, whom he had generously favoured) and beheaded.

Stuart Age

Absolutism and the English Revolution

1603–89

A. EARLY STUARTS (cf. genealogical table, p. 53)

Politically undiplomatic and arbitrary, though with personal dignity and courage, the Stuarts were unpopular through their despotic and Catholic tendencies. Resistance to Stuart despotism led to the revival of Parliamentarism.

James I, 1603–25

James followed his mother, Mary Stuart, as an infant after her abdication as James VI of Scotland, and succeeded Elizabeth I in England as James I. He was well educated, interested in theology and political philosophy but lacked personal vigour. He was dependent on favourites. His chief ministers, Robert Carr, Duke of Somerset, and George Villiers, Duke of Buckingham, were ennobled commoners. James's despotic tendencies are expressed in his essay on *True Law of Free Monarchies*, one of the standard works on the doctrine of the Divine Right of Kings.

1. By inheriting the English crown as Scottish king, James brought about the d y n a s t i c u n i o n o f E n g l a n d a n d S c o t l a n d (the British flag is called the *Union Jack*). Scotland, however, retained its own parliament, church, law and army.

2. Contest between Puritanism and Anglicanism now began to take the place of the contest in the 16th century between Anglicanism and Catholicism. Having tried to come to terms with the Puritans at the Hampton Court Conference 1604, and finding them unwilling to give up their democratic and strict Calvinist principles, James determined 'to make them conform or harry them out of the country'. The only positive result of the Conference was the A u t h o r i z e d V e r s i o n o f t h e B i b l e (1611) based on former translations.

3. C o l o n i z a t i o n i n A m e r i c a : Persecuted 'separatist' bodies emigrated to the Continent, later to America (New England). The 'Pilgrim Fathers', returning from their Dutch exile, left in 1620 for America in the *Mayflower*. Before the Puritan colonization, Raleigh's colony Virginia, which had been destroyed by Indians, was resettled by the London Company, 1607.

4. Catholic G u n p o w d e r P l o t, 1605, to blow up Parliament and seize power was discovered. Guy Fawkes, who was to set fire to gun powder stored in a cellar underneath Parliament, was captured and executed together with the other conspirators. Since that time the 5th November has been celebrated as 'Guy Fawkes Day'.

5. Raleigh, accused of participation in a conspiracy to place James's cousin Arabella Stuart on the throne, was imprisoned for years in the Tower where he wrote *History of the World*. Released upon a promise to find the Eldorado, he started on a new expedition to America and came into conflict with the Spaniards. On his return, the former death sentence was carried out at the demand of Spain.

6. U l s t e r P l a n t a t i o n : After suppression of an Irish rebellion led by Tyrconnel and Tyrone, the northern county of Ireland was taken from the Irish earls and settled by Scottish Presbyterians, who founded towns and industries. This led to the present political division

of Ireland into the industrial north with a Protestant majority and the Celtic, Roman Catholic and agricultural south.

7. Heavy taxation, corruption, monopolies threatening trade, and subserviency to Spain led to c o n f l i c t s   w i t h   P a r l i a m e n t, which was frequently dissolved.

8. James's foreign policy consisted chiefly in the avoidance of a conflict with Spain, which had been the cause of Raleigh's execution. However, the marriage of James's daughter Elizabeth to the leader of the Protestant cause in Germany, Frederick of the Palatinate, led to a conflict with Spain in the Thirty Years' War. When the Spaniards invaded the Palatinate, James tried to appease Spain by offering the marriage of his son Charles to a Spanish princess.

C h a r l e s   I, 1625–49

Charles, although endowed with more vigour and personal dignity than his father, was narrow-minded, obstinate and unreliable in politics.

1. Charles's wars in Spain and France, unauthorized by Parliament, were inspired by the private interests of the King and his favourite, Buckingham. Disappointment over the failure of marriage negotiations led to war with Spain, which was conducted badly and without success. A fleet sent to the King of France to fight against Spain was used to fight against the Huguenots (French Protestants). An attempt to capture the Spanish fleet off Cadiz failed. A later expedition to help the Huguenots against the French government was not supported by Parliament and failed also.

2. C o n f l i c t   w i t h   P a r l i a m e n t, now under the leadership of great champions of liberty, Sir John Eliot, Sir John Hampden, John Pym, resulted in the dissolution of three Parliaments because of opposition to the King's policy: money supplies, formerly granted to the King for life, were now only voted for one year. Buckingham was impeached on the principle (denied by Charles) that Parliament had a right to question the King's ministers.

a) *P e t i t i o n   o f   R i g h t*, 1628, forced from the King by a third Parliament, declared the illegality of enforced billeting of soldiers, of taxes unauthorized by Parliament, and imprisonment without specific charge. Comparable to *Magna Carta,* the *Petition of Right* was, however, soon disregarded by the King.

b) T o n n a g e   a n d   p o u n d a g e (ancient taxes on wine and wool) were collected by the King independently of restrictions imposed by Parliament. Tax collectors were summoned to appear before Parliament. Charles ordered the Speaker to announce the prorogation of Parliament, but the Speaker was held down in his chair till Parliament had carried its resolutions. In great anger the King dissolved Parliament, imprisoning its leaders. Eliot died in the Tower.

c) S h i p   m o n e y, formerly a contribution of seaports to the navy, now collected throughout the country, was generally resented as an unauthorized tax. Sir John H a m p d e n, who refused payment, was tried and declared guilty on the ground that the King had a right over his subjects' person and property. Nevertheless Hampden became immensely popular as a champion against despotism.

3. Personal government of Charles 1629–40: Having dissolved the third Parliament, Charles ruled independently for eleven years. After the murder of Buckingham he was assisted by able advisers, whose subservience to the King, however, made them unpopular:
a) W i l l i a m   L a u d, conscientious, laborious and devoted to the King, became Archbishop of Canterbury. Supported by the Catholic tendencies at court through the French Queen Henrietta Maria, he reintroduced the Catholic ritual into the Church, thus establishing the H i g h   C h u r c h. He persecuted Puritans though these were now stronger than ever before, and strengthened the royal authority. He exercised rigorous supervision over religious and moral life and over the press, inflicting heavy punishments for offences (imprisonment, pillory, mutilation) through the Star Chamber.
b) Sir Thomas Wentworth, formerly a strong supporter of the *Petition of Right*, withdrew from the parliamentary opposition. He took office under the King, who made him E a r l o f S t r a f f o r d, Lord Deputy of Ireland and his principal adviser. Believing in the advantages of a strong government, Strafford ruled efficiently and despotically, estranging the population by imposing high taxes and attempting to build up a strong army.

4. R e b e l l i o n i n S c o t l a n d : When the King tried to reintroduce episcopacy and the High Church ritual with the help of Laud, the Scots pledged themselves to resistance through a national covenant. The Church Assembly, where the laity appeared in arms, despite the King's attempt to dissolve it, restored Presbyterianism and sent troops to the north of England. The 'Short Parliament' (April–May 1640) summoned to vote money for the war against the Scots, presented grievances instead, and was dissolved. The King, unable to beat the Scots with an unwilling army raised by arbitrary means, summoned a new parliament.

5. 'Long Parliament', elected in 1642, contained only the King's opponents. Under the leadership of Pym, Hampden and Cromwell, Parliament soon became stronger than the King, excluded bishops,

abolished episcopacy, executed Strafford and Laud, and effected
CONSTITUTIONAL REFORMS:

a) No dissolution of Parliament without its own consent.

b) *Triennial Act:* Parliament to meet every three years even if not
summoned by the King.

c) Abolition of Star Chamber and Court of High Commission.

d) Ship money declared illegal, tonnage and poundage to be collected
only with the consent of Parliament.

e) *Grand Remonstrance* summarized grievances against Charles once
more, and stated the principle that ministers be appointed with the
approval of Parliament.

An attempt of the King to arrest parliamentary leaders in Parliament
failed, the five Members, including Hampden and Pym, having been
warned in time. United through this latest violation of ancient rights,
Charles's opponents formed a rival government.

6. Civil War, 1642–49, 'Puritan Revolution'

a) Forming of parties: The claim of Parliament to raise and command
forces for suppressing the rebellions in Scotland and Ireland
precipitated war between the
C a v a l i e r s , episcopalian royalists, chiefly nobles, and the
R o u n d h e a d s (name from their close-cropped hair), representing
the parliamentarian middle classes and new gentry, then chiefly
Puritan. They were supported from 1643 by the Scots under the
'Solemn League and Covenant'.

b) O l i v e r C r o m w e l l , country gentleman, Member of Parliament and fervent Puritan, became leader of the troops of the Eastern
Association forming part of the parliamentary army under the
command of Fairfax. Cromwell organized the well equipped 'N e w
M o d e l' army, famous chiefly for its cavalry, the 'I r o n s i d e s',
and inspired it with religious enthusiasm and discipline.

c) First Civil War: Royal troops holding the conservative north and
west of England were at first successful. Owing to the superior tactics
of the King's nephew, Prince Rupert of the Palatinate, who had
served in the Thirty Years' War, they won the Battle of Edgehill
(1642), but failed to capture London and were finally beaten by
Cromwell's troops, which held the southeast. Through the greatest
battle of the war at M a r s t o n M o o r 1644, where Rupert's
armies were routed, the Puritans, under the command of Cromwell
and Fairfax, won the north, and, through a victory at N a s e b y
(1645), the Midlands. When the southwest was conquered through
the capture of the royal headquarters at Oxford, the King fled to
the Scots but was given over to Parliament and imprisoned.

d) Second Civil War: Charles, fleeing to Carisbrooke Castle (Isle of

Wight), made a secret treaty with the Scots, who invaded England but were defeated by Cromwell at Preston, 1648.

7. Pride's Purge: Conflict between Independents (radical Puritans led by Cromwell), who controlled the army, and Presbyterians, who formed the majority in Parliament, led to the exclusion of Presbyterians from Parliament by the army under Colonel Pride.

8. R u m p   P a r l i a m e n t , now consisting only of Independents, established a Court of Justice which sentenced the King to death as a traitor and tyrant and enemy of his people.

9. E x e c u t i o n   o f   C h a r l e s , 1649: The King's dignity in meeting his fate caused a change in public opinion leading to his veneration as a martyr, and hatred against the regicides.

B. COMMONWEALTH (REPUBLIC) AND PROTECTORATE UNDER CROMWELL

I. Commonwealth, 1649–53

Government was chiefly in the hands of Cromwell and other leading generals, Monk and Blake (later admiral). The office of King and the House of Lords were abolished. The executive power was exercised by a newly established Council of State, consisting chiefly of officers, with Fairfax and Cromwell as members.

1. Suppression of rebellions in favour of Prince Charles:
   a) I r i s h   r e s i s t a n c e was cruelly broken by Cromwell: After the conquest of the rebellious towns of Drogheda and Wexford, the garrisons were killed. All land east of the county of Connaught was granted to English landlords and veterans of the army. The Irish remained on their soil as tenants.
   b) S c o t t i s h   r e b e l l i o n : The Scots, who acknowledged the son of Charles I as King Charles II, were defeated by Cromwell at D u n b a r (Scotland). While Cromwell conquered Edinburgh, the Scots invaded England under the command of Prince Charles. Defeated by Cromwell at W o r c e s t e r (1651), Charles fled to France. Scotland was fully united with England under the efficient administration of General Monk.

2. Suppression of radical movements: Lilburne, leader of the 'Levellers', who advocated constitutional and social reforms, was repeatedly put on trial. A communist settlement established under Winstanley to dig common land in order 'to restore the people's birthright of common property' was destroyed.

3. *Navigation Act,* 1651, fought the carrying trade of Holland, which, after separation from Spain, had become one of Europe's foremost trading nations. The Act prohibited all imports not carried on English ships or ships of the country of origin.

4. Attempts to restore Parliamentarism: Upon the forcible dissolution of the Rump Parliament through the ejection of members by the army, the L i t t l e P a r l i a m e n t, consisting of nominated Congregational members, was summoned but was soon dissolved. Failure to restore Parliamentarism led to the

II. Protectorate, 1653–60:

Cromwell was instituted as Lord Protector with more than royal powers. Supported by an officers' council consisting of twelve major-generals, he virtually exercised a m i l i t a r y d i c t a t o r s h i p during the last five years of his rule, though he declined to accept an offer of the crown and re-established a new House of Lords consisting of peers nominated by himself.

1. FOREIGN POLICY: With his highly disciplined army and newly developed navy Cromwell asserted English influence in European politics and established English control of the seas (Cromwell has been called 'the first English imperialist').
   a) First advance into the Mediterranean Sea through victories over Prince Rupert's ships und over pirates.
   b) W a r w i t h H o l l a n d, 1652–54: Brilliant naval victories of Admiral B l a k e secured English success. From now on English *Navigation Acts* founded English control of the seas.
   c) W a r w i t h S p a i n, 1656–58, was waged for free trade with the Spanish colonies: Jamaica and Dunkirk were seized, a Spanish treasure fleet was captured off Teneriffe.

2. INTERNAL POLICY (largely unpopular):
   a) High taxation to finance the army and wars.
   b) P u r i t a n a u s t e r i t y meant the end of Merry England: no theatres, no entertainments on Sundays, no gambling, sports, dancing.
   c) R e l i g i o u s t o l e r a t i o n : Jews were permitted to return to England. The rise of new dissenting groups (Quakers, Unitarians) was not discouraged.

3. End of Protectorate: Oliver Cromwell died in 1658 and was buried with great pomp in Westminster Abbey. His son Richard, who followed him, was not able to cope with disputes between the army and Parliament and abdicated after one year.

C. RESTORATION: Revival of 'Merry England'.

C h a r l e s I I , 1660–85, son of the executed King Charles I.
Charles had lived as an exile in France after the defeat of the royalist cause in England. Though indolent and unreliable in politics, Charles was the most popular Stuart king. Clever, witty and indulging in an extravagant court life, Charles was called the Merry Monarch.

1. Charles's return: Tired of military rule, the English, through mediation of General Monk, recalled the Stuart heir, who landed amid great rejoicings.

2. *Act of Indemnity and Oblivion,* 1660, granted general pardon with the exception of thirteen 'regicides', who were hanged. The body of Cromwell was dug up and hung in its shro·1d. Confiscated estates were returned, estates bought from exiled royalists, however, were left to their new owners.

3. R e v e n g e o n P u r i t a n s , now called Dissenters, was taken by the new Cavalier Parliament (1661–79) through rigorous laws, called the *Clarendon Code* after Charles's chief minister, Edward Hyde, Earl of Clarendon.
   a) *Corporation Act,* 1661, excluded Dissenters from serving on corporations (municipalities).
   b) *Act of Uniformity,* 1662, re-established the Anglican Church, forcing 2,000 dissenting ministers to resign office.
   c) *Conventicle Act,* 1664, forbade Nonconformist services under pain of fines and imprisonment, and, at the third offence, of transportation.
   d) *Five-Mile Act,* 1665, prohibited dissenting ministers from coming within five miles of their former livings without taking an oath of loyalty to the new government.

4. F i r s t w a r w i t h H o l l a n d , 1664–67, was precipitated by colonial rivalry in South Asia and Africa. The English ravaged the coast of Holland, the Dutch captured English ships in the Thames. By the treaty of 1667, Holland ceded New Amsterdam, now called N e w Y o r k after Charles's brother, the Duke of York, and forts in Guinea on the African coast (from whose gold the first English 'guineas' were coined).

5. The P l a g u e (1665) and the G r e a t F i r e (1666): Aggravated by close building and narrow streets, the plague ravaged London, and was followed by a fire, which swept away the ancient city (p. 127).

6. Charles's Ministers:
   a) The Earl of Clarendon, who had shared Charles's exile, was made Chancellor and conducted a wise and moderate government. Losing the favour of Parliament, he was impeached and fled to France.

45

b) **C a b a l   M i n i s t r y** was so called significantly after the initials of the names of its members, who condoned Charles's profligacy. Supported by its two Catholic members, Charles carried on secret dealings with France. Its most important member Ashley, who was later made Earl of Shaftesbury and Lord Chancellor, became the chief opponent of Charles's and his successor's Catholic policy. He organized a lawless opposition and, in danger of prosecution, fled to Holland (later followed by his secretary, the philosopher John Locke).

7. Charles's **s u b s e r v i e n c y   t o   F r a n c e :** Having made France the dominant European power, Louis XIV tried to win England for his policy of conquest on the Continent. Resenting French dominance, Parliament in 1668 ratified the *Triple Alliance* with Holland and Sweden, which ended Louis's war against the Spanish Netherlands, and arranged a marriage between Charles's niece (later Queen Mary) and William of Orange. Charles, however, continued to be strongly under French influence through his French mother, his former exile in France, his Catholic and absolutist tendencies and financial stringency. He

a) received a pension from Louis to compensate for the restricted supplies from Parliament (now granted only annually), which made him largely independent of Parliament,

b) sold Dunkirk to France and

c) concluded the secret *Treaty of Dover* with France, planning joint subjugation of Holland and the restoration of Catholicism in England.

8. Second War with Holland, 1672, was conducted on the English side with little enthusiasm. The naval war remained undecided. Under William of Orange, Dutch territory, overrun by Louis's armies, was saved by the cutting of dykes and flooding of land.

9. Opposition to Charles's Catholic tendencies:
a) **T e s t   A c t ,** 1673: In 1672 Charles, who had secretly become a Catholic, issued the *Declaration of Indulgence* in favour of Catholics and Dissenters. Under pressure from Parliament, this had to be withdrawn, and was superseded by the *Test Act* in 1673. Through requiring that civil service appointments be made dependent upon taking the sacraments of the Church of England, the *Test Act* secured final control of public affairs by the Established Church.

b) The disclosure by an impostor, Titus Oates, of an alleged 'Popish Plot' to murder the King and, through his brother James, to suppress the Protestant religion, caused panic in London leading to several executions of Catholics and the *Exclusion Bill.*

c) *Exclusion Bill* introduced into Parliament in 1679 and 1680 proposed to exclude Charles's brother James, who was avowedly Catholic, from succession. Charles prevented the passage of the bill by repeated dissolution of Parliament.

e) R y e H o u s e P l o t planned in 1683 by Whig partisans to murder the King and his brother James near Rye House, was discovered and led to numerous executions, to which prominent Whig opponents of Catholicism, e.g. the political writer Algernon Sidney, fell victim (p. 267–68).

10. *H a b e a s C o r p u s A c t*, 1679, enacted by Parliament against arbitrary imprisonment (no person to be held prisoner without judicial warrant and speedy trial) later on became a s y m b o l o f E n g l i s h f r e e d o m as against the suppression of subjects in absolutist states.

11. Forming of parties in the course of political and religious struggles in Parliament: T o r i e s represented the landed gentry and clergy supporting a strong government by Crown and Church, W h i g s the commercial classes and Dissenters, whose interests were represented in Parliament by free-thinking Anglican aristocrats. Whigs advocated the restriction of governmental powers, greater individual liberty and therefore religious toleration.

12. Tory reaction to the Rye House Plot strengthened the power of the King, who eliminated Whig influence in towns by annulling municipal charters. He secured Tory control over elections in towns by appointing Tories to offices in municipal governments. The large Tory representation in Parliament thus guaranteed made Charles independent of opposition for the rest of his reign.

J a m e s I I, brother of Charles II, 1685–88

Avowedly Catholic, James was nevertheless acclaimed by the Tories. Trying to restore Catholicism by rigorous measures, he was very unpopular and finally even lost the support of Tories.

1. I n s u r r e c t i o n o f D u k e o f M o n m o u t h : Relying on the strong anti-Catholic feelings, Charles's illegitimate son, the Duke of Monmouth, landed in England, declaring himself his father's successor. He gathered a small army recruited only from the lower classes (chiefly Puritans) and marched on London. Defeated by the King's army at Sedgemoor he was captured and beheaded. In the 'Bloody Assizes' of Justice Jeffreys, which James sanctioned by making Jeffreys Lord Chancellor and his most trusted adviser, many persons were tortured, 150 were hanged, 800 transported to hard servitude in the West Indies.

2. Attempt at Restoration of Catholicism (supported by the French King Louis XIV):
a) James granted livings to Catholics and appointed Catholics to offices in universities. He re-established the Court of Ecclesiastical Commission, which disciplined University Fellows and clergy who opposed him, thus creating universal discontent within three years.
b) James gathered a standing army with Catholic officers, which he stationed near London.
c) A new *Declaration of Indulgence* issued in 1688 favoured Catholics. When bishops and clergy were required to read it during Church services, seven bishops refused. They were imprisoned and tried but acquitted amid the cheers of Anglicans and Dissenters.

3. Birth of Prince James, who was baptized in the Catholic faith, thwarted the hopes of a Protestant succession and prompted Whigs and Tories to concerted action: William of Orange, as husband of James's Protestant daughter Mary, was invited to land with an army to assert Mary's rights of succession.

4. Flight to France: As William landed, November 1688, with 14,000 men, James marched to meet him, but was deserted by most of his army. Returning from Salisbury to London, he left with his family for France.

Beginnings of Constitutionalism and Colonial Expansion

1689–1760

William III of Orange and his wife Mary, 1689–1702

A clear-sighted, dispassionate statesman, William remained a foreigner to the nation owing to his austere character and his preference for Dutch advisers.

1. **Glorious Revolution,** 1689, so called because achieved without bloodshed and with permanent results: William and Mary, proclaimed as joint sovereigns, signed the
a) *Declaration of Rights,* 1689, enacted by Parliament in the same year as the *Bill of Rights.* This made England the first constitutional monarchy of Europe by substituting for the Divine Right of kings the principle of the 'social contract' binding ruler and ruled alike (today: 'constitution').

CHIEF PROVISIONS:
Parliament to control legislation and taxation.
No standing army without consent of Parliament.

No excessive fines and cruel punishments.
Free election of members to Parliament.
Freedom of speech, supplemented in 1695 by abolition of
  censorship in printing (p. 206).
Parliaments to be held frequently.
b) Revenues from taxes formerly granted to the king for life, and
money for the payment of troops were now voted only for one year.
This has made annual meetings of Parliament necessary ever since.
c) *Toleration Act*, 1689, granted Dissenters freedom of worship, in
practice also extended to Catholics. By upholding the *Corporation*
and *Test Acts* the Established Church retained control in politics
(pp. 45 and 46 resp.).
d) *Triennial Act*, 1694, provided that no Parliament should continue
longer than three years.

2. IRELAND:
a) Under the leadership of Tyrconnel and Catholic army officers
appointed by James II, Catholics had gained influence. They
persecuted Protestants, who fled to Londonderry and Enniskillen and
defended themselves against Tyrconnel's troops.
b) James landed in Ireland with French troops and was recognized
as King by the Irish Parliament.
c) William landed in Ireland and won the B a t t l e o f t h e
B o y n e , 1690. James fled to France, leaving the Irish towns of
Dublin and Limerick to be captured by English troops. Londonderry
and Enniskillen were relieved after a three months' close siege and
repeated attacks.
d) Ireland was r i g o r o u s l y s u b j u g a t e d by the English
government despite William's attempt at reconciliation. The Catholics
were excluded from Parliament, 3/4 million acres confiscated. Laws
enacted against the Irish export trade hit Ulster Presbyterians as well
as Catholics. All this led to emigration of the most active part of
the population at an alarming rate.

3. SCOTLAND: Led by loyal nobles, the H i g h l a n d e r s r e b e l l e d
and defeated English troops at Killicrankie. The death of their leader,
the Earl of Dundee, on the battlefield, however, finally led to English
victory. However, the J a c o b i t e s , who strove to recall the
Stuarts, remained a political force throughout the first half of the
18th century, which fact inspired later Scottish uprisings in 1715
and 1745.

4. B a l a n c e o f p o w e r p o l i c y (alliance with smaller nations
against the predominant European power) was initiated by William,
who, as ruler of a small state (Holland), had suffered greatly from

French aggression. This principle has determined British policy ever since (1688–1815 struggle against French predominance, 1900–45 against Germany).

5. War of the League of Augsburg (Pfälzer Erbschaftskrieg), 1688–97: England and Holland, under William, joined Spain and Germany.

a) Causes:
traditional hostility of William towards Louis XIV; Louis's support of the Old Pretender and Catholicism in England; growing military, naval and colonial power of France.

b) Conduct of the war: The French defeated the English-Dutch fleet off *Beachy Head*, 1690. The threat of a French invasion in favour of James was, however, warded off by a brilliant English victory near *Cape de la Hague* on the French coast, 1692, which gave the English full control of the Channel. Even on land the English, after initial defeats, held the position of the allied troops and conquered the fortress of Namur, 1695.

6. B a n k o f E n g l a n d was established in 1694, necessitated by huge loans for continued warfare and the need for safe depositing of money. The stockholders, who subscribed to an initial loan of £1.2 million in return for an annuity of £100,000, were formed into a chartered company. The Bank eventually became the official financial agent of the government with the exclusive right of issuing bank notes.

7. *Act of Settlement,* 1701, which was prompted by fear of Catholic plots to bring back the Old Pretender, provided for the succession of the House of Hanover (descended from a daughter of James I) in case of the childless death of William and his sister-in-law and successor Anne. The Act moreover contained important constitutional provisions:

The Sovereign must be member of the Church of England.

He must not leave the country without the consent of Parliament.

The nation shall not be involved in any war of defence of territories not belonging to the Crown of England without the consent of Parliament.

Foreigners shall not be eligible for offices or membership of either House of Parliament or to have any grant of lands from the Crown.

Persons holding offices under the Crown or receiving pensions from the Crown shall not be members of the House of Commons.

All administrative measures shall be transacted in the Privy Council and signed by the responsible ministers.

Judges shall hold office no longer 'during the King's pleasure', but 'during good behaviour' (quam diu se bene gesserunt), i.e. for life. They can only be removed on address of both Houses of Parliament.

Queen Anne, 1702–14

Anne succeeded as second daughter of James II and was married to a prince of Denmark. Conservative by nature, Anne relied on Tory ministers (Lord Godolphin, Harley and Lord Bolingbroke). Lacking any gifts for ruling, she was greatly under the influence of friendships with ambitious women, esp. Sarah Jennings, later Duchess of Marlborough.

John Churchill, later Duke of Marlborough, was one of England's greatest generals and a dispassionate, skilful diplomat without special party affiliation. He served as officer and courtier under James II, whom he deserted on the landing of William of Orange, who gave him commissions in the Irish and Dutch wars. He was sent to the Tower on the charge of high treason (contacts with James), but released for lack of proof. He reached the height of his power under Queen Anne through the influence of his wife over the Queen. As Commander-in-Chief in the War of Spanish Succession, he won brilliant victories, particularly at Blindheim–Höchstädt (called Blenheim in England), for which he was rewarded by the building of the Palace of Blenheim at the nation's expense. Losing favour with Anne, he was deprived of his offices on the charge of embezzlement of war supplies. Though he was restored to royal favour under George I, he no longer took part in politics. After his death he was buried first in Westminster Abbey, then in Blenheim Palace.

1. **War of Spanish Succession, 1702–14,**

a) *Grand Alliance* between England, Holland and Austria had been formed already by William in response to Louis's recognition of James's son James (henceforth 'the Old Pretender') as English king.

b) The war was fought successfully under the Whig ministry on sea and on land over the whole of Europe. While the English fleet captured Gibraltar and Minorca, allied forces under the command of Prince Eugene and Marlborough drove the French from all territories they had occupied: Prince Eugene from Italy by the victory of Turin, 1706, Marlborough from southern Germany through the victory at Blindheim-Höchstädt.

In the Spanish Netherlands the French were defeated in three battles: at Ramillies (1706) by Marlborough, at Oudenarde (1708) and Malplaquet (1709) by both generals.

c) Peace of Utrecht, 1713, was brought about by a change in the balance of power through the death of the Austrian Emperor

51

Joseph I. This made his brother Karl, for whose succession in Spain England had fought, Emperor of Austria. No longer interested in such accumulation of power by Austria, the new Tory cabinet under Lord Bolingbroke withdrew from the alliance and concluded a separate peace with France: England acknowledged the Bourbon succession in Spain and gained Gibraltar and Minorca (control of the western Mediterranean!), and in America Nova Scotia, Newfoundland and Hudson Bay. The *Asiento Clause* gave England trading rights in Spanish America, esp. the monopoly of the slave trade with Spanish colonies.

3. **P a r l i a m e n t a r y   u n i o n   w i t h   S c o t l a n d** was effected in 1707: Sixteen Scottish lords were to be elected to the House of Lords, as well as representatives to the House of Commons. The ecclesiastical, legal and educational systems, however, have remained separate.

4. Penal code against Irish Roman Catholics forbade acquisition of freeholds and primogeniture for Catholic property in order to split up larger holdings between all children. Catholics were barred from professions, juries, state offices and voting.

5. INTERNAL LEGISLATION:

a) *Property Qualification Act,* 1711, which made a seat in Parliament dependent on the qualification of having landed property, initiated the aristocratic era of the 18th century.

b) *Occasional Conformity Act,* 1711, prevented Dissenters from taking the Holy Communion of the Church of England only to obtain an office, as had been made possible by the *Test Act.*

c) *Schism Act,* 1714, gave the Anglican Church the monopoly of education by making appointments of teachers in Nonconformist schools dependent on a license from a bishop.

6. Death of Queen Anne: Despite efforts of Bolingbroke and the Tories to eliminate the Whigs and recall the Pretender, the Whigs prevailed in securing the succession of the Protestant Elector of Hanover under the *Act of Settlement,* 1701.

House of Hanover

Opposition of the Jacobite Tories to the Hanoverian succession made the first two Georges dependent on the Whigs, who continued ruling for 46 years. The Whig oligarchy was represented by a few noble families, who controlled the House of Lords and largely also the Commons by influencing 'pocket boroughs' to elect their younger sons.

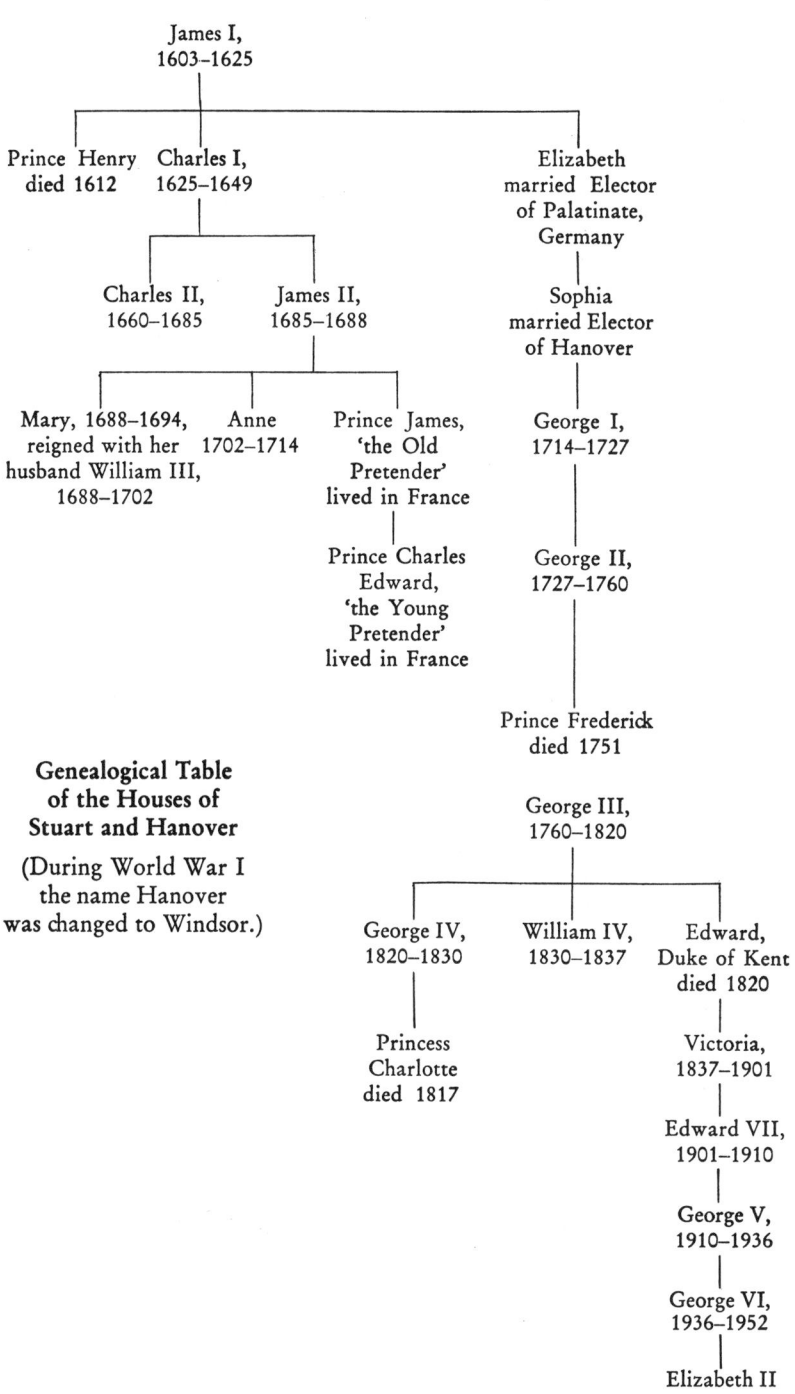

James I,
1603–1625

Prince Henry
died 1612

Charles I,
1625–1649

Elizabeth
married Elector
of Palatinate,
Germany

Charles II,
1660–1685

James II,
1685–1688

Sophia
married Elector
of Hanover

Mary, 1688–1694,
reigned with her
husband William III,
1688–1702

Anne
1702–1714

Prince James,
'the Old
Pretender'
lived in France

George I,
1714–1727

Prince Charles
Edward,
'the Young
Pretender'
lived in France

George II,
1727–1760

Prince Frederick
died 1751

**Genealogical Table
of the Houses of
Stuart and Hanover**

(During World War I
the name Hanover
was changed to Windsor.)

George III,
1760–1820

George IV,
1820–1830

William IV,
1830–1837

Edward,
Duke of Kent
died 1820

Princess
Charlotte
died 1817

Victoria,
1837–1901

Edward VII,
1901–1910

George V,
1910–1936

George VI,
1936–1952

Elizabeth II

George I, 1714–27

George was Elector of Hanover descended from a daughter of James I, who had married the Elector of the Palatinate. An able ruler, he was, however, little interested in English affairs.

1. 'Fifteen Rebellion': A Jacobite rebellion in Scotland under the Earl of Mar and the rising of Catholic nobles in the north of England in favour of the Old Pretender were put down in the battle of Preston. The Pretender, landing too late, returned to France.

2. *Septennial Act*, 1716, increasing the length of Parliament to seven years to keep the Whigs long in power, weakened popular interest in parliamentary life (which is kept alive only by frequent elections).

3. Development of the Cabinet as an independent body: Speaking no English and chiefly interested in Hanover, George I withdrew from cabinet meetings, leaving to the chief minister, Walpole, the task of forming ministries and presiding over their meetings. This gave rise to the office of Prime Minister, who in time became the responsible leader, though not official head, of the government.

Robert Walpole, 1676–1745, ruling for twenty-one years, initiated a long period of prosperity and peace. A Member of Parliament at 25, he served in several offices in the Cabinet and was favoured by George I for having actively sponsored the Hanoverian succession. As Lord Treasurer he considerably reduced the national debt and skilfully managed the South Sea Bubble (panic caused by the bankruptcy of the South Sea Company, the government's support of which had led to frantic speculation). Combining vigour of personality and coarse wit with common sense, diplomatic skill and political prudence, he rose to undisputed leadership despite his descent from the lower gentry. In spite of growing opposition led by Frederick, Prince of Wales, he maintained his authority till failures in a war against Spain forced him to resign in 1742.

4. Conservatism and tolerance: Aware of the continued power of the Tories, Walpole strove to avoid political conflicts at home and abroad by confirming the rights of the Church, universities and corporations, one of his maxims being: 'Let sleeping dogs lie.' In contrast to absolutist regimes on the Continent, he respected personal freedom and favoured a spirit of tolerance, which, however, led to laxity and inefficiency in national institutions.

5. Corruption: In spite of his personal integrity, Walpole initiated an era of corruption by using the general stagnation and egotism to bribe Members of Parliament in accordance with his conviction that 'every man has his price'.

George II, 1727–60

1. War against Spain, 1739, was forced on Walpole by popular feeling against Spain for restricting the English trade with her American colonies. Hatred of Spain was increased by the story of the English captain Jenkins, who asserted that Spaniards had ill-treated him and cut off his ear ('War of Jenkins' Ear'). The unsatisfactory course of the war, in which Spanish ships and colonies in the Indies were attacked without lasting success, led to Walpole's fall.

2. War of Austrian Succession, 1740–48, between Maria Theresa and an alliance of Prussia, Bavaria, Spain and France was joined by England on the Austrian side in continuation of traditional conflicts with Spain and France. English-Hanoverian troops won a victory over the French at Dettingen (1743) under the command of King George II—the last battle in which an English king took part—but were defeated at Fontenoy (Netherlands). The Peace of Aix-la-Chapelle preserved the status quo.

3. 'Forty-five Rebellion': In 1745 the Jacobites rose in favour of the Young Pretender, Charles Edward Stuart (Bonnie Prince Charlie), who, landing in Scotland, won a large following of adherents inspired by his youth and gallantry. Capturing Edinburgh after a brilliant victory near Prestonpans (Firth of Forth), he marched down to Derby (Midlands), but was driven back to the Highlands after another victory at Falkirk and finally beaten in the battle of Culloden Moor, 1746 (last battle on British soil). The story of his gallantry and the faithfulness of the Highlanders who refused to betray him during his long wanderings before escaping to France, closed the era of romance associated with the Scottish Highlands. These were now administered like the rest of the country and 'civilized'. The selfishness of the clan chieftains, who now became feudal landlords of former clan territory and enclosed land for sheep breeding, led to the emigration of about 30,000 Highlanders between that time and the American War of Independence.

William Pitt (the Elder Pitt), later Earl of Chatham, 1708–78, was a fervent patriot and one of the greatest English statesmen and orators. Descended from the landed gentry, educated at Eton and Oxford, he became Member of Parliament at 25. He joined the Young Patriot Party, which was under the leadership of Frederick, Prince of Wales, and against Walpole's policy of corruption. Even after Walpole's fall, 1742, however, and despite wars against Spain and France, the era of corruption continued under the ministries of Lord Carteret, Henry Pelham and his brother, the Duke of Newcastle, till repeated failures in colonial wars necessitated firm, patriotic and incorrupt leadership. In 1756, when Pitt became Minister of War, he began exercising unrestricted control in national and military affairs, directed the war on three continents on land and sea, but lost power on the succession of George III, who favoured the Tories.

During his last years, which were darkened by illness and temporary insanity, he came once more to the fore during England's conflict with her American colonies, appealing for a more generous treatment of the colonists.

His greatness as a statesman lay in his effort to maintain imperial power without infringing constitutional rights, and the fact that he introduced into parliamentary life the force of public opinion.

4. **Colonial War against France,** 1756–63, was waged on three continents for control of the seas, of India and North America.

a) EUROPE: In 1755 England concluded the *Treaty of Westminster* with Frederick II of Prussia. On the outbreak of the S e v e n Y e a r s' W a r between Frederick and France, which was allied with Austria, England declared war on France, sent liberal subsidies to Frederick, and attacked the coast of France, which had meanwhile overrun Hanover.

b) AMERICA: In 1754 French and English colonists came into conflict in the Ohio Valley. Here Duquesne, Governor of the French colony of Canada, declaring all land west of the Appalachians to be French territory, had built a series of forts against infiltration of British settlers. General Braddock, sent with British regulars, was defeated and killed. After an official declaration of war, Pitt raised 40,000 regulars and colonials, appointed able generals, Wolfe, Amherst, Forbes, and cut off all French reinforcements and supplies sent to America. In 1758 British troops began to close in on Canada. Amherst conquered Cape Breton (controlling the mouth of the St. Lawrence River) through the capture of Louisbourg. Fort Duquesne was destroyed and renamed Pittsburgh. The siege and f a l l o f Q u e b e c, where the commanders on both sides, Wolfe and Montcalm, were killed, and the c a p t u r e o f M o n t r e a l in 1760 ended the war in America.

c) INDIA: In 1740 the French and English East India Companies came into conflict in the Carnatic (southeast India) on account of the aggressive policy of the French governor Dupleix, who, after capture of the English trading post at Madras, had become the chief power in India. Following the capture of the British settlement in Calcutta by a native prince (1756), the death of 123 British prisoners in a small cell, 'the Black Hole of Calcutta', led to more active warfare on the British side. Calcutta was recaptured by R o b e r t C l i v e, a clerk of the East India Company, who had already won military fame through the capture of Arcot in the Carnatic. Clive's decisive v i c t o r y a t P l a s s e y, 1757, gave the British control of Bengal. Coote's victory at Wandewash drove the French from the Carnatic.

d) P e a c e o f P a r i s , 1763: England acquired from France Canada, the territory between the Appalachians and the Mississippi, four West Indian islands and parts of India (Bengal and territories in the south).

The Age of Revolutions
1760–1837

A. ENGLAND UNDER THE PERSONAL RULE OF GEORGE III, 1760–82

G e o r g e I I I , 1760–1820, grandson of George II

George was the first Hanoverian monarch born in England with primarily English interests. As a ruler he was able and industrious, but obstinate and narrow-minded. He was insane during the last decade of his reign.

I. **Personal Rule of George III:** George made a last attempt to revive the personal rule of the king by a parliamentary majority known as the 'King's friends', and by appointing chiefly subservient T o r y m i n i s t e r s (Lord Bute, 1762–63, and, after the more liberal ministries of Grenville and the Earl of Grafton, Lord North, 1770–82). No later English monarch held a position comparable to that of George III between 1760 and 1802. Opposition to his government was chiefly expressed in John Wilkes's paper *North Briton* and in anonymous letters signed *Junius* published between 1768 and 1772 in the *Public Advertiser*. Their criticism was acclaimed and the editors were supported by the public in spite of governmental prosecution. Though Wilkes was expelled from Parliament and imprisoned for libel, he was several times re-elected by the voters.

II. **American War of Independence, 1775–83**

1. CAUSES:
   a) B r i t i s h c o m m e r c i a l p o l i c y had greatly impeded colonial development. Manufacturing was forbidden in order to stimulate purchase from the motherland. Heavy duties were laid on imports from other countries. Prohibition of colonial exports except to England and on British vessels led to extensive smuggling.
   b) G r o w i n g d e m o c r a t i c f e e l i n g among settlers, particularly in Puritan New England, resented the spirit of colonialism and aristocratic egotism.
   c) *Stamp Act*, 1765, imposed a tax on all legal documents to finance

a stricter colonial administration and the debts of the late colonial war.

d) A n t i - B r i t i s h   r i o t s in the colonies under the battle-cry 'No taxation without representation' forced the government to repeal the *Stamp Act* in 1766. Under King George's pressure, however, new import duties were imposed to uphold the principle that the motherland had the right of taxation. Riots in Boston, which ensued, were answered by closing Boston harbour.

2. THE WAR, 1775–83, which, in 1778, was extended by the entrance of France, Holland and Spain on the American side, met with passionate criticism from liberal elements in Parliament (Elder Pitt, Burke), who condemned the policy of suppression, and the use of Hessian mercenaries and Indian allies:

a) New England: British troops, defeated at L e x i n g t o n, 1775, and suffering heavy losses in skirmishes at C o n c o r d and Bunker Hill, were forced to evacuate Boston, 1776.

b) New York was captured by the British general Howe, but General Burgoyne was taken prisoner at S a r a t o g a, 1777.

c) Southern colonies: After capture of Savannah and Charleston, British troops devastated the South, but were finally defeated by Washington with French help. The surrender of General Cornwallis at Y o r k t o w n, Virginia, ended the war in 1781.

d) Gibraltar: During a three years' siege by French and Spanish forces, Gibraltar was successfully defended by General Elliot.

3. P e a c e   o f   P a r i s 1783: The thirteen American colonies became independent. Spain received Florida and Minorca, France was given colonies on the western coast of Africa.

III. **Industrial and Agricultural Revolutions:** In 1760 great mechanical inventions began to revolutionize production and society in England, replacing rural domestic industries by the factory system in industrial cities of northern England.

1. INDUSTRIAL REVOLUTION (extending far into the 19th century).

a) S t e a m   e n g i n e developed by Newcomen, 1705, and James Watt, 1769 (first patent), and first used for pumping water out of mines, revolutionized mining, manufacture and transport (first l o c o m o t i v e invented in 1814 by Stephenson).

b) Textile industry developed through invention of the f l y i n g s h u t t l e by Kay, 1733, the 's p i n n i n g - j e n n y' by Hargreaves, 1770, the p o w e r - l o o m by Cartwright, 1785. Since the installation of the first steam engine in a Nottingham factory, 1785, manufacturing towns developed on the coalfields.

c) Iron industry, long centred round the woodlands of Sussex when iron-ore was still smelted with charcoal, was now transferred to the 'Black Country' on the Birmingham coalfield, and increased twenty-fold within 50 years.

d) Transport developed in three stages, aiding in its turn the establishment of new industries:

1760–1810: c a n a l s : first canal the Bridgewater Canal, 1761, first steamship on the Thames, 1801;

1810–25: ' m a c a d a m i z e d   r o a d s ' were constructed by the improved methods of Macadam (engineer and inspector of road construction);

from 1825: r a i l w a y s : The first railway from Stockton to Darlington, 1825, was built in the centre of the largest coalfield; the railway from Manchester to Liverpool, 1830, in the centre of the textile area.

e) Trade was aided by England's industrial advancement over other nations and her predominance on the sea, which secured England the virtual monopoly of overseas trade for over a century.

2. AGRICULTURAL REVOLUTION: Improvements in farming led to new enclosures of land hitherto used as common for grazing. This meant a notable development in arable farming, but resulted in the ruin of small holdings, which were integrated in large estates. Thus rural society broke up into big landowners, tenant farmers and poor land labourers.

a) E n c l o s u r e s of land for improved farming (e.g. roots and new grasses to make possible stall-feeding) were made necessary by the remarkable increase of population and, later, the blockade of England by Napoleon's Continental system. Enclosures by big landlords were sanctioned by Parliament, in which the interests of small farmers were not represented.

b) R u i n   o f   r u r a l   d o m e s t i c   i n d u s t r i e s came about through the factory system.

c) U r b a n i z a t i o n : Deprived of their livelihood (farming and home trades), farmers became land labourers or factory hands.

d) Land labourers were very poor, their wages being fixed by the justices of the peace, who were landowners. The *Speenhamland System*, which had supplemented wages since 1795, was repealed in 1834.

3. MISERY OF THE WORKING CLASSES (extending far into the 19th century):

a) Since manual labourers were now replaced by machines, abundance of labour kept w a g e s   a t   s t a r v a t i o n   l e v e l , making it

59

necessary for the whole family to work (children sometimes from the age of five).

b) In the s l u m s of industrial cities several families were frequently crowded in one room.

c) L o n g w o r k i n g h o u r s : Men, women and children were employed for twelve to sixteen hours in mines and mills.

d) 'Apprentice system' allowed to hire out children as g a n g l a b o u r without pay.

e) S w e a t i n g s y s t e m (domestic piece work) in textile industries ruined the health of women.

f) H e a v y t a x a t i o n due to the Napoleonic Wars.

Interference of the government in favour of the poor was discouraged by e c o n o m i c l i b e r a l i s m , which, by establishing private initiative and free competition as the most productive forces in economic life (see Adam Smith *Wealth of Nations* p. 278), offered an excuse for the egotism of employers and the ruthless exploitation of workers.

IV. **Renewal of Party Struggle** under the influence of internal strain and revolutionary movements abroad:

1. WHIGS, under the leadership of Fox and Burke and supported by Dissenters, merchants and manufacturers, stood for abolition of corruption and sponsored p a r l i a m e n t a r y r e f o r m s and r e l i g i o u s e q u a l i t y. Their sympathy with the American and French revolutions and partial opposition to the ensuing war with France made them an unpopular minority for half a century.
C h a r l e s F o x , one of England's greatest orators and an influential statesman, was a member of the ministry at various times. He advocated political rights for Nonconformists and Roman Catholics and the abolition of pocket boroughs controlled by rich landowners. He sympathized with the French Revolution and with suppressed social groups, particularly slaves. As Foreign Secretary in the short Whig ministry of Grenville, 1807, he carried a measure to abolish the slave trade.
E d m u n d B u r k e , son of an Irish lawyer, exercised considerable influence as a passionate and brilliant orator, politician, and philosophic and political writer. In Parliament he came to the fore through his enthusiastic sponsorship of the American cause and his struggle against corruption at home and in India. This led to the *Economic Reform Bill* against corruption, and impeachment of the Indian Governor-General Warren Hastings. The horrors of the French Revolution led to Burke's separation from the Whigs; his famous pamphlet *Reflections on the French Revolution* became the standard statement of the new conservative views.

2. TORIES, under leadership of the Younger Pitt, stood for protection of tradition, political stability, national power, and exclusion of Dissenting groups from political power.

L o r d   G o r d o n   R i o t s , 1780: Abolition of penal laws against Roman Catholics led to Protestant agitation against religious toleration. Thousands of Protestants under leadership of Lord Gordon gathered in London to present a petition to Parliament. Outbreaking riots resulted in the destruction of Catholic property and a massacre, till the military restored order through the execution of leading rioters.

B. TORY ERA, 1782–1820

Strengthened by the right wing of the Whigs under Burke, who were disillusioned by the French Revolution, Tories maintained their power through successful suppression of revolutionary movements and energetic conducting of the Napoleonic Wars, which appealed to popular nationalism, and, afterwards, through liberal reforms.

W i l l i a m   P i t t , second son of the Earl of Chatham (the Elder Pitt), entered Parliament at 22, and was Prime Minister at 24. Less impetuous and vigorous than his father but with similiar determination and statesmanship, he remained in almost unbroken control for 20 years (1782–1801 and 1804–06). Though appointed personally by George III, he made his party independent of the King. First in favour of liberal reforms (reform of Parliament, abolition of the *Test Act* etc.), he turned Conservative in reaction to the French Revolution. Despite rigorous suppression of liberal movements in England and in Ireland after the French Revolution, his government received sufficient popular support to conduct world-wide war against France.

I. Colonial Policy:

1. INDIA was ruled by a Governor-General and council of the East India Company. After Clive, W a r r e n   H a s t i n g s made new conquests and introduced important administrative reforms. Nevertheless he encountered considerable hostility in the Company and at home, which led to his impeachment for corruption and arbitrary government initiated and conducted by Edmund Burke. Hastings was acquitted, but Pitt's *India Act,* 1784, now placed Indian administration under a Board of Control of the British government. Under later Governors-General L o r d   C o r n w a l l i s and L o r d   W e l l e s l e y , the greater part of the peninsula up to the Himalayas was brought under British rule through new conquests by General Lake and Arthur Wellesley (brother of Lord Wellesley and later Duke of Wellington).

2. AUSTRALIA was discovered in 1642 by the Dutch navigator Tasman and rediscovered in 1770 by the English navigator J a m e s   C o o k . In 1788 the first British colony called after Pitt's Home Secretary, Sydney, was established as a c o n v i c t   s e t t l e m e n t . In 1793 began the free immigration of big sheep and cattle raisers (squatters).

3. CANADA: The *Constitutional Act,* 1791, sought to relieve the growing friction between the original French settlers in Lower Canada and the British colonists, who had increased through the emigration of British loyalists from the U.S.A. Under the Act, Upper and Lower Canada received separate governments.

II. **Suppression of Radical Movements** under the influence of outrages during the French Revolution and of ensuing war against France:

The outbreak of the French Revolution led to the revival of Whig associations (e.g. Revolutionary Society and Constitutional Society) demanding parliamentary reforms, and the forming of radical associations among the labouring classes, e.g. the C o r r e s p o n d i n g S o c i e t y founded by the shoemaker Thomas Hardy. More radical societies, inspired by T h o m a s P a i n e ' s *The Rights of Man,* 1792, demanded abolition of the monarchy, demonstrating in the streets of London for equality and liberty.

1. Radical associations were prohibited.

2. Suspension of the *Habeas Corpus Act,* 1794, enabled the government to keep agitators and suspected persons imprisoned without trial.

3. *Seditious Meetings Act,* 1795, restricted open political discussion.

4. P r o s e c u t i o n o f r a d i c a l l e a d e r s : Agitators, including writers, publishers, Nonconformist ministers, were exiled (e.g. Thomas Paine) or transported to Australia. Thomas Hardy was tried for high treason, but acquitted by an independent jury.

5. C o m b i n a t i o n A c t s , 1799 and 1800, forbade workmen's associations that had been formed to secure higher wages and better working conditions.

III. **Ireland:**

1. Grattan's Parliament: During the American Revolution, the necessity of raising Irish volunteer troops for the defence of their country against a threatened French invasion compelled England to make important concessions demanded by the Irish Parliament under the leadership of Henry Grattan (Protestant lawyer and powerful orator):
a) Free export of Irish goods.
b) Free Parliament through repeal of *Poyning's Law* (enacted in 1494), which had required all Irish laws to be approved by the English government.
c) *Catholic Relief Act* granted to Catholics the right to become jurors and magistrates and to bear arms.

2. Irish rebellion, 1798, caused by the discontent of Catholics (who still could not be M.P.s) and the influence of the French Revolution offset all political gains:
a) The insurrection was put down by General Lake and Lord Cornwallis with the help of Irish loyalists (Orangists); French troops called in to assist the Irish were defeated.
b) *A c t   o f   U n i o n* , 1800: By bribery (£1,250,000) and promises of peerages Pitt obtained a majority in the Irish Parliament for parliamentary union with Britain henceforth called U n i t e d K i n g d o m   o f   G r e a t   B r i t a i n   a n d   I r e l a n d. From now on Irish interests were represented in the English Parliament by 100 Protestant members and 28 Irish peers, whose vote could at any time be overridden by English and Scottish majorities. The immense unpopularity of this measure caused much ill-feeling in Ireland and conflicts in the English Parliament itself.

IV. Napoleonic Wars:

England joined Continental coalitions to preserve the balance of power: Largely unsuccessful in their expeditions on land (Brittany, 1795, and Holland, 1796 and 1809), the British prevailed in all naval battles, thus becoming an important factor in Napoleon's final defeat.

1. WAR OF THE FIRST COALITION, 1792–97, after the French declaration of war on Holland and Great Britain:
a) The English defeated the French fleet off Ushant, 1794. After naval mutinies off Spithead and Nore had been rigorously suppressed, the Dutch and Spanish fleets (which had been confiscated by the French) were defeated off Camperdown (1797).
b) After the conquest of Holland by France, England seized the Dutch colonies: the C a p e   o f   G o o d   H o p e, 1795, C e y l o n and G u i a n a, 1796.
c) Following Napoleon's conquest of Egypt (to cut off England's route to India), Admiral Nelson destroyed the French fleet in the Battle of the Nile (Abukir), 1798.

2. WAR OF THE SECOND COALITION, 1799–1801:
a) The British conquered M a l t a (1800), which Napoleon had wrested from the hands of the Knights of St. John (Johanniterorden).
b) Copenhagen was bombarded by Nelson in 1801 as an answer to Napoleon's attempt to prevent British vessels from entering Danish ports and to place Danish ships under French command.

3. THIRD COALITION, brought about by Pitt, saved England from French invasion prepared at Boulogne. While the Continental powers which Napoleon now attacked instead of England were crushed at Austerlitz

and Jena, the British finally established their naval supremacy by a brilliant naval victory off C a p e T r a f a l g a r over the French and Spanish fleets, 1805, in which Admiral Nelson, who had become the idol of the nation, was mortally wounded.

4. NAPOLEON'S CONTINENTAL SYSTEM attempted to blockade Britain: The *Berlin Decree,* 1806, provided that all vessels coming from England be barred from Continental ports, their wares confiscated; the *Milan Decree,* 1807, ordered that all vessels coming from England be seized. Britain, which, after Pitt's death, was ruled by the Tory ministries of the Dukes of Portland and of Perceval with Canning and Castlereagh as foreign secretaries successively in 1807 and 1812, answered with *Orders in Council* declaring the blockade of the Continent: Neutral vessels were forbidden to trade with ports from which Britain was excluded.

5. SECOND EXPEDITION AGAINST DENMARK, 1807, to prevent Denmark from joining the Continental system led to a second bombardment of Copenhagen and capture of the Danish fleet and Heligoland.

6. PENINSULAR WAR, 1808–14, supported Spanish guerillas against French rule:
a) First expedition to Portugal: When France attacked Portugal for opening its harbours to English ships and captured Lisbon, a British force under Arthur Wellesley (later Duke of Wellington) liberated Portugal through the victory at Vimiera. Under the Convention of Cintra, the French withdrew from Portugal.
b) Second expedition to Spain: In northern Spain British troops were repulsed by Napoleon. While General Moore was mortally wounded, his troops were able to embark from Corunna. Napoleon's Russian campaign in 1812 facilitated Wellington's advance on France. He defeated the French at Talavera, 1809, Salamanca, 1812, Vittoria, 1813, and, after the Battle of Leipzig and Napoleon's abdication, Toulouse, 1814.

7. WAR WITH THE UNITED STATES, 1812–14, was brought about by British *Orders in Council,* forcing neutral ships to call at British ports before landing their cargo in North America, and allowing the search of American ships for deserters. An American attack on Canada was repulsed by United Empire Loyalists. The British attacked Washington and burned the Capitol but were defeated at New Orleans. The *Treaty of Ghent* preserved the status quo.

8. WATERLOO, 1815: Napoleon's escape from Elba, where he had been exiled after his defeat on the Continent, and his return to France during the Congress of Vienna renewed the war. W e l l i n g t o n

and Blücher marched on Paris after a final v i c t o r y a t W a t e r - l o o. Napoleon, surrendering to the British ship *Bellerophon*, was brought to the Isle of St. Helena off the African coast, where he lived under the strict guard of the Governor Sir Hudson Lowe and died in 1821.

9. *Treaty of Vienna*, 1815, was negotiated on the English side by the Foreign Secretary Castlereagh. Of her numerous conquests, England retained Heligoland, Malta, the Cape of Good Hope, Mauritius, the Seychelles, Ceylon, the British part of Guiana, and the West Indian Isle of Tobago.

10. RESULT OF THE WARS: Extension of Britain's n a v a l p o w e r and c o l o n i a l p o s s e s s i o n s compensated for the earlier loss of American colonies. Increased trade made up for the heavy war debt, England becoming the workshop of the impoverished Continent. Heavy taxes and delay of reforms caused by the war increased s o c i a l d i s c o n t e n t.

R e g e n c y, 1811–20: During the growing insanity of George III, his son G e o r g e, P r i n c e o f W a l e s, ruled as Prince Regent. While he played a foremost part in fashionable life (racing, gambling), the Prince Regent was not very interested in politics. His extravagant life and disreputable habits encouraged radical movements, which were rigorously suppressed by the Tory government of Lord Liverpool.

V. Revival of Political Radicalism

1. W i l l i a m C o b b e t t, 1763–1835, son of a farmer, and one of the most powerful English journalists, made himself spokesman of the agricultural interests and rural ideals of Old England as against the profit-making classes of industry, finance and the non-resident gentry living from rents. His *Political Register*, illegally sold at a price available to the working classes, boldly exposed the misery of the poor, and voiced demands for parliamentary reforms. Though he himself spent two years in prison, his widely read periodical became the strongest force in stirring public opinion and bringing about reforms (p. 207).

2. Benthamites or P h i l o s o p h i c a l R a d i c a l s demanded universal suffrage, reform of the penal code and codification of law according to Jeremy Bentham's principle of 'the greatest happiness of the greatest number' (utilitarianism, p. 275–76).

3. S p e n c e a n P h i l a n t h r o p i s t s, propagating the teaching of Thomas Spence, demanded land nationalization (later more successfully sponsored by the American political economist Henry George). Land

was to be rented out by the parish and rents used to pay all public expenditure.

4. Major John Cartwright organized the Hampden and Union Clubs, which demanded parliamentary and tax reforms, and abolition of sinecures.

5. The ex-working man F r a n c i s P l a c e fought for abolition of the *Combination Acts*.

6. 'L u d d i t e s', claiming as their leader one Ned Ludd, whose centre was popularly thought to be Sherwood Forest (cf. Robin Hood!), raised riots in industrial areas, destroying machinery.

VI. Suppression of Working Classes and Radical Movements

1. *Corn Laws* (import duty on wheat), which were introduced in 1815 for the benefit of landowners and farmers to prevent the import of cheap wheat, kept prices of staple food for the working classes high.

2. Abolition of the income tax, 1816, raised indirect taxation, which hit the poor more than the moneyed class.

3. P e n a l l a w s imposed the death penalty on more than two hundred offences (e.g. smashing of machinery, stealing of objects valued at 5s and upwards).

4. 'Luddites' were punished by transportation and hanging. Speeches by Lord Byron and Burdett in Parliament against capital punishment for rioting remained ineffective. Sir Francis Burdett, who represented radical interests in Parliament, was arrested for publishing one of his speeches.

5. Renewed suspension of the *Habeas Corpus Act*, 1817, was caused by a Spencean demonstration, which had led to the arrest and trial of Spencean leaders for high treason.

6. *Gagging Act*, 1817, imposed severer penalties on seditious speech and writing.

7. S p y i n g s y s t e m was employed by the government to encourage and detect seditious agitation.

8. *Six Acts*, 1819, provided for seizure of arms and control of political meetings. The press was muzzled by a newspaper tax of 4 *d.* on every copy, which made the workers' only source of information unavailable to them. Political suspects were sentenced in summary proceedings without assizes.

9. 'B a t t l e o f P e t e r l o o', 1819: The charge of military upon a workmen's demonstration in St. Peter's Fields, Manchester, in which

eleven men were killed and many hundreds wounded, aroused public consternation.

10. C a t o S t r e e t C o n s p i r a c y, 1820: Radicals, especially workers, who plotted to kill ministers at a Cabinet meeting, were betrayed by government agents assisting in the plot and arrested in their meeting place in Cato Street. Leaders were hanged.

C. BEGINNINGS OF LIBERALISM AND SOCIALISM, 1820–38

G e o r g e I V, 1820–30

On his father's death the Prince Regent became King. Owing to his extravagance, his debts, his divorce suit before the House of Lords, his reign marked the lowest moral standard in the modern history of British monarchy. General discontent finally led to liberal and social reforms.

I. **Liberalism at Home** under pressure of the rising middle classes and liberal-minded ministers: R o b e r t P e e l (Home Secretary) and W i l l i a m H u s k i s s o n (Board of Trade) effected reforms in the Tory cabinets of Lord Liverpool and the Duke of Wellington, who, despite his military fame as one of the greatest English generals, was highly unpopular as Premier because of his pronounced conservatism. Lord J o h n R u s s e l l fought in Parliament for parliamentary reforms.

1. R e p e a l o f t h e *C o m b i n a t i o n A c t s,* which had treated trade unions as actionable conspiracies, was carried by Francis Place in 1824.

2. Reforms of Robert Peel (p. 71)
a) Cessation of the spying system.
b) A m e n d m e n t o f c r i m i n a l l a w : death penalty abolished for a large number of minor offences.
c) Organization of the London police armed only with truncheons.

3. Mitigation of the tariff system and *Navigation Acts* by Huskisson was made possible by England's industrial supremacy.

4. R e p e a l o f t h e *T e s t A c t* and *C o r p o r a t i o n A c t,* 1828, urged by Lord Russell, allowed Dissenters to hold public offices, thus preparing the way for the political influence of the middle classes.

5. *C a t h o l i c E m a n c i p a t i o n A c t,* 1829, was forced from Wellington by the Catholic Association, founded in 1823 under leadership of Daniel O'Connell (Irish lawyer and orator). Catholics were admitted to nearly all offices and membership of Parliament. The passage of the bill under pressure of imminent civil war in Ireland, despite opposition of the high Tories, caused the disintegration of the Tory party, but preserved the rule over Ireland.

II. **Liberalism in Foreign Affairs:** After the Napoleonic Wars, Foreign Secretary C a s t l e r e a g h (1812–22) had already withdrawn from the reactionary policy pursued by the Holy Alliance of Continental powers under Metternich's leadership. Foreign Secretary C a n n i n g (1822–27) actively supported struggles for independence in Europe and America.

1. Protest against French interference in constitutional struggles in Spain, 1823.

2. Acknowledgement of the newly gained independence of the Spanish and Portuguese colonies in Latin America against interference of the Holy Alliance; support of the *Monroe Doctrine*, 1823, which demanded that Europe should not interfere in the Americas.

3. S u p p o r t o f t h e G r e e k s t r u g g l e f o r i n d e p e n d e n c e, 1821–29: The united fleets of Britain, France and Russia destroyed the Turkish fleet at N a v a r i n o, 1827. The death of Lord Byron, champion of Greek liberty, at Missolonghi (Greece) inspired enthusiasm for the Greek cause.

W i l l i a m I V, brother of George IV, 1830–37

III. **Democratic and Social Reforms** under the Whig ministries of Lord Grey and Lord Melbourne:

1. *First Reform Bill*, 1832:
   a) PASSAGE OF THE BILL: Under the influence of the July Revolution in France, 1830, and under Radical pressure the Whigs returned to power. The new cabinet of Lord Grey (including Lord Russell and Lord Durham, both of whom advocated reforms) introduced a bill for the reform of parliamentary representation. This was passed in spite of repeated rejection by the House of Lords, after the King had threatened to create new peers who would pass the bill (in German 'Pairschub'), and after violent agitation and riots had brought the country to the brink of civil war.
   b) PROVISIONS: The franchise was granted to the upper middle classes, including independent farmers, owners of house property and tenants in towns paying a yearly rent of £10 ('Ten-Pound Householders'). The seats of fifty-six 'rotten boroughs' were given over to big industrial towns (e.g. Manchester, Birmingham), the rest abolished. Nevertheless the proportion of voters to persons not entitled to vote in England was still 1:17 in towns and 1:24 in counties.

2. *Municipal Reform Act*, 1835, preceded by the *Scottish Burgh Reform Act*, 1833: The aristocratic and often corrupt town governments, which could nominate their successors, were replaced by elected

democratic town councils with councillors (to be elected by the rate-payers for three years) and aldermen (to be elected by the councillors for six years).

3. ABOLITION OF SLAVERY, 1833, came about after untiring agitation by Quakers and Evangelical philanthropists under their leader William W i l b e r f o r c e , who, as Member of Parliament, introduced petitions and bills against slavery.

a) Slavery was abolished on English soil when a court sentence (1772) established the freedom of the negro slave Somerset, who had been sent away by his owner on account of ill health and was later reclaimed by him from his new master. The decision of the court stated that 'a man becomes free the moment he touches our shores.'

b) A b o l i t i o n o f t h e s l a v e t r a d e was carried in the House of Commons by a Whig ministry in 1807 with great ovations for Wilberforce: British warships were authorized to patrol sea routes to seize slave ships. In the Congress of Vienna (1815) Castlereagh secured approval of the suppression of the slave trade by the contracting powers.

c) A b o l i t i o n o f s l a v e r y was effected in the colonies in 1833 under Grey's ministry (important before the opening up of Africa): £20 million were appropriated for compensating slave owners.

4. BEGINNINGS OF SOCIALISM:

a) T r a d e u n i o n s , legalized in 1824, began to fight for e c o n o m i c i m p r o v e m e n t s (higher wages, fixed working hours) by means of collective bargaining or strikes. These were, however, forbidden by law, and were met by military force.

b) C h a r t i s m founded in 1838 under the leadership of O'Connor and Lovett strove for p o l i t i c a l e q u a l i t y through a people's charter demanding annual parliaments, universal male suffrage, vote by ballot, no property qualifications for Members of Parliament, payments for their services. Despite violent agitation of Chartists through mass meetings and the press, the petition, bearing more than one million signatures, was rejected three times by Parliament. Ensuing strikes were severely punished by imprisonments and transportations. In 1848, agitation revived under the influence of Continental revolutions. A mass meeting was summoned on Kensington Common in London. A march to Parliament to present the petition, however, was forbidden and prevented by troops and London volunteer citizens. The Chartists' aims were reached only later when the middle classes cooperated.

c) PRIVATE INITIATIVE

Robert Owen (1771–1858) was the most notable social reformer, whose theories of social improvement exercised a profound influence. Owen left school aged 9, became a worker, at 19 manager of a cotton mill, and later partner and manager of the New Lanark Mills in Scotland, which he organized on socialist principles (satisfactory housing and wages, fewer working hours, no employment of children under ten, elementary schooling for children below this age). Owen founded the first infant school in Britain. The Lanark Mills were visited by numerous reformers and statesmen. In 1813 Owen began to propagate his theory that the human character is the result of outward circumstances. In 1815 he began agitating for factory reforms and demanded that self-interest and capitalism be replaced by cooperation and social justice. He founded c o o p e r a t i v e s o c i e t i e s for building, producing and selling, the consumers' cooperative stores (Konsumvereine) becoming a world-wide movement. Attempts to establish s e l f - c o n t a i n e d c o m m u n i t i e s (one also in the U.S.A.), whose members organized their work, life and pleasures on collective conditions of equality, had no permanent success. Disliked by the upper classes because of his radical views, particulary on religion, Owen was looked upon by the trade unions as their leader.

Anthony Ashley, later seventh E a r l o f S h a f t e s b u r y (1801–85) came, in contrast to Owen, from the highest social class. A Tory, he considered socialism and Chartism as 'the two great demons in morals and politics' and opposed the *Reform Bill* of 1832. On the other hand, he was the chief representative of E v a n g e l i c a l p a t e r n a l i s m. As Member of Parliament he worked untiringly for social legislation against slums, the cruel treatment of lunatics, chimney sweeps and children employed in gangs and mines. He became the chief initiator of f a c t o r y b i l l s and played a part in the foundation of the Young Men's Christian Association and the Ragged Schools for poor children.

5. SOCIAL LEGISLATION:

a) *Factory Act*, 1833, forbade employment of children under 9 and night work for young persons under 18. Children between 9 and 13 were to go to school two hours a day and not to work more than 8 hours. Youths between 13 and 18 were not to work more than 12 hours. Factory inspectors were appointed to enforce the Act.

b) *Poor Law Amendment Act*, 1834, amended the poor law of Elizabeth I by establishing boards of guardians to administer local poor relief. Relief which, under the *Speenhamland System* (in force since 1795 in southern England), had supplemented wages, was no longer to be paid to able-bodied paupers, who were now gathered in newly built w o r k - h o u s e s (cf. Dickens, *Oliver Twist*). Men and women were separated to prevent the growth of families. The harshness of work-house conditions was approved on the principle that relief should be 'less eligible' than the worst working conditions in order to increase the willingness to work.

Victorian Age
Liberalism, Imperialism, Beginnings of Socialism
1837–1901

Victoria, 1837–1901

Well educated, Victoria succeeded to the throne at eighteen. She married her cousin, Prince Albert of Saxe-Coburg-Gotha who, though a noble character and gifted with political ability, was allowed little influence in politics. Combining vitality and determination with strictly moral principles and an acute sense of the responsibility of her royal position, Victoria reformed the moral laxity of her court and lived a life devoted to her royal duties and her family. She thus introduced the 'b o u r g e o i s   e r a' with its high standards of moral and social respectability, not always free from narrow-mindedness and hypocrisy. At the end of her reign she had become the idol of her people, her two brilliant jubilees, 1887 and 1897, demonstrating her i m m e n s e   p o p u l a r i t y throughout the United Kingdom and her vast Empire. Her long reign and the fact that in social and moral life she had restored to the Crown the prestige it had lost in political life, justify the term 'Victorian Age'.

A. PEEL–PALMERSTON ERA, 1841–65, in which Tory and Whig governments frequently alternated.

S i r   R o b e r t   P e e l (1788–1850), son of a wealthy industrialist, entered Parliament at 21. With the Duke of Wellington he was the chief l e a d e r   o f   t h e   T o r i e s. As Secretary for Ireland, 1812–18, he conducted what he called 'an honest despotic government', suppressing agitation for Catholic emancipation. As H o m e S e c r e t a r y from 1821–27 under Liverpool, and 1828–30 under Wellington, he r e f o r m e d   c r i m i n a l   l a w and founded the London police force, called 'Bobbies' after him. He carried with Wellington the *Catholic Emancipation Act* against fierce opposition among his own party. From 1835–39 he reorganized the Tory party under strict party discipline; the new 'Conservatives', though still representing the interests of landowners, took a more liberal attitude towards reforms. As P r i m e   M i n i s t e r from 1841–46, Peel met the economic crisis of 'the hungry forties' by reintroducing the income tax and putting the fiscal system on a sound basis. He was the chief factor in introducing free trade by repealing most duties. Though the abolition of the *Corn Laws* caused his fall and split his party, his adherents formed an important element in the new Liberal party under 'the Peelite' Gladstone, which adopted his principles.
L o r d   P a l m e r s t o n (1784–1865), Member of Parliament at 23, served from 1809–1830 as a minister in Tory cabinets, was F o r e i g n   S e c r e t a r y in Liberal cabinets (1830–51), and was P r i m e   M i n i s t e r for 9 years (1855–58, 1859–65). His audacious, aggressive p o l i c y   o f   e x p a n s i o n and interference in foreign affairs ('Lord Firebrand') gave England political influence in most European disputes and was highly approved of by the nationalistic spirit of the age ('j i n g o i s m'), though his self-assurance and sarcasm were little

appreciated by Victoria. Being less interested in democratic and social reforms at home than in liberal movements abroad (he supported revolutions in Sicily, Sardinia and Hungary, and a coup d'état by Napoleon III), he is sometimes called the last Whig aristocrat.

I. **Economic Expansion** through gradual development of free trade:

1. I n d u s t r i a l   e x p a n s i o n through free competition according to the laissez-faire theory of Adam Smith, Ricardo and Malthus had made England the workshop for the Continent already during the Napoleonic Wars.

2. FREE TRADE MOVEMENT:
   a) *Manchester Doctrine* propagated by Richard Cobden and John Bright from Manchester aimed at securing world markets for British products in order to increase profits and thereby ultimately wages.
   b) A n t i - C o r n - L a w   L e a g u e, founded in 1838 by a group of Lancaster manufacturers, aimed at repealing the *Corn Laws*, since the tax on wheat imports protecting domestic agriculture favoured the gentry at the expense of the industrial classes. In a six-year publicity campaign throughout the country under leadership of Bright and Cobden, who sponsored it in Parliament, the League became a powerful agent for the liberalization of trade.

3. F r e e   T r a d e (leading to an increase of trade by 40 per cent) was finally brought about by a number of measures:
   a) Far-reaching abolition of tariffs (made possible by reintroduction of the income tax).
   b) Gradual repeal of the *Navigation Acts*, which had restricted imports on other than English ships.
   c) Repeal of the *Corn Laws* in 1846 by Peel, after failure of the potato crops in Ireland in two successive years, 1845 and 1846 ('the hungry forties'), had caused the starvation of many thousands (a great wave of emigration to America reduced the Irish population from 8 to 6¹/₂ million).

4. RESULTS OF FREE TRADE:
   a) Industrial and commercial superiority lasted until the increase of foreign competition. Larger imports were balanced by the higher exports of British industry, which profited from cheaper raw materials, and the invisible earnings of shipping and overseas investment. 1850–75 was the g o l d e n   a g e   of   E n g l i s h   c a p i t a l i s m : Britain became the world's clearing house, the English pound sterling the standard of exchange, London the world's exchange centre.
   b) Agriculture, despite fears of landlords, continued to flourish until 1875 when the full development of the steamship made cheap

imports from overseas possible. Livestock developed through the import of new fodder crops, especially maize, arable farming through the invention of the steam plough and threshing machine.

5. G r e a t E x h i b i t i o n (1851) in the newly built Crystal Palace, inspired by Prince Albert, started the line of great international exhibitions and demonstrated British wealth and industrial achievements.

II. Social Legislation:

1. Factory Act, 1833 (p. 70).

2. *Collieries Act,* 1842: Women and children under nine were not to work underground.

3. *Ten-Hours Act,* 1847, limited the working day of women and young persons to ten hours.

4. *Factory Act,* 1850: On Saturdays factories were to close at two o'clock while on the other five working days work was limited to ten and a half hours.

5. Employment of child chimney sweeps was forbidden in 1864.

6. *Gangs Act,* 1868, forbade gang labour of children under eight.

III. **Foreign Policy,** chiefly determined by Palmerston, was marked by an aggressive i m p e r i a l i s m.

1. INDIA:
a) New a n n e x a t i o n s were made as the result of numerous wars: parts of Nepal (1816), which was made a vassal state, Central Provinces through Mahratta Wars (1818), Assam (1826), Sindh (1843), Punjab (1846), Kashmir (1846), Oudh (1856), and Burma after three wars from 1824–85. Beginning in 1850, peaceful expansion through annexations after the deaths of Indian princes without heirs.
Enforcement of P a x B r i t a n n i c a by the paramount power ended the constant strife of Indian princes. A d m i n i s t r a t i v e, s o c i a l a n d l e g a l r e f o r m s were introduced by successive governors-general: Lord Bentinck, 1827–35, abolished slavery and the burning of widows, trained Indian officials for administration and established a commission for the codification of penal law (chiefly through its first president, the notable historian T. B. Macaulay). Lords Auckland and Dalhousie built streets, canals, railways, organized post, telegraph and land surveys, and founded universities, from which Western ideas of freedom began to infiltrate and to undermine British authority. Despite the general economic improvements, the native industries, cotton spinning and weaving, were ruined by cheap imports from Manchester.

c) **Indian Mutiny**, 1857–58: Britain's policy of expansion caused discontent leading to rebellions of native Sepoy troops in Oudh and massacres in Delhi, Lucknow and Cawnpore. The mutiny was finally put down and participants cruelly punished. The *India Act*, 1858, dissolved the East India Company and made British India a **crown colony**. The Governor-General was replaced by a Viceroy, the Board of Control by the **India Office** (a separate ministry). A penal code drawn up by Macaulay was introduced.

2. **Wars in Afghanistan**, 1838 and 1842, aimed at establishing British influence and at relieving Persian and Russian pressure against the northern frontier of British India. Afghanistan remained a buffer state, a prey to foreign rivalries.

3. **New Zealand** was discovered (1642) by the Dutch navigator Tasman and rediscovered (1769) by **James Cook**, who annexed it to the British Crown without the government taking action to occupy the islands. English missions and wholesale purchases of land by the New Zealand Company began in 1814. The North Island was annexed in 1840 through an expedition of Captain Hobson upon news of French colonization plans. The native population of Maoris was gradually driven back by immigrants from Britain.

4. **Chinese (Opium) War**, 1842, was waged by England to protect her opium trade against the Chinese prohibition of opium imports. Being defeated, China had to cede **Hongkong** to England. Shanghai and other ports were opened to European trade.

5. **Crimean War**, 1854–56, against Russia was fought together with France and Turkey in support of Turkish interests in the Near East, in order to prevent Russia from extending her power to the eastern Mediterranean (land route to India). The heroism of the soldiers, e.g. the charge of the Light Brigade in the **Battle of Balaclava**, which was immortalized by Tennyson's poem, stood in marked contrast to the mismanagement of army administration, which caused infinite suffering and losses among English troops. **Florence Nightingale**'s devoted nursing of soldiers saved hundreds of lives. The final **capture of Sevastopol** after a two years' siege stopped the Russian advance to the Dardanelles through the **Treaty of Paris**, 1856. More important results of the war were drastic reforms in the army and the reorganization of London hospitals through Florence Nightingale ('The Lady with the Lamp').

6. **American Civil War**, 1861–65, had important repercussions on England. Raw cotton imports were cut off through the blockade of

Southern ports of the U.S.A., which caused a 'cotton famine' in Lancashire. Despite official British neutrality, the ruling upper classes sympathized with the Southern states. Recognition of the Southern Confederacy by Great Britain and the building of Southern cruisers in British ports caused ill-feeling between England and the Northern Union. In 1872, Great Britain submitted to the *Geneva Award* of an international tribunal to pay a compensation of £3 million for losses sustained by the American government, particularly through the Southern cruiser *Alabama* which had been built in England.

7. CANADA: The year 1837 saw rebellions in the French province of Lower Canada to gain independence, and in the English province of Upper Canada for greater authority of the colonial legislature. Investigation of the causes by Lord Durham led to the *Durham Report*, 1839, sponsoring full union (with automatic predominance of the more populous English province), and full self-government in internal affairs. This was largely realized by the *Act of Union*, 1840, granting representative and responsible government for the united provinces. Finally the *British North America Act*, 1867, granted Canada, as the first British colony, f u l l d o m i n i o n s t a t u s with the right to confederate other territories but not Newfoundland. The F e d e r a t i o n o f C a n a d a made possible the building of the Canadian Pacific Railway, which encouraged further immigration and promoted unity.

B. DISRAELI–GLADSTONE ERA, 1865–86.

B e n j a m i n D i s r a e l i, later Earl of Beaconsfield (1804–81), descended from a Jewish family immigrated from Italy. He first gained prominence through his political tracts anticipating his later conservatism tempered by social responsibility, and by his brilliant novels, the two best-known of which, *Coningsby* and *Sybil* drew public attention to the misery of the working classes. He entered the House of Commons in 1837 after having stood unsuccessfully first as a Radical, then several times as a Tory candidate. As M.P. he was applauded and feared as a brilliant and cynical speaker. After the fall of Robert Peel he became the virtual l e a d e r o f t h e C o n s e r v a t i v e p a r t y, was Chancellor of the Exchequer in the Tory cabinets of Lord Derby, and finally P r i m e M i n i s t e r (1868, 1874–80). He conducted an energetic policy of s o c i a l r e f o r m and i m p e r i a l e x p a n s i o n in Asia and Africa, which reconciled the masses to Conservative leadership. His strong devotion to the Crown and to the cause of imperialism won him the sympathy and support of the Queen, for whom he secured the title of Empress of India.

William E w a r t G l a d s t o n e (1809–98) was one of the most remarkable English statesmen for courage of conviction, personal integrity and administrative efficiency. The son of a rich merchant, an M.P. at 23, he served more than 60 years in Parliament, where he first represented moderate Conservative principles. Under

Peel he served as President of the Board of Trade and Colonial Secretary, under Palmerston as Chancellor of the Exchequer. Prompted by his deep religious sentiment and strong sense of responsibility towards suppressed groups he turned Liberal, and, on Palmerston's death, became l e a d e r   o f   t h e   L i b e r a l   p a r t y , standing for decades in bitter rivalry against Disraeli, whose Conservative ministries alternated with his. In four administrations (the last when he was 83) he introduced s o c i a l   a n d   l i b e r a l   r e f o r m s , withdrew from the expansionist policy of Disraeli, worked untiringly for the b e t t e r m e n t   o f   c o n d i t i o n s   i n   I r e l a n d , and finally split his own party by introducing two *Home Rule Bills* for Ireland (1886 and 1893).

I. Internal Reforms Under Gladstone and Disraeli:

1. PARLIAMENTARY REFORMS finally established u n i v e r s a l   m a l e   s.u f f r a g e   by adding labourers to the electoral roll, and introduced v o t e   b y   b a l l o t .

   a) *Second Reform Bill*, 1867, (under Disraeli) extended the franchise to householders in boroughs paying rates (artisans and workmen) and to lodgers paying a yearly rental of £10.

   b) The secret ballot introduced in 1872 by the *Ballot Act* made possible the founding of the Irish party which, with its obstructionist policy, played an important part in parliamentary life in the 19th century.

   c) *Third Reform Bill*, 1884, (under Gladstone) gave the franchise to householders in rural districts, i.e. land labourers and miners.

2. EDUCATIONAL REFORMS:

   a) *Elementary (Forster's) Education Act, 1870*, provided for p u b l i c   e l e m e n t a r y   s c h o o l s   to be erected by newly set-up school boards, where voluntary schools (usually established by religious bodies) were insufficient (p. 199).

   b) Oxford and Cambridge were opened to Nonconformists through abolition of religious tests, 1871.

   c) School attendance was made compulsory up to the age of ten (1876).

3. ADMINISTRATIVE REFORMS:

   a) Civil service appointments were made dependent on competitive examinations.

   b) The purchase of army commissions and promotions was forbidden.

   c) *Judicature Acts*, 1873 and 1876, simplified the judicial system by grouping former largely independent courts under the new Supreme Court of Judicature.

4. SOCIAL REFORMS: The legal status of workers and trade unions was improved through legislation of Disraeli ('the man who refuted Marx').

a) *Factory Act,* 1874, prohibited employment of children under ten and instituted a work week of 50½ hours.

b) *Employers and Workmen Act,* 1875, placed workmen on an equal footing with employers with regard to breach of contract. The workman was no longer imprisoned for leaving work (as had been provided for by *The Master and Servant Act,* 1824).

c) *Conspiracy and Protection of Property Act,* 1875, 'the great charter of trade unions', l e g a l i z e d s t r i k e s by allowing peaceful picketing, which had been punished as conspiracy.

5. PUBLIC HEALTH:

a) *Public Health Act,* 1875, established p u b l i c h e a l t h a u t h o r i t i e s and public control of drainage, water supply, scavenging, tainted food and infectious diseases. It provided for the appointment of medical officers.

b) *Artisans' Dwellings Act,* 1875, authorized s l u m c l e a r a n c e ; the further building of cellar dwellings was prohibited.

6. IRELAND: Gradual relief of suppression and distress in Ireland was effected by Gladstone, after the coercion acts of former governments had failed to establish peace and order.

a) Disestablishment of the Anglican Church in Ireland, 1869, implicitly acknowledged Roman Catholicism as the dominant religion in Ireland. Church funds were used for charitable purposes.

b) I r i s h L a n d A c t s on pressure of the Irish Land League (founded in 1879 by Michael Davitt) and of agitation for the 'three F's' (fair rent, fixity of tenure, free sale):

Land Act, 1870, fixed rents and disallowed eviction without compensation for repairs done.

Land Act, 1881, reduced rents and gave tenants the right to sell their title deeds to the tenancy.

Land Purchase Act, 1885, provided for r e p u r c h a s e o f l a n d with government loans.

Despite these efforts to relieve grievances, discontent and agitation for full home rule continued, leading to dissolution of the Land League and to the temporary imprisonment of the Irish leader Parnell. The new Irish Secretary Lord Cavendish and his Under-Secretary, who were sent to mediate, were murdered in Phoenix Park, Dublin.

c) *First Home Rule Bill,* 1886: The obstructionist policy of the Irish Home Rule party under its leader Charles Steward P a r n e l l (Protestant Irish M.P. of Anglo-Irish descent), which was backed by the Land League, caused Gladstone to introduce a bill for self-government which, however, was defeated.

II. **Imperialism** 'with all its dazzling appeal' (Cobden) was inspired by poets (e.g. Kipling's *The White Man's Burden*) and historians (Dilke:

77

Greater Britain, Seeley: *Expansion of England,* Froude: *Oceana, or England and Her Colonies).* It was vigorously pursued by Disraeli against the 'Little Englandism' of Liberalism, was propagated by the Imperial Federation League and the Imperial Institute (founded in 1884 and 1887 respectively) and was fostered by the world situation:

a) Opening up of Africa and the Far East, particularly through increased missionary activity (e.g. English missionaries Moffat and Livingstone in Central Africa);

b) Easier access to remote parts through the improvement of transport (from 1870 steamships came into general use);

c) Increased emigration caused by internal depression through industrial competition from the U.S.A. and Germany, and abandonment of tillage at home (cheap import of corn from overseas after development of steamships and building of the Canadian Pacific Railway);

d) New demand for tropical products after exhaustion of West Indian colonies;

e) Free trade calling for opening of world markets;

f) Rivalry of other nations leading to a scramble for colonies (cf. New Zealand, which was annexed upon news of an intended French expedition).

1. Purchase of the Gold Coast from the Dutch and establishment of the Gold Coast Colony, 1874, (today Ghana).

2. Annexation of the Fiji Isles, 1874.

3. Purchase of the majority of Suez Canal shares, 1875, gave England, together with France, control of a new shortened route to India.

4. India was constituted an empire in 1876. Queen Victoria became Empress of India.

5. Acquisition of Cyprus (main stronghold in the eastern Mediterranean) from Turkey at the Congress of Berlin, 1878, in return for support of Turkey in her war against Russia.

6. Occupation of Afghanistan, 1880: The pro-Russian Afghan king was replaced by his son, who acknowledged English suzerainty.

7. South Africa: Between 1836–42 Boers in the Cape Colony, who refused to live under British rule, trekked north, settling in the Natal, Orange and Transvaal territories. While Natal was annexed by Britain in 1843 after British troops had successfully fought against Boers, Orange and Transvaal were acknowledged as free states in 1852 and 1854 respectively. The annexation of Transvaal,

1877, under Disraeli led to a revolt. After the defeat of British troops at Majuba Hill, 1881, Gladstone recognized the independence of Transvaal.

8. Annexation of E g y p t , 1882, after an Egyptian revolt under Arabi against European influence had been crushed: Alexandria was bombarded, an Arabian army defeated at Tel-el-Kebir, Egypt occupied. Remarkable development of Egypt through a Nile barrage and the introduction of cotton culture.

9. Retreat from Sudan which, as a dependency of Egypt, was occupied by Egyptian forces, was necessitated by the revolt of a fanatical religious leader, the Mahdi. General Gordon, who had been sent by the British government to conduct the withdrawal, was besieged in Khartoum and killed before relief from England arrived.

10. B a s u t o l a n d became a protectorate in 1884.

11. B e c h u a n a l a n d , through which ran the 'missionaries road', along which Moffat and Livingstone had opened up the interior from the Cape, was occupied in rivalry with Transvaal Boers and made a British protectorate in 1885.

C. SALISBURY ERA, 1886–1902

The new Conservative period, which was marked by v i g o r o u s c o l o n i a l e x p a n s i o n and the r i s e o f s o c i a l i s m , was interrupted only from 1892 to 1894 by the fourth ministry of Gladstone, whose Irish *Home Rule Bills* split and weakened the Liberal cause. The Liberal party was out of power for 15 years, while the Liberal Unionists, who favoured union with Ireland, strengthened the Conservative party.
Lord Salisbury, a skilful diplomat with aristocratic detachment from popular political doctrines, had served as Secretary for India under Disraeli, after whose death he became leader of the Conservative party. He headed three cabinets (1885–86, 1886–92, 1895–1902), in which he soon served also as Foreign Secretary.

I. **New Imperialism** was inspired by the I m p e r i a l I n s t i t u t e (founded in 1887 at Victoria's Golden Jubilee) and by I m p e r i a l C o n f e r e n c e s to discuss closer trade, post and telegraph connections and a common defence organization.
Great imperialists became champions of British colonialism:

J o s e p h C h a m b e r l a i n (1836–1914), 'the most representative statesman of his period' was the son of a Unitarian, liberal merchant. As Lord Mayor of Birmingham he introduced important liberal and social reforms, making Birmingham the most modern English city. He became Member of Parliament

79

in 1876 and served under Gladstone as President of the Board of Trade. As Colonial Secretary under Salisbury and Balfour he made the Colonial Office one of the most important ministries. Pursuing a highly aggressive policy of colonial expansion, he became one of the chief advocates of a close i m p e r i a l f e d e r a t i o n and, since the Imperial Conference of 1902, of i m p e r i a l p r e f e r e n t i a l   t a r i f f s, despite his earlier support of free trade. A passionate controversy was thus raised, which became one of the important political issues of the early 20th century.

C e c i l R h o d e s (1853–1902), son of a clergyman, emigrated for reasons of health to South Africa, where diamonds had been discovered in 1867, and became a rich diamond prospector. Conceiving the ambitious idea of British colonial dominion reaching ' f r o m   t h e   C a p e   t o   C a i r o   a n d   f r o m   C a i r o   t o   C a l c u t t a ', he worked untiringly for British expansion in Africa and inspired the founding of the South Africa Company, which later colonized the territory called Rhodesia after him. As Premier of the Cape government, he strove for cooperation of the British and Dutch nationalities in a self-governing South African Union under the British Crown, believing in the compatibility of home rule and union with the British Empire. His success in winning over large numbers of Dutch to his idea of a S o u t h A f r i c a n f e d e r a t i o n, and his paternal attitude towards the Negroes, for whom he strove to secure fair wages, individual instead of tribal tenure, and self-government in native affairs, marked the climax of good will between nationalities in South Africa. The unsuccessful British invasion of Transvaal under his friend Dr. Jameson (after the discovery of gold) caused Rhodes's fall, but his popularity with the Negro population remained unbroken. In his testament he instituted the R h o d e s S c h o l a r s h i p for students from British colonies and the U.S.A. studying at Oxford, his own former university.

II. Colonial Acquisitions:

1. The route to India was secured by the occupation of A d e n (1839) and the I s l e o f P e r i m in 1857. After the building of the Suez Canal (1869), the British protectorates of S o m a l i l a n d (1884) and S o c o t r a (1886) were established to strengthen the Suez route.

2. CENTRAL AFRICA:
R h o d e s i a (containing the largest gold mine of antiquity and rich copper deposits) was colonized from 1890 by the South Africa Company, after Rhodes had secured the mining rights through a treaty with the Matabele king in 1888, thus preventing the incorporation of Rhodesia into the surrounding Boer or Portuguese territories.
N y a s a l a n d, acquired in 1891, became a British protectorate in 1893 (Central Africa Protectorate).

3. BRITISH EAST AFRICA: The founding of the East Africa Association in 1886 led to the establishment of the protectorates of U g a n d a and K e n y a (later a crown colony) in 1887 and 1890 respectively.

Z a n z i b a r , which had been acquired by the German East Africa Company, was exchanged for Heligoland in 1890.

4. S u d a n was conquered by Lord Kitchener through his victory at Omdurman in 1898. In 1898 Kitchener led an expedition to F a s h o d a (500 miles up the Nile), forcing a French expedition under Marchand, which had arrived before, to take down the French flag. This incident and the subsequent Anglo-French arrangement which gave England the entire Nile territory from its source to the delta caused considerable ill-feeling in France.

5. SOUTH AFRICA: The d i s c o v e r y o f g o l d in Transvaal in 1886 caused an immense immigration of foreign gold diggers, who soon outnumbered the Boers but were denied a share in the government by Transvaal's president Krüger. When troops of the South Africa Company under Dr. Jameson invaded Transvaal from the Cape, the 'Jameson raid' was repulsed by the Boers in 1895. Jameson was captured, given over to the English and punished with a few months' imprisonment. The Jameson raid caused general ill-feeling against England, also in Europe. The German Emperor Wilhelm II sent Krüger a telegram of congratulation. Nevertheless, continued British intervention by the High Commissioner for South Africa, Lord Milner, on behalf of the uitlanders (foreign immigrants in Transvaal), which was backed by military threats, led to the S o u t h A f r i c a n (B o e r) W a r , 1899–1902, proceeding in three phases:
a) Boers invaded British territory and besieged Ladysmith (Natal), Kimberley and Mafeking (Bechuanaland).
b) British troops advanced under the military command of Lords Roberts and Kitchener with volunteer and colonial reinforcements from Canada, Australia and New Zealand. Kimberley and Mafeking were relieved, the principal Boer cities, Bloemfontein, Johannesburg, Pretoria captured.
c) In a heroic guerilla war, the Boers under D e W e t and B o t h a continued to fight against considerable odds. The British destroyed farms and crops to prevent the provisioning of fighting forces, and interned women and children in concentration camps, where thousands died of starvation. Krüger fled to Europe, asking in vain for help.
d) Peace of Vereeniging, 1902: Orange and Transvaal were annexed but were promised self-government and the rebuilding of farms. Federation with the Cape and Natal in 1910 realized the U n i o n o f S o u t h A f r i c a.

6. N i g e r i a , acquired in 1886 by the Royal Niger Company, became a crown colony in 1900.

7. AUSTRALIA: In 1900 the Commonwealth of Australia was formed through the union of the six Australian colonies, since the vast continent's sparse white population (4.5 million) made necessary cooperation in questions of economy and defence. This was especially the case after discoveries of gold in 1851 and 1884 attracted gold diggers from all parts of the world.

III. **Second Irish Home Rule Bill, 1893:** Defeat of Gladstone's *First Home Rule Bill* had brought the Liberal Unionists and Conservatives to power. They pursued a more rigorous course under Balfour as Secretary for Ireland. Organized resistance under the Irish leader Parnell led to the *Criminal Law Amendment Act, 1887,* which provided for severe punishment of conspiracies, but could not stop riots and occasional murder. Resistance was finally broken, largely owing to the diminishing prestige of Parnell, who was suspected of having connived in the Phoenix Park murders (p. 77) and was involved in a divorce suit which even cost him the sympathies of English Liberals. Nevertheless Gladstone's new government abolished the *Crimes Act* and introduced the *Second Home Rule Bill,* 1893. Its defeat in the House of Lords further increased Irish resistance resulting in a general nationalist revival: The S i n n F e i n party ('ourselves alone') founded in 1900 by Arthur Griffith demanded an independent Irish government and stimulated the revival of the Irish (Gaelic) language.

IV. **Internal Legislation**

1. *Allotments and Small Holdings Acts,* 1882–1908, necessitated by abandonment of tillage and consequent deruralization, empowered local authorities to acquire land to be let out as allotments. These attempts to prevent depopulation of the country by settling a new class of small farmers on the land were, however, made ineffective through lack of compulsory powers and agricultural cooperation.

2. *Local Government Acts* abolished the squirearchy in rural districts by establishing democratically elected C o u n t y C o u n c i l s (1888) and P a r i s h a n d D i s t r i c t C o u n c i l s (1894) with councillors elected for three years and aldermen for six years. These took over the administrative functions of the former appointed magistrates (Justices of the Peace), who were usually squires. County boroughs with over 50,000 inhabitants were granted self-government through B o r o u g h C o u n c i l s.

3. EDUCATIONAL REFORMS: 1891 saw the a b o l i t i o n o f s c h o o l f e e s in elementary schools, 1899 the establishment of the B o a r d o f E d u c a t i o n. The *Education Act (Balfour's Act),* 1902, replaced school boards founded under *Forster's Act,* 1870, by school

committees of the County and Borough Councils, which now became responsible for elementary, secondary and technical education. Finally grants-in-aid established government control over voluntary (denominational) schools.

V. **Rise of Socialism and Labour Movement:** Economic depression, caused by foreign agricultural and industrial competition, u n e m p l o y m e n t, and the increasing influence of unskilled labour led to new social and political agitation.

1. Democratic Federation (later Social Democratic Federation) was founded by Henry Mayers Hyndman, who was influenced by Karl Marx (*Das Kapital,* 1867) and by the American economist Henry George (*Progress and Poverty,* 1879), who demanded complete sozialization of property.

2. Wide-spread s t r i k e s in all trades (the biggest being the London dock strike in 1889) led to a wide development of trade unions and opening of relief funds for supporting workers on strike.

3. F a b i a n S o c i e t y , founded in 1889, propagated in *Fabian Essays* the gradual achievement of state socialism without class war. Its chief pioneers were among the intellectual classes, e.g. Bernard Shaw, Sidney and Beatrice Webb, and H. G. Wells. This socialism, which advocated s o c i a l e v o l u t i o n r a t h e r t h a n r e v o l u t i o n , was grounded on the theories of John Stuart Mill.

4. FOUNDING OF THE LABOUR PARTY:
a) At the parliamentary election, 1868, the working class, hitherto represented by the Liberal party, first put up candidates of its own, who were, however, defeated.
b) The Labour Representation League was established in 1869 to support Labour candidates.
c) First Labour Members (called Lib-Labs because still closely associated with Liberals) were returned to Parliament at the election of 1874.
d) The I n d e p e n d e n t L a b o u r p a r t y was founded in 1893 at a trade union assembly in Bradford under inspiration of K e i r H a r d i e (Labour leader and editor of the first Scottish Labour organ, who, coming from the lowest working class, had worked in mines from the age of ten).
e) Founding of the Labour Representation Committee in 1900 under the auspices of Keir Hardie and Ramsay MacDonald (later Labour leader and first Labour premier) marked the birth of the Labour party with a more national and less Marxist outlook than socialist parties on the Continent.
f) At the election of 1906, the Labour party already won 29 seats.

VI. Monarchy During the Last Years of Queen Victoria's Reign

During her long reign, Victoria gave to the monarchy a new dignity through her personal integrity and high sense of responsibility. Moreover, during the last years of her reign, notwithstanding her strict seclusion after the death of her Consort Prince Albert, 1861, the Queen gained immense popularity when imperial expansion made her the symbol and centre of imperial dominion. While her G o l d e n   J u b i l e e (1887) had gathered in London most European potentates, her D i a m o n d J u b i l e e (1897) became an imperial pageant, to which colonial troops and naval displays added the splendour of military power. The festivities, celebrated with bonfires and illuminations throughout the country, lasted a fortnight.

In 1900 the Queen paid a last visit to London and Ireland during the South African War with visits to wounded soldiers in hospitals, to give encouragement in the year of the worst political depression. Victoria died in 1901, her burial being attended by most of the princes of Europe.

World Wars

Nationalism, Social Legislation

1901–45

A. PREWAR PERIOD, 1901–14

The continuing C o n s e r v a t i v e   g o v e r n m e n t s of Lord Salisbury and Balfour (Premier from 1902–05) pursued an a c t i v e   f o r e i g n   p o l i c y. However, general resentment of Conservative agitation, since 1903, for the reintroduction of protective tariffs drove the Liberal Unionists back into the Liberal camp and brought the Liberals an overwhelming victory by the landslide election of 1905. The L i b e r a l   m i n i s t r i e s of Sir Henry Campbell-Bannerman, 1905–08, and of H. H. Asquith (later Earl of Oxford), 1908–15, included Lloyd George (Exchequer), Sir Edward Grey (Foreign Office) and Winston Churchill (Board of Trade, Home Office, Admiralty, Munitions successively). The Liberal governments enacted extensive s o c i a l l e g i s l a t i o n.

E d w a r d V I I, 1901–10

Edward succeeded his mother at sixty. Amiable, witty, widely travelled and broad-minded, he made the court again the centre of fashionable society and exercised considerable influence in diplomatic circles and on British foreign policy.

I. Foreign Relations until World War I

1. Isolation of Great Britain was caused by the challenge of Russia (Crimean War, support of the Turks in the Russo-Turkish War), estrangement from France (Fashoda), and by the challenge of world public opinion in general through the Boer War. This led to repeated British offers of an alliance with Germany in 1900 and 1901, which, however, were rejected.

2. Anglo-Japanese alliance (1902), intended to check the advance of Russia and other European powers in the Far East, provided for mutual aid in case of foreign aggression. It enabled Japan to wage a successful war against Russia, securing to her half the Island of Sakhalin and Port Arthur in the Peace of Portsmouth, 1905, and led to Japan's entry into World War I on the Allied side.

3. ISOLATION OF GERMANY: Defeat of France in the Franco-Prussian War, 1870, and Germany's discontinuance, in 1890, of her alliance with Russia (Rückversicherungsvertrag) led to a military agreement between Russia and France in 1892. When British naval supremacy was challenged by the German naval programme introduced by Tirpitz, Britain reacted with increased naval armament and alliances:
a) Naval programme: The building of warships was greatly increased; Mediterranean ships were transferred to newly-built naval bases on the North Sea, Rosyth and Scapa Flow, 1906.
b) Entente Cordiale with France, 1904, settled colonial disputes in Africa. Rapprochement of Great Britain and France manifested itself in the international Conference of Algeciras, 1906, summoned at the German Emperor's demand to establish the integrity of Morocco: France was allowed to keep a police force in Morocco. In 1911 France occupied Morocco with British approval despite the German Emperor's protest demonstrated by sending the warship *Panther* to Agadir, which considerably worsened German relations with France and Britain.
c) Triple Entente, 1907, added Russia to the Franco-British alliance after disputes in Asia were settled: Tibet was to remain independent, Afghanistan was recognized as a British sphere of interest. Though Persia's sovereignty was affirmed, northwest Persia was to become a Russian zone of influence, the south and east (Persian Gulf) a British sphere of interest, with a neutral zone in between.

II. Internal Affairs

1. SOCIAL LEGISLATION was intensified under pressure of renewed enonomic depression and agitation by Labour, now increasingly incorporating unskilled workers.

A system of s o c i a l i n s u r a n c e was introduced by Lloyd George on the German pattern initiated by Bismarck:

a) *Workmen's Compensation Act,* 1906, granted workers compensation for injury and industrial diseases.

b) *Trade Disputes Act,* 1906, protected trade union funds from civil actions in cases of strikes. The act was prompted by resentment of the general application of the Taff Vale Case decision, 1901, which had ruled that the Taff Vale Railway Company should obtain damages from the Society of Railway Servants for actions (strikes) against the Company.

c) Coal mines: The *Coal Mine Eight Hours Act,* 1908, established the 8-hour day for underground miners. The *Coal Mines Act,* 1911, increased safety in mines. The *Coal Mines Minimum Wage Act,* 1912, prompted by the coal miners' strike, 1912, (largest up to that time in Britain), prescribed minimum wages.

d) J u v e n i l e w e l f a r e : provision of meals (1906), medical inspection and treatment of school children (1907); legislation for wayward and neglected children and juvenile courts (1908), care of mentally defective children (1913).

e) *Old Age Pensions Act,* 1908, provided for all persons over 70 with incomes under £31 a year to receive a non-contributory pension from one to five shillings a week.

f) L a b o u r E x c h a n g e s were set up under the *Labour Exchanges Act,* 1909, to facilitate the obtaining of employment.

g) *Housing and Town Planning Act,* 1909, provided for public health and planning committees of County Councils responsible for sanitary housing conditions and town planning schemes.

h) *Trade Boards Act,* 1909, was a first attempt at government interference in wage policy since Elizabeth I's wages legislation. It established trade boards consisting of employers, workers and members appointed by the Ministry of Labour, to fix minimum wages in unregulated ('sweated') industries.

i) 'P e o p l e 's B u d g e t ' introduced by Lloyd George in 1909 as 'a war budget for raising money to wage implacable warfare against poverty and squalor' was to meet expenditure on social reforms. It provided for new taxes to be imposed on the wealthy and landed classes: death and luxury duties, surtax on excessive incomes, tax on unearned increment from increase in value of land through industrial or other developments. Persistent opposition of the House of Lords to the Budget made necessary new elections (January and December, 1910). These maintained the Liberal majority, which carried the measure.

2. *Parliament Act,* 1911, prompted by the repeated vetoing of bills by the House of Lords, was passed in the Lords only after the Prime Minister had advised the King to create new peers prepared to vote for the measure:
a) veto of the Upper House was made suspensory: Bills passed by the Commons in three successive sessions were to become law despite rejection by the House of Lords;
b) money bills adopted by the Commons were to be passed by the House of Lords without amendment;
c) payment of Members of Parliament;
d) maximum duration of Parliament fixed at 5 years.

3. *National Insurance Act,* 1911, provided for insurance on a contributory basis.
a) H e a l t h i n s u r a n c e covered workers between 16 and 70 not earning more than £160 a year. It provided for free medical treatment and for sickness and disablement benefits from weekly contributions paid by state, employer and worker.
b) U n e m p l o y m e n t i n s u r a n c e covered only a limited number of trades.

4. Widespread s t r i k e s of railwaymen in 1911, and miners and London dockers in 1912 paralysed economic life.

G e o r g e V , 1910–36

Through his unaffected simplicity, sincerity, and conscientiousness in fulfilling his duties, King George enjoyed great popularity, gaining the respect and loyalty of his people.

III. **Ireland:** *Third Home Rule Bill,* 1912, introduced upon pressure of Irish Nationalists, provided for a separate Irish parliament and ministry. Strong opposition of the Ulster Presbyterians, who feared a Roman Catholic and agricultural majority in a new Irish parliament, threatened civil war between 'Ulster Volunteers' led by Edward Carson and Catholic 'National Volunteers'. Therefore the Bill, though passed by the Commons three times against opposition of the Lords, was not enforced.

L l o y d G e o r g e , 1863–1945, the greatest English statesman during the first quarter of the 20th century, grew up after his father's death in poor circumstances and became a solicitor. Of Welsh descent, he became as M.P. a champion of Welsh nationalism and an eloquent and bitter opponent of the Conservative government on the Radical side (especially on the Boer issue). He came to the fore in 1905 as President of the Board of Trade in Campbell-Bannerman's Liberal ministry. As Chancellor of the Exchequer in 1909, he carried his budget to finance social insurance legislation,—thus laying the foundations of the welfare state—against the fierce opposition of Conservatives and wide circles including the popular press. During World War I he became the leading statesman as Minister of Munitions,

87

then of War and subsequently Premier, creating a highly efficient war machine. His insistence on the unified control of Allied operations helped to bring about final victory. His conciliatory attitude in negotiations of the Treaty of Versailles against public opinion in France and Britain, his concessions to Ireland in 1922 and the conciliation he showed in the railway strike of 1919 diminished his popularity with the Conservatives, who had also supported him. In 1923 he became leader of the Liberal opposition, which, however, through its ignoring of the threat to world peace presented by Hitler, never recovered its former strength.

B. FIRST WORLD WAR

World War I was waged, on the British side, under the governments of Asquith and Lloyd George. Britain entered the war in 1914 upon German violation of Belgian neutrality. The British forces, reinforced by Imperial troops, joined the French army.

I. WESTERN FRONT:

1. In September 1914, Allied forces stopped the German advance across the Marne River. British forces at Ypres prevented the German advance to the Channel.

2. Trench-warfare 1915–16 in wet, vermin-infested trenches strained the perseverance of both sides to the utmost.

3. Franco-British counter-offensive on the Somme River, July-December 1916, did not succeed in pushing the front back more than 10 miles.

4. Successful attacks in 1917, in which the British first used tanks, brought gains at Vimy-Ridge (April), Ypres (July), and Passchendaele (November), but failed to break through the German front.

5. Last great German offensive on the Marne breaking through the British line near Saint Quentin, 1918, was stopped by Franco-British troops and, later, American reinforcements. The German army was obliged to retreat on the whole front.

II. HOME FRONT was strengthened by anti-German propaganda following the sinking of the *Lusitania* (American passenger-ship carrying munitions) in 1916.

1. War Cabinet: General discontent with the conducting of the war forced Asquith to form a coalition ministry including Conservatives, 1915, and to create a separate Ministry of Munitions. This was headed by Lloyd George, who on Kitchener's death through sinking of the cruiser *Hampshire* became Minister of War. On Asquith's resignation, 1916, Lloyd George formed a war cabinet with the new ministries of food and shipping, in which most decisions were made by a small inner circle of only five ministers.

2. British forces, first consisting of the regular army and volunteers, were brought up to two million in 1916 by g e n e r a l c o n - s c r i p t i o n of all men between 18 and 40 (which first raised the problem of conscientious objectors, who were frequently imprisoned).

3. State control over industries: Employment of unskilled workers (by 1917 one million women were engaged in munition works) necessitated the suspension of trade union rules favouring skilled labour by the newly established Ministry of Labour (1916). Ensuing strikes on the Clyde and in South Wales resulted in an extension of state control over shipping and vital industries.

4. Destructive air raids, chiefly on London, by German aeroplanes and Zeppelins (1916) made improvements in the Air Force necessary.

III. NAVAL WAR: Despite the use of submarines by Germany, the British Navy (until 1915 under Churchill) was a decisive factor in victory.

1. On the outbreak of war, the British Navy drove German ships from the high seas, facilitating the conquest of the German Far East and African possessions.

2. B a t t l e o f J u t l a n d (Skagerrak) May, 1916: Though the British Navy sustained severe losses, the German fleet never again sought battle.

3. The Navy made possible the transport of Imperial and American forces.

4. Through the b l o c k a d e o f t h e C e n t r a l P o w e r s , the Navy helped bring about the German surrender.

IV. EASTERN FRONT: War against Turkey

1. D a r d a n e l l e s : A British landing in Gallipoli, 1915, to capture Constantinople and establish connection with Russia failed despite heavy fighting, particularly by ANZAC troops (Australia and New Zealand Army Corps).

2. W a r i n A s i a M i n o r was won by British forces with the aid of Arabs hoping to gain independence from Turkish rule. The Arab revolt was organized by the young British archeologist T. E. L a w - r e n c e , who became the idol and hero of the Arab peoples:
a) In 1917 British forces conquered M e s o p o t a m i a by way of the Persian Gulf, and P a l e s t i n e by way of Egypt. The *Balfour Declaration*, November 1917, addressed to the president of the Zionist movement, Rothschild, promised to make Palestine a national home for the Jewish people.

b) The conquest of S y r i a by General Allenby and the occupation of Constantinople by Allied troops, 1918, ended the war with Turkey.

V. Peace Treaties

1. *Treaty of Versailles*, 1919, was negotiated on the Allied side by Lloyd George (Britain), Clemençeau (France), President Wilson (U.S.A.) and Orlando (Italy):
   a) Founding of the L e a g u e o f N a t i o n s with the Englishman Sir Eric Drummond its first Secretary-General until 1932.
   b) Great Britain obtained from the League the mandate for German East Africa (T a n g a n y i k a), the northwest part of the German Cameroons and the western part of German Togoland. The Union of South Africa was given the mandate for South West Africa; Australia the mandate for German New Guinea.
   c) Germany had to pay reparations for war damage caused to Allies, of which, according to the Spa Conference, 1920, Britain was to receive 22 per cent (France 52 per cent).
   d) German navy, which was to be surrendered to Great Britain, was scuttled by the German crews in the British naval base of Scapa Flow.
   e) Dominions were admitted to separate membership in the League of Nations, gaining equal status with the motherland.

2. *Treaty of Sèvres* with Turkey, 1920: Despite pleadings of T. E. Lawrence, the Arab states were denied independence, Britain was given m a n d a t e s f o r I r a q (Mesopotamia), P a l e s t i n e and T r a n s j o r d a n ; the Dardanelles were internationalized.

C. INTERWAR PERIOD: economic depression, rise of totalitarian states.

I. **Second Lloyd George Cabinet** 1918–22 after the 'Khaki election' (determined by soldier vote and continued war spirit) continued the policy of state control already introduced during the war.

1. *Representation of the People Act*, 1918, abolished plural voting except for university graduates (who had an extra vote for university representatives), and introduced f e m a l e s u f f r a g e from the age of 30. Women's vote had been advocated already by John Stuart Mill, whose bill, 1866, signed by 1500 women, was, however, defeated. Since 1903, ' S u f f r a g e t t e s ', organized in the Women's Social and Political Union, adopted a vigorous policy of militancy, which led to imprisonments, but called public attention to their campaign. Active participation of women in war efforts speeded the passage of the Bill, 1918.

2. *Education Act (Fisher Act)*, 1918, provided for n u r s e r y s c h o o l s and part-time compulsory education after elementary school in c o n t i n u a t i o n s c h o o l s up to the age of 16.

3. *Housing and Town Planning Act*, 1919, intensified efforts of earlier housing acts, 1890 and 1909, providing for state-aided slum clearance and the building of working-class houses.

4. I n d u s t r i a l c o n c i l i a t i o n developed with the establishment of 'Whitley Councils' (recommended by a committee under the chairmanship of J. H. Whitley) and Trade Boards, consisting of representatives of management and labour. The *Industrial Courts Act*, 1919, established a r b i t r a t i o n c o u r t s.

5. *India Act*, 1919, granted self-government to the Indian provinces through a mainly elected parliament and Indian ministers. The central government was still to be administered by the India Office and the Viceroy with an executive council, to which, however, three Indians were admitted. Since 1885 a national movement organized in the I n d i a n N a t i o n a l C o n g r e s s, had been fighting for independence, under the later leadership of M a h a t m a G a n d h i, a Hindu lawyer who had studied in England, fought for the rights of Indians in South Africa and, returning to India, 1914, strove to restore national self-respect through the revival of native industries. Venerated as a religious reformer, an ascetic and a saint, he became one of world's most influential leaders. Cruel suppression of riots (Amritsar massacre cost 375 lives) made Gandhi an inexorable opponent of British government. He strove to liberate India by civil disobedience, i.e. n o n - v i o l e n t r e s i s t a n c e to law.

6. W a s h i n g t o n C o n f e r e n c e, 1921, fixed British naval armament at an equal level with the U.S.A. This estranged Japan, whose naval armament was fixed at a lower level.

7. IRISH FREE STATE: Under the nationalist Sinn Fein movement (founded by the Irish journalist Arthur Griffith), Ireland strove for complete independence:
a) R e v o l t i n D u b l i n, 1916, proclaiming a free Irish republic, was put down by British troops in street fights and artillery from the sea. Leaders were shot: Sir Roger Casement, who had sought help in Germany, was arrested after landing from a German submarine, and was tried and hanged.
b) Establishment of an independent I r i s h r e p u b l i c, 1919: The harsh British suppression of the revolt, together with the extension of general conscription to Ireland, had led to the victory of Sinn Fein over supporters of home rule in the 1918 election. The new Irish

members opened a 'republican parliament' in Ireland *(Dail Eireann)*, which, however, was dissolved by the British government.

c) *Fourth Home Rule Bill*, 1920, dividing Ireland into two parts, was accepted by Ulster, where King George opened the first parliament in 1921.

d) C i v i l w a r in Southern Ireland caused by the Irish rejection of the *Home Rule Bill* led to merciless atrocities on both sides. After 400 policemen had been murdered, the British government introduced 60,000 newly discharged soldiers known as 'Black and Tans' (because of their khaki uniforms with black caps), whose lack of discipline increased hatred and led to 395 new murders.

e) *Irish Free State Act*, 1922, negotiated by the government and moderate representatives of the Dail under leadership of Arthur Griffith, gave Southern Ireland (now called Eire) d o m i n i o n s t a t u s, Great Britain retaining representation by a Governor-General and four naval ports. The refusal of the extremist party under D e V a l e r a to acknowledge the popular vote in favour of dominion status led to renewed civil war, in which supporters of the new Irish government under President William C o s g r a v e prevailed, 50 rebellious republicans being executed, thousands imprisoned. De Valera left the country, Cosgrave remaining in power until 1932.

8. Post-war slump: Growing i n f l a t i o n and u n e m p l o y m e n t (in 1921, 2.5 million), caused by the demobilization of the army and discontinuance of government control over railways and mines, resulted in strikes and made necessary government action:

a) *Emergency Powers Act*, 1921, authorized the government to declare a state of emergency if the safety of the community was threatened, and to preserve order and maintain food supply and essential services by Orders in Council.

b) *Safeguarding of Industries Act*, 1921, under pressure of growing unemployment reintroduced protective tariffs on commodities belonging to key industries and those threatened by dumping.

c) *Empire Settlement Act*, 1922, allocated funds to stimulate emigration.

d) *Unemployment Act*, 1920, extended unemployment insurance to a wider range of industries covering 12 million people.

II. Conservative Era, 1922–29: Ministries of B o n a r L a w, 1922–23, and S t a n l e y B a l d w i n, 1923–29 (with the short interruption of a Labour Ministry, 1924):

1. *Old Age Contributory Pensions Act*, 1925, which introduced contributory pensions for widows, orphans and persons between 65 and 70 supplemented the non-contributory pensions scheme of 1908.

2. G e n e r a l s t r i k e, 1926: The steady decline of the coal industry (competition of oil in transport, antiquated organization, gradual exhaustion of mines) caused much unemployment and great suffering in d e p r e s s e d m i n i n g a r e a s, particularly in Wales. When subsidies paid to coal mines ceased, and miners refused to accept new wage terms, the Trades Union Congress called a general strike, which involved two million men and women, and paralysed public life for twelve days. After the general strike had been brought to an end through prompt government action to maintain the essential services (e.g. milk pool in Hyde Park, London, volunteers for transport services protected by troops), miners continued their strike for 6 months.

3. *Trade Disputes and Trade Union Act*, 1927, forbade sympathetic strikes to coerce the government, as well as picketing (intimidation of persons refusing to take part in illegal strikes). It restricted the levy of trade union contributions for political purposes, and political activity of unions of government employees (first law since 1824 unfavourable to trade unions).

4. *Equal Franchise Act*, 1928: Women were given the same voting rights as men, i.e. from the age of 21.

III. Governments of Ramsay MacDonald, 1929–31, 1931–35

1. DEVELOPMENT OF LABOUR: Strongly under Communist influence during the depression in the first decade of the 20th century, Labour had reorganized in 1918 under its new programme of g r a d u a l s o c i a l i z a t i o n which was put forward in *Labour and the New Social Order* drawn up by S i d n e y W e b b and other Fabians. Labour became the official opposition until the election of 1924 returned the first Labour government under Ramsay MacDonald (Premier and Foreign Secretary) which, however, was forced to resign within one year on account of its unpopular pro-Russian policy.

2. LABOUR CABINET, 1929–31. In 1929 the Labour Party was returned to power, owing to its promises of a more energetic social policy. All efforts of the government on behalf of coal mines, housing, and agriculture (minimum wages, 1924, derating of agricultural land, 1929, marketing schemes, 1931) were, however, made ineffective by the g r e a t s l u m p beginning in 1928 and reaching its peak in 1931. This included a general decrease of output and exports, an increase of unemployment of up to 21 per cent of the insured population. The Emergency Budget of MacDonald and Snowden (Exchequer), proposing a considerable cut in unemployment benefits, which had been made a condition of further foreign credits, split the Labour Cabinet, which resigned in August, 1931.

3. 'NATIONAL' MINISTRY, formed by MacDonald was a coalition government including the Conservatives Baldwin and Neville Chamberlain (Exchequer). After the resignation of Labour and free trade ministers, it relied only on the great C o n s e r v a t i v e m a j o r i t y. Formed to lead the nation through the crisis, it introduced d r a s t i c f i n a n c i a l m e a s u r e s:

a) Snowden's Budget, 1930, raised income tax, surtax and death duties limiting the tax burden almost entirely to the well-to-do class.

b) *National Economy Act,* 1931, reduced unemployment insurance benefits and salaries by 10 to 20 per cent, resulting in riotous meetings of discontented teachers, sailors and unemployed workers.

c) D e v a l u a t i o n o f t h e p o u n d s t e r l i n g to a gold standard of 16s was effected in 1931 after the exhaustion of foreign credits, to revive foreign trade. A new election held in October 1931 to test public opinion on the trade issue, returned the Conservatives to power by an overwhelming majority of 502 against 52 Labour Members confirming the National Ministry's policies.

d) *Statute of Westminster,* 1931, repudiated the right of the British Parliament to legislate for a dominion except with its consent, and the right of the Crown to annul an act passed by a dominion legislature. It allowed dominions to make laws having extra-territorial operation. It thus sanctioned the new status of the British d o m i n i o n s defined in the report of the Imperial Conference, 1926, as 'a u t o n o m o u s c o m m u n i t i e s within the British Empire equal in status, in no way subordinate to one another in any respect of their domestic and external affairs though united by a common allegiance to the Crown'.

e) A b a n d o n m e n t o f f r e e t r a d e, 1932 *(Imperial Duties Act):* Reintroduction of tariffs to improve the trade balance, to raise revenues and encourage British industries led to the resignation of free-trade ministers. The general trend towards economic self-sufficiency doomed to failure efforts to bring about international trade agreements.

f) O t t a w a C o n f e r e n c e, 1932, provided for preferential tariffs for members of the British Commonwealth. I m p e r i a l p r e f e r e n c e established in trade and commerce a tendency towards imperial cooperation which the Statute of Westminster had weakened in the field of politics.

g) A n g l o - G e r m a n n a v a l a g r e e m e n t, 1935, fixed the German naval armament tonnage at 35 per cent of that of England.

h) *India Act,* 1935, following recommendations of the Simon Committee on Indian affairs, appointed in 1928, created the F e d e r a t i o n o f I n d i a to include eleven provinces and the semi-independent states with native rulers. It created a responsible central government for British India chiefly of Indians, though military and foreign affairs remained under British control. In 1937 responsible provincial governments were created with similar safeguards vested in provincial governors.

IV. Conservative Governments of Baldwin, 1935–36, and Neville Chamberlain, 1937–40.

Edward VIII, 1936

Edward, who, as Prince of Wales, had taken an interested part in politics as his father's representative, was highly popular at his succession. After announcing his intention to marry a married American lady, already once divorced, he was compelled to abdicate on the ground that marriage of royalty to divorced persons would not be approved by the British people (cf. Princess Margaret and Townsend). Edward received the title of Duke of Windsor and left England.

George VI, 1937–52

George, Edward's brother, was crowned in Westminster Abbey. His integrity, modesty and devotion to his duty commanded the respect and affection of his people, while his warm-hearted wife, Queen Elizabeth, and his two daughters, the princesses Elizabeth and Margaret, enjoyed great popularity.

1. BRITAIN AND THE IRISH FREE STATE
   a) Growing nationalism in Eire strove to achieve full independence from England. The Irish (Gaelic) language was introduced in schools and as the official language; Irish ambassadors were appointed to other states. The election of 1932 returned the extreme nationalists to power, De Valera becoming President. In 1933 appeals to the British Privy Council and the oath of allegiance to the Sovereign were abolished.
   b) Economic war with England: De Valera cancelled the annuities paid by Irish farmers to the British government for loans to re-purchase farms from their landlords. Protective tariffs, introduced by the British government in retaliation, were abolished in 1938 under a conciliatory agreement which relieved Ireland of further payments. It also provided that naval ports occupied by the British should be returned to Eire.
   c) The Irish Republic, established by the Constitution of 1937, abolished the office of Governor-General. In World War II Eire declared her neutrality. In 1949 she left the Commonwealth.

2. POLICY OF APPEASEMENT BEFORE WORLD WAR II: The peace efforts during the 1920s (Locarno Conference, 1925; *Kellogg-Briand Pact*, 1928, outlawing war; Allied withdrawal from the Rhineland; cessation of reparations, 1932) had not prevented the rise of an

95

extreme nationalism in discontented states. In 1936 Nazi Germany and Italy joined in the Berlin–Rome Axis; Germany and Japan in the Anti-Comintern Pact. All three countries left the League of Nations. In order to preserve peace at all costs aggressions of the three totalitarian states were either not checked at all or else censured ineffectively.

a) Japanese invasion of Manchuria, 1931, and China, 1937, considerably injured British Far-East trade. Japan left the League of Nations in 1933, after the League, following an appeal from China, had demanded withdrawal of her troops from Manchuria.

b) Italian invasion of Ethiopia, 1935, was countered by 'sanctions' on the part of the League of Nations, proposed by England. As they were not applied by all countries, the sanctions remained ineffective and were ended by decree of the League in 1936. Proposals to close the Suez Canal, which would have quickly ended the war between Italy and Ethiopia, were not adopted. In 1938 an Anglo-Italian agreement recognized the Italian conquest in Ethiopia. Eden resigned the foreign secretaryship in protest.

c) Rearmament and expansion of Hitler Germany: German rearmament, facilitated by the Anglo-German naval agreement in 1935, the remilitarization of the Rhineland in 1936, and the German occupation of Austria in 1938 had been effected with occasional protests, but no actual intervention on the part of Great Britain or the League.

When Hitler indicated his determination to support claims of the Sudeten-Germans for independence from Czechoslovakia and annexation of their territory to the Reich, the British and French prime ministers, Neville Chamberlain and Daladier, met Hitler in Munich to negotiate a compromise. The *Munich Agreement*, dictated by Hitler, provided for the German occupation of Sudeten territory. Hailed as a last resort to reason and proclaimed as 'peace with honour', the agreement was later felt to be the greatest humiliation Great Britain and France had suffered at the hands of totalitarian states. The occupation of the Sudeten region by Hitler's troops was followed half a year later by the seizure of the rest of Czechoslovakia, and, despite British and French guarantees to defend Polish integrity (March, 1939), by the invasion of Poland, September, 1939.

D. **SECOND WORLD WAR** waged under the ministries of Neville Chamberlain (till 1940) and Winston Churchill (1940–45):

Sir Winston Churchill, son of the politician Lord Randolph Churchill and an American mother, was born in 1874 at Blenheim Palace. Educated at

Harrow and Sandhurst Military Academy he entered the army in 1895 and served in India, Egypt and the Sudan. In the South African War, 1899–1902, he served as correspondent for the *Morning Post;* he was taken prisoner by the Boers and escaped. He entered Parliament in 1900 as a Conservative Member but turned Liberal when the Conservatives propagated the reintroduction of protective tariffs. Churchill was President of the Board of Trade, 1905–08, and, under Asquith, Home Secretary, 1909–11. As First Lord of the Admiralty he effected reforms of the navy in preparation for a war against Germany, which he strongly supported. When his expedition to the Dardanelles in 1915 failed, he went on active service to France. Under Lloyd George he served as Minister of Munitions in 1917 and as War and Air Minister, 1918–21. Under Baldwin, Churchill became Chancellor of the Exchequer and rejoined the Conservative Party. His opposition to the British policy in India led to his exclusion from the National government in 1931. Having warned for years against aggression by Nazi Germany he entered the War Cabinet in 1939 as First Lord of the Admiralty. After the first crushing defeat of the Allies, Churchill replaced Neville Chamberlain as Prime Minister and also took over the Ministry of Defence. He conducted the war with the greatest energy and perseverance. When the Labour government was returned after the war, he wrote the *History of World War II* in six volumes. The growing rift with the U.S.S.R. made him the leading champion of a United Europe. During his premiership from 1951 until 1955 when he abdicated in favour of his Foreign Secretary Eden, he worked untiringly to bring about summit talks with Russia to relieve international tension. He died in 1965.

1. DECLARATIONS OF WAR: When the British and French ultimatum to Germany to withdraw her troops from Polish territory was ignored by Hitler, the two nations declared war on September 3, 1939, followed by the British dominions Australia, New Zealand, Canada, South Africa and India, which, despite strong opposition from Indian leaders, was made 'the arsenal of the East'.

2. HOME FRONT: Compulsory military service was introduced. Food and clothing were rationed, grassland was ploughed up and industrial conscription for men and women between 20 and 30 introduced. As a protection against German air-raids, administration and industry were decentralized and children evacuated to rural areas.

3. WAR EFFORTS:

a) An expeditionary force was sent to Norway, but was evacuated after the Germans had conquered the country. Governments in exile were formed in London by Polish refugees and the royal families of Norway and Holland.

b) Upon Belgium's surrender, a British expeditionary force of 400,000 men was evacuated from Dunkirk, June 1–4, 1940, with a loss of 30,000 men. When France surrendered, June 17, and declined the British offer of a union of the French and British governments to continue the war from Britain, England was isolated from the Continent.

4. BATTLE OF BRITAIN (August 1940–May 1941): M a s s a t t a c k s o f t h e G e r m a n a i r f o r c e on London, seaports, and industrial cities to weaken the British resistance and prepare an invasion were met by the establishment of a Defence Zone along the south and east coast with anti-tank obstacles and pill-boxes (structures covering machine guns). The destruction of Coventry (November 12) and an air raid on London City (December 29) through incendiary attacks mark the first climax of the bomb war. Later the air raids weakened until the resumption of the 'b l i t z' by Germany with flying bombs (V1 and V2) on London from June 13, 1944.

5. BATTLE OF THE ATLANTIC: U n r e s t r i c t e d n a v a l w a r f a r e included bombarding of harbours, submarine warfare, and capture, after the French defeat, of French ships by the British Navy at Oran and Dakar. The German attacks were countered by the convoy system and the development of the radar system virtually eliminating German submarines. The U.S.A. was allowed naval bases in the West Indies in exchange for U.S. destroyers.

6. WAR IN THE MEDITERRANEAN was chiefly caused by the Italian ambition to expand her power over independent or British-controlled Mediterranean territory.
a) C o n q u e s t o f G r e e c e (October–May, 1941): The Italian attack on Greece was repulsed by the Greek army which received reinforcements (60,000 men) and naval support from Britain through attacks on Italian-controlled ports. The German invasion, April 6, however, forced the Greek army to surrender within a fortnight.
b) C r e t e, to which the British troops were evacuated, was conquered by German airborne troops with heavy losses to the British Navy, the British force being evacuated to Egypt on May 21.
c) AFRICAN WAR, 1940–43, on the coastal strip of North Africa: Italians conquered British Somaliland and advanced into British-occupied Egypt under Marshal Graziani, but were driven back by General Wavell, Commander-in-Chief in the Middle East. In 1941 the British had conquered Italian East Africa (Ethiopia and Somaliland) and advanced into the Italian colony of Libya, but were repulsed on the arrival of German troops under General Rommel. The German advance into Egypt within 70 miles of Alexandria was finally stopped by General Montgomery in the furious tank battle of E l A l a m e i n after reinforcements had been received from India, Australia, New Zealand, South Africa and the Free French under

leadership of General de Gaulle. The American-British invasion of French North Africa, November 1942, trapped Rommel's forces. Nevertheless in the Tunesian campaign the Axis forces held out for 6 months against overwhelming odds until their unconditional surrender, May 9, 1943.

d) WAR IN ITALY (1943–44): The Allied invasion of Sicily, July 10, with 2,000 ships led to the surrender of the Italian troops in Sicily within 5 weeks and the downfall of the Fascist party and Mussolini. The new anti-German government facilitated the Allied conquest of Sicily and the invasion of Italy through three landings. Despite the unconditional surrender of Italy, which joined the Allies against Germany, German forces continued to hold two thirds of Italy until 1944.

7. RUSSIAN WAR (1941–45): Upon the German invasion of Russia, treaties between Great Britain and the U.S.A. provided for military aid to Russia. After a staggering German advance, the tide finally turned in the five months' battle at Stalingrad. From 1943 the Russians, reinforced by American war supplies, reconquered their own territory and the Baltic States, advancing into the Balkans, Poland, Czechoslovakia and, in 1945, eastern Germany.

8. PACIFIC WAR: Japan, feeling hampered in her expansionist policy by the U.S.A. and Britain, attacked Hongkong and simultaneously the American port of Pearl Harbour (December 1941). Thereupon Britain declared war on Japan but could not prevent the conquest of the British colonies Hongkong, Malay, Singapore, Burma, and island groups in the Pacific within three months. The further expansion of Japan in the Pacific was finally halted by the Allies. Losses inflicted on the Japanese navy made possible the recapture of the Pacific island groups in 1943–45.

9. UNITED NATIONS (UN), January, 1942: The widening of the European conflict into a global war led to a close alliance of 26 'United Nations' including Russia and China.

10. JOINT CONFERENCES laid down common policies for continuance of the war and subsequent peace.
At a conference in the Atlantic in August 1941, Churchill and Roosevelt issued the *Atlantic Charter*, which established principles for the restoration of peace after the defeat of the Axis powers: self-government for all peoples, equal access by all nations to basic raw materials, greater freedom of trade and 'freedom from fear and want'. It stated that neither Britain nor the U.S.A. would seek territorial aggrandizement after the war.

Conferences between the Western powers and their Eastern allies were held in M o s c o w, October 1943, between Stalin and the Foreign Secretaries Eden and Hull; in C a i r o, November 1943, between Churchill, Roosevelt and Chiang-kai-Shek; in T e h r a n, 1943, between Churchill, Roosevelt and Stalin. At the conference at Y a l t a, 1945, between Churchill, Roosevelt and Stalin, Churchill's proposal to establish a common Allied front in the German-occupied Balkans (in order to prevent an occupation of eastern Europe by Russia only) was not adopted.

11. ALLIED INVASION OF FRANCE, June 5, 1944, was effected between Le Havre and Cherbourg with 4,000 transport ships and a superiority of aeroplanes of 200:1. The slow advance in Normandy and Brittany was supported by an invasion from the Mediterranean. Paris was liberated, August 25, Brussels occupied by British forces, September 3. Southern France was invaded on September 15. A strong counter-offensive by von Rundstedt was repulsed in heavy fights. The invasion of German territory, aided by pitiless air raids, and the Russian advance into eastern Germany ended with the unconditional s u r r e n d e r o f G e r m a n y, April 1945.

12. TERMINATION OF THE EUROPEAN WAR:

a) P o t s d a m C o n f e r e n c e of the Allies, August 1944, provided for the joint occupation of Germany and Austria.

b) Peace treaties with Hungary, Rumania and Bulgaria, 1946–47, ended the war with Germany's eastern allies.

13. RESULTS OF THE WAR:

a) At home: destruction of towns, decline of industry through the bombing of industrial plants, diminution of manpower, and a thorough social levelling through rigorous taxation.

b) Overseas: loss of one half of British overseas investments as a result of war borrowing; loss of world markets through industrial progress in Commonwealth countries; shipping cut by one third; disintegration of Empire through the growing independence or secession of former colonies; loss of world leadership to the U.S.A.

14. SOCIAL POLICY:

a) *Beveridge Report (Report on Social Insurance and Allied Services)*, 1942, proposed a comprehensive scheme of social security irrespective of salary and occupation.

b) *Education Act (Butler Act)* in 1944 raised the higher classes of the elementary schools to the standard of 'secondary education' in an attempt to avoid social discrimination (p. 199).

Postwar Period

Welfare State, Disintegration of Empire

LABOUR GOVERNMENT of Clement Attlee 1945–51 included Ernest Bevin (Foreign Secretary), Hugh Dalton (–1947) and Sir Stafford Cripps (Exchequer), Aneurin Bevan (Health).

I. Postwar Reconstruction and Social Welfare

1. FINANCE: The exhaustion of gold reserves necessitated borrowing:
a) U. S. l o a n of $3,750,000,000, 1945; Canadian loan of $1,250,000,000, 1946.
b) E u r o p e a n R e c o v e r y P r o g r a m m e (ERP): Britain received a major share of U.S. aid extended under the Marshall Plan beginning in 1948.
c) D e v a l u a t i o n o f t h e p o u n d sterling, 1949, to recapture foreign markets.

2. N a t i o n a l i z a t i o n of industries and services, 1946–49, was effected to increase efficiency through streamlining and standardization, and to protect smaller industries from monopolistic practices of big concerns. Owners were compensated by interest-bearing government securities.
1946: Bank of England, wireless, aviation, coal.
C o a l - m i n i n g, which had reached an alarming employment and production level, was put under control of the National Coal Board to make possible the modernization of technical equipment and industrial structure. The Board appointed by the Minister of Fuel took over not only mines but also subsidiary undertakings (coke plants, chemical works). B a n k o f E n g l a n d, which had been one of the world's few private central banks, was nationalized to bring the note issue, national credit and investment policy under national control.
1947: Electricity, railways and road transport.
1948: Gas.
1949: Steel: Despite fierce opposition on the ground that steel was not, like coal, in a state of general depression, the *Iron and Steel Act* was passed in 1949, but before it really came into force steel was reprivatized in 1953 under the subsequent Conservative government together with road transport.

3. A u s t e r i t y P r o g r a m m e, carried by Sir Stafford Cripps to pay off war debts and postwar loans:

101

a) Reduction of imports (e.g. meats, fats, sugar), which made necessary the continuation of rationing; (an ambitious groundnut scheme in the East African colonies failed).
b) Production chiefly for export.
c) Heavy taxation to curb inflation.
d) Severe currency restrictions (precluding travel abroad).
e) Cessation of Marshall Aid, 1950.

4. The Welfare State fully realized social welfare as a right of every citizen, removing the last stigma from the acceptance of social benefits (criticized by Conservatives as 'getting something for nothing'). It aimed at a juster distribution of income and responsibility and strove to raise the living standard of the working classes through higher wages, shorter working hours (made possible by increasing automation) and full employment. Social welfare, which came into full operation in 1948, was based on the following acts (for detailed provisions see pp. 165–67):

a) *Family Allowances Act,* 1945, provided family allowances (Kindergelder) for second and subsequent children.
b) *National Health Service Act,* 1946, provided that medical services and the dispensing of prescriptions should be free of charge to every person including visitors to England who fall ill in Britain. Hospitals and the medical profession were brought under state control.
c) *National Insurance Act,* 1946, and subsequent measures extended social insurance for sickness, unemployment, industrial injuries and disability, and old age pensions to all groups of the population.
d) *Children Act,* 1948, made local authorities responsible for children under 17 who were without parents or guardians or abandoned by their parents.
e) *National Assistance Act,* 1948, established a comprehensive state service of financial assistance to any needy person over 16, to be administered by the National Assistance Board.
f) Municipal and housing programmes provided for subsidized house building made necessary by war damage, while private building was restricted, owing to shortage of raw materials. *The New Towns Act,* 1946, authorized the Minister of Housing and Local Government to designate any area of land as the site of a proposed new town to be acquired and developed by a development corporation appointed for this purpose.
g) Foodstuffs were subsidized.

5. REARMAMENT: Conscription for a one-year military service was introduced in 1947 as a result of the deterioration of relations with the U.S.S.R. The Rearmament Budget of 1951 and the explosion of the first British atom bomb off the

northwest coast of Australia caused a split in the Labour party through a revival of socialist radicalism under Aneurin Bevan, who resigned his post as Minister of Health in 1951.

6. CONSTITUTIONAL REFORMS:

a) A b o l i t i o n   o f   u n i v e r s i t y   r e p r e s e n t a t i o n, 1948, on the principle of 'one man one vote'. University representation, which had given university graduates a second vote (made by post) besides that exercised in their constituencies, had existed since 1604 and had returned twelve Members to the House of Commons.

b) V e t o   o f   t h e   H o u s e   o f   L o r d s   was reduced from two years to one year. Proposals to constitute the Upper House on a representative rather than hereditary basis on the ground that one party (Conservative) possessed a permanent and overwhelming majority in it, were not adopted.

c) *Representation of the People Act,* 1949, legislated on the conduct of elections and illegal and corrupt electoral practices.

II. European and Atlantic Integration

1. *Treaty of Dunkirk* between Britain and France, March 1947, provided for an alliance and mutual defence against possible aggression (by Germany).

2. GATT (General Agreement on Tariffs and Trade), October 1947, between 23 states including Britain, provided for a reduction of tariffs. It was extended through an agreement at Torquay, 1951, to include 35 states handling 85 per cent of world trade.

3. *Brussels Pact* with France and the Benelux states, March 1948,* provided for common defence and economic, social and cultural cooperation as a result of the growing breach between East and West.

4. OEEC (Organization for European Economic Cooperation) including Britain was formed in April, 1948, to administer the ERP (European Recovery Programme) within Europe.

5. ICU (International Clearing Union), October 1948, established an international bank for clearing transactions between member states including Britain.

6. NATO (North Atlantic Treaty Organization) was established in April 1949, for mutual defence in case of aggression. It included 12 nations situated on both sides of the North Atlantic.

7. E u r o p e a n   C o u n c i l   propagated by Churchill, was established in Strasbourg through a ten-power statute drafted by a conference of Foreign Ministers in London, May 1949.

---

* Dates given generally refer to the enactment of a law or ratification of a treaty (not enforcement)

III. Disintegration of Empire

1. INDIA: Britain withdrew from India, 1947, after India had been divided into two dominions according to the religious divisions of the country: the I n d i a n U n i o n (comprising 29 Hindu states), and P a k i s t a n, including the Moslem parts of former British India: the Northwest (Indus Basin and Beluchistan) and East Bengal. Both Indian states remained members of the British Commonwealth, though they were later proclaimed republics, recognizing the British sovereign as the 'symbol of union'. The Indian Union's first President, Jawaharlal N e h r u ruled India until his death in 1964. (The son of an Anglophile family of the Brahmin caste, Nehru spent seven years in England at Harrow and Cambridge, later practising law at the Inner Temple. On his return to India he joined the Indian National Congress. After the Amritsar massacre he became a follower of Gandhi and a passionate enemy of British rule in India. He spent several years in prison.) As Premier and Foreign Minister of the newly founded Indian Union Nehru enjoyed considerable prestige in Asia through his firm stand against colonialism in any form and his strict neutrality between East and West. The Chinese invasion of Indian territory in 1963 dealt a severe blow to his ideas of non-alignment.

2. B u r m a left the Commonwealth in 1947.

3. C e y l o n (hitherto a crown colony) obtained dominion status in 1948, British troops being withdrawn in 1957.

4. P a l e s t i n e : Jewish immigration into Palestine (British mandate since 1920) had caused friction between Jews and Arabs, worsened by increased Jewish immigration since the persecution of the Jews in Hitler Germany. In 1947 the British mandate authorities appealed to the UN, which worked out a plan for the partition of the country between Jews and Arabs and the termination of the British mandate. On May 14, 1948, one day before the withdrawal of the British troops, the Jews proclaimed the independent state of Israel.

5. S o u t h e r n I r e l a n d left the Commonwealth in 1949.

IV. Britain between East and West

1. Participation in the B e r l i n a i r l i f t against the Russian blockade of Berlin together with the U.S.A., 1948–49.

2. Participation in the K o r e a n w a r , 1950, to stop the invasion of South Korea by Communist North Korea.

3. R e c o g n i t i o n o f R e d C h i n a , 1950, Hongkong remaining a British colony.

4. **C o l o m b o P l a n**, January, 1950, in agreement with the nations of south and southeast Asia, provided for financial and technical aid for the development of south and southeast Asian countries from Britain and other members of the Commonwealth.

CONSERVATIVE ERA, 1951–64

A. **SECOND CHURCHILL CABINET**, 1951–55, included Anthony Eden (Foreign Secretary) and R. A. Butler (Exchequer).

The election of 1950 held when people were generally tired of Labour austerity and controls gave Labour a bare majority of eight seats and necessitated a new election in 1951 resulting in a Conservative victory.

E l i z a b e t h I I succeeded her father in 1952, aged 25. Her coronation in 1953 was followed by a Commonwealth tour, 1953–54. She married Prince Philip, Duke of Edinburgh, and gave birth to four children: Charles, Prince of Wales, Princess Anne, the princes Andrew and Edward.

I. **Internal Affairs:** Liberalization, encouragement of private enterprise.

1. **R e p r i v a t i z a t i o n o f s t e e l** and road transport 1952–53.

2. Intensification of the house-building programme through encouragement of private enterprise.

3. Cuts in subsidies, taxes and general controls.

4. **T e r m i n a t i o n o f r a t i o n i n g** and the government purchase monopoly, 1954.

5. Abuses of the Health Scheme abolished through introduction of small payments for medicines and dental treatment.

6. **A b o l i t i o n o f c u r r e n c y r e s t r i c t i o n s :** new overseas investments to aid underdeveloped countries.

II. **Foreign Affairs**

1. Dispute with **I r a n**, 1951–52, was precipitated by the nationalization of Persian oil, which meant heavy loss to the Anglo-Iranian Company.

2. **M a u M a u r e v o l t** in Kenya was suppressed, 1952–56.

3. **B a g h d a d P a c t** between Turkey and Iraq, February 1955, which had been encouraged by the U.S.A. in order to create a Western alliance system in the Middle East, was joined, April 5, by Great Britain, and later in the year by Pakistan and Iran.

4. **W e s t   E u r o p e a n   U n i o n** : European integration and defence were subjects of conferences in London and Paris, 1954. The German Federal Republic and Italy joined the *Brussels Pact,* 1954, which was henceforth called West European Union. Britain promised to station four British divisions permanently on the Continent.

5. '**S u m m i t   t a l k s** ' to terminate the cold war between East and West were held in Berlin, 1954 (German question), and Geneva, 1955 (disarmament).

6. SEATO: The South-East Asia Treaty Organization for collective defence was established in 1955 after Communist expansionism had driven the French from Indochina. It included the U.S.A., Britain, France, New Zealand, Australia, the Philippines, Thailand and Pakistan. In 1977 SEATO was replaced by ASEAN (Association of South-East Asian Nations), which, unlike SEATO and NATO, does not provide for common defence.

B. **EDEN CABINET** (after Churchill's resignation), April 1955–57, with Harold Macmillan as Foreign Secretary.

1. **S u d a n** became an independent republic, 1956.

2. **F e d e r a t i o n o f M a l a y a** , which had been formed out of the British Malayan dependencies, obtained an independent constitution, 1957. Singapore remained separated from it because of its importance as a British military base and member of SEATO, to which the Malayan Federation did not belong.

3. Conflict with Egypt after the withdrawal of British forces from the Suez Canal Zone, 1956, was precipitated when Egypt nationalized the Suez Canal. Britain, after futile attempts at a peaceful settlement, joined France and Israel in a **m i l i t a r y e x p e d i t i o n i n E g y p t** , which was stopped by the influence of world disapproval at the demand of UN. Sharp criticism also in Britain was one of the causes of Eden's resignation.

C. **MACMILLAN CABINETS**, 1957–59, 1959–63, with Selwyn Lloyd and Lord Home as Foreign Secretaries successively.

I. **Internal Policy:**

1. *Life Peerages Act,* 1958, provided that the Crown could create life peers, and that these could also be women.

2. *Immigrants' Act,* 1962, restricted immigration from Commonwealth countries.

II. Commonwealth Developments: see p. 291–92 see p. 291–92

III. British Near East Policy

1. Revolution in Iraq, 1958, led to the temporary o c c u p a t i o n   o f J o r d a n   a n d   L e b a n o n by British troops, 1958, in order to prevent Communist subversion also in these countries.

2. The new Iraq government left the Western defence alliance (Baghdad Pact), which was renamed CENTO (Central Treaty Organization).

3. Temporary British occupation of Kuweit, 1960, prevented its annexation by Iraq.

IV. Britain and European Economic Integration: EFTA (European Free Trade Association) formed in 1960 to include the European states not members of the Common Market (Britain, Norway, Sweden, Denmark, Austria, Switzerland, Portugal) provided for the gradual elimination of protective tariffs between member countries.

D. MINISTRY OF SIR ALEC DOUGLAS-HOME (previously the Earl of Home), October 1963–October 1964, with R. A. Butler as Foreign Secretary.

1. Under the *Peerage Act* 1963, peers may disclaim their peerage for life and can be elected to the House of Commons (cf. Douglas-Home).

2. T a n z a n i a : A Communist revolt in Zanzibar, where the Sultan and the Arab ruling classes were overthrown, and riots in Tanganyika, January 1964, resulted in the intervention of British troops and warships at the request of the Tanganyika government. In April 1964, Zanzibar and Tanganyika formed a union, now called Tanzania, under the moderate president of Tanganyika, Nyerere.

3. Heavy fighting between Greeks and the Turkish minority in C y p r u s throughout the year made necessary the intervention of U.N. forces. British troops strove to restore order.

LABOUR GOVERNMENT OF HAROLD WILSON, 1964–66, 1966–70, with J. Callaghan (Home Secretary) and Barbara Castle (Minister of Employment and Productivity).

1. Wilson included trade union officials, social workers and members of the socialist intelligentsia in his ministry. He created new ministries in order to increase governmental efficiency.

2. In order to fill the trade gap Wilson introduced tariffs and decreed a drastic increase of the bank rate.

107

3. The p o u n d s t e r l i n g was saved in 1964 by the greatest concerted action in history: 11 nations (including the U.S.A., Canada, Japan, and West Germany) extended a credit of $2,800,000,000 after rumours of the imminent devaluation of the pound had resulted in alarming sales of British stocks and the withdrawal of foreign assets from London. In 1965 a new credit was granted. In 1967 the pound was finally d e v a l u e d.

4. Commonwealth:
a) Rhodesia: While Northern Rhodesia became independent in 1964 under the name of Zambia, the independence of S o u t h e r n R h o - d e s i a was delayed because the British government was not satisfied that the Africans would be granted a share in the government proportional to their numbers. In 1965 the white government of Ian Smith declared u n i l a t e r a l i n d e p e n d e n c e after futile negotiations with Wilson. Britain and the U.N. announced an economic boycott and an arms embargo.
b) In a war between Nigeria and the rebellious Nigerian province Biafra, Britain supplied arms to the Nigerian government, 1966.
c) Aden and the South Arabian Federation gained full independence in 1967. In 1968 Wilson committed himself to withdraw the British forces from east of Suez. For Malaysia and Singapore see p. 292.

5. *Iron and Steel Act*, 1967, brought into public ownership most major steel companies under the British Steel Corporation.

6. Race Relations: The unrestricted influx of c o l o u r e d w o r k e r s from Commonwealth countries (chiefly Pakistan and West Indies) led to unrest in industrial cities, intensified by the powerful speeches of the Conservative MP Enoch P o w e l l, who demanded that immigrants be repatriated and new ones prevented from entering.
a) *Commonwealth Immigrants Act,* 1968, restricted immigration but provided against discrimination of coloured people resident in Britain.
b) *Race Relations Acts,* 1965 and 1968, prohibited discrimination on grounds of colour or national origin. A Race Relations Board was set up to investigate complaints and, if necessary, to seek remedies in the courts.

7. Death penalty was abolished under the *Murder Act,* 1965.

8. Laws relaxing former legislation on divorce, abortion and homosexual activities heralded the greater tolerance of a 'permissive society'(the Conservatives, however, favoured the principle of 'law and order'). The age of attaining majority was reduced from 21 to 18.

9. V o t i n g a g e was reduced to 18 under the *Representation of the People Act,* 1969.

10. Education:
    a) The Labour government's policy was to establish c o m p r e -
    h e n s i v e s c h o o l s wherever new schools were needed, and to
    integrate the Public Schools into the state system.
    b) Student demonstrations against South African apartheid and the
    Greek regime, and teach-ins to bring about educational changes (e.g.
    students' participation in university administration and access to
    university files) led to students being suspended or sentenced in the
    courts.
11. Industrial Relations: The government's repeated attempts to bring
    about a price and wage stop and to disallow unofficial strikes failed
    in 1969 owing to trade union opposition.
12. N o r t h e r n I r e l a n d : see p. 124

CONSERVATIVE GOVERNMENT OF EDWARD HEATH, June 1970–
74, with Sir Alec Douglas Home (Foreign Office)

1. Industrial Relations: The government's problem was to limit inflation while avoiding economic stagnation.
   a) Prolonged strikes in vital services (dustmen, dockers, electricity
   and municipal workers) caused a loss of 6.6 million work days within
   8 months. Ensuing wage increases accelerated inflation.
   b) *Industrial Relations Act,* 1971, which passed the House of
   Commons after 450 hours of bitter debate, imposed a number of
   controls on trade union activity, penalizing violations with financial
   penalties, and set up an Industrial Relations Court, whose rulings,
   however, were ignored by a number of trade unions. The act was
   repealed under the later Labour government.
2. In 1971 IRA men planted a bomb in the Post Office Tower in
   London.
3. D e c i m a l c o i n a g e s y s t e m was introduced February 1971
   (pound has now 100 pence, shilling abolished).
4. The government's supply of arms to South Africa to halt the spread
   of Russian influence around the Indian Ocean met with sharp
   criticism in Britain and the coloured Commonwealth states.
5. C o m m o n M a r k e t : In 1972 the treaty of accession to the
   Common Market, signed by Edward Heath, was approved by a
   parliamentary majority of eight against strong Labour opposition.
6. Oil crisis 1973/74: The severe oil shortage caused by the decision of
   the Arab countries to reduce their oil supplies led to an alarming
   increase in unemployment and bankruptcies as a consequence of

contracting production. The government tried to meet the crisis by introducing a three-day working week.

7. Miners' strike: The government's counter-inflationary policy of wage control and a ban on overtime working was boycotted by the National Union of Mineworkers, which made new demands for higher wages. Heath's refusal to yield to the miners' pay claims led to new elections and the consequent fall of the government.

LABOUR GOVERNMENTS OF HAROLD WILSON (1974–76) and JAMES CALLAGHAN (1976–79)

1. The fact that Labour had won the election as a consequence of Heath's unpopular policy of wage control caused Wilson to seek an understanding with the trade unions by means of a *Social Contract*. The trade unions agreed to voluntary wage restraint while the government cut back on public expenditure to help finance industrial investment and export. The Social Contract reduced the inflation rate from 26⁰/₀ to 10⁰/₀ within three years.

2. In 1975 Iceland unilaterally extended its territorial waters from 12 to 200 miles to protect its fishing industry. This led to a 'cod war' (p. 138), which ended in 1976 with a compromise reducing the British catch.

3. The conflict in Northern Ireland continued unabated, with bomb explosions and killings throughout Ulster. Acts of terror extended as far as London.

4. Continuing opposition to membership of the EEC prompted a referendum, 1975, resulting in a 2 to 1 vote in favour of continued membership.

5. The *Sex Discrimination Act* 1975 and *Race Relations Act* 1976 made it illegal to discriminate in employment, education or housing on the grounds of sex or race.

6. Devolution bills for Scotland and Wales (see pp. 122, 124).

7. Continued immigration from Commonwealth countries increased racial tension in industrial cities, leading to outbreaks of violence. In 1976 the annual celebration of the West Indian carnival in the London district Notting Hill ended in a severe clash between black youths and the police. Other disturbances occurred in the London suburbs Lewisham and Southall and in two Birmingham suburbs, Handsworth and Ladywood.

8. The cancellation of the Social Contract by the TUC brought about new industrial strife. A three-month strike of the firemen 1977–78 cost several lives, because the soldiers called up by the government were inadequately trained and equipped.

9. An acute depression in 1977 was relieved by the International Monetary Fund (IMF) with the help of a credit of 1.3 billion* pounds bringing the national debt up to 20 billion pounds.
10. In 1977 Britain celebrated the 25th anniversary of Queen Elizabeth's accession to the throne. The Silver Jubilee celebrations included pageants and festivals in all parts of the country.
11. In January 1979 strikes of lorry and train drivers initiated a wave of strikes and secondary picketing, which paralyzed public life. Public service strikes crippled hospitals, shut down schools and left streets clogged with uncollected garbage.
12. Decline of Labour: The growth of a more radical wing under the leadership of Anthony Wedgwood ('Tony') Benn caused an ideological split in the party. Committed to an extreme socialism, it demanded the abolition of the House of Lords and peerages, of private education and health services. All tenanted farmland and privately rented property were to be transferred to public ownership, denationalized industries nationalized without compensation. Further demands were unilateral nuclear disarmament and withdrawal from NATO and EEC. The left-dominated National Executive Council (NEC) was to elect the party leader instead of MPs and to draft the election manifesto.
13. In 1979 Callaghan was defeated in a censure motion by one vote. This brought about an election prematurely.

CONSERVATIVE GOVERNMENT OF MARGARET THATCHER

Mrs Thatcher won the election with a majority of 43 seats over Labour – the greatest election victory since the war. Although her polemic sharpness irritated many voters, the desire for change proved overwhelming. Coming from the lower middle class, but educated at Oxford (and Minister of Education in Heath's Tory Cabinet), 'the iron lady' pursued her conservative course with remarkable determination and consistency admired even by her critics.

She had been leader of the Conservative party since 1975. Re-elected in 1983, she won a third time in 1987, again with a considerable lead over Labour. Mrs. Thatcher is the only British prime minister in this century to serve three successive terms.

I. Internal Affairs

1. Financial and social policy: Mrs. Thatcher was committed to economic liberalism, believing that industry could recover only if private initiative was restored. Public spending was to be cut, private investment encouraged. Her first budget, denounced by the trade unions as benefiting the rich and penalizing the poor, put up the

---

* The Americans call one thousand million a billion, a practice gradually being adopted in Britain.

minimum lending rate and lowered income tax (in the top brackets to the Continental average of 60% instead of 83%), but raised interest taxation at the consumer's expense. Social services (e.g. health and education) and local government jobs were to be reduced. Tenants of council houses (sozialer Wohnungsbau) were encouraged to buy their homes, while councils often found it difficult to find housing for the poor. The abolition of exchange controls making it possible to invest abroad drained much capital and did not create jobs at home.

2. Abuses in industrial action were limited by an Employment Act (p. 163).
3. Although Labour moved towards left-wing goals, members of the hardleft Militant Tendency were expelled.
4. In 1981 former right-wing Labour ministers founded the Social Democratic Party, which soon formed an alliance with the Liberals, today Liberal Democrats.
5. Violent rioting in Brixton 1981 was followed by unrest in other cities. In Toxteth (Liverpool) three days of ferocious attacks on the police by black as well as white youths caused alarming police injuries.
6. The IRA bombing campaign extended to mainland Britain. In 1984 a bomb exploded in a Brighton hotel where Mrs. Thatcher and her Cabinet were attending a Conservative Party Conference.
7. Encouraged by the 'Falkland factor' (p. 113), which had increased her popularity immensely, Mrs. Thatcher called a premature election, and, after her landslide victory over Labour, reshuffled her cabinet to include ministers who were even more in accord with her policies.
8. The Coal Strike of 1984–85 was directed against the Coal Board's policy of closing uneconomic mines. It failed ultimately when, after much violent confrontation between pickets and the police, most miners returned voluntarily to their pits.
9. For privatization see p. 145.
10. The introduction of a general 'Poll Tax' met with great hostility throughout the country and diminished Mrs. Thatcher's popularity considerably.

II. Foreign Affairs

1. Falklands: In 1982 a British colony, the Falkland Islands (a group of islands at the southern tip of South America), was occupied by the Argentine army after long-standing attempts by Argentina to negotiate a transfer of sovereignty had failed. Mrs. Thatcher sent a task force which recaptured the islands within 50 days. Britain's victory was hailed enthusiastically throughout the country despite the loss of two warships, 250 lives and the expenditure of £3 billion.
2. EEC: The common agricultural policy (CAP) required Britain as the

largest importer of food from non-EEC countries to make the greatest contribution to the common budget. This disadvantage was mitigated when Britain was granted rebates at several summits.

3. The Sino-British Treaty of 1984 provided for the return of Hong Kong to China in 1997 (p. 293).

4. The Anglo-Irish Treaty, which provided for the cooperation of Eire in matters of Northern Ireland was passionately resented by Ulster's Protestants. In Belfast Protestants hooligans terrorized mixed neighbourhoods which had been created to integrate Protestants and Catholics. Many Catholics moved out, preferring to live in Catholic ghettos.

5. Unwilling to submit to international control of sea-bed mining, Britain, like the USA, declined to join a UN convention drafted to adjust the interests of 150 nations on the principle that the mineral wealth of the ocean floor was 'the common heritage of mankind'.

6. The Commonwealth Development Corporation increased its funding for development in more than 40 Commonwealth countries.

7. Gulf War: In the conflict with Iraq, Mrs. Thatcher sided with the US government and sent troops to the Persian Gulf to join the UN forces.

8. Originally concerned about the growth of Soviet power, Mrs. Thatcher had given defence priority in public spending. Britain modernized its missile system and allowed US cruise missiles to be stationed on British soil.

9. European union: A closer union of Europe beyond the EEC area had long been discussed. Provisions for a monetary and political union, laid out by a summit at Maastricht, were approved by the EEC countries except Denmark and Britain. Mrs. Thatcher rigorously opposed the prospect of having to subject British policy to the dictates of a centralized bureaucracy ruled from Brussels. This led to a conflict with many of her ministers which brought about her resignation.

Although Mrs. Thatcher had triumphed over Labour in three consecutive elections, her uncompromising style of government and domineering attitude towards her ministers had undermined her cabinet's support as well as her popularity in the country. Nevertheless, not prepared to leave the political scene, she remained a member of Parliament and was enthusiastically acclaimed in the party conference at Brighton 1992 by her supporters. She was awarded the title of Baroness by the Queen.

CONSERVATIVE GOVERNMENT OF JOHN MAJOR (1990–)

John Major, the son of a circus performer (who had later engaged in a variety of small business ventures with little success), left school at 16 to help support his family. Banking jobs gave him his first training in business matters. He

113

pursued his early political interests in private studies and passed exams in several subjects. He soon felt that the pragmatic approach of Liberal Tories appealed to him more than Labour's more doctrinaire handling of political problems. He therefore stood as a conservative candidate for a seat in Parliament and actually became a Tory MP. He served in Mrs. Thatcher's cabinet as Chancellor of the Exchequer and was chosen Prime Minister by his colleagues when Mrs. Thatcher was compelled to resign.

As the youngest British premier of this century and with yet little political profile or social background, Major enjoyed little sympathy until he made it clear that he was determined to join the Maastricht Treaty. The General Election, which Major called in April 1992, upheld the Tory majority.

1. Major tried to alleviate the gloom concerning the general recession and steadily rising unempolyment by increasing child benefits and support to victims of Aids. His plan to close 31 unprofitable coal mines met with such general disapproval that he reduced the number of closures to 10.

2. Gulf War: Britain's disproportionate contribution to the allied forces in the Security Council's war against Iraq was backed by a vote of 453 to 57 in the House of Commons (obviously a lingering sense of involvement expressed by a nation that had been the leading colonial power in the Gulf).

3. A blow to British finance was the drastic increase in interest rates by the German Bundesbank as a consequence of German reunification. The ensuing higher capital requirements affected the European exchange rate mechanism (ERM) and was disastrous for weaker currencies. Britain and Italy left the ERM.

4. The Edinburgh Summit substantiated the Maastricht provisions, allowing Denmark to revise its first negative referendum and Britain go join later when its reservations would have been overcome.

5. Royalty: Despite a forty-year reign by Queen Elizabeth, which was marked by her integrity and self-discipline, royality became a matter of deep national concern in the '90s because scandals in the royal family, liberally publicised by the media, began to undermine respect for the institution of monarchy. Prince Charles and his wife Diana separated, though both continue to perform their royal functions independently. Prince Andrew separated from his wife Sarah, who had had an affair with a Texan millionaire. Princess Anne, who had divorced her husband Mark Philips, remarried against Church-of-England tradition.

6. Labour: In 1992 John Smith replaced Neil Kinnock as labour leader on the pledge of a moderate left-of-centre course (e.g. abolition of trade union block votes).

British Cabinets

Prime Ministers	Party	Duration	Important Cabinet Ministers
Duke of Newcastle	Whig	1754–62	Elder Pitt
Lord Bute	Tory	1762–63	
Lord Grenville	Tory	1763–65	
Lord Rockingham	Whig	1765–66	
Duke of Grafton	Coalition	1766–70	Elder Pitt
Lord North	Tory	1770–82	Charles Fox –1774
Lord Rockingham	Whig	1782	Charles Fox
Lord Shelbourne	Whig	1782–83	Younger Pitt
Duke of Portland	Coalition	1783	Fox, Lord North
William Pitt (the Younger)	Tory	1783–1801	
Harry Addington	Tory	1801–04	
William Pitt	Tory	1804–06	Henry Castlereagh
Lord Grenville	Coalition	1806–07	Charles Fox
Duke of Portland	Tory	1807–09	George Canning
Spencer Perceval	Tory	1809–12	
Lord Liverpool	Tory	1812–27	Robert Peel, Huskisson
George Canning	Tory	1827	
Lord Goderich	Tory	1827–28	
Duke of Wellington	Tory	1828–30	Robert Peel, Huskisson
Lord Grey	Whig	1830–34	Russell, Durham, Palmerston
Lord Melbourne	Whig	1834	
Robert Peel	Tory	1834–35	
Lord Melbourne	Whig	1835–41	
Robert Peel	Tory	1841–46	Gladstone
John Russell	Whig	1846–52	Palmerston
Lord Derby	Tory	1852	Disraeli
Lord Aberdeen	Coalition	1852–55	Palmerston
Lord Palmerston	Liberal	1855–58	
Lord Derby	Conservative	1858–59	Disraeli
Lord Palmerston	Liberal	1859–65	Gladstone, Russell
Lord Russell	Liberal	1865–66	
Lord Derby	Conservative	1866–68	Disraeli
Benjamin Disraeli	Conservative	1868	
William Gladstone	Liberal	1868–74	
Disreali, Lord Beaconsfield	Conservative	1874–80	
William Gladstone	Liberal	1880–85	Joseph Chamberlain
Lord Salisbury	Conservative	1885–86	

Prime Ministers	Party	Duration	Important Cabinet Ministers
William Gladstone	Liberal	1886	
Lord Salisbury	Conservative	1886–92	Balfour
William Gladstone	Liberal	1892–94	
Lord Rosebery	Liberal	1894–95	
Lord Salisbury	Conservative	1895–1902	Joseph Chamberlain
Arthur Balfour	Conservative	1902–05	
H. Campbell-Bannermann	Liberal	1905–08	
Herbert Asquith	Liberal	1908–15	Lloyd George, Grey, Winston Churchill
Herbert Asquith	Coalition	1915–16	
David Lloyd George	Coalition	1916–18 1918–22	Austen Chamberlain, Baldwin, Churchill
Andrew Bonar Law	Conservative	1922–23	Baldwin
Stanley Baldwin	Conservative	1923–24	
James Ramsay MacDonald	Labour	1924	Henderson: Home Office
Stanley Baldwin	Conservative	1924–29	Churchill
Ramsay MacDonald	Labour	1929–31	Snowden
Ramsay MacDonald	Coalition or 'National Cabinet'	1931–35	Neville Chamberlain
Stanley Baldwin	Conservative	1935–37	
Neville Chamberlain	Coalition	1937–40	Churchill: Admiralty
Winston Churchill	Coalition	1940–45	Eden, Lord Beaverbrook, Bevin, Attlee
Clement Attlee	Labour	1945–51	Cripps, Bevin, Bevan
Winston Churchill	Conservative	1951–55	Eden: Foreign Office
Anthony Eden	Conservative	1955–57	Harold Macmillan
Harold Macmillan	Conservative	1957–63	Lord Home, Maudling
Sir Alec Douglas-Home	Conservative	1963–64	
Harold Wilson	Labour	1964–70	Callaghan, B. Castle
Edward Heath	Conservative	1970–74	Douglas-Home, Carr
Harold Wilson	Labour	1974–76	Healey, A. W. Benn
James Callaghan	Labour	1976–79	Healey, A. W. Benn
Margaret Thatcher	Conservative	1979–90	Carrington, Howe
John Major	Conservative	1990–	

PHYSICAL GEOGRAPHY
OF THE BRITISH ISLES

A. **Situation of Britain** in the past was very favourable.

1. I n s u l a r p o s i t i o n afforded 'splendid isolation', but proximity to the Continent allowed close connection with Europe. The Straits of Dover separate England from France by a distance of only 22 miles, i.e. an hour and a half by ferry from Dover to Calais.

2. C o m m a n d o f s e a r o u t e s made Britain the greatest naval power of Europe.

3. Position in the c e n t r e o f t h e l a n d h e m i s p h e r e allowing ready access to overseas countries made England the world's foremost commercial and colonial power.

B. **Coast Line and Rivers**

1. The coast line is much broken by deep bays and estuaries forming fine harbours, many not approachable today by large tankers.

2. No place in the island is more than 75 miles away from the sea.

3. The gradual slope of the Continental Shelf (raised part of the ocean floor), on which England lies, makes the tides rise high and penetrate far inland allowing vessels to take their cargo far up the estuaries of rivers.

4. Strong tidal flow keeps estuaries from silting, thus aiding navigation.

5. R i v e r s are numerous. Their slow and slight gradient made them n a v i g a b l e for small vessels. They are linked by numerous canals, too small for efficient transport today.

C. **Physical Regions**

I. **England** consists of two main types of landscape:

1. LOWLAND ZONE occupies the southeast of England roughly extending from Exe to Tees. It is scarpland composed of soft younger rocks and consists of a series of limestone ridges separated by c l a y v a l e s with deep, rich soils. The actual lowland parts are the London and Hampshire Basins, the Midlands, East Anglia, the Fenlands, Lincolnshire and eastern Yorkshire. The lowland, especially in the south and west, is softly rolling country with meadows enclosed by

Regions of the British Isles

hedges, a notable feature of the English landscape. In the flat eastern part, which is England's granary, fields are more extended and less often enclosed.

The escarpments fall into two groups: the chalk Downs, chiefly in the southeast, and the Jurassic l i m e s t o n e   s c a r p s (oolite) extending roughly from Portland Bill on the Channel to the Tees. These include the Cotswold Hills, the Northampton and Lincolnshire Heights and the Cleveland Hills. The   c h a l k   D o w n s   radiate from Salisbury Plain: the Dorset Hills run southwest, the North and South Downs, inward-facing scarps, enclose the upfold of the Weald and terminate at the Straits of Dover and Beachy Head; the Chiltern Hills extend to the northeast and, after interruptions, continue in the chalk outcrops of the Lincoln and Yorkshire Wolds.

2. HIGHLAND ZONE is composed of Palaeozoic rocks:

a) The western highlands form two peninsulas separated by the Bristol Channel: C o r n w a l l, a dissected plateau with the high desolate moorlands of Dartmoor, Exmoor and Bodmin Moor, and W a l e s consisting of the deeply dissected central plateau and the rugged northern highland, which contains Wales's highest mountain, Snowdon (1085 m). Both areas are largely waste and moorland suited only for sheep rearing.

b) The northern highlands consist of the P e n n i n e s extending north-south through the middle of the island and bordered by important coalfields,* and the rugged, picturesque C u m b r i a n M o u n t a i n s of the Lake District, one of England's most attractive tourist areas.

II. Scotland (90 per cent mountainous) is divided into three regions:

1. SOUTHERN UPLANDS with the Cheviot Hills are treeless, melancholy hills rising to 800 m. As borderland much devastated in medieval wars, they contain the ruins of famous monasteries (e.g. Melrose, Dryburgh), which, in the Middle Ages, constituted the main centres of settlement and culture.

2. CENTRAL LOWLANDS: The fertile Midland Valley contains ³/₄ of the Scottish population and the two great cities, E d i n b u r g h, the beautiful capital below the steep volcanic castle rock, which has been called the Athens of the North, and G l a s g o w, the industrial and ship-building centre. The eastern part of the Lowlands is farming land, the west Scotland's chief industrial area. As the eastern coast of Scotland, which is flat throughout its length, is the main route to the north, its

---

* Since the coal measures formed the highest strata, and were worn away from the top of the uplifted arch, coal is now found only on the flanks of the Pennines.

deep inlets, the Firth of Forth and the Firth of Tay are crossed by huge bridges.

3. NORTHERN HIGHLANDS covering two thirds of the total Scottish area are wild and rugged, and contain Britain's highest mountain B e n N e v i s (1343 m). They are famous for the beauty of their deep glacial glens (valleys) and lochs (lakes). Glen More with Loch Ness, which is followed by the Caledonian Canal, divides the Highlands into the G r a m p i a n M o u n t a i n s in the south and the north-west Highlands. The Highlands with their heavy rainfall are the chief source of Britain's hydro-electric power. The mountains decline from west to east. On the flat east coast, which is suited to agriculture, are the main towns of the region, Aberdeen and Dundee. The Aberdeen area is now benefiting from North Sea oil.

4. ISLANDS: The H e b r i d e s (rugged and desolate) lie off the western coast. To the north lie the S h e t l a n d s and O r k n e y s, which became centres of the oil industry in the 1970s. The Shetlands are famous for their sheep yielding high-quality wool.

III. Ireland is called the 'Emerald Island' because of its lush green pastures (heavy rainfall).

1. Coasts, steep and indented, consist of rugged mountain groups which are chiefly wasteland.

2. The Central Plain is a region of vast peat bogs, which, in the absence of coal, provide the chief fuel, and of meadows, which make Ireland a grazing land of pastoral farms. Because of the island's saucer shape, rivers stagnate and form lakes.

D. Climate is oceanic, i.e. h u m i d and t e m p e r a t e with small seasonal contrasts. The indented coast allows maritime influences to penetrate far inland. The climate is healthy and invigorating, favouring outdoor work and exercise.

1. Temperature is mild, despite Britain's comparatively northern latitude. Owing to the influence of the Gulf Stream, the west is warmer than the east.
a) Summers are cool and not suited for ripening fruits requiring much sunshine (e.g. grapes).
b) Winters have only short spells of frost and snow. Harbours are never ice-bound. Plants like laurels, azaleas and rhododendrons are not damaged by frosts and are therefore frequently found in southern England. Grazing is possible throughout the year. It was only during the

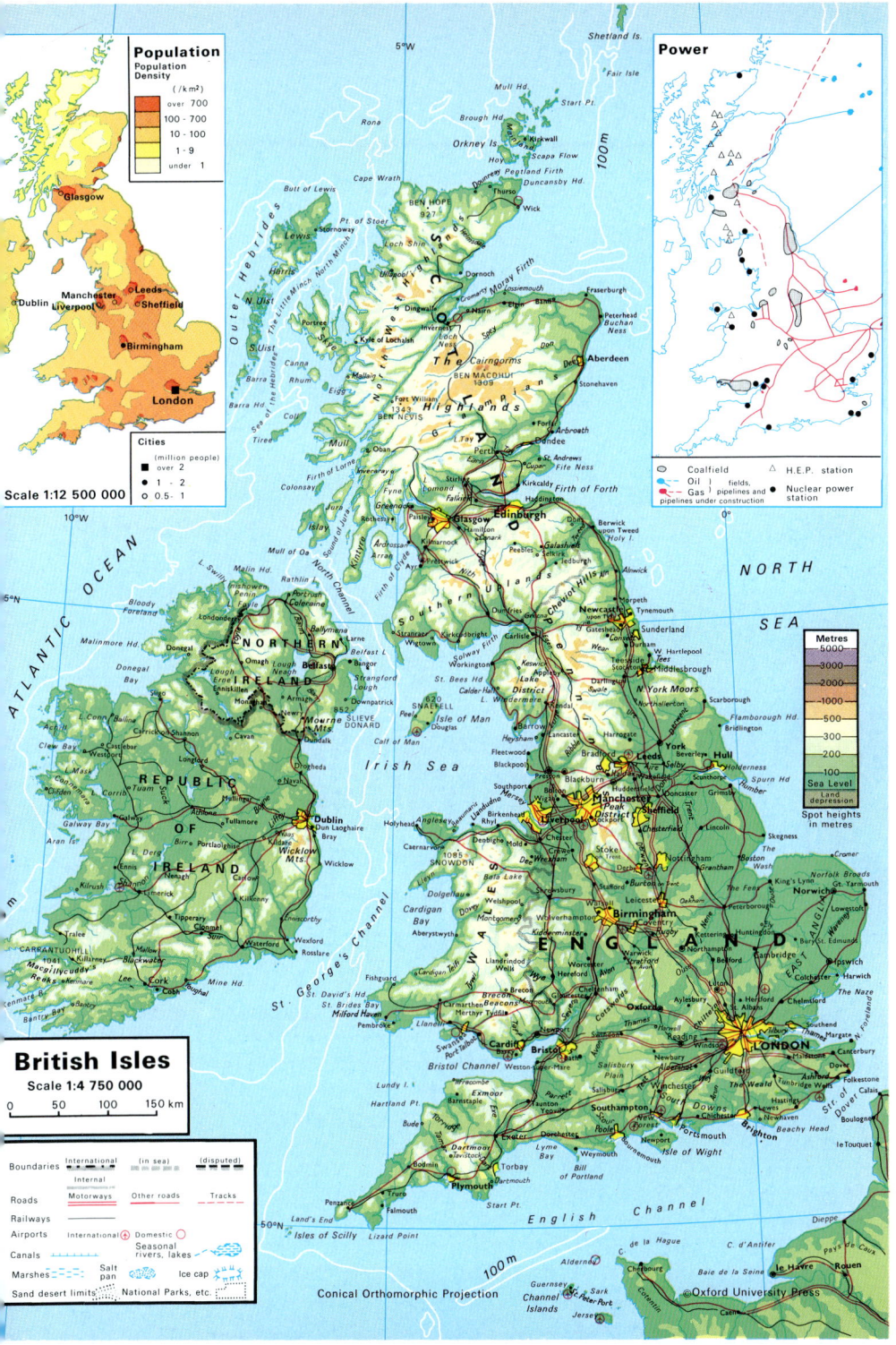

British Isles

Population

Population Density

(/ k m²)

- over 700
- 100 - 700
- 10 - 100
- 1 - 9
- under 1

Cities
(million people)
- ■ over 2
- ● 1 - 2
- ○ 0.5 - 1

Scale 1:12 500 000

Power

- Coalfield
- Oil } fields,
- Gas } pipelines and pipelines under construction
- △ H.E.P. station
- ■ Nuclear power station

Glasgow · Manchester · Leeds · Sheffield · Dublin · Liverpool · Birmingham · London

Metres
- 5000
- 3000
- 2000
- 1000
- 500
- 300
- 100
- Sea Level
- Land depression

Spot heights in metres

British Isles

Scale 1:4 750 000

0   50   100   150 km

Boundaries
International | Internal | (in sea) | (disputed)

Roads Motorways | Other roads | Tracks

Railways

Airports International ⊕ Domestic ○

Canals

Marshes Salt pan | Seasonal rivers, lakes | Ice cap

Sand desert limits National Parks, etc.

Conical Orthomorphic Projection

©Oxford University Press

ATLANTIC OCEAN

NORTH SEA

Irish Sea

St. George's Channel

English Channel

SCOTLAND

NORTHERN IRELAND

REPUBLIC OF IRELAND

WALES

ENGLAND

EAST ANGLIA

ENGLAND AND WALES : Political

Projection: Conical with two standard parallels

West from Greenwich 0 East from Greenwich

1:2 500 000

COPYRIGHT.
GEORGE PHILIP & SON LTD.

The DISTRICTS of Northern Ireland have been numbered and can be identified by reference to this table.

1 Londonderry
2 Limavady
3 Coleraine
4 Ballymoney
5 Moyle
6 Larne
7 Ballymena
8 Magherafelt
9 Cookstown
10 Strabane
11 Omagh
12 Fermanagh
13 Dungannon
14 Craigavon
15 Armagh
16 Newry & Mourne
17 Banbridge
18 Down
19 Lisburn
20 Antrim
21 Newtownabbey
22 Carrickfergus
23 North Down
24 Ards
25 Castlereagh
26 Belfast

1 Merseyside
2 Greater Manchester
3 West Yorkshire
4 South Yorkshire
5 West Glamorgan
6 Mid Glamorgan
7 South Glamorgan

IRELAND AND SCOTLAND:
Political

Projection: Conical with two standard parallels

Copyright, George Philip & Son, l

last decades that dwelling houses have installed central heating. Even today some have still merely open fireplaces and electric stoves.

2. Rainfall is abundant and well distributed throughout the year. It is heaviest (100 in.) in the high mountains of the west where the prevailing south-westerly winds, extremely moist after their long passage over the warm waters of the Gulf Stream, are forced upwards with a consequent lowering of temperature and condensation. The sunniest and driest part is the southeast, which has less than 30 in. of rainfall and is therefore suited to agriculture. Autumn and winter are the wettest seasons.

3. Fogs were frequent over London and industrial areas where moisture condenses on carbon particles in the polluted atmosphere. Meanwhile, larger cities have enforced 'smokeless zones'. Coastal fogs are usually due to the mixing of two air currents at the junction of land and sea.

POLITICAL DIVISIONS
OF THE UNITED KINGDOM

The United Kingdom of Great Britain and Northern Ireland (UK) has a population of 57.4 million according to the 1991 census. Its population density (235 per square km) ranks it fifth among the major states after the Netherlands, Belgium, Japan and Germany). The United Kingdom consists of four countries.

1. *England* with a population of 47.6 million and 54% Britain's land area, contains over 83% of the total population and has a density of 366 per square km.
2. *Wales* has a population of 2.87 million and a population density of 138 square km; 19% speak Welsh (a Celtic language).
3. *Scotland,* with a population of 5.09 million and 32% of the land area, has 9% of Britain's total population. It has a density of 66 people per square km. 1.6% of the population, mainly in the Highlands and the Hebrides, speak Gaelic (a Celtic language).
4. *Norther Ireland* (Ulster) has a population of 1.58 million. It has a density of 112 people per square km. The original Gaelic language is all but extinct.

The Channel Islands, where the French language is spoken, and the Isle of Man, where the Manx variety of the Celtic language is no longer spoken, are Crown dependencies, not parts of the United Kingdom. They have their own legislative assemblies (in the Isle of Man, the Tynwald, in the Channel Islands, the States). For economic purposes they are treated as parts of the mainland.

In recent decades nationalist movements in Scotland and Wales have made both countries more conscious of their own identities. Moreover, two decades of civil war in Northern Ireland have raised the question of the country's future political status.

Scotland

Despite its dynastic and parliamentary union with England, which took place in 1603 and 1707 respectively, Scotland has a very strong sense of its importance as an independent cultural unit within the United Kingdom and resents the traditional use of the term 'English' for the whole of Britain. This has led to a much more general use of the word 'Britain' unless reference is made only to England.

A number of factors have contributed to stimulate Scottish nationalism: the memory of centuries of warfare with England in the Border country, which has bred nostalgia for a heroic past, Highland romanticism fostered by wearing kilts with patterns of the ancient clans, a separate Church founded by Britain's greatest reformer John Knox, independent systems of law and education and – throughout the history of a united kingdom – the feeling of being neglected by a government in far-off London.

The rough and desolate nature of a country consisting mainly of barren mountains has bred a stern, hardy spirit, accustomed to coping with economic stringency (which in turn has given rise to the notorious jokes about Scottish thrift). However, more than the physical environment, the stern and democratic spirit of Calvinism introduced by John Knox in the Reformation has contributed to shaping the Scottish character. John Knox's principle that every person should be able to read the Bible led to the early establishment of parish schools supported by local taxation. Scotland's democratic tradition in Church matters as well as education has had its influence on the Scottish way of life and thought. In a speech made at the Scottish university of St. Andrews in 1925, Earl Baldwin remarked: 'There is nothing that fills me with more admiration than the way in which your people for generations have held up that standard of plain living and high thinking ... Nothing has made Scotland what she is more than the magnificent system of parochial education, which she had years before any other part of the British Isles. The picture of the Scottish student with his sack of oatmeal, leaving his work for part of the year, living and drawing on the frugality and self-sacrifice of his parents, in the pursuit and attainment of knowledge for the sake of knowledge, is an example to the whole world, and what you Scots have to be mindful of is that in this age, when education is tending to become spoonfed, you do not allow yourselves to lose sight of the ideals of past generations'. Part of these ideals may be seen as symbolized by the fact that Scotland had four universities centuries before England's third university in London was founded.

The Scots have made considerable contributions to British culture in other ways too. Walter Scott, one of the greatest novelists of British literature, gave his countrymen a vision of their heroic past. Robert Burns has been described as the first great poet of the common people. Allan Ramsay and Sir Henry Raeburn won fame as portrait painters. The 18th contury saw a Scottish school of thought. The Ossianic Poems of the Highlander Macpherson, which professed to be translations from a legendary third-century Gaelic bard called Ossian, created a sensation in Europe stimulating the Romantic movement, esp. the German Sturm und Drang.

Scottish efficiency and technological skill played an important part in the development of industry, not only in Scotland and Northern Ireland, where Scottish Presbyterians had settled in the 17th century, but also in Britain as a whole. The invention of the steam engine by James Watt started the Industrial Revolution. Adam Smith, who laid the foundation of economic liberalism, is considered one of the world's greatest economic thinkers.

The extinction of the clan system after 1745 eventually doomed the Gaelic language, which had survived in the Highlands. However, the small number of children who speak only Gaelic when they first go to school get their first instruction in Gaelic until they have acquired a sufficient knowledge of English.

The discovery of great oil resources in British waters, which has meanwhile revolutionized life in the Aberdeen area and the Shetlands and Orkneys, strengthened the Scottish Nationalist Party (SNP), which argues that exploitation by an independent Scottish state could relieve poverty and make Scotland economically self-sufficient. In the 1974 election, the SNP gained 11 seats in Parliament. In 1979, however, Labour recovered its traditional dominance in Scotland, while the SNP lost 9 of its seats. In 1975 and 1979 the British government sought to stifle the clamour for independence by elaborating two devolution bills granting Scotland a Scottish Assembly with limited powers of home rule. The first bill was defeated in the Commons, the second did not get the required number of yes-votes.

Thus Scotland is still ruled from London, where it is represented by a Secretary of State for Scotland, whose responsibilities are exercised by five departments in Edinburgh.

An important source of Scottish revenues is tourism. Visitors of Scotland are attracted by the beauty of its mountains and lakes and by its romantic castles. The Edinburgh Festival attracts thousands to the 'Athens of the North' every year. Some romantics may even hope to find out whether 'Nessie', the legendary Loch Ness monster, really exists – as many claim.

(As a matter of fact, fears were already expressed in the Commons that the catching of salmon in Loch Ness might threaten Nessie's survival. The Scottish Secretary soothed these fears by remarking that having looked after itself for 70 million years, Nessie was probably not in any immediate danger in the present session of Parliament.)

Wales

The British inhabitants of Wales, who were called 'foreigners' (*Wealas*, today *Welsh*) by the Anglo-Saxon invaders, are no less proud than the Scots of their contributions to the British heritage: the Arthurian legends, which became an integral part of mediaeval literatures in Europe, a long choral tradition and the annual gatherings of bards and musicians, the eisteddfod, going back to the 6th century. Being a competition conducted entirely in Welsh, in which many choirs take part, the Royal National Eisteddfod has helped to preserve the Welsh language and, with it, an awareness of national identity (see also p. 255). It was the Britons, not the Anglo-Saxons, who gave the whole island its name.

Although Wales was conquered by the English as early as the 13th century, the inaccessible nature of the interior prevented English influences from penetrating far inland, so that until the 20th century the physical difference between the Welsh, who had mixed with the dark-complexioned aboriginal population, and the English was still discernible. Meanwhile tourism and the general mobility of our age has largely wiped out physical and linguistic differences.

The number of persons speaking Welsh is steadily declining (since 1950 from 29 per cent to 19 per cent), although in a few western areas a majority of people still speak it. There has been considerable local pressure to revive the Welsh language. Children in Wales who speak Welsh at home now receive the early stages of primary education in Welsh with English as a second language. The *Welsh Language Act* 1967 confirmed the equal validity of Welsh in the administration of law and the conduct of official business. The Welsh Language Council, an official body, promotes the use of the language. The Welsh Arts Council helps with the publication of literary works in Welsh. Television provides programmes in Welsh.

Wales has a strong nonconformist tradition. The Anglican Church was therefore disestablished. The main religious organizations are the Presbyterian Church of Wales with about 94,000 members and the Union of Welsh Independents (see also p. 192). Since 1921 there has been an Anglican Church in Wales with its own archbishop.

Wales has a certain measure of home rule. In 1964 the Labour government, which had come to power with strong Welsh backing, appointed a Secretary of State for Wales with a seat in the Cabinet. He is advised by a Welsh Council nominated by him. The greater part of his department's work is carried on in Cardiff. There is a Welsh Nationalist Party (Plaid Cymru) demanding full independence, but it has far less backing than the Scottish Nationalist Party. The fact that 70 per cent of the population live in the Anglicized industrial south-east, while the Celtic-speaking population with the most pronounced Welsh characteristics live in the poor mountainous north and west, tends to make Welsh nationalism a marginal and romantic movement. A devolution bill in 1979 did not win more than 11.9% of the Welsh vote.

The TV series *How Green was my Valley* based on a famous novel, where the scene is set in a Welsh coal district, brought the problems of this area and of the Welsh in general home to the attention of the English public.

Northern Ireland

When, after a prolonged struggle for independence, leading to civil strife even in Ireland itself, Southern Ireland became a Free State in 1922, Northern Ireland, which had a Protestant majority, decided to remain a part of the United Kingdom. Ulster was granted its own regional Parliament, convening in Stormont (Belfast) and its own government, which, however, was subject to the Parliament in Westminster.

As the C a t h o l i c   m i n o r i t y felt discriminated against by the Stormont government, which was formed by the permanent Protestant majority (Ulster Unionist Party), it began to voice its demands in the sixties through the C i v i l   R i g h t s   m o v e m e n t. In August 1969 the Protestant extremists, who feared that a victory of the civil rights movement might ultimately lead to a reunion with Catholic Southern Ireland, began to attack civil rights marchers and Catholic areas in Belfast and Londonderry. Thereupon the government in Westminster sent army forces to support the local police, the Royal Ulster Constabulary. A   t e r r o r i s t   c a m p a i g n conducted by a break-away group of the Southern Irish Republican Army (IRA), the *Provisional IRA,* was answered by the prorogation of the Stormont parliament. In 1972 the British government introduced d i r e c t r u l e under a Secretary of State for Northern Ireland with a seat in the U.K. cabinet. Two attempts to form a new government in which Protestants and Catholics would share power were thwarted by the uncompromising attitude of the Protestants under their leader, the Reverend Ian Paisley, and IRA extremists who would accept nothing short of a united sovereign Ireland. The escalating cycle of violence, in which acts of terror extended even to London, has meanwhile claimed 3,000 lives.

In 1976 two Catholic women, Betty Williams and Mairead Corrigan, following an act of terrorism which had bereaved Miss Corrigan's family, founded a Peace

Movement, which organized demonstrations. In 1977 the two women received the Nobel Peace Prize, but the movement eventually collapsed.

In 1981 Mrs Thatcher refused to yield to the demands of convicted IRA terrorists to get political-prisoner status. Ten men, who had gone on hunger strike, died. One, Bobby Sands, had been elected MP.

The Northern Ireland Development Agency (NIDA), which tries to remedy some of Ulster's economic grievances, is improving housing and transport and setting up new industries to relieve unemployment. However, more and more people, even Protestants, emigrate.

Britain has promised that Ulster shall remain part of the UK as long as the majority of the people there (61% are Protestant) wishes. But it is the very problem of majority rule which will perpetuate the strife. As things stand, direct rule from London is the least bad solution as it is impartial.

LONDON

London is the capital of the United Kingdom and centre of the British Commonwealth. Until 1964 it consisted of the City of London proper and the London County area, which included the City of Westminster and the Metropolitan Boroughs. London has now absorbed large parts of the surrounding counties and, with a population of 6.7 million, is one of the three largest conurbations in the World. 'Greater London' consists of 32 Boroughs, while, under its own Lord Mayor, the City of London has retained its ancient rights, though the resident population is not more than 5,000. The Greater London Council, which was responsible for local services requiring large-scale planning, was abolished in 1986. A danger facing London, the tidal surges from the Thames caused by the progressive decline of the Continental Shelf towards the east, was averted in the mit-80s. A gigantic barrier now prevents flooding, while at the same time allowing ships to pass through.

History

Since London as a capital has absorbed much of national life to the detriment of the provinces, its history may be considered as an epitome of English history.

1. ROMAN LONDON: It has generally been assumed that the Roman name 'Londinium' derived from a previous Celtic settlement Lyndyn, the hill ('dune', later 'down') on the water. The Romans realized the importance of a site in the marshy land of the Thames estuary, where two elevations afforded firm

ground which made possible a river-crossing. About 60 A.D. they encircled the hills with a w a l l , fragments of which still exist. This square mile (still called the City of London) near the tidal limit of the river which formed the natural entry from the Continent, soon developed into a commercial and administrative centre and became the junction of the country's two main arteries, the Roman Ermine and Watling Streets. Approach to the steep slope of the western hill was across the little harbour of F l e e t R i v e r (hence 'Fleet Street') through the gate bearing the name of the British king Lud. L u d g a t e H i l l (called after this gate) was separated from Cornhill, later Tower Hill, by Wallbrook, where after German bombings important Roman remains were found. East of these two rivers (now filled in) the Thames was later crossed by L o n d o n B r i d g e , which made Fleet harbour useless and has up to this day remained the limit of navigation.

2. MIDDLE AGES: When the London area was occupied by the East Saxons the town was Christianized from Kent, whose king Ethelbert built O l d S t . P a u l ' s on its present site. Farther up the Thames were various low elevations rising above the flood level of the marshes, which are recalled by the Saxon endings -ea or -ey (island) found in the names of Chelsea and Battersea. The most famous is Thorney, where 400 years later Edward the Confessor built a monastery with a church already called Westminster. During the time of Alfred the Great, London (now fortified) became a political power, which William the Conqueror acknowledged when he had himself elected King by the citizens of London and crowned in Westminster Abbey. However, he tried to overawe the city by erecting the T o w e r (begun 1078), which later served as a state prison, the place of execution being outside on Tower Hill. Owing to its commercial strength London soon gained a large measure of independence from the government in Westminster, its liberties being confirmed by Magna Carta. Its government was largely in the hands of the guilds and centred in G u i l d h a l l . The annual election of the Lord Mayor in November was celebrated by an official ceremony, the L o r d M a y o r ' s S h o w , which is still one of the most magnificent pageantries in the London year. Followed by a colourful procession, partly on the Thames, the Lord Mayor proceeded to Westminster Hall to swear the oath of allegiance.
The kings reigned in W e s t m i n s t e r P a l a c e , were crowned and (since Henry III) buried in the Abbey. Later the House of Commons met in the Chapter House of the Abbey. Law was administered in Westminster Hall, begun in 1097 by William II (Rufus). The lawyers' guilds established themselves in t h e T e m p l e , grounds bought from the medieval order of the Knights Templar. At the Temple the city was entered through T e m p l e B a r G a t e , on which the heads of executed criminals were exposed as a warning.
The walk from Westminster to the city was called the S t r a n d . Here bishops and dukes had their crenellated palaces with gateways upon the Thames, the main highway of London.

3. SIXTEENTH CENTURY: When in the course of the Reformation private chapels were abolished, the Commons began to meet in the Royal Chapel of St. Stephen within the Palace of Westminster. Thus Westminster Palace, where the Lords

had from the first been accommodated, became the Houses of Parliament. Henry VIII transferred the court to W h i t e h a l l   P a l a c e. On the site of an ancient leprosy hospital he built S t.   J a m e s ' s   P a l a c e, which became the official residence of the sovereigns after Whitehall had burnt down in 1698. Henry drained the swampy wasteland between St. James's Palace and Whitehall as a deer park. Elizabeth I built the R o y a l   E x c h a n g e in 1567 to provide a meeting place for merchants, to be followed by the S t o c k   E x c h a n g e when the founding of chartered joint-stock companies for foreign trade necessitated the trading in stocks. L o m b a r d   S t r e e t, where Lombard merchants had established themselves as money lenders in the 12th century, remained the financial centre. The only bridge across the river was L o n d o n   B r i d g e, which had houses on both sides and two fortified gates, on which the heads of executed criminals were displayed as a warning. South of the river, the flourishing borough of Southwark was famous for its r i v e r s i d e   t h e a t r e s associated with Shakespeare.

4. SEVENTEENTH CENTURY: In the hot summer of 1665 London was decimated by the P l a g u e and, one year later, ravaged by the G r e a t   F i r e, which raged for four days and nights reducing the greater part of the City within the walls to ashes. St. Paul's Cathedral, then a Gothic building, and 87 parish churches were destroyed. The City, including St. Paul's, was rebuilt by England's greatest architect, Sir Christopher Wren. The medieval town with its narrow lanes and thatched wooden houses became a modern city with broad streets and stately stone houses. Another fire (1695) destroyed Whitehall Palace, sparing only the Banqueting Hall (p. 230), from one of whose windows Charles I had stepped on to the scaffold for his execution.

5. THE EIGHTEENTH CENTURY saw the development of a rich civic culture, which was almost wholly concentrated in London. Dr. Johnson wrote: 'When a man is tired of London he is tired of life, for there is in London all that life can afford.' Its coffee houses and taverns, 'the thrones of human felicity' (Johnson), became meeting places of various trades. C o v e n t   G a r d e n was the centre of actors and literary men, P a t e r n o s t e r   R o w of the book trade; S t.   M a r t i n ' s   L a n e, with an art school, and L e i c e s t e r   S q u a r e, with the studios of famous painters, were the homes of art. The coffee houses in Pall Mall and Piccadilly later developed into gentlemen's clubs. P i c c a d i l l y itself probably derived its name from the piccadillos, small stiff collars worn by the gallants who frequented a place of entertainment in this street.

The removal of the medieval walls, which had replaced the Roman wall, made it possible to extend the city beyond its narrow limits. The 'rows' and 'terraces' of semi-detached houses with a small front garden became the distinguishing feature of London's residential quarters. The ' W e s t   E n d ' between the City and Westminster was occupied by fashionable society. The mansions of the nobles with smaller houses of their dependents grouped around them formed squares (or 'gardens'), which frequently bore the noble's name (e.g. Berkeley and Grosvenor Squares).

In the number of its pleasure gardens London was unsurpassed. Concerts, masquerades, fireworks took place in famous entertainment establishments like V a u x h a l l, the Rotunda, Ranelagh Gardens and the Pantheon. London parks had become an important feature in all aspects of London life. When Queen Caroline, who embellished H y d e P a r k with an artificial lake, the Serpentine, asked Robert Walpole how much it would cost to transform Hyde Park into a Palace Garden, his answer was only: 'Three Crowns'. She succeeded, however, in changing its western part according to the new style of landscape gardening and barring the lower classes from this part, which became K e n s i n g t o n G a r d e n s. Westminster Bridge, built in 1749, afforded a new crossing over the river.

6. THE NINETEENTH CENTURY saw the development of industry, which grew up near the Port of London in the East End. The great expansion of shipping congested the quays along the Thames so that much of the unloading had to be done in midstream into lighters (still a distinctive feature of the river traffic). The marshes below the City afforded cheap land for new docks, which could accommodate larger ships in closed dock-basins, where deep water could be maintained even at low tide. As London became the focus of the country's main railway lines, new bridges had to be built. The world's first underground railway, opened in 1863, relieved traffic congestion within the city.
The manifold activities of civic life concentrated in functional zones: commerce and banking in the City, which had become the world's financial centre, the printing presses and newspaper offices in Fleet Street, where the first printing press had been established in 1501 by one of Caxton's pupils, administration in Westminster, entertainment and shopping in the West End.
The Regency period introduced the new principles of town planning by grouping several buildings in uniform architectural complexes (R e g e n t S t r e e t, p. 234). B u c k i n g h a m P a l a c e, which George III had bought in 1762 from the Duke of Buckingham, became the royal residence. Under Queen Victoria, who had grown up in Kensington Palace, the site south of Kensington Gardens became a centre of museums and important institutes, with the Royal Albert Hall and Albert Memorial built in commemoration of her consort. Government buildings in Whitehall and museums (British Museum, National and Portrait Galleries) were constructed in the neoclassical style, while the Houses of Parliament, which burnt down in 1834, were rebuilt in the 'national' Perpendicular style (p. 235). The first great product of civic engineering, the Crystal Palace, which was built for the great Colonial Exhibition in 1851, burnt down in 1936.

7. TWENTIETH CENTURY: In World War II, large parts of the City were destroyed by the blitz and were re-erected in a modern style. Wren's parish churches were rebuilt largely by London Livery Companies. When in 1951 the Festival of Britain in commemoration of the first Great Exhibition took place, the Royal Festival Hall was opened on the chief exhibition site on the south bank of the Thames. In 1976 the National Theatre was built next to it.
In the late sixties Carnaby Street and King's Road, Chelsea, became centres of a youthful pop culture. Hence the image of 'swinging London'.
1982 saw the opening of the Barbican Centre for Arts and Conferences in the City. The largest centre of this kind in Western Europe, it contains a concert hall, two theatres, an art gallery, cinemas and conference rooms.

Principal Sights of London

The most important sights of London are in the City of London proper, which is the centre of business, and in the City of Westminster, which is the seat of government and includes the Houses of Parliament, the royal palaces, the University of London, the principal museums and centres of entertainment.

The eastern boundary of the City on the Thames is marked by the T o w e r guarded by the picturesque Yeomen Warders, which has served as fortress, palace and prison. The original square Norman 'keep', the White Tower, contains the oldest chapel in London. In the Wakefield Tower are the heavily guarded Crown Jewels. Nearby is T o w e r B r i d g e with its massive Gothic towers, one of the distinctive London sights (built in 1894). Its carriage-way can be raised hydraulically in a minute to let big ships through to the limit of navigation below London Bridge.

Not far from the Tower, the M o n u m e n t built in commemoration of the Great Fire of 1666 affords a wide panoramic view of London, in which the spires of Wren's churches (p. 230) form a characteristic feature. The importance of the City as the centre of banking and insurance (which employs 350,000 people and is inhabited by only about 5,000 residents at night) is marked by the B a n k (p. 232) and the R o y a l E x c h a n g e, which stand in a triangular area opposite the M a n s i o n H o u s e, the official residence of the Lord Mayor. Nearby is B o w C h u r c h, (properly St. Mary-le-Bow), which is famous through the saying that true Londoners or 'cockneys' are those born within the sound of Bow Bells. Not far from the Bank are G u i l d h a l l, seat of the City Corporation, and the Norman church of S t. B a r t h o l o m e w t h e G r e a t, the oldest ecclesiastical building in London (founded in 1123).

On the summit of Ludgate Hill (p. 126) stands S t. P a u l ' s C a t h e d r a l. Its famous dome, which is the distinctive feature of the London skyline, is the largest in the world after St. Peter's in Rome. From the bottom of Ludgate Hill, F l e e t S t r e e t, the centre of the British press, leads to T e m p l e B a r, where a monument surmounted by a bronze griffin marks the boundary between the City and Westminster.

From this point the street is called the S t r a n d, the busiest thoroughfare between the City and the West, and the centre of law. The neo-Gothic L a w C o u r t s were built opposite the Temple, the oldest Inn of Court (p. 126), which contains T e m p l e C h u r c h, built by the Knights Templar as a replica of the Church of the Holy Sepulchre in Jerusalem.

On an island in the middle of the Strand stands S t. C l e m e n t D a n e s on the site of a Danish settlement in Saxon times, one of the finest churches designed by Wren. Not far from this part of the Strand, Waterloo Bridge affords the most impressive view of the Thames as it sweeps in a wide curve from Westminster down to Tower Bridge.

North of the Strand is the site of the old Covent Garden vegetable and

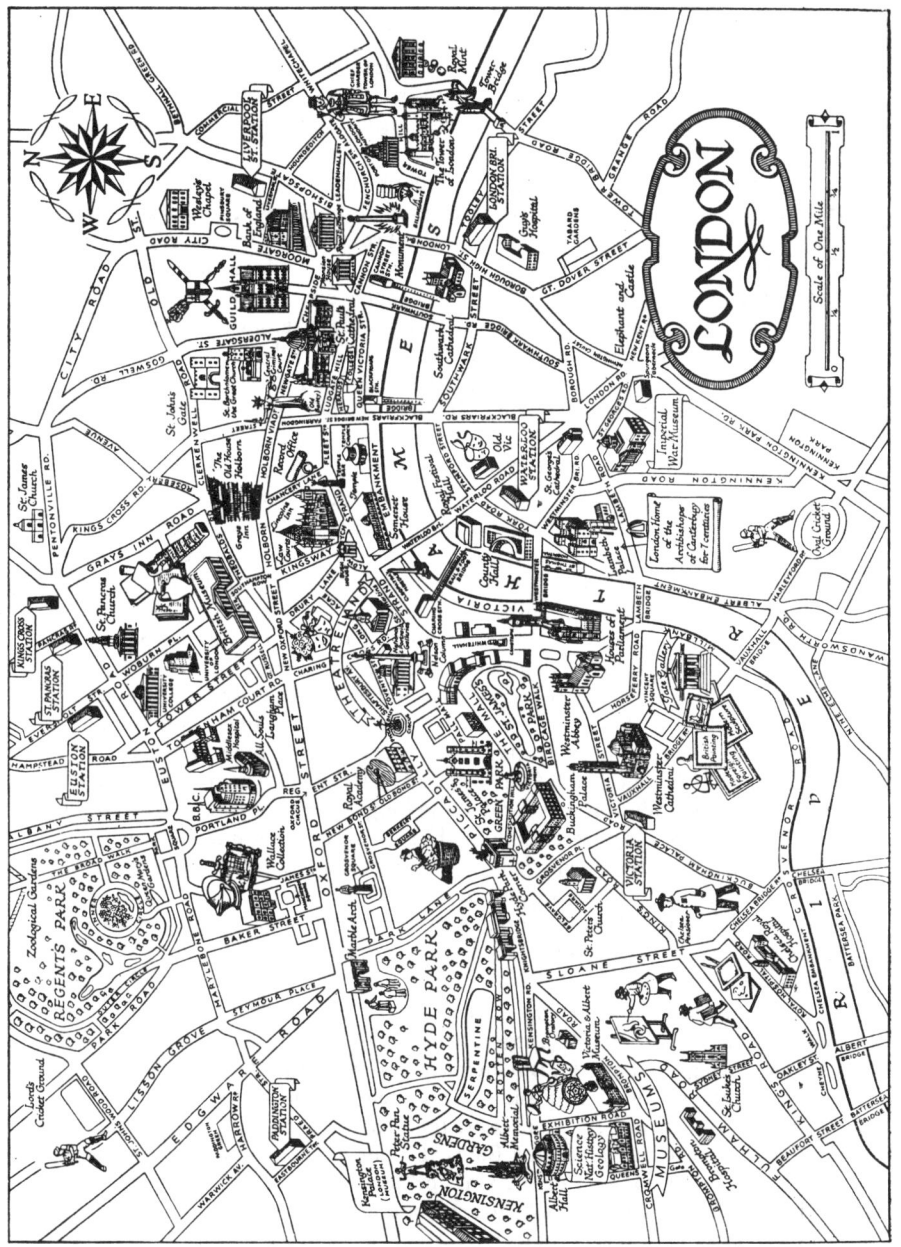

flower market, which has now moved to Nine Elms, south of the River Thames. The site has now become a vast shopping area. Opposite this is the Royal Opera House, Covent Garden, which takes its name from the Convent Garden of the monks of Westminster Abbey which occupied this site in the Middle Ages.

From here one reaches the centre of entertainment, L e i c e s t e r S q u a r e, with its large cinemas, and S o h o, with its night clubs and exotic restaurants, the principal foreign quarter of London. From Leicester Square, Charing Cross Road leads to T r a f a l g a r S q u a r e, where demonstrations and political meetings take place in the open air. A Corinthian column surmounted by the statue of Admiral Nelson commemorates the victory of Trafalgar. The square, which has two fine fountains, is bounded on the north side by a terrace, on which stands the N a t i o n a l G a l l e r y containing a vast collection of paintings from all countries and schools of art.

From Trafalgar Square W h i t e h a l l, a broad street lined with imposing government buildings, leads to Westminster Abbey. In front of the H o r s e G u a r d s (p. 231), the picturesque scene of the Changing of the Guard takes place every morning. Walking through its archway one reaches H o r s e G u a r d s P a r a d e, the yard of the ancient Whitehall Palace where the year's greatest military ceremony, the Trooping of the Colour, takes place on the Sovereign's official birthday in June.

Branching off from Whitehall to St. James's Park is D o w n i n g S t r e e t, which has contained the residence of the Prime Minister ever since George II gave House Numer 10 to his Premier, Robert Walpole, in 1732. The famous S c o t l a n d Y a r d, headquarters of the Metropolitan Police, is in Victoria Street. From the Thames Embankment one may see across the river C o u n t y H a l l, until 1986 seat of the Greater London Council, which was dissolved in 1986. Beyond Westminster Bridge the long frontage of the H o u s e s o f P a r l i a m e n t (p. 235) stretches along the river side. The sound of B i g B e n, the bell of its clock tower, which is frequently broadcast, is known throughout the world. The only remaining part of the medieval palace is W e s t m i n s t e r H a l l, which was for many centuries the seat of jurisdiction and is now the place where most of the important state ceremonies and coronation festivities take place.

Close to the Houses of Parliament is W e s t m i n s t e r A b b e y, representing the epitome of British history, where English sovereigns are crowned and many kings lie buried. Its monuments, notably the P o e t s' C o r n e r, commemorate many of England's great men. Its most sacred part is the Chapel of St. Edward the Confessor, founder of the Abbey, which contains the Coronation Chair made for Edward I and, underneath it, the Stone of Scone, the coronation seat of the kings of Scotland. The finest later addition is H e n r y V I I's C h a p e l, which contains the tombs of the two great enemies, Elizabeth I and Mary Stuart. S t. J a m e s's P a r k near the

Abbey affords one of the most picturesque views of London: in the foreground the gentle lawns of the park with drooping willows reaching down to the lake, in the background the spires and cupolas of Whitehall against the horizon.

St. James's Park is bounded in the north by the M a l l, a broad processional avenue leading from Admiralty Arch in Trafalgar Square to B u c k i n g h a m P a l a c e, the London residence of the sovereigns since 1837. When the Sovereign is in residence, the royal standard is flown. At the palace gates the guards in their red coats and bearskins are a popular sight.

Not far from Buckingham Palace is H y d e P a r k C o r n e r. Walking through a big archway and then along the Serpentine, an artificial lake, one reaches the western continuation of Hyde Park, K e n s i n g t o n G a r d e n s with K e n s i n g t o n P a l a c e where Queen Victoria was born.

From Hyde Park Corner, P i c c a d i l l y, lined with most of London's clubs and big hotels, leads to P i c c a d i l l y C i r c u s with a fountain surmounted by the famous figure of Eros. From here R e g e n t S t r e e t sweeps in a big curve north towards R e g e n t ' s P a r k, with the Zoological Gardens. B l o o m s b u r y, the district northeast of Piccadilly Circus, contains the university centre and the B r i t i s h M u s e u m with one of the world's most remarkable archaeological and ethnographic collections and the largest collection of books and manuscripts in the Commonwealth.

Not far from here is O x f o r d S t r e e t, together with Regent Street the main shopping centre, with London's biggest department stores. It leads to M a r b l e A r c h at the northeast corner of Hyde Park, where the speeches of the popular Sunday orators (also held on work-day evenings) form a characteristic feature of London life.

The main sights south of Hyde Park and Kensington Gardens are the T a t e G a l l e r y with a big collection of British and modern art, and W e s t - m i n s t e r C a t h e d r a l, the Roman Catholic Metropolitan Cathedral Church, in a sumptuous neo-Byzantine style. The only place in the East End worth a visit is the R o y a l N a v a l C o l l e g e on the Thames at Greenwich (p. 231) below G r e e n w i c h O b s e r v a t o r y with imposing buildings by Inigo Jones and Wren.

Two principal sights near London lie up the Thames. H a m p t o n C o u r t (p. 229) is a magnificent palace which became royal property when its builder, Cardinal Wolsey, lost the favour of his king, Henry VIII. W i n d s o r C a s t l e, farther west, has been a royal residence for 900 years since William the Conqueror built it on a steep eminence rising above the Thames. Its principal architectural features are the large round tower and the beautiful St. George's Chapel (p. 228).

On the Thames opposite Windsor is the famous Public School of E t o n C o l l e g e built in the Tudor style.

BRITISH ECONOMY

Britain's geography and position, and the fact that largely British inventions initiated the Industrial Revolution have made Britain a nation dependent on trade and industry rather than farming.

By the beginning of the 20th century, Britain had become the workshop of the world and a great trading nation, whose commercial fleet, protected by the world's biggest navy, dominated the seas. The colonies provided cheap supplies of raw materials. London had become the world's banking and insurance centre, the pound sterling the standard of exchange in which international business was transacted.

With growing competition from new industrial nations, Britain, however, gradually lost its lead over other countries. In World War II it suffered crippling losses through bombings, the sinking of ships and the sale of overseas investments to pay for military aid. After the war most colonies became independent. Extensive w e l f a r e p r o g r a m m e s prevented capital from being used productively, and h i g h t a x a t i o n stifled private initiative. The U.S.A. became the world's economic giant. The dollar replaced the pound sterling as the standard of exchange, while sterling declined as a consequence of war losses and diminished industrial efficiency (despite repeated billion-dollar loans from other countries). Wages and salaries in Britain, even salaries of high executives in industry, are well below levels in countries like the U.S.A., France and West Germany.

One of the main forces paralyzing the British economy since World War II has been the strikes called by the powerful trade unions. Increasing wage demands thwarted all efforts to introduce wage and price freezes, leading to galopping wage-price inflation.

Britain has suffered its share of the worldwide recession, with growing unemployment (3.1 million in 1987) and an inflation which has brought down the value of the pound sterling from DM 12 in the fifties to under DM 4.

Flight of capital became a common phenomenon. With taxation on investment income extremely high, the British found little incentive to invest their money at home. The wealthy began to seek tax shelters in other countries encouraging investment. Many of the ablest men in business and science left Britain to work in other countries with lower taxes, the more so as membership of the Common Market has increased mobility. On the other hand floods of weekend shoppers from the continent took advantage of the depreciation of sterling, while Arab oil sheiks bought up whole businesses, real estate and country mansions. As the value of the British currency rose as a result oil production, the tourist flood subsided.

North Sea oil has not only had a beneficial effect on the balance of payments, with foreign currency reserves trebling in 1977, but the strength of the pound has already begun to reduce Britain's export opportunities.

Industrial relations remain a problem. Employees are threatened with layoffs, while employers blame labour for stagnant production and find it annoying to be compelled to negotiate with several unions within one plant. There are also conflicts within trade unions, where the shopfloor has no influence on their officials' decisions. In recent years the workers of plants have increasingly decided to got to work rather than follow their officials' call to strike (p. 163).

Entry into the European Economic Community, effected in 1973 met with such criticism across party lines that in 1975 the nation was called on to decide on its continued membership by means of a referendum (the only one ever held in Britain). The result was a two to one majority in favour of staying in the EEC. But criticism of EEC policies is as strong as ever. Anti-marketeers would prefer the old Commonwealth ties to what they consider dependence on Britain's competitors, the more so as the Commonwealth countries resent the protectionist policies of the EEC, which threaten to deprive them of their most important customers. Moreover, the change-over to decimal weights and measures (cf. p. 109) offends the insular sentiments of the British and is widely ignored.

The Conservative government effected vital changes. Mrs. Thatcher's policy of monetary restraint (including public spending on social services) brought down inflation. Her encouragement of private initiative promoted private ownership in housing and industry. She curbed trade union power and triggered a moderate productivity growth. She did not succed in bringing down unemployment, largely the result of automation (cf. p. 210) and plant closures in the steel industry. Her critics accuse her of having widened the gulf between the rich and the poor (including more than 3 million unemployed), whose needs, they argue, are ignored in a profit-seeking society forgetful of social responsibility. Her sucessor John Major has so far not succeeded in stimulating the economy.

Agriculture

History

1. ANGLO-SAXON OPEN-FIELD SYSTEM employed c o m m o n g r a z i n g on village pastures (the 'common'), while arable land was tilled individually according to the t h r e e - f i e l d s y s t e m (a three-year rotation of winter crop, summer crop and fallow).

2. FEUDALISM, especially since the Danish invasions, introduced the m a n o r i a l s y s t e m, which made the inhabitants of the village ('villeins') serfs of the

lord of the manor. Serfs had to perform feudal services on the demesne (Domäne) three or four days a week, beside work on their own fields.

3. SHEEP RAISING AND ENCLOSURES: Scarcity of labour after the plague of 1348, and the rise of wool prices induced land-owners to take the demesne out of cultivation and to use it for sheep raising, which required fewer workers if pastures were enclosed. This enclosure movement was halted by Elizabeth I to protect small farmers.

4. DRAINAGE OF FENS (marshes of Lincolnshire and Cambridgeshire) in the 17th century yielded fertile arable land.

5. AGRICULTURAL REVOLUTION: General interest in experimentation, e.g. with winter roots to supplement grazing, immensely improved farming but encouraged new enclosures of common land, which ruined the small tenants. Two factors contributed to an unprecedented development of arable farming: the blockade of England during the Napoleonic Wars and the *Corn Laws* protecting home-grown wheat.

6. DERURALIZATION: In the second half of the 19th century, the gradual shift of the population to the industrial cities and the cheap transport of wheat from overseas since the mechanization of navigation made English arable farming the victim of overseas competition. England became a country of industry, grazing and parks.

7. ENCOURAGEMENT OF AGRICULTURE in the 20th century: Attempts by the government to create small owner-occupied holdings (e.g. Liberal programme of 'Four acres and a cow') and mechanization promoted farming and increased production considerably. During the two World Wars, moreover, the need to become independent of overseas food supplies led to increased tillage. During World War II the area sown with wheat, barley and potatoes was doubled. Since 1945 there has been a gradual return to grass, but the area of crops is still above pre-war level. Mechanization has encouraged larger farms.

Agriculture Today

Agriculture employs only 2.5% of the working population and provides 1.5% of the gross domestic product (gdp). It produces about two thirds of the food consumed in Britain. The EEC's common agricultural policy (CAP) is the main target of British criticism of the Common Market (p. 113). 78% of the total U.K. land area is used for farming, 50% for tillage and grass, 28% for rough grazing (bracken etc.). In Scotland rough grazing constitutes 75% of the total area.

In England, Scotland and Wales about 35% of the farms are still operated by tenant farmers, though legislation in 1977 established a right of succession to farm tenancies. Farms are large by continental standards (averaging 135 ha). But many can only be worked part-time. In Scotland small farms ('crofts') average 5 ha.

Lately there has been an increase in the purchase of farmland by financial institutions or corporations, either as saleable investments or to be operated by a manager. It is feared that this development will increasingly oust farmers, who have traditionally been the mainstay of local affairs.

Besides, there are complaints that more efficient farming methods, for instance the removal of hedges and trees to make fields bigger, damage the landscape. This has given rise to movements like Greenpeace and Friends of the Earth, and an Ecology Party, which demand legislation to protect the countryside. Beautiful areas have already been set aside as National Parks and Areas of Outstanding Natural Beauty.

1. **Arable farming,** chiefly in the eastern part of England, is the most highly mechanized in Europe and is therefore very i n t e n s i v e , though only 30 per cent of the land is tilled (in Western Germany 55 per cent):

   a) *Wheat* and *barley* are grown on the fertile and drier plains of the southeast of England and the eastern Scottish Lowlands. The temperate climate allows the growth of winter wheat, which is very productive (heavy soils, more than 30 inches of rainfall; the average yield per acre is one of the highest in the world). For bread, English 'soft' wheat, which is excellent for making biscuits, must, however, be blended with 'hard'

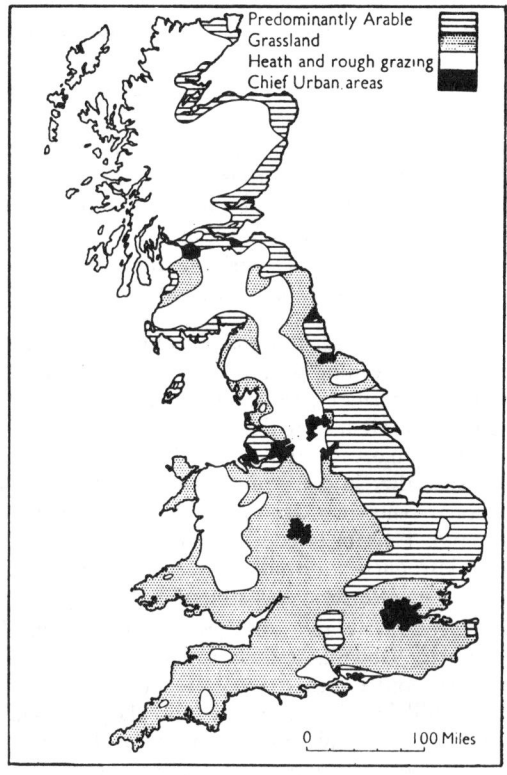

Land Utilization in Britain

137

wheat grown in the drier climate of the North American prairies. Thirty per cent of the wheat consumed in Britain is home-grown as against 12 per cent pre-war. Production of barley (for malting and stock-feeding) has more than doubled since 1960.

b) *Oats* grow in less fertile, cooler and wetter parts, especially in west England, Ireland and Scotland. As oats have no longer been used for horse feeding since the mechanization of traction, production has considerably declined in favour of barley. Even in Scotland, one of the few countries where oats are an important food, acreage under oats has decreased by one third.

c) *Sugar beet,* grown in the Fens and East Anglia, has gained in importance as Britain's supply of cane sugar has declined. Being subsidized and therefore a popular crop, it now provides one third of Britain's requirements though the sugar content is only 20 per cent of the weight of the beet. The pulp which remains after the extraction process and the leaves provide fodder and valuable by-products such as molasses and industrial alcohol.

d) *Hops* for the brewing industry grow chiefly in Kent, Worcestershire and Herefordshire.

e) *Potatoes* are the chief crop in Ireland (failure of the potato harvest in Ireland in 1846 caused a disastrous famine and emigration of a large part of the population). In England potatoes are grown everywhere but chiefly in the east (Essex, Fenlands, Yorkshire).

f) *Apples,* grown in Somerset, Devonshire and Kent are partly used for the cider industry, cider being a popular drink.

2. **Livestock** is favoured by rich pastures. Britain is the largest exporter of pedigree animals for breeding purposes (horses, sheep and cattle):

a) *Cattle* are reared chiefly on moist alluvial lowlands of western Britain, where abundant rainfall makes the grass rich, and mild winters allow grazing throughout most of the year: The Cheshire Plain, Somerset, Devon, Dorset specialize in dairy products. Cheshire and Cheddar cheeses have international renown. Cattle are also reared on the east coast of northern Scotland. Herefords and Aberdeen Angus are important beef cattle. With the introduction of milk quotas as a result of over-production in the EEC, farms now suffer reduced monthly 'milk cheques'.

b) *Sheep* are reared on upland areas (especially Scottish Highlands and Uplands, Pennines, Downlands, Dartmoor and Exmoor, Cotswolds, Welsh Mountains), and on good arable farms in the Midlands and the southeast, where hill breeds are crossed with larger lowland breeds for early maturity and fat lamb production. W o o l, chief export in the Middle Ages, is now of little importance, 90 per cent of home consumption being imported from the southern hemisphere. Chief purpose of sheep breeding in Britain today is the production of fat lambs, lamb being a most popular meat.

c) *Pigs* are reared on most farms, especially in Ireland. Bacon is an Irish national speciality and the invariable breakfast dish in England and Wales.

d) *Horses* on farms have, since 1939, declined by 90 per cent, but English race horses, being the finest in the world, are a major item of export.

Fishing

Fishing is one of the most ancient British industries and the original object of British seafaring. It is favoured by Britain's position on the shallow Continental Shelf providing good feeding and spawning grounds, by constant supplies of fish food brought by the Gulf Stream, by a great variety of fish due to differences in salinity and temperatures, and by deep estuaries for fishing ports. The North Sea is one of the world's richest fishing grounds (e.g. Dogger Bank). The chief fish are c o d, h a d d o c k, p l a i c e and h e r r i n g. Lobsters, crabs and shrimps are taken by 'inshore' fishermen from beds in the shallow waters of creeks. Herring fisheries are seasonal because different varieties of herring come inshore to spawn in their accustomed localities at different times. In June the season opens in Scotland (Shetlands, Aberdeen), in autumn it reaches its peak at Yarmouth and Lowestoft (southeast England). By December herring are caught in Devon and Cornwall.

The fishing industry, formerly pursued in every little port, is now highly organized and centralized in a few large fishing ports (p. 151). The wholesale distribution centre in London, Billingsgate Market on the Thames, has declined as a consequence of the shift from ship to motor traffic.

A 'Cod War' with Iceland concerning fishing rights in Iceland's part of the North Sea, in which even the Navy was deployed to protect British trawlers in their clashes with Icelandic vessels, ended in 1976 with a compromise. The British catch was reduced, but Britain followed Iceland's lead and extended its fishery limits to 200 miles in 1977, although EEC countries have the right to fish up to 12 miles from the coast. In 1983 agreements were reached between the member countries covering access to coastal waters, allocation of catch quotas, conservation regulations and effective enforcement of EEC rules.

The considerable drop of deepwater fishing by 36% since the 1976 agreement with Iceland has caused severe unemployment among fishermen, especially in Hull, Britain's main fishing port. Moreover, there have been complaints that oil rigs sited in good fishing grounds have put fishing villages out of business.

Forestry

Only 9 per cent of the British land area is forested. The ancient dense forests were long ago destroyed for shipbuilding and iron-smelting with charcoal. The largest tracts of forest land in England are the Wealds of Kent and Sussex, the New Forest in Hampshire, and Sherwood Forest in Nottinghamshire (the latter the haunt of the legendary Robin Hood). These forests owe their survival largely to the fact that in the Middle Ages they were reserved as Royal Forests for hunting. Since World War I the Forestry Commission has acquired land, mainly in Scotland and Wales and planted conifer forests. As Britain imports the greatest part of its timber and wood products, the government now supports new planting to reduce dependence on imports and to favour employment in forestry and related industries.

Minerals

Britain has the greatest energy resources of any EEC country, while non-fuel minerals have to be largely imported.
T i n in Cornwall, which has been mined since antiquity, is now largely exhausted. Little mining survives, and that partly below the sea. The School of Mines at Cambourne, which trains mining engineers for service in all parts of the world, recalls the ancient local skill in mining.
Iron ore is no longer mined in the British Isles. The high-grade ore supply of the Cleveland Hills on which the Middlesbrough iron industry was founded has long since been exhausted. Extensive deposits in Northamptonshire and Lincolnshire, which are low-grade but could be worked opencast, have also been abandoned. There is an abundance of other industrial minerals, such as china clay (Cornwall), salt (Teesside and Cheshire), limestone (Pennines), potash (Cleveland), gypsum, and chalk (the Downs and Chiltern Hills).

Coal

Coal, accounting for the greatest share of the mineral output, has been the basis of British industry and overseas trade. South Wales coal, shipped from Cardiff, was long the world's main steamship coal. Coal has been mined since the 13th century. Thus many deposits have been exhausted. Since the mining of thinner and deeper seams requires heavy investment, many pits closed down after World War I, making the traditional mining regions of South Wales, and the Tyne and Clyde valleys critical areas.

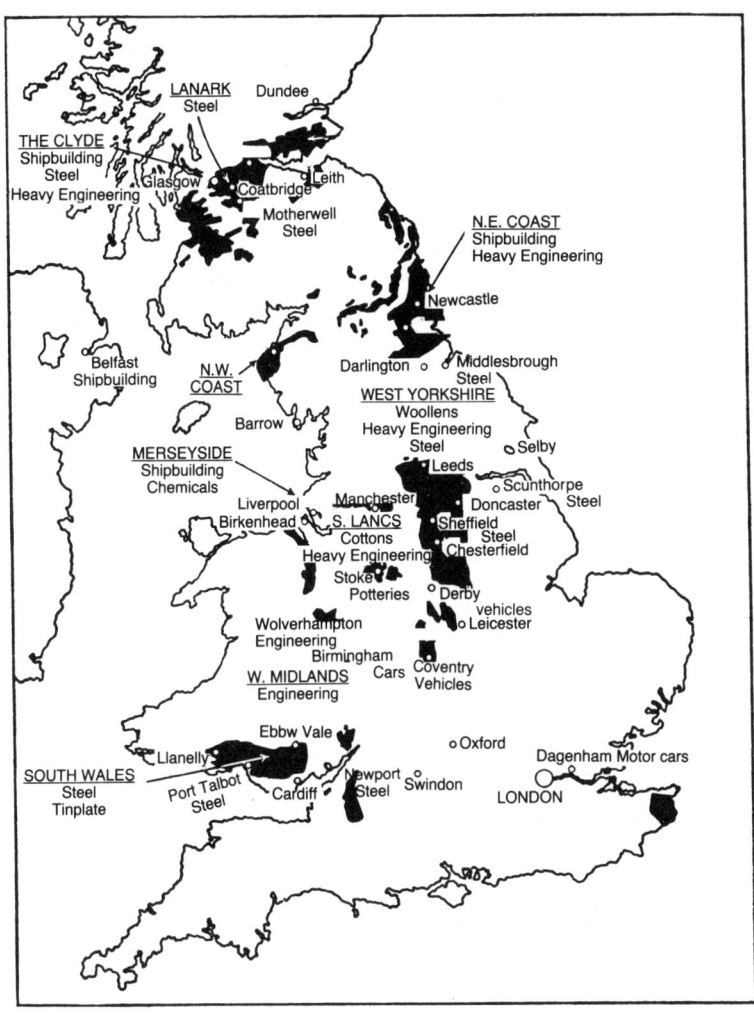

Relationship of the Principal Industries to the Coalfields

In 1947 the mines were nationalized. Today the British coal industry provides the fuel for 80% of electricity generation. As large new coalfields have been found, it is estimated that known British deposits will last for another 300 years. However, mining today meets with serious environmental objections. Thus there have been heated controversies over the exploitation of large deposits in the Vale of Belvoir. It is hoped that such handicaps and the world's growing energy demand will speed projects for coal to be turned into liquid fuel. The c o a l f i e l d s, chiefly on both sides of the Pennines, have become the centres of the chief industrial areas:

a) Coal from the S c o t t i s h L o w l a n d s between Edinburgh and Glasgow gave rise to the Scottish heavy steel industry, shipbuilding on the Clyde river (Glasgow), and textiles.

b) D u r h a m a n d N o r t h u m b e r l a n d : Newcastle coal has been mined since the Middle Ages (cf. 'to carry coal to Newcastle' means doing something superfluous). The industrial area stretching from Newcastle to Middlesbrough, once the chief centre for steel, heavy engineering, shipbuilding and chemical industries, is now a depressed area. The majority of the coal mines and shipbuilding plants had to close.

c) Y o r k s h i r e , D e r b y s h i r e a n d N o t t i n g h a m s h i r e account for more than half the total coal output. Yorkshire produces woollens, Sheffield cutlery, Nottinghamshire and Derbyshire textiles and engineering products.

d) C u m b r i a : The last mine in Cumbria is closed. It was associated with an iron industry and shipbuilding at Barrow-in-Furness.

e) The small L a n c a s h i r e field around Manchester is the centre of the cotton industry and engineering.

f) Midland fields exploit deposits in Staffordshire, Shropshire, Warwickshire and Leicestershire. The small N o r t h S t a f f o r d s h i r e coalfield contains the Potteries, centered in Stoke-on-Trent. The S o u t h S t a f f o r d s h i r e field, now exhausted, gave rise to the 'B l a c k C o u n t r y '. The important industrial centres which grew up around this coalfield, e.g. Birmingham and Wolverhampton, specialize in multifarious engineering industries, domestic metalware and jewellery.

g) S o u t h W a l e s produces chiefly high-quality coal. It is the only source of anthracite (smokeless) and almost smokeless coal, once the fuel of most of the world's steamships. Today mining has drastically declined, but industries have become important. The steel industry has been greatly developed at Port Talbot and Newport. The tin-plate industry, once based on tin from Cornwall, has been modernized. Oil refineries are found at Milford Haven and near Swansea, where they gave rise to the petrochemical industry.

Oil and Gas

Since the invention of the combustion engine, oil has played a major part in British economy and – for that matter – in the forming of policy. As

England's oil resources were negligible, British and Dutch oil companies were, up to World War II, instrumental in exploiting the resources of many overseas countries, chiefly in the Middle East. After the Persian Gulf was established as a zone of British influence (1907), the Anglo-Iranian Co. (now nationalized) operated in Persia, while the granting to Britain of mandates over Iraq, Transjordan and Palestine after World War I made possible the exploitation of Iraq petroleum. A pipeline was built from Kirkuk (Iraq), where the oil was produced, through Transjordan to the port of Haifa in Palestine. Since the sixties, Kuweit, Saudi Arabia, Venezuela, Libya and Nigeria have become major suppliers, one quarter of the British supply coming from Kuweit (cf. British occupation of Kuweit in 1960 to prevent its annexation by Iraq).

Large oilfields in the North Sea, exploited since 1975, have made Britain the world's fifth largest oil producer. They are estimated to be productive till about 2020. After the initial policy of granting licences to multi-national companies had begun to threaten national interests, the British National Oil Corporation (BNOC) was formed to secure majority state participation and government control of the rate of depletion. BNOC soon sold its oil at prices comparable to those for which OPEC was being criticized. Moreover, Britain's largest company, British Petroleum (BP), which is largely nationalized, has considerable interests in offshore oil and gas exploration and in refining and petro-chemical plants. Britain has large refineries and important research centres supported by the big companies BP, Shell, Esso, which supply the British petrol stations. Since oil has come to be used more for heating, consumption of oil as a source of energy has increased to 42% of the total energy consumption. Britain has a number of pipelines for carrying crude oil from harbours to refineries and refined oil to marketing areas, especially to London Airport and intustrial areas.

Gas, for over a century produced from coal, is now almost wholly supplied from North Sea sources. The industry, nationalized since 1949, is controlled by the British Gas Corporation, which is responsible for the search for and the extraction and transmission of gas. Natural gas from the North Sea, exploited since 1967, accounts for nearly all the gas consumed and for 24% of British energy consumption.

Electricity

Most electricity is produced from coal, but the use of oil has increased markedly. Since England has few water power resources owing to the low gradient of its rivers, only 1.9% of the energy demand is supplied by hydro-electric power stations, which are entirely confined to Scotland and Wales. Two pumped-storage stations cater for the peak load by using falling water to generate electricity at peak hours and pumping it up again during the night with power from the national grid (public network of transmission lines).

Recently much research has been done on generating electricity from the motion of waves along the stormy west coast, which would guarantee perpetual energy supplies. There are also schemes for using wind power and geothermal energy by extracting heat from hot dry rocks at great depths. Nuclear energy has been supplied since 1956 when the British reactor was built at Calder Hall in Cumbria, the world's first nuclear station to produce electricity for public use. Today nuclear power stations produce 13% of the country's electricity. Most of them are located well away from population centres and on the coast.

Opposition to nuclear power is voiced by the environmentalist movements, Greenpeace and Friends of the Earth, and an Ecology Party. Because of the pressure of their peaceful demonstrations, the government has suspended plans for the disposal of nuclear waste in several designated regions.

Industry

History

1. GUILD SYSTEM IN MEDIEVAL TOWNS (12th–16th century): Trades in the Middle Ages were organized by the craft guilds of the towns, which also controlled social and corporative life. The main industry was the spinning and weaving of wool in the Cotswolds, East Anglia and Yorkshire. Since the 14th century Flemish immigrants settling chiefly in East Anglia developed the weaving of fine cloth from firmly twisted yarn called worsted after the village of Worstead near Norwich, where it was chiefly produced. The richest textile towns were Norwich, Lincoln, Beverley and York, whose former wealth is testified by their magnificent cathedrals.

2. RISE OF RURAL INDUSTRIES: Since the 15th century master clothiers organized industries on a capitalistic basis in rural communities by employing 'servants' for spinning, weaving and dyeing. These industrial villages (e.g. Manchester, Leeds, Halifax) were the beginnings of the later factory system. Small domestic industries existed in most rural communities. Defoe wrote in 1725 in his *Tour Through Great Britain* about a Yorkshire area: 'The houses are full of lusty fellows, some at the dye-vat, some at the looms, others dressing the cloths; the women and children carding and spinning; being all employed, from the youngest

to the oldest'. Employment chiefly of unmarried women in spinning is reflected in the word 'spinster'.

3. NEW INDUSTRIES: In the 16th century Walter Raleigh introduced dyeing, Huguenot refugees developed the s i l k and g l a s s industries and paper trades. In the 18th century Josiah Wedgwood brought English p o t t e r y to perfection. C o t t o n manufacture developed with the imports of raw cotton from India and America.

4. INDUSTRIAL REVOLUTION, 1760–1900, heralded by the invention in Britain of the s t e a m e n g i n e led to an unprecedented development of manufacturing on rich coalfields, leading to a shift of population to the north of England. The textile industry was encouraged by the invention of the s p i n n i n g j e n n y and the p o w e r l o o m. Factories, which began to replace domestic industries, were first operated by water (cf. 'cotton mill'), from 1785 onwards by steam power (p. 58). Iron manufacture, which, until the Industrial Revolution, had been based on the primitive method of smelting iron by charcoal, increased with the use of coke, while steel production was improved by the B e s s e m e r and T h o m a s p r o c e s s e s, invented by English engineers, Sir Henry Bessemer and Gilchrist Thomas. By the 19th century Britain, the first industrialized country, had become the workshop of the world.

5. THE TWENTIETH CENTURY saw serious depressions owing to competition from new industrial countries (e.g. the U.S.A., Germany and Japan), whose equipment was often more modern.

In the great slump of the early thirties when a number of areas like South Wales, Tyneside and the Clyde Valley suffered severe unemployment, the *Special Areas Act,* 1934, made the government responsible for assisting in their development. Industries were attracted to Industrial Estates where factories were built for leasing and subsidies were offered to intending builders.

This policy was continued after World War II. Labour governments after 1945 nationalized a number of industries and public services with the aim of increasing their efficiency.

The insatiable demand from a war-shattered continent favoured industrial recovery, which secured the working population full employment and a comparatively high living standard. But increasing demands for higher wages and shorter working hours backed by strikes lowered industrial efficiency. Every year many million man-days were lost through strikes. Moreover, while Germany was compelled to install new equipment to replace industrial plant dismantled as a consequence of the war, British industry largely failed to modernize its plant. All this encouraged Labour's policy of f u r t h e r n a t i o n a l i z a t i o n. The o i l c r i s i s of 1974 had a disastrous effect on British industry, which was then still almost wholly dependent on oil from the Middle East. In 1975 the government bailed out the leading motor company, *British Leyland,* when it was threatened with bankruptcy. In 1968 the quickly developing firm, Leyland Motors, had merged with the British Motor Corporation. From the start the British Leyland Motor Corporation was handicapped by constant strikes, widely dispersed and overstaffed plants and the large number of models it produced. After Leyland had lost a million cars through strikes within seven years, the government bought 95 per cent of the shares – the greatest public investment programme Europe had ever seen. Under Mrs. Thatcher's programme of denationalization, BL shares are now being sold to private investors.

The building of Europe's first nuclear plant at Windscale (Cumbria), now Sellafield, initiated the nuclear age. A fallout in 1957 caused many deaths. Investigations published 30 years later in 1987 revealed the full scale of the catastrophe. The rate of deaths from leukemia in this region is three times higher than the normal average incidence.

Industry Today

Although Britain is among the foremost nations for inventing and developing new products, productivity per head in many industries is considerably lower than in comparable industries abroad. The decline in efficiency has led to formidable competition from cheaper imports. Since World War II there has been a considerable shift from the traditional industries centred on the coalfields (steel, shipbuilding, textiles) to high-technology branches not dependent on coal, such as electronics or aerospace products. Thus Central Scotland has become a focus of the electronics industries, north-east Scotland of products related to North Sea oil. In the London region science-based industries are thriving beside London's traditional food, printing and clothing industries. Moreover Greater London has large oil refineries, aircraft and engineering plants. Other industrial centres are Bristol (tobacco, aerospace) and Southampton with large ship-repair yards, oil refineries and cable manufactures.

Many of the most important industries, including coal, electricity, steel, shipbuilding, railways and airlines are still nationalized. They are managed by public corporations with management boards, whose members are not civil servants but are accountable to Parliament. The minister gives general directions but does not interfere in the actual management. Privately owned industries are represented by the Confederation of British Industries (CBI) and the Association of British Chambers of Commerce.

In the eighties Mrs. Thatcher carried out her programme of privatising state-owned industries in order to boost personal initiative and industrial efficiency. So far British Aerospace, the National Freight Corporation, British Ports, British Telecom and British Gas have been privatised. The sale of British Gas to 5 million small shareholders was the world's greatest sale of shares to individuals so far.

But Mrs. Thatcher's policy of revitalizing British industry was not as successful as she had hoped. The early '90s saw serious depressions in many industries.

An important development of the post-war era has been the dispersal of industries away from industrial centres to areas with a high level of unemployment and to peripheral areas around industrial cities. Factories and grants were made available to firms willing to move to such assisted areas. Today specially designated Enterprise Zones offer advantages to potential investors and developers.

In recent years, however, the decay and unemployment in the centres of large cities like Liverpool have reached such proportions that efforts to move industry away from such cities are being rapidly abandoned. In the wake of the 1981 riots, inner city aid began to soar.

1. *Textiles* produced in Britain are renowned for their high quality. Although GATT's Multifibre Arrangement allows for some restraint on imports, British industry has suffered formidable competition from countries with low-cost labour, especially from Hong Kong.

a) *Cotton industry*, formerly Britain's largest exporter, developed on the L a n c a s h i r e coalfield, which offered a number of advantages: The coalfield lay nearest the principal source of raw cotton, the U.S.A. The Pennine streams provided power. Their soft water was suitable for use in dyeing. The moist atmosphere prevented threads from breaking in the spinning process. Cheshire salts were of value for bleaching.

Cotton production is highly specialized. Spinning is done in the southern towns of Rochdale, Oldham, Bolton, weaving on the northern edge of the coalfield in Nelson, Blackburn, Preston. The commercial centre is Manchester. The ship canal to the cotton importing port of Liverpool is now closed. In central Scotland the G l a s g o w - P a i s l e y area, with advantages similar to those of Lancashire, developed a cotton industry which produces poplins, muslins and the famous Paisley shawls. Since the forties the cotton industry has considerably declined as a result of competition from Eastern countries and and man-made fibres.

b) *Woollen industry*, the oldest English manufacture, is still one of the largest in the world. Since the rise of the cotton industry in the west, woolens have been largely confined to the W e s t R i d i n g district in Yorkshire with a large supply of coal and soft water for bleaching and dyeing. Huddersfield produces high-quality cloth, Leeds ready-made clothes, Halifax carpets. Bradford is the marketing centre. Halifax and Bradford are the chief producers of worsted. In the west of England, the industry has continued in Kidderminster, which produces carpets, and Witney, which makes blankets. Nottingham, where the stocking frame was invented, and Leicester specialize in knitwear (hosiery). In Scotland the Tweed Valley, where the ancient woollen manufacturers of the Upland monasteries moved when power was needed for driving machinery, is still famous for its high-quality 'tweed' and knitwear industries. Hand-woven tweed is produced in the Hebrides.

c) *Linen* is the traditional industry in Northern Ireland.

d) *Silk*, formerly worked in the Spitalfields district of east London, is now concentrated in Macclesfield.

e) *Jute,* a coarse Indian fibre used for ropes and sacking, for the reinforcement of plastic and decorative wall-coverings is manufactured in Dundee, Scotland, which has the world's oldest jute industry.

f) *Synthetic fibres,* a part of the chemical industry, are produced in the existing textiles centres in Lancashire and West Yorkshire. Rayon has been produced since 1905, nylon was introduced from America in 1941. A number of the other fibres – polyester, courtelle and terylene (sold in Germany as Trevira) – were invented in Britain. Among the world's leading firms are Courtaulds and ICI (p. 149).

g) *Clothing industry,* which is centred in London, Leeds and Manchester, is now greatly handicapped by cheap imports. London has begun to be a leader in fashion.

2. *Steel industry,* formerly favoured by the proximity of British coal and iron deposits, relies now only on imported ore. While heavy steel products are produced near the sea (Teesside, Humberside, South Wales) to facilitate export, smaller articles like Sheffield's renowned cutlery are manufactured in inland centres. Britain's largest steel plant, is Port Talbot, South Wales.
Nationalization of steel has long been a political issue between Labour and Tory governments, till, under a Labour government, in 1967, thirteen major companies were merged in the British Steel Corporation (BSC), Europe's biggest steel maker, which produces 85% of Britain's crude steel. Since the first oil crisis in 1974, there has been a considerable worldwide recession in the industry, with plant closures in Britain as elsewhere. Mrs. Thatcher has therefore failed so far to make progress with her aim of denationalizing British Steel.

3. *Mechanical engineering,* which is based on an early tradition of machine-tool making, is one of Britain's major industries and exporters. It produces machinery for agriculture, mining, industry, earth-moving, construction. As a matter of fact, construction services are among Britain's main exports because many plant projects overseas are carried out by British contractors.

4. *Non-ferrous metals industry* is one of the largest in Europe. It produces aluminium, copper, zinc, lead and specialized alloys for the nuclear, aerospace, electronic and petrochemical industries. The oldest of such manufactures is the Welsh tin-plate industry, once processing Cornwall tin.

5. *Shipbuilding industry,* which once produced half the world's tonnage, has greatly contracted, mainly as a result of world-wide competition and the virtual end of the passenger liner. The main centres are Clydeside (Glasgow), Tyneside

(Newcastle), Teesside (Hartlepool), Merseyside (Birkenhead), and Belfast with Britain's largest shipbuilding dock, Harland and Wolff. Clydeside, which was once the greatest shipbuilding area of the world, with docks stretching along 20 miles of the river, is now a depressed area. In 1977 most of the larger ailing companies were nationalized under the British Shipbuilders' Corporation.

6. *Motor industry*, dating from 1896, is in obvious decline. It is centered in Coventry, Birmingham, Oxford, Sunderland and Luton, the chief producers being Ford, Vauxhall (GM) and the Rover group. Britain's most expensive high-quality car is produced by Rolls Royce. Cars are increasingly imported from Japan and Germany. On the other hand, the sporty Jaguar sells well abroad.

7. *Aerospace industry* is the largest and most comprehensive in Western Europe and produces civil and military aircraft, aero-engines and missiles. It is centred on Coventry, Bristol and Derby. The main producers are British Aerospace (BAe), now largely privatized, and the publicly-owned companies Short Brothers (Belfast) and Rolls Royce (Derby), which is responsible for almost the whole output of aero-engines. The manufacture of the world's only supersonic airliner, Concorde, which was developed jointly by Britain and France, has been stopped because of the aircraft's enormous cost and the difficulty of obtaining permits to fly it on the main world routes, though Concorde planes fly profitably. Britain takes part in the manufacture of communications satellites and is a partner in the European consortium *Airbus Industrie*.

8. *Electrical and electronic engineering* is one of Britain's chief industries, Tyneside and the Glasgow area being noted for heavy electrical equipment, central Scotland for electronics. Britain has made some of the most important contributions to electronics (radar, the first public TV service and, recently, laser technology). It has the largest computer industry outside the U.S.A. It is a major producer of radio, TV and video equipment, navigational aids and telecommunications networks, whose main customer is *British Telecom* (now privatized).

9. *Nuclear industry* is the world's largest manufacturer of radio-isotopes and provides the design of nuclear plant, the processing and enrichment of uranium. Sellafield (formerly called Windscale) in Cumbria reprocesses spent nuclear fuel. Plans for depositing nuclear waste in several British regions were abandoned on ecologist pressure.

10. *Chemical industry* is the second largest in Europe (after West Germany). Originally it was centred on the saltfields of Teesside and Cheshire, and on

the coalfields, where the by-products of the coke ovens were used. Now North Sea oil has given rise to a rapidly expanding petrochemical industry, which grew up chiefly near the big oil refineries (e.g. Shellhaven on the Thames estuary). While the plastics industry goes back to 1865, when a Birmingham chemist patented celluloid, British scientists today have made important contributions to the development of pharmaceuticals, detergents, chemical fertilizers, herbicides and pesticides.

Imperial Chemical Industries (ICI) is the world's fifth largest chemical company with a workforce of 123,800 and thousands of people permanently engaged in research. Like BP Chemicals, it is closely connected with North Sea oil and gas interests – as are their American competitors Esso and Dow Chemicals.

11. *Food and drink industries:* Britain's main exports are Scotch whisky, produced since the 15th century, chiefly in north-east Scotland, and marmalade, produced in the same area (chiefly Dundee). English exports are chocolate products, the chocolate industry being largely in the hands of the Quaker families Cadbury (Birmingham) and Rowntree (York). Other important products are biscuits, gin, and cider, chiefly from the apple counties Devon and Somerset. Grimsby and Yarmouth have big fish processing plants. Unilever, one of the world's biggest producers of food and household products, is an Anglo-Dutch firm.

12. *Pottery,* a British industry since pre-Roman times, still uses indigenous china clay from Devon and Cornwall. In the 18th century, when British potters began to imitate the porcelain imported from China (hence 'chinaware'), Josiah Wedgwood established his famous factory near S t o k e - o n - T r e n t in the North Staffordshire coalfield, which has remained the industry's centre. 80 per cent of the production is concentrated in the 'Potteries' area, though Worcester and Derby have other important factories. The best-known British makes are Wedgwood, Spode, Royal Worcester.

13. *Rubber:* The British rubber industry, the oldest in the world, ranked third after the USA and Russia, but is now declining. It is centred near the car industries, Coventry, Manchester, Birmingham. Two Scotsmen made important contributions to its development: Macintosh invented waterproof garments, Dunlop the pneumatic tyre.

14. *Paper, printing, publishing:* Printing goes back to 1476, when Caxton established the first printing press in England. As the paper manufacture relies chiefly on timber imports· from Canada and the Baltic countries, it has grown up near seaports (Thames estuary, Lancashire, rivers Forth and Clyde). The printing industry, which is also supplied by British paper firms in Newfoundland, is largely centered in London and Edinburgh, which are also Britain's principal publishing centres.

Ports

Ports lie in favourable positions in deep estuaries with great tidal range. Ports lying inland have outports, e.g. London: Tilbury, Bristol: Avonmouth. Since the seventies, three factors have changed the structure of British overseas trade considerably: North Sea oil, membership of the Common Market, and roll-on/roll-off traffic through the use of containers.

1. COMMERCIAL PORTS:

a) *London*, at the head of ocean navigation on the Thames estuary, was once the largest port in the Commonwealth, favoured by the big tidal range of the Thames as well as its inland position. Today its focus has shifted from the city to *Tilbury* 25 miles downstream. The wharves and cranes characteristic of the ancient port have disappeared as the modern container port only needs road and rail access and adequate berths. London/Tilbury handles a great variety of goods and a large amount of re-export.

b) *Liverpool* serves five large industrial centres (West Riding, Lancashire, Black Country, North Staffordshire, Cheshire). It is a major port for importing raw cotton, crude oil and grain, but has declined greatly from being a world port. Manchester, connected with Liverpool by the Manchester Ship Canal, has lost its importance as an inland port since the canal was abandoned.

c) *Glasgow* (Clydeside) serves the industrial area of the Scottish Lowlands and is the main exporting port for Scottish textiles, steel products and Scotch whisky.

d) *Belfast* is the principal port in Northern Ireland, handling most of its imports and exports (cattle, dairy produce).

e) Ports in South Wales: *Milford Haven* is a major oil port. *Port Talbot* and *Newport* import iron ore and export steel and tin-plate products.

f) *Bristol* (the cradle of British sea-faring, whaling and exploration) serves the industrial Midlands and imports tobacco, oil, grain and cocoa.

g) *Southampton*, in a protected position opposite the Isle of Wight with four tides a day, was formerly the chief ocean passenger port for America, where big ships could enter. With the decline of sea travel except by ferries and cruise liners, Southampton has greatly expanded as a trading port handling a wide range of exports and imports. With its easy access to London, it handles especially highly perishable fruits. Nearby Fawley imports oil for its large refinery.

h) *Felixstowe* and *Harwich* in East Anglia have greatly developed as container ports since Britain joined the Common Market.

i) *Hull* on the Humber estuary serves the industrial centres of Yorkshire and the Midlands. It imports grain, oil and timber from Baltic countries. Facing the Common Market it has greatly increased in importance.

k) *Tees* and *Hartlepool* are the main ports for iron ore imports (especially from Sweden) and for steel and heavy engineering products.

151

m) *Grangemouth* on the Firth of Forth handles great quantities of petroleum and petrochemicals.

n) *Sullom Voe* (Shetland) and *Flotta* (Orkney) are North Sea oil ports. Sullom Voe became the largest oil exporting port in Europe in the mid-1980s.

2. FERRY PORTS: With the increase in package holidays and links with the EEC, ferry ports have become very busy, e.g. *Dover, Folkstone, Southampton* and a number of other ports along the south coasts specializing in the transportation of vehicles. In addition, *Harwich* and *Felixstowe,* together with Hull and ports further north have increased their ferry trade with northern Europe. *Holyhead* is the ferry port for Ireland.

3. FISHING PORTS are chiefly on the east coast: in Scotland *Aberdeen*, in England *Grimsby* and *Hull* for whitefish (cod, haddock, plaice, sole), *Yarmouth* for herring, *Lowestoft* for both.

4. NAVAL PORTS: With the shrinking of the Navy, naval ports remain at *Portsmouth* (favoured, like Southampton, by double tides), at *Devonport-Plymouth* with a big naval dockyard, and at *Rosyth* (Firth of Forth, Scotland), which was established when alarm at the German naval programme prompted the transfer of British ships from the Mediterranean to the North Sea. Scapa Flow, where the German Navy, after its surrender, was scuttled by German crews in 1919, was given up in 1956.

Transport

Owing to its technical start over other nations, England was the first European country to develop a dense network of canals, roads and railways. The first canal was built in 1761, roads were 'macadamized' by the improved construction methods developed by M a c a d a m in 1810, the adaptation of steam to locomotion by S t e p h e n s o n led to the building of the first railway lines from Stockton to Darlington in 1825 and from Manchester to Liverpool in 1830. In the 20th century Britain was also ahead of other European nations in the construction of asphalt roads, but the building of motorways (Autobahnen) was not begun until the 60s. Regular air transport services started in 1919 (London–Paris), the first through service on an intercontinental air route (England–India) in 1929.

1. RAILWAYS AND ROADS: A dense railway network, nationalized in 1947, competes with a highly developed road transport system which now carries 80% of Britain's freight (railways 16%). As roads and motorways multiplied, many railway lines were closed down, but inter-city trains running at a speed of more than 200 kph have gained importance.

2. CANALS: Owing to faster traffic on railways and roads, the dense network of navigable inland waterways (about 2,500 miles) has lost its importance, the more so as English canals are narrow and have many locks. Britain's

broadest waterway, the *Caledonian Canal* in the Scottish Highlands following Loch Ness, which provides the straightest connection between the North Sea and the Atlantic, is too far away from the main traffic and therefore little used.

Canals handle only 4% of the total tonnage in Britain. The *Manchester Ship Canal* to Liverpool, which once carried a substantial volume of overseas trade, is now closed. The commercial use of British canals has been replaced by recreational boating. However, there are now attempts to revitalize canal shipping.

3. AIRLINES: The British airline company BA has one of the largest route networks in the world. London Airport, *Heathrow*, is the world's busiest airport for international travel. *Gatwick* (south of London) is the airport for charter flights, which are undertaken by independent companies. *Stanstead* has been developed to cater for the boom in air travel. In 1976 BA and Air France inaugurated the world's only supersonic passenger service with the jointly developed aircraft Concorde. Sir Freddie Laker's non-reservation Skytrain Service across the Atlantic at less than half the normal fares, which had become a formidable competition to convential air travel, went brankrupt in 1982. Nowadays the *Virgin Airlines*, owned by Richard Branson, offer cheap alternative transatlantic flights.

Airlines carry twice as many passengers to and from Britain as ships. Britain's offshore oil industry is mainly served by helicopters, Aberdeen (Scotland) being the world's biggest airport for helicopters.

Trade

History

1. IN PREHISTORIC TRADE Britain was important through its mineral treasures: g o l d in Ireland, t i n in Cornwall, l e a d in the Mendips and Derbyshire.

2. DURING THE MIDDLE AGES markets were the first settlements to be granted self-government for money loans to kings and nobles. M e r c h a n t g u i l d s secured rights of coinage and the privilege of holding annual fairs, the most important being Winchester and Stourbridge. Crusades opened up trade routes to the Mediterranean and the East, through which luxuries like spices and rich Eastern materials entered England. A provision of *Magna Carta* secured merchants freedom to travel and trade throughout the realm.

England's main export was raw wool, taxes and payments to foreign countries being calculated in sacks of wool, whose importance is symbolized by the Woolsack, on which the Lord Chancellor sits in the House of Lords. Under Edward I the monopoly of selling a special product was first granted to 'staple towns', later also in Flanders (Antwerp, Ghent, Bruges). Foreign trade, however, was carried on chiefly by the H a n s e a t i c L e a g u e from their centre in London, the Steelyard, and by the Venetian fleet, landing annually in Southampton. Banking was developed by L o m b a r d m e r c h a n t s; cf. 'Lombard Street', amidst the banks today.

3. THE TUDOR PERIOD saw the beginning of English trading initiative. Henry VII subsidized the building of a commercial fleet. He granted the *Merchant Adventurers* the virtual monopoly of the wool and cloth trade with Europe, and restricted the import of Gascon wines not carried on English ships. Elizabeth I founded the R o y a l E x c h a n g e and eliminated the influence of foreign traders by closing the Steelyard. She supported explorers who opened up trade with new countries, which soon came to be controlled by big c o m m e r c i a l c o m p a n i e s (Russia: Muscovy Comp.; America: London Comp.; Asia: Levant and East India Companies). When Antwerp was sacked during the Dutch rebellion against Spain, London took the lead in European overseas trade.

4. NAVAL AND COMMERCIAL ASCENDANCY encouraged m e r c a n t i l i s m (1650–1846): In successful commercial wars against Spain, Holland and France, c o l o n i e s were established as sources of cheap raw materials and were linked during the 19th c. by trading posts along great sea routes, e. g. Singapore, Hong Kong. Since Cromwell, Navigation Acts prohibiting imports not carried on English ships strove to secure for England the monopoly of shipping. Restrictions imposed on the trade of British colonies in America were the main cause of the American War of Independence.

5. FREE TRADE 1846–1932: E c o n o m i c l i b e r a l i s m led to the repeal of the Navigation Acts, the Irish famine of 1846 resulted in the a b o l i t i o n o f t a r i f f s. Free trade, made possible by England's industrial lead and the virtual monopoly of the carrying trade, made Britain the world's biggest trader with the world's largest commercial fleet. Sterling became the standard currency, London the world's financial centre.

6. RETURN TO PROTECTIONISM: Competition from Germany and the U.S.A. and, after the World Wars, from many other countries, necessitated t h r e e d e v a l u a t i o n s o f t h e p o u n d sterling (1931, 1949, 1967) and reintroduction of p r o t e c t i v e t a r i f f s (1932), preferential tariffs being granted to Commonwealth countries ('imperial preference'). Losses through World War II (debts for war supplies from overseas, loss of overseas investments, bombing, sinking of ships) were to some extent made good by U.S. and Canadian loans and Marshall Aid from the U.S.A. under ERP (European Recovery Program). The A u s t e r i t y P r o g r a m m e of the Labour government, which imposed import and currency controls, made Britain independent of foreign aid in 1950.

7. LIBERALIZATION OF TRADE: In 1954 the Conservative government abolished rationing, the government import monopoly and most restrictions on the convertibility of sterling. Import duties were reduced under GATT (General Agreement on Tariffs and Trade). In 1959 Britain established a European Free

Trade Association (EFTA) with Sweden, Norway, Denmark, Switzerland, Austria and Portugal, providing for a gradual reduction of tariffs on industrial products. In 1972 Britain and Denmark left EFTA to join the Common Market. Today the EEC is EFTA's biggest trading partner.

British Trade Today

British trade ranks fifth in the world (after the U.S.A., Germany, Japan and France). It has the third largest and one of the most modern commercial fleets, but a number of British ships are registered abroad.

Moreover, England has some of the world's chief commodity markets, e.g. the London Exchange (for tropical products, wool, tea, furs and metals), the London Gold and Gold Futures Markets and the Liverpool Exchange (for cotton and maize). London is the chief commercial and insurance centre.

Britain imports more goods than it exports. The deficit is balanced by 'invisible exports' – shipping, banking, insurance, overseas investments, tourism. Britain has, after the U.S.A., the largest share of the world's invisible trade, which today includes also expert advice and teaching abroad. Britain's chief invisible earnings result from the transactions of the London banks, of the Foreign Exchange Market and the Baltic Exchange, the world's largest market for the chartering of ships. The ship insurance company Lloyds of London, which orginated as a merchants' coffee house in the 18th century, has become the world's biggest insurance market, with three quarters of its premium income from overseas.

Today tourism has become a major source of invisible earnings. The Queen's Jubilee in 1977 attracted more than 10 million visitors, a boom that lasted as long as weekend shoppers from the continent could take advantage of the low value of the pound. Now Britain's oil-inflated currency has not only improved the balance of payment but also the opportunity for travelling abroad. But it is a disadvantage to British exports.

As a result of Britain's membership of the EEC, the preferential tariff treatment of Commonwealth countries was replaced by the Convention of Lomé (Togo) in 1975, which established new trade and aid links and industrial co-operation between the EEC and developing countries in Africa, the Caribbean and the Pacific, including 24 Commonwealth countries. Until World War II Britain was the central banker for those countries dealing in sterling ($^{1}/_{4}$ of the world's population). With the disintegration of Empire, the 'sterling area' has ceased to exist. But many Commonwealth countries still maintain currency reserves in Britain.

Seaborne trade has shrunk drastically as other countries have built up their own fleets. Moreover, many ships of other nations are registered under 'flags of convenience' (chiefly Panama and Liberia). They pay lower taxes and can employ low-cost crews while British shipowners are restricted with regard to wages and manning levels laid down by the unions.

I m p o r t s are mainly primary products and semi-manufactured goods, which are now increasingly produced by the former exporters of raw materials themselves. Britain imports nearly all the raw materials needed for its industries and nearly 50% of the food consumed: butter from New Zealand and Denmark; beef from Argentina, wheat from Canada, mutton from New Zealand, which greatly suffers from the EEC's protectionist policy. Raw cotton is imported from the U.S.A., India, Egypt and Sudan; wool from Australia, New Zealand and South Africa; rubber and tin from Malaysia; iron ore from Canada, Sweden, Brazil and Australia. Tobacco comes from the U.S.A. and Zimbabwe; timber from Scandinavian countries and Canada. Inefficient domestic production has been widely blamed for stimulating demand for cheap foreign products (e.g. Japanese cars or Hong Kong textiles). Britain is self-sufficient in oil, but imports special types from the main world sources.

E x p o r t s are chiefly manufactures, which account for 80% of the total. Britain is among the largest exporters of machinery, aerospace products, vehicles and electronic plant. The export of chemicals has risen spectacularly, while textile exports are declining (from 18% of total exports in 1948 to 3.3%). The chief articles of re-export are wool, tea and rubber. An important item of British export is the sale of education programmes, technician training and distant-learning methods of the Open University.

Trade with Commonwealth countries has decreased, while 43% of British trade is now with other EEC countries. Depending on exports to pay for its many vital imports, Britain has reason to be more concerned about the current trend towards protectionism than other countries.

SOCIAL STRUCTURE

History

The foundations of the social structure in England are to be found in the f e u d a l s y s t e m of the Middle Ages. The king was the supreme owner of land, which he granted as fiefs to barons or tenants-in-chief (Kronvasallen), who sublet it to knights or tenants-in-mesne (Aftervasallen). Big feudal lords or barons formed the nobility, which was represented in the House of Lords. Their estates could not be divided between several heirs: The law of *primogeniture* (which still holds) provided that only the eldest son should inherit title and estate. Younger sons of nobles were only commoners. Subtenants (knights) formed the gentry, which was represented in the House of Commons. Before the coming of the 'English gentleman', John Bull,

Social Structure   Political Representation

Middle Ages	Present Structure	Parliament since 14th Century
Sovereign (Supreme landowner)	Sovereign	Sovereign
Barons (Nobles) (Tenants-in-chief = Kronvasallen)	Lords { Spiritual: Archbishop, Bishop; Temporal: Duke, Marquess, Earl, Viscount, Baron } = Nobility	Peers { Lords Spiritual, Lords Temporal } = House of Lords
Knights (Holders of subsidiary fiefs = Aftervasallen)	Lower Aristocracy { Baronet, Knight } / Substantial landowners = Gentry	Commons = House of Commons
Freemen: Yeomen (Freeholders), Burghers	Upper Middle Classes (Professional classes and substantial businessmen), Lower Middle Classes (Smaller businessmen, craftsmen, clerks, shop assistants) = Middle Classes	
Serfs	Workers { industrial, agricultural } = Working Classes	

157

the boisterous country squire indulging in sound habits and coarse manners, was generally seen as the embodiment of the typical Englishman.

1. DEVELOPMENT OF THE RURAL POPULATION: Already in Saxon times feudalism with its principle: 'no land without a lord' had reduced free peasants to serfdom. After the Norman conquest, the rural population consisted of s e r f s, who were bound to the soil and to feudal service (Frondienst) on the lord's demesne (Domäne). From the 14th century many serfs became free tenants (y e o m e n) by paying a fixed rent ('firma', hence 'farmer'), while the rest became agricultural labourers working for wages on farms or the lord's manor. The law of *entail*, which prohibited partial alienation of landed property and which applied to ²/₃ of the entire land, operated to prevent the rise of an independent peasantry which owned the land it tilled.

When during the Agricultural Revolution most small farmers lost their land as a consequence of enclosures, the proud yeomanry of the 16th and 17th centuries finally disappeared. England became a land of large estates, cultivated by b i g t e n a n t - f a r m e r s and poor a g r i c u l t u r a l l a b o u r e r s, whose social status was the lowest of all classes. Even attempts by the government, since 1882, to resettle small independent farmers on the land could not substantially change this situation.

2. DEVELOPMENT OF THE INDUSTRIAL POPULATION: In the Middle Ages the urban population was represented by independent traders and a r t i s a n s, who were represented in the House of Commons by two burgesses for each borough. After the Industrial Revolution urban society broke up into factory owners and factory hands, the capitalists and proletariat of the modern industrial city.

By the 18th century the Parliamentary seats of decayed medieval towns (rotten boroughs) had passed into the hands of the neighbouring gentry, and it was not until the *First Reform Bill* of 1832 that the wealthier population in the new industrial towns gained political importance by obtaining the electoral vote and seats in Parliament. The labourers were the last to gain social and political status. While social reformers and t r a d e u n i o n s since 1824 struggled to improve their economic conditions, political associations (e.g. Chartists) succeeded in securing them political representation through the *Second* and *Third Reform Bills* (1867 and 1884, respectively). Since 1900 their political influence has increased steadily owing to efforts of the L a b o u r P a r t y. From 1908 *Pensions* and *Insurance Acts* provided a measure of social security. The Labour Government after the Second World War extended insurance to all groups not reached by former legislation and established the W e l f a r e S t a t e. Since the 50s coloured immigrants have formed part of the industrial population.

3. EMANCIPATION OF WOMEN: In England the struggle for the emancipation of women began earlier than in any other country, when in 1796 M a r y W o l l s t o n e c r a f t wrote her *Vindication of the Rights of Woman*. Soon women began to play a part in literature (e.g. Jane Austen, Elizabeth Barrett Browning, George Eliot) and in social work. E l i z a b e t h F r y introduced prison reforms, F l o r e n c e N i g h t i n g a l e reorganized the London hospitals. In 1848 F. D. Maurice (p. 189) founded Queen's College, London, the first educational institution of university type for women. In 1861 John Stuart

158

Mill demanded in his *Subjection of Women* that women be given equal educational facilities, realized in Cambridge through the foundation of the first girls' colleges, Girton (1869) and Newnham College (1871). But women were long barred from university examinations. Married women were not allowed to hold property or to be guardians of their children. Women were only employed in domestic service – until the Industrial Revolution made them eligible for the lowest paid jobs, where they often worked for more than 12 hours under extremely unhealthy conditions. The only paid occupations for educated women were those of governess or 'companion', until the invention of the typewriter opened secretarial work for women.

On the other hand, women of the upper classes held unlimited sway in households where all the work was done by servants and where the husband's gentlemanly ideals made him subservient to his wife's caprices. It may be argued that men's clubs in which women were not admitted except as occasional guests, were founded as refuges from domestic bliss.

In the 20th century suffragettes under the leadership of Mrs. Pankhurst fought with the greatest militancy – including hunger strikes – for the woman's vote, which, after rejection of 28 bills submitted to Parliament, was granted in two stages in 1918 and 1928.

In the two World Wars women began to replace men who had joined the armed forces. Their achievements also in higher occupations brought about a certain change in public opinion. Beatrice Webb was instrumental in setting up trade boards to regulate wages in unorganized industries, in which women were chiefly employed. The *Equal Pay Act* 1970 and the *Sex Discrimination Act* 1975 provided (not altogether successfully) against discrimination against women in education, employment, pay, housing and advertizing.

4. POSTWAR SITUATION: The 20th century has worked a radical change in the social pattern. Education in publicly maintained schools, the influence of the popular press, of wireless and television have had a levelling effect and created a mass society with uniform instincts and habits. Moreover, the two World Wars have done much to sweep away traditional values. After World War II a disillusioned post-war generation substituted pleasure and license for moral restraint. 'Angry young men' gathered in gangs often given to violence and crime. Gangs of young people, like the Mods and Rockers, went about smashing furniture and telephone kiosks, fighting the police and each other for no obvious purpose but to shock. Recently football violence has become a major problem.

In an age of affluence and full employment, in which the younger generation enjoyed early financial independence and relatively much leisure time without much ambition to use both for educational advancement, the young people were apt to suffer from boredom and thus to become a prey to an entertainment industry strongly influenced by America, which caters especially for adolescent appetites. The film star, the pop singer, and pop music have become the idols of the young generation, which gathers in discos to hear records and dance. It has been observed that vandalism has diminished where young people indulge in their musical ecstasies. Such phenomena may help to account for the fact that the long-haired pop singers from Liverpool, the Beatles, received a decoration at the hands of the Queen. The old institutions, which had formed the young: family, Church and school have ceded their influence to those who determine

159

mass communication and entertainment. The Beatles with their defiance of bourgeois society, gave rise to many thousand beat groups.

British Society Today

As in most other Western countries, society in Britain has changed considerably since the two world wars. The Labour Part'y commitment to an egalitarian society has reduced the gap between the upper and lower classes, and industrial society is more than in other countries dominated by the trade unions, which fight for a higher living standard for the working classes. Their considerable political influence was restricted by a number of employment acts issued by the conservative governments of Mrs. Thatcher and John Major.

The striving for security has eroded the 'Victorian work ethic' and the spirit of enterprise which had marked the era of liberalism. The 'elevenses' tea break in offices two hours after work has started symbolises for many the modern indulgence in leisure practised by white-collar workers. Heavy taxation has played its part in discouraging initiative. People see no point in working hard if most of their earnings are taxed away.

Among all classes of the population the postwar desire to enjoy life has done away with the fetters of Victorian society, especially in the sexual sphere. In the sixties 'swinging London', pop groups of international renown and British fashion trends set the pace for the modern pop scene.

On the other hand, the loss of empire, the stagnation of industry exacerbated by continuous strikes has diminished wealth and much of the outer refinement and luxury that goes with it. All this has created in the middle classes a certain nostalgia for an ordered, structured society, indicated by the enormous success of the two TV series, the *Forsyte Saga* and *Upstairs, Downstairs* (about an upper class family and its servants, which ran for several years; in Germany: 'Das Haus am Eaton Place').

Conservatism finds an ally in most of the capitalist newspapers with mass circulation, which exert a strong influence on the lower classes. Primogeniture has worked to keep the nobility as a social institution intact. The standards of the aristocratic Public Schools continue to colour social life in England. This has in a way worked out to the detriment of the economy because the elite has not tended to engage themselves in technological development or industrial management. The hidden residual class consciousness of English society is described somewhat ironically in an article in *The Times* on *Singular Saxon Attitudes:* 'That queer web of custom and inanity that the English, with a mystical smile, like to call tradition, puts a premium on snobbery ... The class distinctions of England have long been hazed or mangled by history. But they still exist, irremovably, arrogant upon the surface or mysteriously beneath it. However toneless your accent and anonymous your clothes – your school forgotten and your parents abroad, the paper you read a compromise, the cut of your suit a self-effacement, your mayonnaise a mean between the plebeian and the exquisite – however warily, modestly, gently you tread, some snob or other will find a category for you, and drop you into your class like a wayward pea returned to the pod.'

Because of its relative stability, English society has been able to cope with the problem of coloured immigration. But with the growth of race consciousness among the English in mixed neighbourhoods and among coloured youths insistent on their legal right to equal opportunities, English society faces a serious challenge. Moreover, mass unemployment is beginning to alienate growing numbers of whites, especially jobless youths with little hope for the future.

I. Grouping of Population:

1. *Royalty:* A nation throughout its history dedicated to tradition could be expected to support the institution of monarchy more than most other contemporary nations. But changing patterns of social life have begun to destabilize the principles on which the very idea of royalty is based. In 1936 King Edward VIII abdicated because he married a divorcee. Today the completely unconventional conduct of some royals is publicised by the media with embarrassing relish. The general public follows the situation with deep concern, wondering what monarchy may stand for in the future. So far members of the royal family still play a part in high society and public life.

2. *Nobility:* Despite the democratization of life since the 19th century, the nobility has still its separate political representation in the hereditary House of Lords, whose members are not required to undergo the inconveniences of an electioneering campaign. It still exercises a certain influence in social and cultural life, recalling Emerson's statement in 1856: 'The nobility have the lead in matters of state and expense, in questions of taste, in social usages, in convivial and domestic hospitalities. In general, all that is required of them is to sit securely, to preside at public meetings, to countenance charities, and to give the example of that decorum so dear to the British heart . . . The frame of society is aristocratic, the taste of the people is loyal.

It is true that much of this has changed since the two world wars. Many big estates have been broken up or have become public property. 'Stately mansions' are often sold to rich foreigners, they may become a company headquarters or a training college for executives.

Nevertheless the English nobility has remained firmly rooted in the conservative instincts of the people, its love of grandeur and pageantry. The nobility is divided into five ranks, ranging from b a r o n up to v i s c o u n t , e a r l , m a r q u e s s and d u k e , the latter also

161

being the title of younger sons of the monarch. Dukes are addressed 'Your Grace'; holders of the other titles 'My Lord'. The nobility normally do not use their family name. Thus the Elder Pitt became Earl of Chatham, Disraeli Earl of Beaconsfield, while the famous general John Churchill (18th century) became Duke of Marlborough, a title still extant in the Churchill family.

3. *Gentry:* The landed gentry, too, enjoys considerable prestige, which is reflected in the age-old tendency of successful businessmen to acquire landed property. Some of the gentry may hold the title of b a r o n e t (hereditary) or k n i g h t (not hereditary). Holders of these titles have 'Sir' prefixed to their Christian names and their wives are, like the wives of nobles, called 'Lady'.

The lines between the upper classes were never clearly drawn. While younger sons of noblemen became gentry, rich businessmen and men who gained eminence in political, economic and cultural life could be knighted or even rise into the nobility.

4. *The upper middle class,* long influential in business, has, since the 19th century, gained an ascendancy in politics, administration and the Church, all of which had been preserves of the aristocracy in the 18th century. The development of science and technology, and the widening tasks of administration have enhanced the importance of higher education, and have thus given the professional classes (Akademiker) greater influence in public life. The civil service can now only be entered through competitive examinations.

5. *Lower middle class:* As small workshops and businesses are being more and more superseded by large-scale concerns, white-collar workers and other employees in business and public services (the 'suburbia' of modern cities) have replaced the independent trader more and more. The Tory government now encourages small businesses.

6. *Labour:* In the 19th century a number of factory acts improved the abominable conditions of the working population during the Industrial Revolution. In the 20th century insurance acts provided greater security. Working hours of manual workers average 45 for men and 40 for women in full-time work over a five-day week. The normal lenght of holidays for manual workers and shop assistants is 4 weeks. Additional public holidays are Christmas Day, Boxing Day (26th December), Good Friday, bank holidays on New Year's Day, Easter Monday and the Spring and August bank holidays (the last Monday in May and August) and, since 1978, May Day (1st May). There are various systems for worker participation in the management of industries, but the functions of works councils have so far been

consultative only. The Department of Employment is responsible for employment policy, industrial relations and pay policy. It is assisted by the Manpower Services Commission, which operates through nearly 1,000 employment offices (formerly 'labour exchanges'), concentrating chiefly on regions most affected by the recession in the coal-mining, steel and shipbuilding industries (north-east England and Merseyside, parts of Scotland and Wales, and Northern Ireland). Successive governments have developed programmes of job creation especially for long-term unemployed young people and of training opportunities to ease a transfer to new industries.

Immigrant workers need a work permit, applied for by the prospective employer and issued for a specific job and for not longer than one year, but extendable at the employer's request. Legislation in the sixties extended these restrictions to Commonwealth immigrants who had not acquired the right of residence. Since Britain's entry into the EEC, workers of Community countries may move freely within member states.

W a g e s are usually determined by collective bargaining between management and the trade unions concerned. Disputes may be referred to the Central Arbitration Committee. The average weekly earnings of manual workers are lower than those of their continental colleagues. But wage increases outpace those on the Continent and partly account for the uncompetitiveness of British industry.

W o r k i n g h o u r s of manual workers average 44 for men and 39.5 for women in full-time work, over a five-day week. People employed in non-manual work usually work several hours less.

The normal length of holidays for manual workers and shop assistants is 3 weeks, though two-thirds of manual workers already get more than 4 weeks. Additional public holidays are Christmas Day, Boxing Day (26th December), Good Friday, bank holidays on New Year's Day, Easter Monday, and the Spring and August bank holidays (the last Mondays in May and August), and for the first time in 1978 May Day (1st May).

There are various systems for worker participation in the management of industries, either in the form of works councils or individual directors appointed by the trade unions or the workforce. However, their functions have so far been consultative only. If, in the course of the planned denationalization of public industries, shares were sold to employees, this might help to promote their appreciation of managerial problems and discourage Labour from sponsoring renationalization.

The t r a d e u n i o n s ar the chief representative of the working population's interests. The influence they have gained in political life has made them the most important pressure group in the country. The fall of two governments in the 1970s was caused by 'industrial action'. Even if the central organ of organized labour, the Trades Union Congress (TUC) endorses wage restraint, 'wildcat' strikes by single unions representing just one skill within a workshop can paralyze a whole industry. This happened in 1977, when a strike of the toolmakers' union in British Leyland brought the production of 11 out of 18 car models to a standstill.

While Labour legislation in the '70s sought to protect the worker against unfair practices by the employer, thus encouraging strikes, Tory legislation in the '80s limited industrial action by 5 employment acts. Now the individual worker is protected from arbitrary expulsion and from pressure to join a union where there is a 'closed shop', which requires industries to employ only union members. During strikes those willing to work (blacklegs) have a right to enter the workplace. Secondary picketing against firms not involved in the actual dispute has been made illegal. Penalties for violating these regulations may include sequestration of the unions assets. Industrial action must be preceded by postal votes of union members.

There are now far fewer unions than before the Tory governments. Total membership is about 10 million.

Unions have officials (local, district, national), who must be elected by secret ballot. Those representing the individual workshop are called shop stewards.

Major unions are the Transport and General Workers' Union (TGWU), the Amalgamated Union of Engineering Workers (AUEW), the National Union of Mine Workers and the Union of Shop, Distributive and Allied Workers.

7. *Women:* English women tend to be more independent and wilful than their sisters on the Continent (cf. Lady Winston Churchill's burning of the portrait of her husband, a masterpiece by Graham Sutherland). British women were pioneers in the struggle for the right to vote, the English suffragettes being the first militant group to use hunger strikes as a means to reach their aim. Upper-class women tend to dominate in the domestic sphere, which gave rise to the slogan of the 'henpecked' husband (see also p. 158).

Although equality of men and women before the law has as yet not been established by statute (as in the German Grundgesetz of 1949), women are now virtually admitted to all offices and educational institutions. They are members of Parliament, can sit in the House of Lords as hereditary peeresses and can (since 1958) be created life peeresses. They serve as councillors, mayors and ministers of the Crown. Margaret Thatcher is the first woman in the Western World to lead a major political party and to head a government.

In the field of law women serve as jurors and judges. One third of magistrates in England and Wales are women. However, the number of women who are High Court judges or barristers is small. In the teaching profession they constitute 75 per cent of the staff in primary schools, but only 43 per cent in maintained secondary schools. At universities, where 11 per cent of the teaching staff are women, only 1.7 per cent are professors.

Considerable discrimination remains between the career prospects and average earnings of men and women in industry and commerce. Women get lower wages than men, usually on the ground that their work is unskilled. The *Equal Pay Act* of 1970 established the principle of equal pay for work of equal value (though women's salaries in the teaching profession and the civil service had been raised to the level of men's pay before). But continuing discrimination in recruitment, promotion and dismissal prompted a new piece of legislation, the *Sex Discrimination Act* of 1975.

Women constitute almost 40 per cent of Britain's work force, but one third work only part-time. This is due to the great number of married women (63 per cent of all women in employment). Many married women go back to work after their children have grown up.

In family matters women's rights have increased considerably. The right of a wife to own property independently of her husband was recognized as early as the late 19th c. The *Guardianship Act* of 1973 gave her equal rights in respect of the guardianship of her children.

Recent legislation has made divorce much easier than it used to be. The *Divorce Act* 1969 recognizes as the only ground for divorce the irretrievable breakdown of marriage, though a divorce may be granted for intolerable conduct like adultery, desertion or cruelty. Between 1960 and 1980 divorces soared from 25,000 to 143,000. Over the same period, illegitimate births nearly doubled (many of them voluntary).

The Abortion Act of 1967 considerably relaxed legislation with regard to abortions. Though a new bill in 1979 tightened restrictions, there were still 138,000 legal abortions in 1982.

8. *Coloured population:* Britain's racial problem, the integration of black and coloured people, grew out of the imperial heritage. Until 1962, citizens of any Commonwealth nations (Indians, Pakistanis, West Indians and blacks direct from Africa) could settle in Britain without formalities. With growing unemployment, these immigrants became

formidable competition to working-class whites. Since 1962 therefore, legislation has restricted immigration but has also provided protection for those immigrants already in Britain (p. 108). These are even allowed to bring in dependants (wives, children, fiancées, aged parents), who came to Britain in considerable numbers. Moreover the fact that Commonwealth citizens are allowed to visit Britain for a limited time has led to much illegal infiltration. The number of coloured people in Britain is estimated at 2.2 million, i.e. 4% of the total population. Half the population of Southall, a London suburb, are Indian. The 1981 census has dropped the question about a person's race or ethnic origin.

However, large-scale coloured immigration is over. Due to the depression, emigration from Britain (especially to Australia and Canada) has been larger than immigration.

Despite the country's tradition of tolerance, racial tension has risen sharply. In London and industrial cities of the Midlands, Lancashire and Yorkshire, where 60% of the immigrants are concentrated, clashes have occurred between white and coloured residents, between coloured youths and the police, between the racist National Front and the extremist Socialist Workers' Party. Many of the problems of American cities in the sixties have begun to flare up in Britain. Many black youths look on the police as their enemies. Disturbances in London, Birmingham and Liverpool resulted in hundreds of injuries and arrests (pp. 110 and 112).

The second generation of coloured people, which was born in Britain, feel that they are entitled to the same opportunities as whites (confirmed by repeated legislation) and sneer at their parents for their acceptance of white privilege, of low-grade work and housing.

II. **Social Services:** While Labour governments extended social security, the Tory government since 1979 has cut back on a large number of social services, especially by reducing the number of people entitled to benefits, or by increasing charges (e.g. for school meals and in the public health service).

1. NATIONAL INSURANCE, to which contributions are made by the insured person, the employer and the Exchequer, applies in general to all persons over school-leaving age including employed, self-employed and non-employed persons. It provides sickness and unemployment benefits and invalidity pensions.

Pensions are paid to men over 65, to women over 60, who have retired from regular work, and to widows if they have reached the age of 50 or have dependent children. They are not affected by other unearned income or previous level of earnings. Retirement pensions are paid to men over 70 and women over 65 even if they continue to work. If pensioners under 70 (65 for women) are employed in gainful work, their pensions are reduced in proportion to their earnings. Special widow's allowances are paid to widows during the first 26 weeks of bereavement. Employees in jobs providing them with a higher occupational pension can be contracted out of the scheme. Unemployment benefits are paid for a maximum of one year, sickness benefits for 28 weeks. If after that time the beneficiary is still incapable of work, he receives an invalidity pension. Injury benefits are paid for a maximum of 26 weeks. All these benefits are supplemented by allowances for adult dependants and dependent children. Disablement benefits depend on the extent of disablement as assessed by a medical board.

2. THE CHILD BENEFIT SCHEME, which replaced family allowances in 1977, grants tax-free child benefits to the mother of children below the school-leaving age of 16 and for children under 19 if they are in full-time education.

3. SUPPLEMENTARY BENEFITS can be drawn by people not in full-time work, whose financial resources fall below a certain level. Such families are also entitled to other benefits like free school meals and exemption from the medical charges of the National Health Scheme for prescriptions and dental treatment.

4. NATIONAL HEALTH SERVICE, introduced by the Labour government in 1948, provides a national system of personal health services available to every person. While under the Labour Government from 1945–51 medicines and medical treatment including vaccination, ambulance and hospital services were absolutely free of charge, the subsequent governments reintroduced charges for dental and optical treatment. Dentures, spectacles and medicines must be paid for in proportion to their cost, children and the very poor being exempt.

Medical treatment under the National Health Service is provided by practitioners in public service, who receive capitation fees according to the number of their patients. Pharmacists are paid according to the prescriptions they dispense. Doctors and dentists usually practise at their surgeries, and over three quarters are in partnership or group practices. A doctor may treat patients privately. The scheme provides for the treatment of narcotic and alcohol addiction. The licencing of medicines is subject to public control. Although most people in Britain approve of the principles of the Health Scheme, critics have pointed out that it is an enormous strain on public revenues and thus on the taxpayer, that doctors might be inclined to spend more effort on their private patients, and that pensioned people, who have time, are encouraged to crowd the doctor's waiting room to the detriment of working patients. The number of the aged ('senior citizens') is rising steeply and the government contends that pensions will shortly become an unbearable burden on the nation. It advocates private insurance.

The fact that the Government spends only 5% of the budget on health services (European average 7%) has led to an alarming decline of the NHS. The insufficient number of beds and medical staff, which delays necessary operations, has prompted sharp criticism. Low wages do not encourage young people to become nurses.

5. VOLUNTARY SOCIAL SERVICES: There have always been numerous voluntary bodies in Britain assisting people in need, e.g. The British Red Cross Society, the Women's Voluntary Service, the National Society for the Prevention of Cruelty to Children, etc. Welfare organizations of various kinds maintain about half of all homes for children and old people, and most of the homes for unmarried mothers and for children sent by the juvenile courts. Many of the residents in these homes are maintained by public funds. Several hundred community associations manage community centres serving as neighbourhood meeting places. Residential settlements in poorer districts, still largely voluntarily maintained, are centres of local social service and educational and youth activities.

6. YOUTH SERVICES: Youth groups with a total membership of over six million young people under 21 have been developed and financed mainly by voluntary effort, though they now receive grants from education authorities which also cooperate in organizing youth centres and clubs, providing premises and employing youth organizers. Full-time youth and community workers receive a two-year training at certain universities or higher education colleges. The government has initiated a Youth Training Scheme to help unemployed youths to develop skills for future employment.

The chief organizations with a mainly religious purpose are the Young Men's Christian Association (Y.M.C.A.) and the Young Women's Christian Association (Y.W.C.A.), the Boys' Brigade, the Methodist and Salvation Army Youth Organizations. The Boy Scouts and Girl Guides, both with a membership of more than 600,000 are undenominational. Founded in 1908 by Lord Baden-Powell to develop character and good citizenship in young people (who are usually under 16), the Scouts movement has now spread to most other countries in the Western World. The Youth Hostels Association maintains hostels for walkers and cyclists.

7. HOUSING: To cope with the enormous destruction caused by the war, public house-building programmes have been carried out on a large scale since 1948. The fact that one third of all dwellings in Britain were

rented from public housing authorities has, in Mrs. Thatcher's opinion, created a 'council-house mentality', which the Tory government now seeks to break by giving all council tenants the right to buy their homes. It also considers home-ownership an advantage because maintenance costs become the owner's responsibility, thus cutting council spending. Moreover, the restriction of rents for council houses had often resulted in deterioration of property. Many former tenants have made use of the opportunity to buy their homes.

Whereas after 1945 rebuilding and slum clearance were the major concerns, the government now gives priority to the modernization of houses to regenerate declining inner cities, the more so since high-rise estates produced by the large-scale redevelopment programmes of the 1950s and 1960s have proved generally unpopular. The average Briton prefers a house with two stories. 78% of families in Britain live in individual houses, only 22% in flats.

8. TOWN PLANNING: One of the outstanding developments of this century has been the uncontrolled decentralization of the city population into less crowded areas, intensified by the fact that the English prefer living in separate houses with small gardens to dwelling in flats. This 'urban sprawl' has not only created the featureless suburbia of Metropolitan London and other big cities, but has absorbed many towns and villages in the adjoining counties. From the *Towns Act* of 1909 onwards the necessity of a planned use of land has been one of the major concerns of the government. In 1937, the *Barlow Report on the Geographical Distribution of the Industrial Population* first advocated new satellite towns for the overspill of the great conurbations, and successive acts since 1946 have provided for new towns to be built in Great Britain, thirty-two of which are already established: five in Scotland, three of which are designed to absorb the excess population of Glasgow, twenty-three in England and Wales, eight of which serve the London area, e.g. Crawley, Basildon, Stevenage, Hemel Hempstead, four in Northern Ireland. In contrast to the former dormitory suburbs, these towns are self-contained communities with residential and industrial quarters, with civic buildings, schools, shopping and entertainment facilities. Green belts are designed to prevent a further sprawl of the towns, which are planned to accommodate a population of not more than about 100,000. Britain's town planning policy has become an important social investment and has encouraged similar experiments in other countries.

In recent years this policy of population dispersal has, together with the environment problems of larger cities, called for government action against the decline of inner cities – now a phenomenon in most industrialized countries. Within the last twenty years several million people in Britain have moved to suburbs and peripheral towns, leaving the inner cities to the poorest classes and to decay.

Seasonal Customs

Like all Western countries Britain is subject to the levelling influence of modern civilization, which has eroded most of the ancient traditions underlying national and local customs. Of the two forces which usually combine to develop national customs, i.e. religion or superstition on the one hand, and the need for social and civic conventions on the other, the irrational forces have always been particularly marked in Ireland, while England has become the stronghold of customs that contribute to good civic conduct and social well-being. In Britain many of the ancient religious customs have only retained their outward forms, serving mainly as a pretext for conviviality and feasting.

Christmas in England has long been more a season of merry-making than of religious celebration, and the Christmas holidays are, in certain respects, the same to the English as carnival is to the Catholic countries on the Continent. In the Middle Ages, Christmas was a season of uninterrupted entertainment and feasting, which was intended to cheer up long winter nights and lasted from Christmas Eve (24th December) till Twelfth Night (6th January). Some popular observances still continue today, like hanging up a twig of mistletoe, under which one has the privilege of kissing girls, and, in places, the burning of the yule log, an ancient winter ceremony which originated in Scandinavia. While the yule log is burning in the fireplace, the assembled family will drink, sing and tell stories to each other. On Christmas Eve children hang up their stockings for Santa Claus to fill during the night. On Christmas morning the presents are opened under the Christmas tree, which most English families decorate for the occasion. The rooms are decorated with holly and coloured papers, while coloured lights are hung in the windows. The Christmas dinner in the early afternoon includes the traditional roast turkey, mince pies, plum pudding and a Christmas cake. Frequently children go round singing carols. *Boxing Day* (a name derived from the old habit of giving one's employees Christmas presents in boxes) is the first weekday after Christmas. It is a public holiday for further eating and drinking and sleeping off the effects of the day before.

Twelfth Night on 6th January is the twelfth day after Christmas and coincides with the festival of the Epiphany. It is the last day of Christmas festivities, on which Christmas trees are removed.

On *Valentine's Day*, 14th February, young persons choose 'Valentines', to whom they send decorative cards, often in verse.

Shrove Tuesday is the day before Lent when people used to be shriven i.e.

to confess their sins to the priest. Nowadays people eat pancakes and the meaning of the day has been forgotten by everybody except the religious.

On *April Fool's Day*, 1st April people play practical jokes on each other.

On *Good Friday* spiced buns marked with a cross in memory of Christ's crucifixion are eaten.

May Day, 1st May, used to be celebrated by setting maypoles adorned with garlands for the villagers to dance around. The May queen held her court. This custom is now more a matter of fun than conviction. Britain does not follow the continental fashion of socialist celebrations in any marked degree, though 1978 saw May Day as a public holiday for the first time.

On *Guy Fawkes Day*, 5th November, groups of boys burn a dummy representing Guy Fawkes (p. 39). A popular rhyme runs 'Please to remember the fifth of November, gunpowder, treason and plot. I see no reason why gunpowder treason should ever be forgot.' Children collect money from friends and relatives and buy fireworks, which they let off as the dummy of Guy Fawkes in burnt on a bonfire. The exploding of bangers, the lights of the fireworks, the cheers of the crowd contribute to make Guy Fawkes Day the year's most picturesque custom.

Lord Mayor's Day on 9th November is one of the big London civic days of pageantry. The first Lord Mayor's Show was recorded in 1236. The newly elected Lord Mayor sets off to Westminster to swear his oath on taking office. The Lord Mayor's coach, which is gilded and brightly decorated, is followed by a procession of the Mayor's own livery company and mounted soldiers with banners as well as brass bands playing march tunes. The procession is joined by many decorated vehicles which illustrate various themes. The speeches made at the banquet at Guildhall after the procession include one by the Prime Minister, which always contains some important announcement.

London's royal pageantry includes the *State Opening of Parliament* by the Sovereign in the House of Lords, and the military ceremony of *Trooping the Colour*, which takes place on the Sovereign's official birthday on 3rd June. The Sovereign, accompanied by a gorgeous cavalcade of horsemen, rides on a white charger from the Mall to the Horse Guards Parade, where she is joined by the Foot Guards. The solemn march of the troops ends when the bands play 'God Save the Queen' and the colours are dipped to the ground. Nowadays the national anthem is rarely sung.

A number of s p o r t i n g e v e n t s in or near London have, in the course of time, assumed the character of seasonal customs. The *University Boat Race* between Oxford and Cambridge takes place on the Thames in March. The most famous horse races are the *Grand National* at Aintree, Liverpool, the *Derby* on Epsom Downs and the *Royal Ascot* (Ascot, Surrey). The *Henley Regatta* on the Thames and the popular cricket *Test matches* and *One-Day* matches against visiting national teams at Lord's (Marylbone, London) take place in the summer. Other important sporting event are the *Cup Final* at Wembley and the *All England Lawn Tennis Championships* at Wimbledon.

THE BRITISH GOVERNMENT

Central Government

History

The British government is not, like those of the U.S.A. and most Continental countries, based on a written constitution, but on an organic development beginning far back in the Middle Ages and never, since 1066, interrupted by military invasions or other interference from outside. In contrast to Continental constitutions, which were largely the results of revolutions, the British constitution is an agglomeration of a number of declarations claiming merely to reassert ancient rights (e.g. Magna Carta). As the royal prerogative was restricted, the three basic principles of the modern conception of democracy emerged:

I. The idea of government as a 'social contract' between the ruler and ruled, binding ruler and ruled alike (today 'c o n s t i t u t i o n').

II. R e p r e s e n t a t i v e g o v e r n m e n t by a Parliament in which all classes of the nation are represented.

III. D i v i s i o n o f p o w e r s (legislative, executive, judicial).

I. **The British Constitution,** a mother of constitutions (e.g. for the many former colonies becoming independent states) is the sum of political practices and laws of a constitutional nature enacted in the course of English history:

1. *Magna Carta,* 1215: no imprisonment without trial by the accused's equals; no taxation without consent of the Common Council.

2. *Petition of Right,* 1628, opposing Stuart absolutism, largely re-enacted the above provisions.

3. *Bill of Rights,* 1689, made England the first constitutional monarchy by substituting the constitutional principle for that of Divine Right and by establishing parliamentary control of legislation and taxation, while the King retained the executive power.

4. *Act of Settlement,* 1701, made ministers responsible for the acts of the sovereign.

172

5. **Shift of governmental initiative** from the Monarch to Cabinet occurred during the reigns of the first Hanoverians (George I and George II), when the actual leadership of the government passed to the Prime Minister while the Monarch remained official head of the government, signing all Acts of Parliament.

II. Development of Parliament (representative government).

1. MIDDLE AGES: The Royal Council since William I was, like the Saxon Witenagemot which it replaced, a meeting of the nobles (barons) to advise the King on administrative and legal (i.e. legislative and judicial) matters, whose advice, however, the King was not bound to take. Whereas administration was soon placed in the hands of permanent officials (since Henry VII centered in the Privy Council), the feudal council (the 'Common' or 'Great Council', or 'Parliament') continued to meet intermittently to be consulted on t a x a t i o n and other matters of importance and to present petitions for the redress of grievances. Having lost its administrative functions, it gradually developed into an instrument for the c o n t r o l o f g o v e r n m e n t and a l e g i s l a t i v e b o d y.
The representative system developed after 1265 when, for the first time, elected commoners were summoned: two knights from each shire and two burgesses from each borough. The Model Parliament of Edward I (1295) permanently established the r e p r e s e n t a t i o n o f c o m m o n e r s, who, since the 14th century, met separately from the House of Lords as House of Commons. Summoned chiefly to be consulted on taxation, the Commons soon gained financial control and a measure of ascendancy over the House of Lords, which, however, retained its importance as highest court of justice.

2. PARLIAMENT IN THE AGE OF DESPOTISM AND OLIGARCHY: The popular Tudor monarchs were able to use Parliament as an instrument of their despotism, while the Stuarts failed in their attempt to eliminate it altogether (execution of Charles I). The oligarchy of the 18th century restricted the vote in many ways, so that even the House of Commons was largely controlled by the aristocracy, the gentry and younger sons of nobles holding 'pocket' and 'rotten boroughs'.

3. True representation was achieved when in the 19th century general m a l e s u f f r a g e, and in the 20th century f e m a l e s u f f r a g e were introduced.
a) *First Reform Bill* (1832) gave the franchise to the upper middle classes and abolished many rotten boroughs, giving seats to the new industrial towns.
b) *Second Reform Bill* (1867) gave the franchise to the lower middle classes and industrial workers in towns.
c) *Third Reform Bill* (1884) enfranchised the rural population.
d) *Representation of the People Act* (1918) gave the franchise to women over 30.
e) *Equal Franchise Act* (1928) gave the vote to all women over 21.

173

5. *Parliament Act* (1911) made the veto of the hereditary House of Lords merely suspensory.

6. Abolition of plural voting (1918), and of university representation during the Labour government (1948), finally established the principle 'one man, one vote'.

III. **Division of powers** was virtually already established in the later Middle Ages by the principle that legislation should be the province of Parliament, and that law should only be administered in ordinary courts by independent judges. This principle was challenged by the Stuarts, who held that the king was the source of law and that judges were dependent on his will. The Glorious Revolution re-established the principle that laws are made by Parliament, and guaranteed the independence of jurisdiction. In Britain, however, the division of powers was not realized as fully as in the U.S.A., where secretaries (ministers) were not given seats in the legislature, and where the President is only allowed to 'deliver messages' to Congress. British ministers have seats and vote in Parliament and today introduce all important bills. Moreover, the House of Lords has remained the highest court of justice. The Lord Chancellor is not only Speaker of the House of Lords, but also an active judge and, as the highest judicial authority, member of the Cabinet.

The British Government Today

In contrast to economic and social life, where striking changes have occurred during the last fifty years, Britain's political institutions have shown a remarkable stability. Britain has no terrorism with the aim of changing the political system. Acts of terror have been perpetrated only in connection with the problems of Northern Ireland.

In spite of all criticism, Britain, alone among European countries, has still that relic of feudal times, an upper House representing the country's nobility. The monarchy, although deprived of political power, has retained much of its pomp and its full popular appeal. To what extent it is cherished was made manifest in the enthusiastic celebrations of the Queen's Jubilee in 1977.

The British government is a p a r l i a m e n t a r y m o n a r c h y in which Parliament is supreme. Parliament is neither bound by a written constitution nor by former legislation, nor can its laws be revised by a constitutional court. But the growing complexity of modern administration has gradually given the executive a certain predominance over the legislature. Moreover the national government's authority is already considerably restricted by international institutions like the EEC, NATO and GATT, and the modern media have made Parliament much more subject to public opinion and criticism.

I. **The Sovereign** is the official head of the UK and the only remaining constitutional link with the Commonwealth countries. 'The Queen in Parliament' is the supreme legislative authority. As the 'fountain of justice' she is the official prosecutor in criminal proceedings. She is the head of the Church of England (not in Wales and Northern Ireland, where the Church is disestablished) and the protector of the Church of Scotland. However, as royal prerogatives have been largely abolished, the Sovereign today 'reigns but does not rule' and actually holds only a limited number of rights: the right to summon, prorogue and dissolve Parliament, to veto legislation (a right not used since the 18th century), to make appointments to high church and government offices, and, as 'fountain of honour' to create peers and knights. She is the dispenser of pardons. The Sovereign exercises these rights on the advice of and through her ministers and is thus not accountable for the acts of government ('the King can do no wrong'). Therefore the Crown is an enduring institution, while the government resigns when it loses the voters' confidence. Embodying the unity of the nation and Commonwealth, the Sovereign performs a wide range of social and ceremonial functions (e.g. opening of Parliament in the House of Lords with the annual Speech from the Throne).

II. **Parliament** (the legislature), sitting from November till July, with sometimes about ten days added in October, has the following functions: legislation, appropriation of funds, control of government with the right to criticize its policy, and, by custom only, the right to be consulted before ratification of international treaties. England has 523 members of parliament, Scotland 72, Wales 38, Northern Ireland 17).
Parliament consists of two chambers:

1. H o u s e o f L o r d s (with about c. 1200 members) consists of Lords Spiritual (two archbishops and 24 bishops), and Lords Temporal, including all hereditary peers and peeresses of the United Kingdom who have not disclaimed their peerages, and, since 1958, a number of life peers (persons appointed for their merits in public life) including ladies. Law Lords appointed for life represent the judicial functions of the House as highest court of appeal. The House of Lords is presided over by the Lord Chancellor, who sits on the Woolsack. The Upper House cannot initiate or veto Money Bills and can hold up other laws for one year only (pp. 87, 103). Despite proposals to reform or even to abolish it, the House of Lords still has an important function as moderator and safeguard against rash legislation. It constitutes an element of stability, is not dependent on the favour of the electorate and not dominated by party strife.

2. H o u s e o f C o m m o n s consists of 650 members (private members and members of the ministry), who are elected by universal, direct and secret ballot and receive a salary of £17,000 per annum. It is presided over by the Speaker, who is elected by the Members of Parliament. His function is to

175

conduct, not to take part in, debates (since ancient times he has been supposed to be the spokesman for the House). His political neutrality is emphasized by the fact that he may only vote in cases of a tie, when he has the casting vote. The House of Commons is elected normally every five years unless some crisis makes the dissolution and re-election of Parliament necessary.

TV was allowed in the House of Lords in 1986, in the Commons in 1988.

3. Parliamentary control is exercised mainly by the power of the House to pass a vote of 'no confidence' on the government, by the daily Question Time, when ministers are questioned about matters for which they are responsible, and by the right, through the Committees of Supply and of Ways and Means of the whole House, to examine the administrative and financial measures of the government. 14 permanent Select Committees scrutinize the main government departments.

4. Debates are conducted by the Speaker, in whose discretion it lies, which member he calls upon to speak, who guards against abuse, and sees to it that all opinions are equally expressed. Members speak from their places and address the Speaker, not the House. They refer to other members not by name but as 'the honourable member'. The obstructionist policy of the Irish members in the 19th century, who tried to defeat bills by endlessly drawing out debates, has made necessary the introduction of the 'closure' of the debate (1882), which requires 'that the question be now put' when the motion is supported by a prescribed number of members.

5. Bills (except Money Bills, which must be introduced in the Commons) can originate in either House, Public Bills being introduced by ministers or other members of either House, Private Bills by individuals or organizations outside Parliament. The Bill receives three readings. After the First Reading on introduction it is printed. After the Second Reading it is referred to a standing committee or the whole House sitting in committee (presided over by a chairman instead of the Speaker). When the House has decided on the committee's amendments, the Bill receives a Third Reading. It is then voted upon either by a summary procedure or, in cases of doubt, by a 'division', when members pass through two doors, where the 'ayes' and 'noes' are counted. When the Bill has been passed, it is sent to the other House, where it can be amended (except Money Bills). If both Houses come to an agreement and the Royal Assent is given, the Bill becomes a law and is entered on the Statute Book. Bills can be held up by the House of Lords only for one year. When after that period it has been passed a second time by the Commons, it becomes a law.

6. Elections are normally held every five years. Each of the present 650 constituencies returns one member to Parliament, who has been elected by secret and direct vote. Members of the House of Lords are not allowed to vote. Civil servants, members of the armed forces and the police forces, and the clergy of the Churches of England, of Scotland, of Ireland and of the Roman Catholic Church are among those who cannot stand as candidates for election. Special by-elections held to fill vacancies in Parliament often serve as important indicators of political trends during the rule of one government. General elections are usually attended by c. 78 per cent of the electorate. Money spent on an election campaign is strictly regulated by law, and anybody infringing such regulations may incur severe punishments (including annulment of the candidate's election). British subjects are entitled to vote from the age of 18.

III. **Her Majesty's Government** represents the executive branch and consists of ministries charged with the administration of national affairs. Ministers are appointed by the Crown on the advice of the Prime Minister, who is leader of the majority party and chooses his ministers from among the Members of Parliament belonging to his party. Ministers as well as Junior Ministers assisting them and representing them in Parliamentary debates are thus p o l i t i c a l a p p o i n t-m e n t s and usually possess no professional qualifications. They are therefore dependent on their permanent staff of civil servants for the routine work of administration. Ministers lay down the general line of policy and are liable to answer in Parliament any questions or criticism relating to their spheres of administration. Chief ministers are the P r i m e M i n i s t e r, who, by tradition, holds the title of First Lord of the Treasury, the C h a n c e l l o r o f t h e E x c h e q u e r, who presents the budget; the L o r d C h a n c e l l o r, who, as highest legal authority, is a member of the House of Lords, the highest court of justice, the Secretaries of State for the Home and Foreign Offices and for Commonwealth Affairs. Other major ministries are the Departments of Trade and Industry, Employment, Education and Science, Environment, the Department of Health and Social Security, and the Department of Transport. The Ministry of Defence coordinates the activities of the army, navy and air force.

1. CABINET: The work of the ministries is coordinated by the Cabinet, which determines the national policy and exercises supreme control over the national executive. The Prime Minister decides which ministers belong to the Cabinet (c. 20). A minister cannot act as an individual, he must resign if he disagrees with Cabinet policy. This rule of the c o l l e c t i v e r e s p o n s i b i l i t y of the Cabinet

gives considerable power to the Prime Minister. The meetings of the Cabinet are secret. As all important bills are introduced by the appropriate minister, the Cabinet, in which the principal ministries are represented, has become the chief initiator of policy within Parliament.

2. PRIVY COUNCIL: Until the 18th century the Privy Council, which was an inner council of officials, was the chief executive body. Most ministries have developed from the Privy Council, the Cabinet itself as a committee for foreign affairs. The Privy Council, to which Cabinet ministers belong automatically, is entitled to issue O r d e r s i n C o u n c i l by virtue of the royal prerogative or of legislation delegated by Parliament. Having grown too big to act efficiently (c. 340 members), the Privy Council now meets only occasionally. The actual work is done in committees.

IV. Civil Service

The term Civil Service, which goes back to the 18th century, applies to those servants of the Crown who are employed in a civil (as a contrast to military or political) capacity, and who are remunerated from money voted by Parliament. The Civil Service has a permanent staff, whose members (about 1 million) remain in office when the government changes.

History:

In the Middle Ages the king's clerks, headed by the Lord Chancellor, were recruited from the clergy, the only people who could read and write. Until the 19th century, patronage was the chief means of entry into the service. The widespread habit (esp. in the 18th century) of buying and selling offices was first criticized by Edmund Burke, whose *Economic Reform Bill* undertook to abolish the sinecure offices and the system from which certain officials profited by lending the public money in their trust at interest. This led to the appointment of commissioners who had the right to enquire into the accounts and emoluments in public offices. In 1870 an Order in Council introduced competitive examinations open to everybody, which had been demanded by the *Northcote-Trevelyan Report* of 1854. This created an independent, impartial service subject to the authority of Parliament. The setting-up of a National Whitley Council for the Civil Service established the principle of joint consultation, already accepted in industry, also for government service.

Present Structure:

A civil servant is legally a servant of the Crown. Although he works under the authority of the minister of his department (who is a political appointee dependent on the outcome of elections), a change of minister does not involve a change of staff. The political neutrality of the service guarantees the stability of administration. Although a civil servant must resign his office if he stands for Parliament he may engage in private political activities, e.g. in local government, subject to the provisions of the *Official Secrets Act* and the *Prevention of Corruption Act*. Persons associated with the Communist Party or Fascist organizations are not employed in work in which secrecy is of vital importance (cf. betrayal of the atom bomb to Russia by the physicist Klaus Fuchs, who, as a Communist, had emigrated from Nazi Germany to Britain). A civil servant may not use official information for writing, lecturing or broadcasting purposes without express approval of his department.

For the purposes of pay, recruitment and personnel management the Civil Service is divided into occupational groups (administration, police, legal category, secretarial group etc.) Posts for the three grades at the top level – permanent secretary, deputy secretary and under secretary – are filled by the people most suitable for them without regard to their academic background. All other permanent appointments are made by the department concerned on the strength of a 'certificate of qualification' issued by the Civil Service Commission, for the system tries to ensure that candidates are selected on the basis of fair and open competition. Promotions are made partly through centrally conducted examinations, partly by the departments themselves.

The organization representing the Civil Service in negotiations on conditions of service is the National Whitley Council.

Political Parties

The two original parties, Tory and Whig, originated in the constitutional struggles during the reign of Charles II in the 17th century, when the T o r i e s represented the interests of Crown and Church, and the W h i g s the interests of liberal aristocrats, the commercial classes and Nonconformists. They changed their names to Conservative and Liberal in the 19th century, when the C o n s e r v a t i v e s pursued a vigorous imperialistic policy, the L i b e r a l s reforms at home. By 1900 the growing needs of the workers had given rise to the L a b o u r   P a r t y, which represented a moderate type of socialism. Gaining strength as the importance of Liberals declined, Labour has, since 1924, held office on five occasions. In the 70s it split into a moderate and a radical wing (cf. p. 111). Although it eliminated the Trotskyite faction of the 'Militant Tendency', which propagated open class war, Labour's platform adopted a more uncompromising socialism. It introduced left-wing principles for electing its leaders and MPs, and intends to retain the option of withdrawal from the EEC, and unilateral disarmament.

179

The left-of-centre Social Democratic Party (SDP), which was founded in 1981, gathered strength by forming an alliance with the Liberals (cf. p. 112). During the racial disturbances of the 70s, two extremist parties were formed: the Socialist Workers' Party and the Fascist National Front, which demands repatriation of immigrants and segregation of immigrants' children in schools. The National Front however never gained more than 1.3% of the national vote.

However, despite the existence of such 'third parties' (including the Scottish, Welsh and Irish Nationalists, Ecologists and Communists), Britain has to all intents and purposes a t w o - p a r t y s y s t e m. At elections votes are cast for candidates in a constituency, not for parties, the candidate with the majority of votes winning the seat. This 'direct vote' all but eliminates the weaker parties, which, in countries with proportional representation, gain seats in proportion to the total votes cast for them. Thus Communists in Britain have consistently failed to obtain seats in Parliament. In the British election for the European Assembly in 1979, the Liberals polled 13% of the votes, but did not secure a single seat. In the general election of 1983, the alliance of SDP and Liberals, which gained 25% of the votes, got only 4% of the seats in Parliament. One of its aims is therefore proportional representation.

Moreover, the requirement that candidates deposit £500, which are forfeited if they fail to obtain one eighth of the votes cast in the constituency, discourages many from standing for Parliament.

The Ecology Party – although too small to have gained a seat in Parliament – has nevertheless become an important pressure group opposing actions threatening the environment.

The majority party in Parliament forms the government, while the defeated party plays an important role as parliamentary opposition, whose responsibility is stressed by the leader of H e r M a j e s t y ' s O p p o s i t i o n receiving a salary. A group of leading members of the opposition party forms the 'shadow cabinet', whose members could at any time take over ministerial functions if a new election brought their party to power. The division of the House into Government and Opposition is emphasized by the seating arrangement in Parliament. Members from each party sit opposite each other, not in a semi-circle, their leaders (in the case of the majority party, the ministers) occupying the front benches. A strong opposition party acts as a natural moderator of government (e.g. during Question Time, when every legitimate question must be answered). Party control in Parliament is exercised by the W h i p s, who ensure attendance of their members when important issues are decided.

Apart from the recent upsurge of extreme socialist and nationalist thinking, parties in Britain are less ideologically orientated than parties on the Continent, more committed to practical issues.

Local Government

History

1. IN ANGLO-SAXON TIMES a large measure of local self-government was exercised by the freemen in folk-moots ('hundreds' and 'tithings') under the supervision of royal officials: aldermen and sheriffs (p. 16).

2. AFTER THE NORMAN CONQUEST had reduced most of the freemen class to serfdom, local government in counties was controlled by the local gentry. Justices of the peace, who from the reign of Edward III were appointed from this class, held also administrative functions. Self-government in towns began when boroughs, in return for loans to their overlords, obtained favours, e.g. election of mayors, exemption from the sheriffs' interference in matters of tax levy. These corporative rights, which gave them the status of 'c o r p o r a t i o n s' were largely exercised by guilds (in London, Guildhall is the town hall).

3. 16TH–19TH CENTURY: After the decay of medieval boroughs under the Tudors when the guilds were deprived of their privileges, local government, even in small towns, was again largely controlled by local gentry ('s q u i r e a r c h y').

4. 19TH–CENTURY REFORMS replaced the rule of justices of the peace by democratic bodies. The *Municipal Reform Act* 1835 established Borough Councils with councillors elected for three years and – at the higher level – aldermen elected by the councillors for six years. County Councils, and District and Parish Councils created by later acts (1888 and 1894) were organized broadly on the same lines.

The reorganization of local government in 1974 ended the divorce of town and country reflected by the division between borough and district councils, changed county divisions and abolished aldermen.

Local Government Today

I. LOCAL DIVISIONS: On the new map of Britain small and thinly populated counties (Huntingdon, Rutland, Westmorland) have disappeared, while heavily populated industrial conurbations have been made separate 'metropolitan counties', which have replaced the former borough councils. These are Merseyside, Greater Manchester, West Midlands, West Yorkshire, South Yorkshire, Tyne and Wear. The two sides of the Humber estuary now form one county, Humberside, the Tees estuary has become Cleveland. There are also changes in Scotland, and in Wales, where all counties were given Welsh names.

II. LOCAL AUTHORITIES: Local government today is exercised by local authority councils of the various administrative areas, of counties and their subdivisions – districts and parishes.

1. LOCAL COUNCILS consist of elected, unpaid councillors usually elected for four years and a chairman elected for 1 year. In districts which still carry the ceremonial title 'borough' conferred on them by royal

charter the chairman is known as Mayor, in large cities, e.g. London, Birmingham, as Lord Mayor.

2. LOCAL OFFICIALS: The Lord Lieutenant is the Queen's representative in the county with few duties except on symbolic occasions. The ancient office of sheriff has been abolished in England (in Scotland there are still 'sheriff' courts). The actual administrative work lies in the hands of salaried officers and employees, including administrative, professional and technical staff, teachers and manual workers.

3. FUNCTIONS: In England all county councils are responsible for planning and administration over wider areas, e.g. education, the police, the fire service, personal social services, traffic regulation, transportation planning. The chief functions of district councils are the levy and collection of rates (local taxes), environmental health and housing (council houses = sozialer Wohnungsbau). In the metropolitan counties (with populations up to 2.8 million), the county councils (chiefly Labour) were abolished in 1986, their functions are exercised by their constituent districts.

4. FINANCE: Local authority expenditure is chiefly financed from grants of the central government (c. 50 per cent), and local rates (c. 30 per cent). The remaining 20 per cent come mainly from the rent from council houses. Housing and education are the main items of expenditure.

ENGLISH LAW

HISTORY

I. In Anglo-Saxon times jurisdiction was the function of various p o p u l a r
c o u r t s (e.g. hundred court, shire court) presided over by royal officials (alderman, sheriff). The legal usage which emerged and gradually superseded family vengeance was codified by various kings (Athelbert of Kent, Athelstan, Alfred, Cnut, Edward the Confessor).

II. After the Norman conquest, A n g l o - S a x o n l a w, f e u d a l l a w introduced by the Normans, and C a n o n (C h u r c h) l a w were applied concurrently in secular and Church courts till legal reforms, particularly under Henry II, created common legal usages and institutions.

1. COURTS

a) Central courts developed through the separation of certain bodies from the curia regis: *Court of Exchequer* (financial administration plus jurisdiction), *Court of Common Pleas* (civil actions), *King's Bench* (chiefly criminal and supervisory jurisdiction), *Chancery Court* (providing remedies for wrongs irremediable in other courts).

b) Local jurisdiction was administered by manorial courts and, since Edward III, by j u s t i c e s o f t h e p e a c e, unpaid judges with no legal training recruited from the landed gentry.

2. LEGAL SYSTEMS

a) *English Common Law* emerged under Henry II when uniformity of legal custom was achieved by itinerant judges, who went on circuit from the royal court. Moreover Henry II made the jury system an integral part of English jurisdiction.

b) *Statute Law* developed from parliamentary legislation, which since Edward I was collected in Statute Rolls. It became an important supplement to the unwritten Common Law.

c) *Equity* developed after the 14th century in the Chancery Court. It was applied in cases where Common Law did not provide adequate remedies. Its basis being the Chancellor's conscience, equity was less dependent on legal formalities and could thus develop more freely. Today Equity and Common Law are applied concurrently. The nature of the case determines which will apply.

III. STRUGGLE FOR INDEPENDENCE OF THE JUDICATURE: Jurisdiction outside ordinary courts through courts controlled by the government was always resented in England. In 1215 *Magna Carta* abolished arbitrary royal jurisdiction through the provision that no freeman should be imprisoned without trial by his equals. This principle was upheld in the struggle of Parliament against the S t u a r t k i n g s who maintained that kings were 'judges over all their subjects, yet accountable to none but God' (James I: *True Law of Free Monarchies*). This maxim was contradicted by the great lawyer Edward C o k e , who held that Common Law was supreme alike over King and Parliament, that even Parliament had only to defend the law, not to make it. 'Magna Carta is such a fellow that he will have no sovereign.' When during the Puritan Revolution the Long Parliament abolished the detested Star Chamber and Court of High Commission (for Church matters), which had become instruments of royal tyranny, it decided the victory of the Common Law. In 1679, the *Habeas Corpus Act* restated the principles of *Magna Carta* by providing that no man should be held prisoner without a warrant of arrest and that all prisoners were entitled to a speedy trial. The *Act of Settlement* 1701 provided that judges be appointed for life.

IV. REFORMS IN THE 19TH AND 20TH CENTURIES: The severity of English Law (e.g. death penalty for stealing objects worth more than 5s.; imprisonment of debtors) led to frequent demands for legal reforms, particularly by Jeremy Bentham, who also made proposals for a codification of English Law. These proposals resulted in the r e f o r m o f c r i m i n a l l a w by Sir R. Peel, who abolished more than 100 capital crimes, and a r e o r g a n i z a t i o n o f E n g l i s h c o u r t s in 1873 and 1875 (which, from 1882, were housed in the new Law Courts in the Strand).

183

The death penalty was abolished in 1965. The judicial reform in 1972 established crown courts to replace the existing local criminal courts of Quarter Sessions and Assizes held by itinerant judges.

V. **Standard Works** recording the development of English Law:

1. Ranulf de Glanville: *Tractatus de legibus et consuetudinibus regni Angliae,* 1189;

2. Henricus de Bracton: *De legibus et consuetudinibus Angliae,* 13th century;

3. *Year Books* (collection of cases from Edward II to Henry VIII);

4. Edward Coke: *Law Reports* with comments, and *Institutes of the Law of England,* 1628;

5. William Blackstone: *Commentaries on the Laws of England,* 1765;

6. F. W. Maitland: *History of English Law,* 1895.

CHARACTER OF ENGLISH LAW

Britain has no written law code. The law administered by the English courts is derived from u n w r i t t e n C o m m o n L a w and S t a t u t e L a w, i.e. Acts of Parliament (and local by-laws enacted under them), which take precedence over Common Law, because Parliament is the supreme law-making body in the realm. Though Scotland has a separate system of law and courts, the parliamentary union with England during the last 280 years has tended to abate differences. Since 1973 a new source of law has been provided by the European Community law – chiefly confined to economic and social matters – which in the case of conflict takes precedence over domestic legislation and the English Common Law.

1. Importance of p r e c e d e n t o r c a s e l a w : In the absence of a written law code judgments are rendered according to a statute or to precedent (i.e. cases tried before). Thus Law Reports recording previous judgments take the place of the paragraphs of a law code as legal authority. The English judge is therefore not only interpreter of the law but may be said to 'create' the law, though statutes are increasingly gaining importance in jurisdiction. Respect for precedent accounts for the conservatism of the English legal system, expressed outwardly in the wearing of the wig, and the civic respect shown for everything connected with the law.

2. P r o t e c t i o n o f t h e r i g h t o f t h e i n d i v i d u a l against executive pressure was repeatedly guaranteed by law, above all by the writ of *Habeas Corpus,* which, since its enactment in 1679, has remained a symbol of freedom from arbitrary arrest. Under the *Habeas Corpus Act* the police must release the accused on bail if his case cannot be tried within twenty-four hours, unless the offence for which he was arrested was a serious one. The principle that

a defendant is considered innocent until his guilt has been proved stands in contrast to the legal attitude in despotically ruled countries where the defendant is considered guilty until his innocence has been proved. The trial judge is in no way concerned with investigations before the trial, which is largely conducted through pleadings and cross-examination by counsel (prosecuting and defending). The judge only sums up the evidence for the benefit of the jury and pronounces the sentence should the jury pass a verdict of guilty. During the trial the defendant has the right to hear and subsequently to cross-examine (normally through his lawyer) all the witnesses for the prosecution and to call his own witnesses, who may be legally compelled to attend. He cannot be questioned unless he consents to be sworn as a witness in his own defence. No confessions made by him are admissible unless it can be proved that they were made voluntarily. At the trial the defence has the right to the last speech. In England less use is made of public prosecutors than on the Continent. Queen's Counsel appear only in important cases.

3. I n d e p e n d e n c e   o f   j u r i s d i c t i o n from State control is symbolized by the fact that England has no Minister of Justice. The central responsibility is vested chiefly in the Lord Chancellor, who functions as judge in various courts and is responsible for the appointment of magistrates. The judges' training and career are in no way influenced by the State; they are controlled by the independent Council of Legal Education. The English have never favoured a separate administrative law. Civil servants were until recent years sued in ordinary courts. It was not before the state had to assume more and more social responsibility, and complaints that the executive was encroaching on the individual's constitutional rights increased, that administrative tribunals were set up.

4. The n o n - p r o f e s s i o n a l   e l e m e n t is strongly represented.
a) *Magistrates* (justices of the peace) are unpaid lay judges in local courts, men of local repute who until 1888 had also many administrative functions.
b) The *jury* usually consists of 12 citizens who give the verdict of 'guilty' or 'not guilty'. In Scotland there is a third verdict of 'not proven'. Formerly the verdict had to be unanimous. Now judges may accept a majority vote provided that there are not more than two dissentients. A jury is completely independent of the judiciary. If the jury returns a verdict of 'not guilty', the prosecution has no right of appeal against it and the defendant cannot be tried again for the same offence. But the defendant has a right of appeal against a verdict of 'guilty'.

185

COURTS OF JUSTICE

I. Courts in England und Wales

1. *Magistrates' courts,* which usually consist of three unpaid lay magistrates (originally known as 'justices of the peace') try minor offences without a jury in summary procedure. They have also limited civil jurisdiction, mainly in domestic matters. Magistrates are advised on points of law by a legally qualified clerk of the court. About 97 per cent of all criminal cases are dealt with in these courts, which also conduct preliminary inquiries into indictable offences (more serious crimes) to determine whether there is sufficient evidence to justify a trial in a higher court.

2. *Crown Court* (since 1972) is responsible for all criminal cases above the level of magistrates' courts and appeals from magistrates' courts. It sits regularly at about 90 centres. All trials are held with a jury. The central criminal court in London is still popularly known as the Old Bailey.

3. *County courts* (300 in England and Wales) are conducted by a professional circuit judge assisted by a jury if either party wishes it. They cover almost all types of civil suits including complaints of race or sex discrimination.

4. *High Court of Justice* has original and appellate jurisdiction in all civil and some criminal cases. It has three subdivisions: the Family Division, the Chancery Division (for the administration of estates and the interpretation of wills) and the Queen's Bench for all cases not dealt with by the other two divisions.

5. *Court of Appeal* (Criminal and Civil Division) hears appeals from the High Court and the Crown Court.
   The Crown Court, the High Court and the Court of Appeal together form the Supreme Court of Judicature.

6. *House of Lords* is the ultimate civil court of appeal for cases which involve a point of law of general public importance. It is presided over by the Lord Chancellor and consists, when it sits as a court, of three to seven Lords of Appeal in Ordinary appointed as life peers, and such peers as hold, or have held, high judicial office.

7. *Judicial Committee of the Privy Council,* the last remnant of the jurisdiction of the 'King in Council' is now the final court of appeal from decisions of the courts of dependencies and those independent members of the Commonwealth that have not abolished it. It is presided over by the

Lord Chancellor and may include judges of the Commonwealth countries. There are a number of courts with special functions: *courts martial, juvenile courts* dealing with young people under 17 and *coroners' courts* investigating cases of violent and unnatural death.

Lately the law courts have come in for a good deal of criticism. Criminal justice has not been able to cope with the enormous increase in crime, especially among young people. Pre-trial inquiries are not conducted by judges as on the Continent. The police decide whether charges are to be brought in most criminal cases. The fact that their interrogations are not tape-recorded may encourage the guilty to disclaim confessions and say that they were extorted by police brutality. In 1986 a new service of solicitors was set up to decide whether a prosecution shall take place.

Civil justice is slow and costly. In cases of compensation for damage or injury by accident, for instance, delays of four to five years are commonplace, and lawyers' fees are high. Though the poor get free legal aid, this does not extend to most tribunals, whose decisions are often of great importance for people on welfare or workers who feel that their job rights are being impaired.

II. Courts in Scotland

Scotland has its own legal system, which has more affinity with the law systems of Continental countries, civil law being based on the principles of Roman rather than English Common Law.

1. *District courts,* staffed by justices of the peace, are the lowest criminal courts, which deal with minor offences under summary procedure.

2. *Sheriff courts,* which have also civil jurisdiction, try less serious crimes, in some cases with a jury.

3. *High Court of Justiciary* is the supreme criminal court for more serious cases, which are always tried with a jury. Its seat is in Edinburgh, but the judges go on circuit to preside at trials in other towns.

4. *Court of Session* is the supreme civil court with a division for appeals. There is no final appeal to the House of Lords.

THE LEGAL PROFESSION

1. *Solicitors* (in the U.S.A. the older term 'attorney' is still in use) often practise after only a practical training of three to five years in a lawyer's office, after an examination held by the Law Society (solicitors' organization). They prepare cases and generally act as private business advisers.

2. *Barristers* are counsel trained at the barristers' headquarters in London, the Inns of Court, which are self-governing societies. They may also receive some of their legal training at universities, the degrees

of which (LLD and Bachelor of Law) however are purely academic and do not qualify the holder to practise the law. Barristers are called to the 'bar' when they have passed the legal examinations conducted by the Council of Legal Education, and must be members of one of the Inns of Court, the Inner or Middle Temple (p. 129). Gray's Inn, Lincoln's Inn. Barristers conduct legal proceedings in higher courts and also advise on legal problems submitted through solicitors. Leading barristers are briefed to prosecute for the Crown as Queen's Counsel. In Scotland, barristers are called advocates.

3. *Judges* are highly respected. They are appointed by the Crown on the advice of the Prime Minister or the Lord Chancellor and can only be removed by action of Parliament. Their authority sanctioned by tradition is outwardly stressed by the wearing of wigs. Very strict rules against *contempt of court* have so far prevented occurrences as in some trials against terrorists on the Continent.

RELIGION

A. CHURCH OF ENGLAND (ANGLICAN CHURCH)

History

1. *A national Church* was founded in 1532 by Henry VIII, who separated the English Church from Rome and made himself 'Supreme Head of the Church of England', but retained Catholic doctrines.

2. *Protestant doctrines* were introduced under Edward VI by Archbishop Cranmer, who wrote the 39 Articles of Religion and compiled the *Book of Common Prayer*, henceforth the great inspiration of Anglicanism.

3. Re-establishment of the Anglican Church with Protestant doctrines was effected by Elizabeth I in 1559 after Mary Tudor had restored Catholicism.

4. *High Church ritualism* was introduced by the Stuarts, who inclined towards Catholicism. William Laud, Archbishop of Canterbury under Charles I, may be considered as the founder of the High Church. High Church forms of worship were disallowed under Cromwell, but reintroduced at the Restoration.

5. *Latitudinarianism,* the result of the Enlightenment in the 18th century, brought religious tolerance, but encouraged laxity among the clergy and prompted a reaction against High Church formalism among more serious believers.

6. *Evangelicals (Low Church)* sided with Dissenters in the demand for a more Christian social outlook and humanitarian activities. William Wilberforce and the Quakers fought for the abolition of slavery (effected in 1833), Lord Shaftesbury for factory legislation.

RELIGION IN BRITAIN

Denominations with Times of Foundation

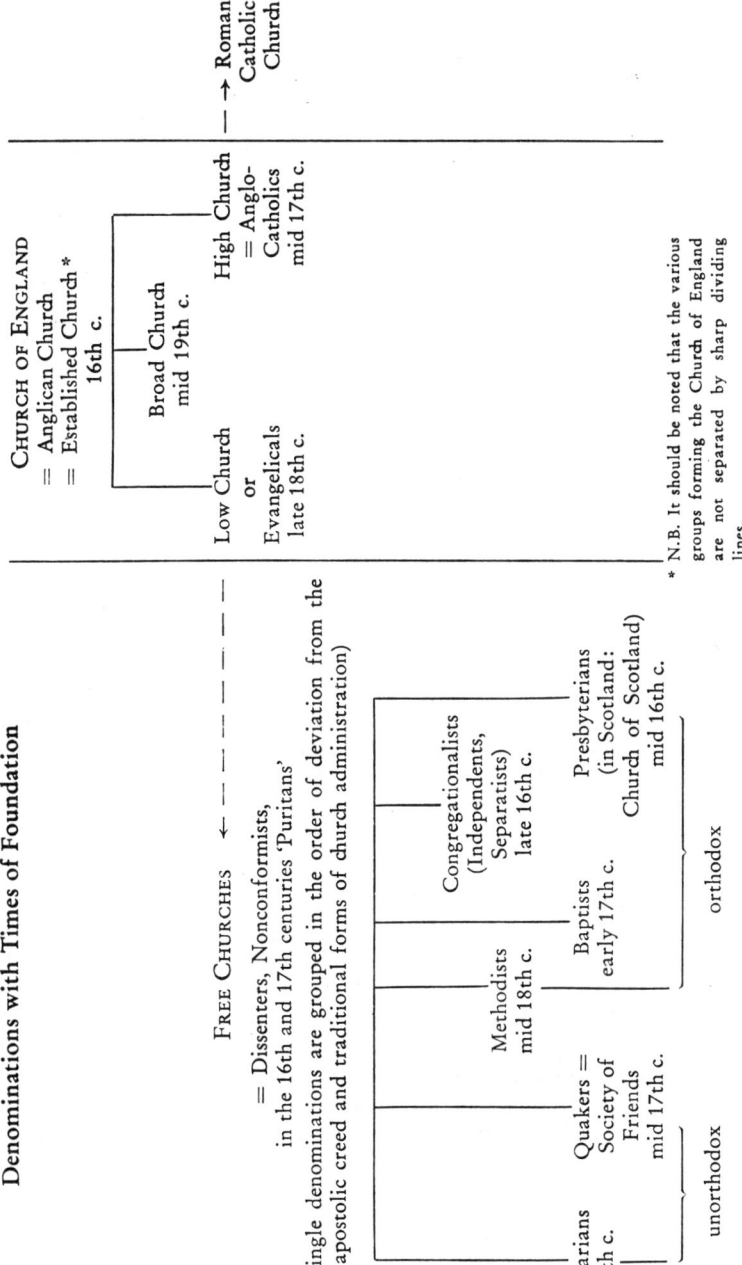

CHURCH OF ENGLAND
= Anglican Church
= Established Church *
16th c.

Broad Church
mid 19th c.

Low Church
or
Evangelicals
late 18th c.

High Church
= Anglo-
Catholics
mid 17th c.

⟶ Roman
Catholic
Church

FREE CHURCHES ⟵ — — — —
= Dissenters, Nonconformists,
in the 16th and 17th centuries 'Puritans'

(The single denominations are grouped in the order of deviation from the
apostolic creed and traditional forms of church administration)

Unitarians
17th c.

Quakers =
Society of
Friends
mid 17th c.

Methodists
mid 18th c.

Baptists
early 17th c.

Congregationalists
(Independents,
Separatists)
late 16th c.

Presbyterians
(in Scotland:
Church of Scotland)
mid 16th c.

unorthodox

orthodox

* N.B. It should be noted that the various
groups forming the Church of England
are not separated by sharp dividing
lines.

189

7. *Catholic Revival (Oxford Movement):* The Oxford theologians H. Newman, Dr. Pusey, John Keble, who wrote *Tracts for the Times* (1832) and were therefore also called Tractarians, endeavoured to restore the beauty of ancient ritual as against the sober outlook of Evangelicals. High mass was considered an essential part of religious services, religious orders were re-established. The group was called Anglo-Catholic, though it has never recognized the supremacy of the Pope. However, the Anglo-Catholics' aim to assert the independence of the Church from the State led to the revival in England of the Roman Church itself (assisted by Newman's conversion to Roman Catholicism).

8. *Broad Church* group, whose founders Frederick D. Maurice, James Martineau and F. W. Robertson were influenced by 19th century German Bible criticism, sponsored theological liberalism in the effort to make the way into the Church as broad as possible. This group, which included poets like Tennyson, and Matthew Arnold, remained, however, small.

9. *Christian Socialism,* led by Charles Kingsley and Frederick D. Maurice, saw Christianity as a source of social reform.

10. Disestablishment of the Irish and Welsh Anglican Churches was effected in 1869 and 1919 resp.

11. *Church Assembly* was established in 1919 to give the Church greater independence from Parliament through a more effective central representation.

11. *British Council of Churches* consisting of representatives of almost all British Churches except Roman Catholics was founded in 1942 to facilitate cooperation with all other Churches in Britain.

12. *World Council of Churches* including the Anglican Church was established in 1948 in Amsterdam to work for closer cooperation between Christian Churches. It links together some 300 churches in over 117 countries. The Roman Catholic-Church did not then join this ecumenical movement.

Church of England Today

1. ADMINISTRATION:

a) *Episcopacy* gave rise to the name 'Episcopal' for Anglican churches in Scotland and in America. The Church of England has two archbishops ruling the two provinces of Canterbury and York and 43 diocesan bishops. The Archbishop of Canterbury holds the title Primate of All England. The parish clergy consists of rectors and vicars (incumbents of livings), and curates (assistant priests). In 1970 the General Synod took over the powers of the Church Assembly and the Convocations of the two archdioceses, though the Convocations continue to meet (less often than before). The General Synod is the central governing body dealing with spiritual questions as well as administrative matters, such as the training of clergy, schools and church work at home and overseas. Since 1867, bishops of the Anglican Churches all over the world have

met at the Lambeth Conference at Lambeth Palace (the London residence of the Archbishop of Canterbury), which enjoys great prestige.
b) *Established Church* (disestablished in Ireland and Wales): The Church of England is a State church. The Monarch is head of the Church, all clergymen taking the oath of allegiance to the Crown. He holds the title 'Defender of the Faith' (F. D. is imprinted on British coins). Appointments to bishoprics and Crown livings are made by the Sovereign on the advice of the Prime Minister, though, in some places, the lord of the manor has still the hereditary right to nominate the incumbent (patronage). The Church is also linked to the State through the House of Lords, in which the two archbishops and 24 senior diocesan bishops have seats. Church legislation, in the hands of the General Synod, requires the consent of Parliament and the Crown. Though considerable endowments in land and investments make the Church financially indepedent of the State, these resources are controlled by Church Commissioners, who include laymen. In 1992 The General Synod decided that women should be allowed to be ordained as priests.
c) *Membership* figures can only be given approximately, as no inquiries about religious beliefs are made in population censuses. Membership of the Church of England is about 27 million (about ²/₃ of the English population). Membership of the Anglican Communion, which includes 25 independent Churches in the United Kingdom and overseas (the U.S.A. and territories formerly ruled by Britain in Africa and India), is 70 million, the majority being black.

2. RITUAL: Services are held according to the ancient liturgical form of worship embodied in the *Book of Common Prayer*. High churches lay emphasis on the beauty of worship with vestments, incense and High Mass. Low churches stress Bible reading and preaching. '*The Alternative Service Book*' (1980) in modern English has partly replaced the Common Prayer Book.

3. CHARACTER OF THE ANGLICAN CHURCH: The Church of England prides itself on having achieved a c o m p r o m i s e between Catholic and Protestant elements, most evident in the co-existence of the High Church (Anglo-Catholic) and Low Church (Evangelical) groups. This compromise may be seen in many respects: The Anglican Church has retained the Catholic episcopate and ritual, but has Protestant doctrines. It claims to be both 'Catholic' and 'reformed'. It has separated from the Roman Church, repudiating the supremacy of the Pope, yet retains the principle of Apostolic Succession, believing that English bishops have been consecrated in direct, unbroken succession since primitive Christianity. The Church of England is ruled by ordained priests, not laymen, but Parliament has control of Church legislation. On the other hand, the Church has a certain amount of influence on government through the bishops in the House of Lords. The Anglican Church has retained the Catholic liturgy but has,

191

from the Reformation, held its services in the English language. It has abolished celibacy of the clergy, yet has monasteries. The *Articles of Faith* do not acknowledge marriage as a sacrament, yet the Church does not remarry divorced persons (cf. abdication of Edward VIII because of his marriage to a divorcée). The absence of rigid tenets permits religious instruction on a general Christian non-denominational basis in schools of the public system. The Church allows its members, including the clergy, great freedom, not only of religious practice but also of opinion. In 1963 Dr. John A. T. Robinson, Bishop of Woolwich, started what he called 'a reluctant revolution' in his widely read book *Honest to God,* which saw nine editions within one year. Robinson considers 'a radical questioning of the established religious frame' to be 'a genuine defence of faith'. Other Anglican theologians have expressed similar views.

B. THE FREE (NONCONFORMIST) CHURCHES

I. General History

1. *Puritan conventicles* striving to represent the pure form of primitive Christianity formed under Elizabeth I. In Scotland John Knox established the Presbyterian Church in 1559 as the national church in Scotland, while in England the Act of Uniformity, 1559, made churches other than the Anglican Church illegal.

2. Persecution under the Stuart kings James I and Charles I caused emigration to America and the establishing of British colonies in New England. Moreover it strengthened Puritan opposition in England, where Puritanism grew particularly strong among the gentry.

3. *Puritan Revolution* under the control of Independents led to the establishment of a Puritan Commonwealth under Cromwell and to the introduction of an austere Puritan culture. Comparative tolerance in matters of religious belief, however, favoured the foundation of new religious societies, Unitarians and Quakers (Society of Friends).

4. *Discrimination against Puritans* lasting 170 years was established during the Restoration through exclusion laws. The Conventicle Act, 1664, forbade Puritan services, the Corporation Acts barred Puritans from town governments, the Test Act from general public service. Puritans were since that time called Dissenters or Nonconformists.

5. *Methodist Revival:* The Toleration Act, 1689, granting freedom of worship by repealing the Conventicle Act, gave a new impetus to Dissent. Methodism founded in 1739 soon became the most powerful dissenting group in England, Wales and America.

6. Education was strongly influenced by Dissenting groups, who established the first voluntary denominational schools. The Quakers exercised an influence on legislation through their campaigns against slavery and for prison reform.

7. *Equal status* in politics was attained through the abolition of the Test and Corporation Acts in 1828, in education through the admission of Nonconformists to Oxford and Cambridge in 1871.

II. **Free Churches** (formerly 'Dissenters', 'Nonconformists') are mostly Calvinistic in faith, differing largely in their forms of church government. Their membership has fallen but appears now to have stabilized.

1. *Presbyterians* are a group ruled by presbyters (elected church elders and ministers), the two offices having equal status. The minister conducts services and dispenses sacraments, the church elders (laymen) assist in matters of administration.
Presbyterian communities tend to be more firmly organized, less individualistic than Congregational and Baptist groups. The biggest Presbyterian community is the Church of Scotland (p. 195). The Presbyterian Church in Northern Ireland (originally founded by the Presbyterian settlers in the Ulster Plantation) has 125,000 members, that of Wales 94,000. For England see below.

2. *Congregationalists* (the oldest dissenting community in Britain) believe in the autonomy of the single congregation, whose head is Christ. They were also called Independents because the doctrine of the priesthood of all believers made them independent of outward authority, even of ministers (the Pilgrim Fathers had no minister for nine years). They were called Separatists because they believed that Christians must be prepared to separate from the world, and, if necessary, even from the Church, which has no control of the individual conscience. There is consequently great individualism also with regard to the interpretation of the Bible. Services are very simple, without altar, prayer book or vestments.
The original founder was R o b e r t B r o w n e, who emigrated with his sect to Holland in 1582 after having been imprisoned several times. He returned to England, however, and conformed. Members of his sect, which was re-established by the English emigrant, John Robinson, migrated to America. These 'Pilgrim Fathers' established the first English colony in New England, where the Congregationalists remained the chief Puritan denomination. The English Congregationalists in Holland returned during the Puritan Revolution and became the dominant power in Cromwell's Commonwealth.
In 1972 the Congregationalist Church in England and Wales united with the Presbyterian Church of England to form the United Reformed Church, the first union between two different denominations since the Reformation. Its membership is some 148,000.

3. *Baptists* believe in adult baptism by immersion as essential for membership of the community of Christ. The English Baptists were

founded in 1609 by two members of the English Separatists in Holland, John S m y t h and Thomas H e l w y s, who had adopted Baptist beliefs under the influence of Mennonites. They returned to England under Helwys and established the first Baptist Church in England in 1612. Like the Congregationalists from which they stem, Baptists have a loose organization. They are important in the mission field. The greatest Baptist writer was John B u n y a n, who wrote *Pilgrim's Progress* (1684), the most powerful preacher C. H. S p u r g e o n (1832–92). The Baptist churches have about 170,000 members.

4. *Quakers* (Society of Friends) founded by G e o r g e F o x (1624–90) are a humbly individualistic and therefore small group. Believing in individual inspiration by God, they base religion on personal experience rather than on a fixed creed or the authority of ordained ministers. They hold no services, but sit in silent meditation and prayer, anybody who feels inspired by the Holy Ghost being encouraged to address the meeting. Sacraments are not observed. Their belief in the 'Inner Light' common to all people, Christian and heathen alike, has made the Quakers extremely tolerant of religion and race. In America, Pennsylvania, founded by the Quaker William Penn, was the only colony which entertained friendly relations with the Indians. Quakers were the first to give up slave-holding, respecting blacks as their fellow-men. Their doctrinal liberty, which made them pioneers of non-denominational religious education, is offset by a very strict attitude in private and business life. They shun amusements and will not take the oath in law courts or to obtain an office, in order not to set two standards of truth. In the 18th century the Quakers started agitation for the a b o l i t i o n o f s l a v e r y, in the 19th century Elizabeth Fry was the first to call for prison reform. Since Quakers are strict pacifists, not even allowed to be engaged in the manufacture of weapons, they were the first c o n s c i e n t i o u s o b j e c t o r s in World War I when general conscription was first introduced in English history. After the world wars they instituted organizations in a i d o f w a r - s h a t t e r e d c o u n t r i e s. Throughout their history their influence on public life has been considerable in comparison to their small number (18,550).

5. *Unitarians,* founded in the 17th century, are anti-Trinitarian, denying the deity of Christ. They are a small but important group mainly of intellectuals, who, on account of their sceptical attitude towards the authority of Scripture, have played a more important part in philosophy than theology (e.g. Transcendentalism in America).

6. *Methodists* were so called because their founder J o h n W e s l e y
(1703–91) and his college friends at Oxford engaged in a methodical
form of Christianity. Under the influence of German pietism, Wesley
founded strictly organized religious communities, which soon grew
into a great religious movement. Though Wesley himself was a loyal
Anglican priest, he was driven out of the Church because of his
unconventional practices necessitated by m a s s - o r g a n i z a t i o n.
He organized mass meetings in the open air, employed l a y
p r e a c h e r s, and ordained ministers (the function of bishops).
The co-founder and powerful preacher George Whitefield later broke
with Wesley because of the doctrine of predestination, which Wesley
rejected.
Methodists made an important contribution to the general revival
of religious fervour by their immense emotional rather than logical
appeal (stress on personal salvation through sudden conversion as a
gift of grace rather than conformism with Church teaching). Being
the first modern movement to recognize that the missionary principle
hitherto pursued only in non-Christian countries should also be
applied to the needs of Christian society (Innere Mission), Methodism
often won for Christianity the new industrial proletariat, which on the
Continent fell a victim to class hatred. Today the Methodist Church, with
430,000 adult members, is the largest of the Free Churches. Its
administration through a centralized system of meetings resembles the
Presbyterian organization. The Methodists favour reunion with the
Church of England, which, however, has voted against it.

7. *Salvation Army* was foundet in 1878 by William B o o t h, an
ex-Methodist, to intensify evangelical work among the very poorest
people, esp. by fighting against drunkenness. Holding their religious
gatherings in streets an using popular slogans and tunes, they win the
masses rather than the intellectual classes. Their organization as an
'army' stresses the idea of 'soldiers of Christ'. Today it helps victims
of drug addiction, prostitution and Aids. The Church has spread to
86 countries with a total membership of c. 2 million.

8. *Christian Science* is a religion which originated in the U.S.A. The
founder, Mary B a k e r E d d y, defined it as 'the scientific system of
divine healing', which is to prove that sickness and sin are unreal
'because they are not of God'. The Christian Scientists have some 262
churches and societies in Britain. The American paper *The Christian
Science Monitor* has a noted international weekly edition.

III. General Characteristics

1. *Calvinistic doctrines* are held by most groups, though some reject

predestination, e.g. Wesleyan Methodists (who stem from Anglicanism) and 'General Baptists', who believe in general redemption (in contrast to 'Particular Baptists').

2. *Practical Christianity* emphasized by Dissent has greatly influenced education and prompted social reform.

3. *Missionary zeal* appears in active foreign missions (especially of the Baptists) and in the endeavour of the Methodists and Salvation Army to convert the masses to Christianity.

4. *Internal democracy* gives the laity an important share in church administration. Clergy are chosen by laymen. In contrast to the Church of England, the Free Churches have recruited their members chiefly from the urban middle class, especially the lower middle classes. Puritan political philosophy, which favoured democratic institutions, has greatly influenced political life, particularly in America.

5. *Religious individualism* has led to division and a narrow outlook on life. On the other hand, the belief in the inwardness of true religion the 'searching of the soul' cultivated by many groups has created an introspective frame of mind. This psychological interest has had some influence on English philosophy (Locke, Hume, pp. 269, 573) and literature, particularly on the novel from Richardson onwards.

6. *Puritan austerity* and self-discipline (cf. the English Sunday) exercised an important positive influence on the British character. On the other hand, the strict control of private life favoured self-righteousness and hypocrisy, the classical expression of this being Nathaniel Hawthorne's novel *The Scarlet Letter* about Puritan life in New England.
In the Victorian Age, English society was strongly influenced by the moral principles of these evangelical groups – their work ethic, their struggle against brutality, duelling and cruel sports. Evangelicalism imposed on society, even on people indifferent to its religious motivation, its code of Sunday observance, philanthropy, discipline at home and honesty in business affairs. The spectacular change of moral attitudes in our century is often attributed to the extreme cult of virtue in the Victorian Age, its prudery and social discrimination of persons not conforming with its strict morality.

7. *Churches* (often called 'chapels') are very simple, usually without altar, images and ornaments, and therefore sober and unattractive.

C. **The Established Church of Scotland,** which was founded by Britain's greatest reformer, John K n o x, is Presbyterian. Its membership is estimated at 1 million. Though it is based on the d e m o c r a t i c principle that ministers and elders have equal status, it has a hierarchical centralized government represented by a system of elected church assemblies ranging from the local *Kirk Session* through the *Presbytery* and the *Synod* to the *General Assembly*. The Presbytery, consisting of all the ministers in a larger district and one elder from each parish, forms a court of appeal from the Kirk Session. A similar relation exists between the higher courts. The Synod meets twice a year. The General Assembly, which meets once a year and is presided over by an elected Moderator, is the highest church authority and conducts missionary enterprises. The Sovereign is represented at the General Assembly by the Lord High Commissioner.

The Church of Scotland enjoys full self-government in matters of doctrine and administration. Its decisions are not subject to modification by Parliament. This independence was upheld in a bitter struggle against the Stuarts' attempts to establish royal control by introducing episcopacy. It was acknowledged in the Act of Union, 1707, and re-stated in the Church of Scotland Act, 1921. Though ceremonious forms of worship are rejected, emphasis is laid on dignified and beautiful services. Since the days of John Knox, who, in his *First Book of Discipline* (1560), demanded that every parish should maintain a school by local taxation, the church has played its part in developing an educational system on democratic lines, which has become one of the most efficient in Europe and has established the high academic standard of intellectual life in Scotland.

A number of Presbyterian groups have separated from the Established Church of Scotland, e.g. the Free Church of Scotland founded by Thomas Chalmers in 1843 and the Free Presbyterian Church of Scotland. Among the higher classes there is a certain tendency to join the Episcopal (Anglican) Church of Scotland, which has seven bishops and some 94,000 members.

D. Roman Catholic Church

After England's separation from Rome, Roman Catholicism remained suppressed until 1829 when, one year after Dissent, Roman Catholics gained political rights through the Catholic Emancipation Act. The modern Roman Catholic hierarchy was established in England in 1850 under the primacy of the Archbishop of Westminster who officiates in Westminster Cathedral in London. Membership is c. 5 million in the United Kingdom (including children). Roman Catholicism in England, was strengthened by immigrants from Ireland and a trend towards conversion after the wars. It is supported by a separate system of education in schools largely maintained by the Roman Catholic orders. A subcutaneous fear of Catholics still persists in Britain.

Recent Developments

While traditional religious belief and practice have declined, there has been an upsurge of cults like *Jehovah's Witnesses, Seventh-Day Adventists* and *Pentecostals.* The many Indians and Pakistanis in the country have spread interest in Indian cults and Islam. Moslems have built mosques. West Indian sects, which like singing and preaching with an enthusiastic response from the congregation, also attract white people. Occultism and black magic have adherents.

Since the 70s youth sects exploiting their members' devotion by subjecting them to complete mind control have caused growing concern. Cults like the Krishna movement and the Korean Moon's Unification Church usually compel their adherents to give up their career and, by giving the sect all their property and day-long begging, to help their leaders become millionaires. When the Moonies in Britain sued the Daily Mail for accusing them of brain-washing and breaking up families, they lost their case and had to pay close to £400,000 in legal costs. Scientology, which styles itself 'Church' as well as 'Modern Science of Mental Health', is a bizarre system of thought tracing the individual's mental life back billions of years. It excels in selling expensive courses.

EDUCATION

English education has to a large extent been the result of voluntary (chiefly religious) effort, and is thus characterized by a certain lack of unity and central control, which was not established until 1870. It still provides t w o s e p a r a t e s y s t e m s o f e d u c a t i o n : publicly maintained or aided schools attended by 94 per cent of the school-children, and independent boarding-schools for the wealthier classes.

HISTORICAL SURVEY

    I. **Universities.** Oxford and Cambridge were founded in c. 1170 and 1210 respectively, the four old Scottish universities St. Andrews in 1411, Glasgow in 1451, Aberdeen in 1494, and Edinburgh in 1583. Scholars entering at 14 studied the seven Liberal Arts, first the 'trivium' of verbal arts (grammar, dialectic, rhetoric), then the 'quadrivium' consisting of music, arithmetic, geometry and astronomy. They proceeded to the degree of Bachelor of Arts after four years, to the Master of Arts after six years, and sometimes, after additional years of professional studies, to a doctorate: D.D. (Doctor of Divinity), M.D. (Medicine) and LL.D. (Laws). Universities were organized loosely in colleges (separate places of residence). The c o l l e g e s y s t e m , the study of humanities (' A r t s ') and the degree system are still characteristic of Oxford and Cambridge. Since the Tudors, when the two universities became schools for training the new gentry for government service, Oxford and Cambridge have been schools mainly for the aristocracy. In 1826 the founding of

University College, London, which became the nucleus of L o n d o n U n i v e r s i t y first gave the dissenting middle classes the chance to acquire a university degree. In 1871 Oxford and Cambridge were liberalized through the abolition of religious tests, and recently by an extensive scholarship system.

M o d e r n u n i v e r s i t i e s were established in the 19th and 20th centuries to meet the demand for scientific and technical education created by the Industrial Revolution and the admission of new classes to higher education. The 'Red-brick' universities of the 19th and early 20th centuries usually developed from local colleges preparing their students for external degrees of London University, till royal charters gave them university status.

Since World War II 22 new universities have been established, ten of which were completely new foundations (Keele, Sussex, York, East Anglia. Essex, Lancaster, Kent, Warwick, Stirling, Ulster). Since 1963 another twelve universities have been created from existing institutions of higher education, mostly from former Colleges of Advanced Technology (CATs). The target of the Robbins Report of 1963, which proposed a doubling of the student population, has already been almost achieved.

II. **Grammar Schools** to prepare pupils for universities were founded as charities by royalty, nobility, merchant guilds, wealthy individuals and from Church endowments (e.g. W i n c h e s t e r C o l l e g e, 1382, by the Bishop of Winchester, E t o n C o l l e g e, 1440, by King Henry VI). Many of these schools later became preserves of the wealthier classes, nine of them gained national reputation. The educational system of these Public Schools was created by Dr. Thomas Arnold, headmaster of Rugby (and father of the poet Matthew Arnold), who wanted to educate the future leaders of England to become what he called Christian gentlemen. Since 1902, state-aided schools, open to all social classes, have been founded by local authorities. The sixties saw the development of comprehensive schools admitting children between 11 and 18 regardless of their abilities.

III. **Elementary Education.** While Scotland, since 1696, has had a system of parish schools, based on the principle, already expressed in John Knox's *First Book of Discipline* (1560), that every parish should maintain a school by local taxation, elementary education in England grew up haphazardly and, until 1870, entirely through voluntary effort.

1. *Voluntary Schools* on a denominational basis (provided and maintained by voluntary subscriptions) were established chiefly in the 18th century, first by religious societies with a Nonconformist bias: C h a r i t y S c h o o l s for Dissenters by the Society for Promoting Christian Knowledge, S u n d a y S c h o o l s, first founded by Robert Raikes, by the Sunday School Union, Sunday being the only day children were not employed in factories or mines. The 19th century saw the foundation of 'National Schools' by the Anglican Society for Educating the Poor in the Principles of the Established Church, and of 'British Schools' by the non-denominational British and School Society, and further schools by the Nonconformist British and Foreign Schools Society. These schools based teaching on the monitorial system of mass

199

instruction developed by the Anglican educationist Andrew Bell and the Quaker Joseph Lancaster, by which older pupils taught smaller children under the direction of an adult teacher. The system being inexpensive, was soon introduced in other countries and thus constituted the first large-scale attempt at promoting popular education. After 1833 all these schools received government grants-in-aid, which, from 1862 to 1895, were made dependent on teaching results. Introduced to increase efficiency, this principle of payment by results virtually restricted the curriculum to the 'three R's' (reading, writing, arithmetic).

2. *Public Elementary Schools* on a non-denominational basis were first founded under the *Education Act* of 1870 by locally elected school boards and made compulsory in 1876. As these 'B o a r d   S c h o o l s' were established only where Church schools did not exist, they initiated the 'dual control' system which still exists. The *Fisher Act*, 1918, allowed for the creation of nursery schools for the age-group 2 to 5, and part-time continuation schools (Berufsschulen) for the age-group 14 to 18. The *Education Act* of 1944 abolished the old type of elementary school by applying the term 'secondary school' (formerly used only for higher education) also to the post-primary level of compulsory education (ages 11 to 14), thus creating the secondary modern school. In 1947 the school-leaving age was raised to 15, in 1972 to 16. In Scotland the *Act for the Settling of Schools* ordered as early as 1696 that every parish must have a school and schoolmaster.

IV. **Vocational Education.** T e c h n i c a l   s c h o o l s   for vocational training (Fachschulen) were established under the *Technical Education Act*, 1889, by county and borough councils under the auspices of the Science and Art Department, but their growth was stunted when the *Education Act* of 1902 made government grants dependent on the provision of 'general education'. From 1919 on, technical colleges, part-time day courses and evening classes were developed on a larger scale.

PRESENT SCHOOL SYSTEM

The school system in England and Wales is still largely decentralized though Labour governments have increased centralized control with a view to creating a more egalitarian society. Although state schools are controlled by the local education authorities, headmasters are given wide discretion in determining their curriculum and textbooks. Her Majesty's Inspectors of Schools have the task of advising teachers and providing the Minister with information.

Full-time education is compulsory from the age of 5 to 16. Lessons extend into the afternoon, midday meals being provided at subsidized rates by the School Meals Service. Schools are closed on Saturdays. A small proportion of children between 2 and 5 attend nursery schools or nursery classes in primary schools.

Education in Great Britain

Ages	Scotland		Public Education	Private Education (for the wealthier classes)	Ages
				England	
5	Primary Department		Infant School	Prepreparatory School	5
6			Primary* School	Private Infant School	6
7			Junior School		7
8				Preparatory School (often with a day school for the 5—8 year-olds)	8
9					9
10					10
11					11
12	Junior Second. School	Secondary Modern School	Compreh. School (incl. all types of sec. educ.) / Gram-mar School		12
13	Senior Secondary School			Common Entrance Exam	13
14				Public School	14
15					15
16	Scot. Cert. of Educ. 'O' Grade		Gen. Cert. of Sec. Educ.		16
17		Part-time Release	Sixth Class College		17
18	Scot. Cert. of Educ. Higher Grade		Gen. Cert. of Educ., 'A' Level	Gen. Cert. of Ed. 'A' Level	18
19	University		University Undergraduate Level	University (preferably Oxford or Cambridge)	19
20					20
21	Bachelor		Bachelor	Bachelor	21
22	Master		(Post)graduate Level		22
23	Master (Honours)		Master and Doctorate	Master	23

* Sometimes organized on the lower level as 'first schools' followed by 'middle schools'.

Note that in England the education of the wealthier classes may thus be entirely separate from that of the general public.

I. **Public education** consists of county schools maintained by local education authorities, and denominational voluntary schools (chiefly Church of England and Roman Catholic), which are mostly publicly maintained. Those which are only aided are more independent. About one third of maintained schools in England and Wales are voluntary schools. Maintained schools, which comprise 94 per cent of the school population, do not charge fees.
Public education is organized in three progressive stages.

1. PRIMARY EDUCATION (age group 5 to 11) consists of *infant schools* (5 to 7) and *junior schools* (7 to 11). In Scotland primary schooling in undivided schools continues until the age of 11 or 12. Many local authorities in England have established *first schools* for children from 5 to 8 or 9 followed by *middle schools,* whose pupils move on to comprehensives at 13.

2. SECONDARY EDUCATION: The general system of allocating children to the school best suited to their abilities through an examination at the age of eleven or more, which is known as the eleven-plus exam, has, since the sixties, come in for a great deal of criticism on the ground that it passes a final judgement on a child's later career at too early an age and that children whose parents can afford high fees may be sent to private schools. With the Labour Government's policy to hasten the reorganization of the secondary school system along comprehensive lines, the division into grammar and secondary modern schools has largely disappeared and with it the eleven-plus. Today about 80% of pupils of secondary-school age go to comprehensives. The Tory government wants to give parents full choice of schools for their children.

Comprehensive schools take all pupils over 11 without reference to ability. Catering for a wide range of interests they are usually big. The pupils alre often streamed into different classes according to ability. Comprehensive schools are organized in a number of ways, either for the age-group 11 to 18 (leading to university), or for pupils between 11 and 16, with a sixth-form college for pupils over 16.

Comprehensives are favoured by Labour governments on the ground that they eliminate selection and separation. The *Education Act* 1976, which required local authorities to establish a comprehensive school system, was reversed by the Conservative government in 1979 (as happened in 1970 after similar Labour legislation).

Children not attending comprehensives are allocated to the traditional schools by a variety of methods. Those *secondary modern schools* remaining (11 to 16) provide a general education with a practical bias for less gifted children.

Grammar schools (11 to 18) provide a mainly academic education for pupils who want to go on to the university. Conservatives deplore their widespread phasing out to the advantage of comprehensives and to the disadvantage of bright children, for they maintain their standards are higher. On the other hand, comprehensives complain that grammar schools 'weed out' their best pupils.

Secondary technical schools (11 to 16) are few in number. They, too, offer a general education but stress subjects related to commerce and industry. In contrast to Scotland there is no national school-leaving examination in England and Wales, but pupils of secondary schools can take part in examinations which attest their attainments or qualify them for further education.

A new system of examining pupils at 16 has been introduced. The new General Certificate of Secondary Education (GCSE) for all 16 year olds makes allowance for a wide range of abilities. At 18 pupils take the General Certificate of Education (GCE) at Advanced (A) level. Most study 2–3 subjects for A levels, which is necessary for University entrance. If pupils wish to study more than 2–3 subjects in the 6th form, they can take a combination of A and AS level (Advanced Supplementary level, worth half an A level).

3. Post-school education

a) Part-time vocational training for young people of 16 or more who have entered employment is provided by part-time release from work one day a week *(Day Release)* or in periods of several consecutive weeks *(Block Release)*. This takes place at Colleges of Further Education and Technical Colleges.

b) Full-time professional education is provided in universities, polytechnics and colleges of higher education (e.g. commercial colleges). In liberal arts colleges – the former colleges of education for teacher training – the existing courses may be of four years' duration with a view to making teaching a fully graduate profession. Non-obligatory vocational training (chiefly part-time in evening courses) can be obtained by young employees and workers in technical, commercial and art colleges after entering employment and is concurrent with it. The most popular advanced full-time courses in recent years have been the 's a n d w i c h   c o u r s e s'. They consist of short periods of full-time study at a technical college alternating with practical experience in industry, and extend over three to five years. Many courses in these colleges lead to an external degree of London University or some technical diploma.

c) Non-vocational education in a d u l t e v e n i n g c o u r s e s is provided by local education authorities, the Extramural Departments of the universities with a full-time staff for this purpose, by voluntary organizations like the Workers' Educational Association, and statutory bodies. The courses are held in community or adult education centres.

II. **Private Education** is provided in independent schools maintained by school fees and, in some cases, endowments. The proportion of children in independent schools is much higher in England than in Scotland.

1. *Private infant (prepreparatory) schools* exist for children from 5 to 7 (formerly 'dame schools maintained by some lady of the district).

2. **Preparatory schools** (i.e. preparatory to Public Schools) offer private education for boys and girls from the age of 5 to 13. Many 'prep' schools offer boarding places from the age of 8 upwards. At the age of 13 pupils take the Common Entrance Exam to try to gain a place at Public School.

3. **Public Schools** provide education for some 5% of the population, predominantly boys. Most are boarding schools, although nearly all accept 'day pupils' in increasing numbers. There has also been a trend towards co-education. Most 'boys' Public Schools now admit girls in the sixth form and some, such as Rugby School, are completely co-educational.

Public Schools still use the prefect system giving older pupils a share in administration and the supervision of younger boys. Public Schools lay special emphasis on sports as an instrument of character training (cf. the slogan 'that's not cricket' to emphasize unfairness).

Public Schools charge high fees for a boarding place and so tend to be attended by the wealthier classes. However, they have tried to change their image of being anachronistic bastions of privilege and offer scholarships for gifted pupils from less-well-off families.

The best-known schools are E t o n (which has supplied sixteen prime ministers!), H a r r o w, R u g b y, Winchester and Charterhouse. The Public Schools' aristocratic reputation, which is today repudiated by the younger generation, stems from the school system of Dr. Arnold (p. 198), whose ideal was to look first for religious and moral principles, secondly gentlemanly conduct, thirdly intellectual ability, principles which have thus determined the education of the upper classes and, through their leadership in public life, permeated the nation at large. It testifies to the unique power of this ideal that the qualities traditionally held to be characteristic of the English gentleman: moral restraint, fear of sentiment, civil behaviour, dislike of exaggeration (the famous English 'understatement'), and fair play have set the standard of behaviour even for the lower classes. The worst accusation which can be levelled at a person is that he is not a gentlemen.

III. **Universities** are independent and self-governing bodies, although they receive about 80 per cent of their income from public grants. 90 per cent of their students are aided from public or private funds. In 1992 many polytechnics, which train the country's technologists and managers, were allowed to assume university status; the number of universities has therefore almost doubled. Although the former polytechnics offer also liberal arts courses, the Tory governments show little interest in financing them through university grants.

The British student's studies are still divided into an u n d e r - g r a d u a t e c o u r s e of 3–4 years (medicine 5–6) completed by the *Bachelor of Arts* (in Scotland *Master of Arts*), and p o s t g r a d u a t e studies leading to the degree of *Master of Arts* or the higher research degree of a doctorate, including the *Doctor of Philosophy (Ph.D.)* since World War I. About 90 per cent of the students leave the university after the first degree, which may be taken in a great variety of subjects: on the Arts side e.g. in history, languages, economics, law, on the Science side in natural sciences, engineering, medicine. Many universities have now introduced special degrees of *Bachelor of Science, Law, Medicine*. The *B.A.* may be taken as an ordinary Pass Degree (more general), or Honours Degree (more specialized and exacting) which is taken by the majority of students. University degrees, however, are not usually considered professional qualifications, which are acquired later: Legal and medical degrees are obtained in the I n n s o f C o u r t in London and in the M e d i c a l S c h o o l s of the various universities.

1. OLDER UNIVERSITIES, O x f o r d and C a m b r i d g e , are still a federal group of separate colleges, i.e. boarding establishments, which make possible individual supervision of each student's work by his tutor (this 'tutorial system' is now spreading to the new universities). While the separate colleges maintain their own bodies of instructors ('dons'), the university as a whole has its own professorial and lecturing staff. It examines, grants degrees and owns lecture halls, the main libraries and laboratories for the whole body of students.

Once the preserves of the aristocracy, Oxford and Cambridge are now accessible to all who can pass their entrance and scholarship examinations (though the *Robbins Report* showed that still one half of their students come from private schools). They still enjoy a unique social prestige, which attracts the ablest students and staff to the detriment of the modern universities. The M.A. in Oxford and Cambridge is granted without examination some time after the B.A., upon payment of a small fee. Oxford is famous for the study of the humanities, Cambridge for mathematics and science.

2. MODERN UNIVERSITIES (e.g. Birmingham, Liverpool, Leeds) are more like Continental universities. They are organized in faculties, not colleges, and are fully co-educational (whereas 'Oxbridge' colleges began to admit women not before the seventies). They are governed by a Senate composed of their professors and other teachers, and a council containing also persons drawn from outside (representing the interests supporting them).

London University with 32,000 students, is the largest and most comprehensive British university, consisting of some 30 separate federally organized colleges and institutes (e.g. Medical Schools) having a common centre in Senate House. London University occupies a unique position in that its external degrees can be obtained by candidates from all parts of the world who pass its examinations. Legal education and admission to the legal profession are controlled by the Inns of Court, which are not part of any university.

'Civic' or 'Red-brick' universities of the 19th century, which are usually situated in great industrial towns, have a technological bias. They are non-residential, though all have halls of residence. Recent universities founded since World War II are largely residential to ensure a better community life. In accordance with the modern trend towards decentralization, they tend to be in smaller towns away from the main industrial centres, e.g. Colchester (University of Essex), Canterbury (University of Kent), Brighton (University of Sussex).

Work of university standard is also undertaken by specialist institutes like the Royal College of Art, the Manchester Business School and the famous London School of Economics, which, in 1968, made headlines through its student demonstrations. In 1971 the non-residential *Open University* started its work of organizing part-time courses, for which students can register without formal academic qualifications. These courses make use of a number of teaching methods, including television and radio broadcasts, summer schools and correspondence courses together with a network of listening and viewing centres. Its degrees (obtained by more than 5,000 students a year) are equivalent to those of other universities.

3. SCOTTISH UNIVERSITIES are, like the modern English universities organized centrally. The four old universities, E d i n b u r g h (with

a famous medical faculty), G l a s g o w , S t. A n d r e w s and A b e r d e e n , which were founded in the 15th and 16th centuries, were renowned for their philosophical teaching. Since World War II four new universities have been established: Strathclyde (also in Glasgow), Stirling, Dundee and Heriot-Watt (Edinburgh).

THE BRITISH PRESS

HISTORY

1. STRUGGLE FOR FREEDOM OF THE PRESS (17th century): The *Star Chamber Decree,* 1588, which restricted the freedom of printing, impeded the development of the press during the time of absolutism. The first English papers *Weekly News from Italy, Germany, Hungarie, Spaine and France,* 1621, and *Mercurius Britannicus,* 1625, were confined to news from abroad. When the strict control of printers, which had ceased with the abolition of the Star Chamber, 1642, was reintroduced in 1643, Milton wrote his famous treatise *Areopagitica,* in which he demanded free speech as a right of citizenship and a benefit to the State: 'Give me liberty to know, to utter and to argue freely according to conscience above all liberties'. The gains of the Puritan Revolution were but temporary, for in the last years of Cromwell's rule censorship was reintroduced. Through the Glorious Revolution licensing and censorship were finally abolished in 1695 (a century before the Continent), while the *Libel Bill* of Charles Fox, 1792, provided for offences of libel through the press to be tried exclusively by jury.

2. LITERARY JOURNALISM:
The early 18th century is marked by the journalistic activity of great writers, who introduced the e s s a y p e r i o d i c a l. Defoe may be considered the founder of modern journalism. In his *Review,* 1704–13, he introduced comment and criticism. Swift, who wrote political articles for the Tory organ *Examiner,* introduced the leading article.
The didactic and moralizing trend of the Age of Enlightenment was reflected in the m o r a l w e e k l i e s , which attempted to influence taste and manners in general: Steele's *Tatler,* Addison's and Steele's *Spectator,* and Samuel Johnson's *Rambler* and *Idler* combined moral essays with portraits of invented characters. The first magazine or miscellany of a modern type was *The Gentleman's Magazine.*

3. THE STRUGGLE FOR DEMOCRATIZATION OF THE PRESS began in the second half of the 18th century, when John Wilkes' *North Briton* and the anonymous *Junius Letters* published in the *Public Advertiser* attacked influential politicians, even the King. Both voiced the general demand for the publication of Parliamentary debates. Though reporters were not admitted to Parliament, P a r l i a m e n t a r y r e p o r t s appeared as second-hand information as early as 1733 in the

Gentleman's Magazine. It was not before 1772 that the right to publish parliamentary reports was finally established. As a result of the French Revolution, which for some time crushed liberalism in English politics, even the press ceased to be an instrument primarily of liberal interests. The most influential papers *Morning Post* and *The Times,* which had been founded as liberal organs, became the standard conservative papers. Political suppression in its turn stimulated radicalism.

THE RADICAL PRESS exercised a strong revolutionary influence among the middle and lower classes. The *Six Acts,* which raised the Stamp Tax (first introduced in 1712) to four pence on each issue, had made newspaper reading a privilege of the educated classes. Despite prosecution and imprisonment, W i l l i a m   C o b b e t t sold his *Political Register,* which exposed oppression and corruption, illegally at a price which made it available to the lower classes. In 1855 the Stamp Tax was finally abolished as a consequence of agitation in Parliament by men like Bulwer Lytton and Cobden. After 1878 the government even subsidized *Hansard's Parliamentary Debates* or *Hansard,* which Cobbett had started under the name of *Parliamentary Debates* as a means of controlling governmental proceedings by public opinion, and which had passed into the ownership of their printer Hansard.

THE LIBERAL PRESS reached its height in the second half of the 19th century, when the principal liberal reforms were effected. The *Daily News,* founded in 1846 under the editorship of Charles Dickens, championed liberalism and gained a high reputation for its foreign correspondence. The liberalism of industrial Manchester found expression in the *Manchester Guardian.* The *Daily Telegraph,* founded in 1855, was published by J. R. Levy as the first penny paper, which soon secured it the highest circulation in the world. The chief organ of the liberal middle classes, it turned Unionist after Gladstone's Irish Home Rule Bill. It made a name by financing Stanley's expedition to Central Africa. When, during the Boer War, the *Daily News* was in financial difficulties, the Quaker philanthropist George Cadbury, who wanted to save it from falling into the hands of the pro-war party, came to its rescue. He made the historic paper, which had been founded to speed the repeal of the Corn Laws, the advocate of better conditions for working people and old age pensions. In 1928, the *Daily News* bought the liberal *Westminster Gazette,* which had been the chief organ of liberal thought in London, also famous for its literary criticism.

4. PERIODICAL JOURNALISM produced the first high-class critical journal in the *Edinburgh Review,* 1802–1929, which supported the Whigs. Carlyle, Hazlitt and Macaulay wrote for it. Its eminent Tory rival in England, the *Quarterly Review* (1809), which counted Walter Scott among its contributors, still survives. The third of the famous 19th century journals was *Blackwood's Magazine,* which still publishes stories and accounts of travels. The chief literary review was the *Athenaeum* (founded in 1828).

5. THE DEVELOPMENT OF CAPITALIST NEWSPAPER CONCERNS initiated the era of the p o p u l a r   p r e s s during the last hundred years. With the development of elementary education and the extension of the franchise, which aroused political interest among the masses, the reading public multiplied. The result was the

p e n n y and h a l f p e n n y p r e s s, which appealed to the more primitive instincts of readers who had not yet been reached by the printed word, through sensationalism, scandal-mongering, and the ample use of illustration. The actual creator of the new style was the brilliant journalist and organizer Alfred Harmsworth (who became L o r d N o r t h c l i f f e in 1905). His *Daily Mail* (founded in 1895), the first paper sold for a halfpenny, replaced the *Daily Telegraph* as the most widely read daily paper in the world. In 1904 Harmsworth started the *Overseas Daily Mail*, in 1905 the *Continental Daily Mail* published in Paris. These as well as Northcliffe's connection with important foreign papers, which were allowed to use the Northcliffe telegraphic news service, spread Northcliffe's political influence all over the world. Northcliffe bought the Sunday paper *Observer* and founded the *Daily Mirror*, a woman's paper, which soon became the first illustrated daily. He reached the workmen through the *Evening News* (bought in 1895), women through magazines of a family kind, and catered for the simplest tastes with the *Sunday Pictorial*. In 1905 Northcliffe united all his dailies and periodicals in the Associated Newspaper Ltd., which soon became a self-contained empire with its own telegraphic service, its brilliantly organized system of special night trains (now aeroplanes), and forests in Newfoundland supplying the concern with wood pulp. Northcliffe's political bias, propagated in all his papers, was conservative and imperialistic. In World War I Northcliffe formed public opinion throughout the world by his systematic anti-German propaganda, which helped to draw the U.S.A. into the war. After Northcliffe's death, the tradition he had created was continued by his brother, L o r d R o t h e r m e r e.

The chief liberal papers, the *Daily News* and the *Daily Chronicle,* remained independent, but were amalgamated in 1929 to become the *News Chronicle.* The *Daily Herald,* founded in 1912 to voice trade union policy, was taken over in 1923 by the Labour Party. In 1929 Odham's Press Ltd. bought 51 per cent of its shares and saved the only Socialist daily from financial ruin by a great capitalistic publicity campaign, which became a general feature of the time. Free insurance policies for subscriptions, competitions of all kinds, and gifts ranging from books to race horses were among the inducements offered in the competition for mass circulation, which could only be afforded by capitalist concerns. Thus, since Northcliffe's death in 1922, most of the important English newspapers came under the control of a few large concerns mostly owned by great newspaper magnates (Lord Rothermere, Lord Beaverbrook, the Berry brothers, Lord Camrose and Lord Kemsley, and the Quaker families Rowntree and Cadbury).

6. DEVELOPMENT OF ILLUSTRATED MAGAZINES began in the 19th century, when the *Illustrated London News* with 32 woodcuts made its first appearance in 1842. The *Graphic* (1869) and the *Sketch* (1892) followed suit. In the 20th century when process engraving was introduced, illustrated magazines reached a wider circulation and provided light entertainment on the principle which the great journalist George N e w n e s (initiator of inducements for subscriptions) had established: that magazines 'should give wholesome and harmless entertainment to crowds of hard-working people craving for a little fun and amusement'.

7. THE TWO WORLD WARS considerably impeded the development of the press. The *Defence of the Realm Act* in World War I subjected military information to

censorship. In World War II the press submitted to a system of voluntary censorship to avoid violation of *The Official Secrets Act,* but comment and criticism were not restricted. The Communist *Daily Worker* (founded in 1932) was suppressed for opposing the war effort, but reappeared when Russia became an ally.

Since 1951 the increase of the price of newsprint has meant the end of the penny press and has compelled important papers to close. Illustrated papers like *Picture Post* 1938–57 and *Illustrated* became the victims of television. In 1953 a voluntary Press Council was set up to prevent monopolies, but has not yet become very effective.

THE PRESS TODAY

I. General Features:

England, which has always been proud of allowing freedom of opinion and expression, has no official press. The *London Gazette* is a mere leaflet publishing official announcements. No English newspaper is even an official party organ. The press is much rather considered as an instrument for controlling government through public opinion. On the other hand, the fact that in Britain more persons buy newspapers than in any other country has made the press an important instrument for forming public opinion in the conservative spirit of its capitalistic owners. The popular press with the highest circulation is independent conservative and has eclipsed the appeal of liberal papers. In 1960 the only liberal mass paper *News Chronicle* was compelled to close.

The necessity of catering for the more emotional instincts of the masses (including women) has produced the typical features of the popular press of our age: superficial information, local gossip and s e n s a t i o n a l i s m. The stunt, introduced to give a thrill to dull objective news, sporting news and pictures are examples of this tendency. Scandalous news appeal to the lowest instincts (cf. Profumo scandal in 1963 when Christine Keeler sold the story of her affair with the Minister of War Profumo first to the *Sunday Pictorial* for £1,000, then to the *News of the World* for £23,000).

A Royal Commission on the Press set up in 1947 to inquire into management, ownership and monopolistic tendencies in the press stated 'that the gap between the best of the quality papers and the general run of the popular press is too wide', and, moreover, regretted the tendency of the larger chains to expand.

Strict laws against libel, trespass and contempt of court (if information is published on cases that are still sub judice) aim to protect the fairness and decency of public information and discussion. They are approved of by public opinion although journalists tend to complain that in Britain, the home of free expression of opinion, 'you have the most rigorous battery of laws to stop people finding out what is going on' (Harold Evans, editor of the *Sunday Times*).

As in other Western countries, newspapers in Britain have to fight against formidable odds. Soaring costs, declining circulations due to competition from TV and union contracts requiring considerable overmanning of machines got several of the national newspapers into such financial straits that they had to merge or close down, unless rescued by rich firms. Thus the press is now increasingly controlled by international interests.

The Times and the *Sunday Times* were sold in 1981 to the Australian press magnate Rupert Murdoch, who also bought *The Sun* and *News of the World*. Murdoch defied the unions in 1986 when he transferred the production of his four papers to Wapping in London's industrialized dock area to introduce new labour-saving technologies. He dismissed 5,000 workers, replacing the striking typesetters with electricians, who were promptly excluded by the TUC. For some time his modernized plant worked practically in a state of siege defying union action. Two new papers, the daily *Today* and the evening paper *London Post* already use the most modern technologies.

As the press is now increasingly controlled by international interests, it is feared that this development may not promote the objectivity of papers or improve their quality.

II. News Centres and Agencies:

The chief British press centre is Fleet Street, London, the second largest Manchester, which also publishes northern editions of ten London papers. The principal news agencies are:

1. Reuters Ltd., (founded in London in 1850), a world news agency owned by the newspapers of Great Britain, Australia and New Zealand with correspondents in all larger capitals;
2. The Exchange Telegraph Company Ltd.;
3. Press Association Ltd. owned collectively by British provincial newspapers, distributes home news, also to the London dailies.

III. National Dailies and Sunday Papers

1. The Popular Press ('Populars')

a) Dailies: The *Daily Mirror* is very widely read, especially by workers, and supports a practical socialism which does not voice doctrines but attacks privilege and social injustices without regard to taboos.

The *Daily Express* is described as independent, but actually represents that self-righteous conservatism which was a special feature of the popular press at the beginning of the century. It makes a special appeal to the semi-educated middle classes whose tradition it embodies: belief

211

in personal initiative and efficiency, dislike of red-tape and controls impeding free competition, and distrust of modernism in life and thought. Its evening edition is the *Evening Standard*.

The *Daily Mail* is a distinctly conservative paper, which tries to present its news in a responsible though popular form. Its Evening News merged with the *Evening Standard* in 1980.

Today is similar in standard to the *Daily Mail* and *Daily Express* but puts forward a Liberal viewpoint.

The *Sun*, originally the successor to the socialist *Daily Herald,* has changed its character since it was bought by the Australian tycoon Rupert Murdoch. It now caters for the tastes of a less discriminating public. In the Gulf War 1991 it excelled in an extreme jingoism. *The Star* has a similar level of writing to *The Sun*, but it is a more left-wing paper.

b) 'Sunday Populars': The Sunday papers, which have by far the highest circulation, are *The Sunday People*, the *Sunday Mirror* and *News of the World* (4.3 million). They represent the more irresponsible side of British journalism, being mainly committed to sensationalism, sex and crime. The *Sunday Express* and the *Mail on Sunday* are slightly higher-quality tabloid Sunday papers.

2. PAPERS WITH A HIGH STANDARD ('QUALITIES')

a) Dailies:

The Times, an independent daily, occupies a unique position in Britain and in the world. R e l i a b l e and o b j e c t i v e in its information, it is read by the educated classes, which accounts for its small circulation (300,700). Founded in 1785 as a private concern of the Walter family, it employed the world's first steam press to compensate for the high Stamp Tax by lower production costs. It retained its independence from telegraphic news agencies and government news services by keeping its own correspondents in all capitals of the world, supported in times of war by a large staff of war correspondents. *The Times* has its experts on all economic, scientific and social subjects, who cater for the needs of professional groups through special weekly supplements: *The Times Literary Supplement, The Times Educational Supplement, The Times Trade and Engineering Supplement,* and the *Law Reports* recording court decisions. True to its founder's promise 'to publish nothing that might wound anyone's delicacy or corrupt the mind and to abstain from unfair partisanship and scandalous scurrility', *The Times* has remained the symbol of moderate, reliable information given in a sober, lucid style, and has become 'a n a t i o n a l i n s t i t u t i o n'. Even from

1909–22, when the Times passed into Northcliffe's ownership and was drawn into his anti-German campaign, its world-wide reputation for objectivity was skilfully maintained. When Northcliffe died, *The Times* became an independent concern with some of the shares held by its previous owners, the Walter family, and was secured by its chief new proprietor and chairman, I. T. Astor, from undesirable financial and political infiltration by the formation of a board of trustees. To-day, *The Times* is still the newspaper most strongly committed to tradition. Its layout was till 1966 that of the 19th century with the front page occupied by advertisements and special pages devoted to special subjects. In its social columns it gives detailed reports of social events though it abstains from discussion of the affairs of the royal family or popular film stars. It voices conservative views on political and social issues and has no political cartoons. Making few concessions to modern taste, it has a comparatively small percentage of young people among its readers. But its excellent news service, its comprehensive reports on legal and financial affairs and its correspondence columns, to which some of the most influential personages of public life contribute, enjoy a unique prestige.

The Daily Telegraph is a more popular conservative paper of a high standard, which is read by a wider middle-class public, devoted to tradition, disliking stunts and sensation. Its news coverage is remarkably comprehensive. Its circulation is 1.47 million.

The Guardian, with a circulation of 420,271, which was founded in 1821 as a provincial paper (the *Manchester Guardian*) and has long become a national paper, is now published only in London. Long the mouthpiece of Manchester liberalism, it has, since the closing of the *News Chronicle* in 1960, been the chief liberal paper, though it is described as independent. *The Guardian* has a national, even international, reputation for its commercial information, its foreign section, and the high standard of its book reviews.

b) The Sunday papers of a high standard are the independent *Observer* (845,431) and *The Sunday Times* (1.37 million), both of which issue colour supplements, and the more popular *Sunday Telegraph* (850,326). All three appeal to intelligent readers of all persuasions. The *Observer*, now again in British hands, even makes a profit.

IV. **Specialist daily papers** are *Financial Times, Lloyd's List and Shipping Gazette* (founded in 1695 as *Lloyd's News) and Sporting Life*.

V. **Provincial and Scottish papers:**

Provincial papers tend to decrease in numbers. The chief are the conservative *Yorkshire Post* (founded in 1759) and the *Birmingham*

Evening Mail Post (founded in 1857), which hold the leading positions in the North and Midlands resp. In Scotland the leading newspapers are still the *Glasgow Herald* (founded in 1783) and *The Scotsman* (founded in 1815), which have a national reputation. The widest circulation, however, is reached by the Scottish editions of the English mass papers, by Kemsley's conservative Glasgow *Daily Record* subsidiary of the national *Daily Mirror* and Glasgow's *Evening Times*.

VI. **Periodicals** numbering over 4,250 weeklies, monthlies and quarterlies are growing rapidly in numbers and specialization.

1. GENERAL PERIODICALS of the older type, catering for the educated classes, enrich the reader's general education rather than his specialist knowledge. The articles are written not so much by experts as by educated men with scholarly tastes. They give information on a great number of subjects, politics, economics, science, literature, art. In the past, the finest examples of this type were the Liberal *Edinburgh Review* (1802–1929) and the Conservative *Quarterly Review*. The independent conservative *Spectator* is chiefly influential among progressive Conservatives. The liberal periodical *Time and Tide* has ceased publication. *Statesman* (77,539), an intellectual Socialist periodical founded by the Fabians, Sidney and Beatrice Webb (p. 93), provides reliable information on politics, literature and art. Despite their political bias, most of these periodicals are not particularly partisan and reflect a high degree of culture. The BBC periodical *The Listener* reprints radio talks and book reviews. *Punch* is a humorous periodical of international reputation. Formerly tending to political satire, it represents today that unbiased generous humour characteristic of the general English attitude towards life.

2. SPECIALIST JOURNALS began to develop towards the end of the 19th century. Commercial interests are mainly represented by *The Economist*, which contains also political comments, book reviews and articles of general interest. Literary subjects are now dealt with in *The Times Literary Supplement* (since 1902), which has become the leading critical literary organ. A periodical devoted to s c i e n c e is *Nature*. Two recent and very important weeklies are the *New Scientist* and *New Society* on development in science and sociology. There are about 1,800 trade and technical publications and innumerable magazines dealing with sports and hobbies, reflecting the spare-time interests of the nation.

3. PERIODICALS WITH A MASS APPEAL are the *Radio Times* founded in 1923, the *TV Times*, magazines for women, such as *Woman* and *Woman's*

Own, all with circulations in the millions, and innumerable journals for children, and periodicals for young people containing fiction, science and practical suggestions for hobbies and crafts. Since the middle of the century there has been a tendency for American comics to swamp the market.

4. PICTURE MAGAZINES are *Vogue* (society, sport and fashion), *Illustrated London News* with a coverage of world events, art, archeology etc., and the rural magazines *Country Life* and *Field.* The renowned picture magazines *Sphere* and *Tatler* had to close' in 1980.

SOUND BROADCASTING AND TELEVISION

History

Sound broadcasting began in 1922 when the British Broadcasting Company Ltd. was founded, which, in 1927, was transformed by Royal Charter into the public British Broadcasting Corporation (BBC). In 1936 the BBC started the world's first regular public service of television, which was suspended during World War II and resumed in 1946. The rapid development of television led to the establishment of the Independent Broadcasting Authority (IBA). Britain was the first European country to introduce Breakfast TV (in the USA since 1952).

Present Situation

Sound broadcasting services are provided by the BBC and some local commercial stations, television by both the BBC and ITV (Independent Television). Some 96 per cent of British homes have television. The BBC provides 5 national radio stations. Radio 1 broadcasts pop music, Radio 2 light music, Radio 3 classical music, while Radio 4 provides the principal news, a wide range of drama, talks and information on hobbies. Radio 5 broadcasts sports, light entertainment and educational prgrammes.

The BBC's External Services, which have been called the calmest and fairest source of international news there is, broadcast in English and 35 other languages (e.g. the Asian service in 14 Oriental languages). The 'English by Radio and Television' lessons are the world's most extensive language service supplying recorded lessons in 90 countries. The BBC publishes its own magazine, *The*

215

Listener. While its External Services depend on government grants, which have been considerably cut since 1980, the domestic services are financed by the income from television licenses, from the sale of records and publications, and the export of TV programmes.

ITV programmes are provided by companies having their own production studios (although the IBA builds, owns and operates the TV transmission stations). As they depend for their revenue on commercial advertising, ITV, in contrast with BBC television, broadcasts advertisements, subject, however, to the statutory provision that they should be recognisably separate from the programme and not so long as to impair the value of TV as a medium of entertainment and instruction. Some types of advertisements, e.g. cigarettes and betting, are prohibited. The IBA supervises the quality of programmes, e.g. with regard to the broadcasting of programmes containing violence at times when children are likely to be viewing. In general it may be said that British radio and TV are renowned world-wide for the technical and artistic excellence of their programmes.

Britain is a member of the European Broadcasting Union and a regular contributor to the network of Eurovision. It is a partner in Visnews, the world's most widely used newsfilm agency serving 94 countries.

Britain played an important part in the development of telecommunication systems by satellite. The first satellite broadcast across the Atlantic began in 1962, simultaneous two-way transmission between Europe and the U.S.A. in 1965.

The new age of information technology has brought video and cable TV. Many families have bought satellite dishes to receive 'Sky TV' and other European satellite channels. Linking households by glass-fibre technology, 'the cable revolution' is expected to open the way to multiple TV and communications channels – although there are fears that with the uncontrollable multiplication of services the infiltration of horror and porno films will become as inevitable as in the video cassette business.

Prestel, the Post Office's viewdata service, was the world's first system transmitting computerized information through telephone lines for display on a television screen in the form of words, figures and graphics.

SPORT

England is the country in which most of the modern sports originated. Not even in America, the country of pioneers, do sports form such an important aspect of national life.

This is partly due to the physical conditions of the country, the ample possibilities for water sports and the temperate climate favouring outdoor pastimes throughout the year. Other reasons may be found in national features of the British people: the predilection for life in the country, the belief in the value of social activities and team work, the gift for establishing and keeping to social rules. In the Middle Ages the chivalrous sporting instinct of the aristocracy was not absorbed by wars as on the Continent, and later a wealthy leisured class became the chief patrons of sport. An aristocratic system of education perpetuated the chivalric educational ideal in the Public Schools and colleges. The catch-phrase 'that's not cricket' is used as a form of protest against unfairness and cheating.

The inclination to idealize sport, which was bred by this tradition, is expressed in a speech made by the late Duke of Windsor (then Prince of Wales) in 1929:

'There is one attribute which Englishmen, Irishmen, Scotchmen, and Welshmen share in common. That common attribute is the love of sportsmanship. To be a good sportsman becomes the ideal of every British boy born within the Seven Seas as soon as he can understand the meaning of the word. ... We owe to this ideal our sense of fair play, our capacity for team work, and our love of justice. It is the source of our ability to tolerate, to allow for the widest differences of opinions amongst ourselves and it is always a wonderful help to us in our dealings with other nations and races. It preserves what was meant in the old ideal of chivalry, but is larger and more human. It bridges all distinctions of class, all differences of education, occupation, or opportunity; and we have taken it with us into every part of the globe. Till today, it forms a link to hold together each unit in a world-wide Empire.'

History

MIDDLE AGES: Already in Saxon times sports like hunting, wrestling and archery were considered important means of physical training, particularly for the sons of the nobility. The Saxon passion for h u n t i n g is reflected in the story of Robin Hood, the national Saxon hero, who, as an outlaw, challenged the Norman conquerors' monopoly of the English forests. Towards the end of the Middle Ages hunting (boars, deer, foxes, hares, pheasants, partridges) had become a national sport, in which h a w k i n g and c o u r s i n g greyhounds played an important part. The Normans introduced the chivalric sports of the j o u s t (between two contestants) and the t o u r n a m e n t (between any number of knights). A r c h e r y, which had largely secured the Normans' victory over the Saxons at Hastings, was soon made compulsory for all men, and under Edward I even for boys above the age of seven. In the Hundred Years' War the English archers decided the English victory over the French chivalric army. The 14th century was the peak of *Merry England*, when even the lower classes engaged in some rude form of most later sports: r o w i n g, w r e s t l i n g, b o x i n g, c o c k - f i g h t i n g and a n i m a l b a i t i n g (boars, bears, bulls), b o w l s in the open and on tables (shovelboard, later billiards), handball, first hit against the church wall by hand ('f i v e s') or with a racket (t e n n i s). The roughest game was f o o t b a l l which, when played on the cobbled pavements of city streets, caused so many deaths that it was forbidden under punishment of imprisonment as a public danger. The usual scenes of village a t h l e t i c s were the country fairs, the churchyard, where people gathered on Sundays after church, or the village green, which also saw the annual ceremony of erecting the maypole, with dancing and singing around it on May Day.

Skating (on bone skates) was much more common in the Middle Ages when there were still vast stretches of land under water (e.g. Fens), and when as elsewhere in Europe the winters were much colder than now (in 1410 the Thames froze for 14 weeks!). Many match sports were already connected with a vast amount of gambling.

Tudor England: Renewed pleasure in life and bodily exercise during the Renaissance immensely favoured sport. Henry VIII was the most notable sportsman of his court, excelling in wrestling, archery and putting the weight. He organized tournaments and made t e n n i s fashionable by building the first tennis court at his palace of Hampton Court. He constructed the Royal Cockpit and laid out bowling alleys at Whitehall. He encouraged f e n c i n g, which became an important item in the training of the sons of the nobility, by licensing a fencing school known as 'the Noble Science of Defence'. R i d i n g was greatly encouraged by Henry VIII, who, also for military reasons, decreed that every man of rank should keep horses of his own, the number being determined by rank. C o c k f i g h t s and b e a r b a i t i n g were favourite pleasures even of the Court, which kept a special Master of Bears. Though a r c h e r y lost its military importance with the introduction of the powder gun, it was still encouraged and practised as a sport even for women. Queen Elizabeth was admired for her skill with the bow as well as for her passion for hunting, in which she indulged till a few years before her death.

The 17th century brought new ball games under the earlier Stuarts. James I introduced g o l f from Scotland where the natural 'bunkers' (obstacles) of the scenery had favoured the development of the game. He encouraged the new game of p a l l - m a l l, a cross between golf and croquet, in which a ball was hit with a mallet along an alley about 800 yards long, with a number of iron arches serving as hazards. The area adjoining St. James Palace, where it was played by the Court, is still called *Pall Mall*. When this area was built over in the time of Cromwell, Charles II laid out a new ground inside St. James's Park itself, which he called the *Mall*.

Most sports, dancing round maypoles included, declined or were banned during the Commonwealth which considered sports as sinful amusements. Consequently, the Restoration brought about a tremendous revival of entertainment and sporting activities under the patronage of the Court. Water sports (swimming, skating) became very popular. King Charles II himself initiated the sport of y a c h t i n g by matching his yacht against his brother's. Walton's *The Compleat Angler* helped to make angling a national hobby. Football, which, according to James I, was 'meeter for laming than making abel the users thereof' became still more popular.

Common entertainments were r u n n i n g r a c e s between 'footmen', who were often employed for their athletic abilities, particularly since the aristocracy had begun to maintain two establishments, one in the country and one in London. By far the most popular sport, however, was still c o c k f i g h t i n g which had become a real science, the cocks being carefully trained and fitted with silver spurs, which were made by expert craftsmen centred in *Cockspur Street*, London. B e a r b a i t i n g a n d b u l l b a i t i n g were still common, specially trained dogs ('bulldogs') being used to bait the animal, which was chained to a wall or a post. Under the Stuarts h o r s e r a c i n g became 'the Sport of Kings'. Under James I N e w m a r k e t became a centre of well-organized horse races run by carefully

218

trained horses whose pedigree was now, for the first time, improved by Arabian and Barb stallions. The actual 'Father of the Turf' however was Charles II, who at Newmarket became owner, jockey and judge all in one, while the gambling houses of his mistresses became 'the resort of the highest and most depraved in the land'.

THE 18TH CENTURY became the g o l d e n   a g e   o f   s p o r t, when under the influence of Enlightenment sports began to be 'humanized' and to be played according to standard rules. Racing developed further through the establishment of new race courses. The *Royal Ascot* was founded through Queen Anne's patronage. In Doncaster, Yorkshire, two noblemen, who were prominent riders, gave their names to two classic races, the *Rockingham* and the *St. Leger* stakes. On Epsom Downs, Lord Derby instituted two races, *the Derby*, 1780, called after him, and the *Oaks*, 1779, called after his house near the Epsom course. Later, steeple chases, esp. the *Grand National*, the 'Derby of the Sticks' (1839) supplemented the flat course races. From about 1750 the Jockey Club, formed by prominent sport patrons (e.g. Lord Derby), provided the first strict rules and properly elected officials. The authority of the club stewards was so generally accepted that in one instance the Prince of Wales (later George IV), who at the end of the century had become the royal patron of sports, was 'warned off the course'. In 1766 Richard T a t t e r s a l l opened his famous auction room at Hyde Park Corner (now Knightsbridge) where it became the custom of 'the Gentlemen of the Turf' to assemble for sales and the transactions of the gambling business in a strictly gentlemanly way. A q u a t i c   s p o r t s increased enormously. Rowing contests began when in 1715 one I. Doggett instituted a race for six Thames watermen, which is still an annual event.

The aristocracy began to frequent m i n e r a l   s p a s. T u n b r i d g e   W e l l s and B a t h became the chief centres of fashion outside London, followed by C h e l t e n h a m, Leamington, Harrogate etc. When the beneficial results of swimming in saltwater became known, this discovery led to the development of great s e a s i d e   r e s o r t s like Scarborough, Worthing, Weymouth, Margate and, above all, B r i g h t o n, which became the chief centre of fashion during the Regency. As bathing dresses were not yet worn, the bathers were drawn into the water by special closed bathing machines in which they could undress.

H u n t i n g was still a national passion, but changed its character when the ancient forests gave way to enclosed meadowland. S t a g   h u n t i n g, still most popular, became an artificial affair, the stag being taken to the scene of the chase in a deer cart and then let loose to be taken back to the cart when it had been lassoed, the utmost care being taken that it was not killed. From 1750 onwards f o x h u n t i n g on horseback with packs of hounds became the great fashion among the country gentry. The most famous pack was the *Quorn* of Hugo Meynell, 'the Father of the modern English chase', who made his mansion, Quorndon Hall, the headquarters of fox hunting. The necessity of galloping over fences and hedges required considerable daring and skill, but the damage caused was one of the less pleasant features of this aristocratic sport. Hunt balls lasting for several days became a new social feature in country life.

As duelling declined, a new method of defence came to the fore, which one James Figg taught the aristocracy in his Academy of Boxing. Soon prize fights, held in a

219

specially built amphitheatre in Oxford Road, were attended by huge crowds including the highest and the lowest.

By 1750 c r i c k e t, which in a less organized form had been played since the 16th century, had developed into an organized game. Gathering rich and poor alike on the village grounds, it soon enjoyed enormous popularity. In 1787 a Yorkshire man Thomas Lord opened a cricket ground, 'Lords', in Marylebone, London, which in 1788 gave rise to the Marylebone Cricket Club which remained the controlling body.

THE 19TH CENTURY saw the development of modern sport through the establishment of rules still binding for most sports, in which the universities and Public Schools began to play a major part. From 1805 the cricket matches between Eton and Harrow at Lord's became a major attraction. By 1812 the two universities had their eight-oared boats. From 1856 the famous *University Boat Race* between Oxford and Cambridge crews (first rowed in 1829) became an annual event of the Easter vacation. It was rowed on the Thames between Putney and Mortlake, the river banks being thronged by immense crowds. In 1839 the first *Henley Regatta* was staged with a pageantry even exceeding that of the 'Varsity' race, with church bells ringing throughout the day and music bands and river barges providing music. The chief yachting races were now held at Cowes (Isle of Wight), where fashionable society began to spend a few summer weeks.

As water sports increased, s w i m m i n g was promoted by the establishment of public baths, which soon made swimming a sport of the masses. W a t e r p o l o became a popular entertainment. In 1842 the first attempts were made to produce artificial ice in indoor rinks for skating and iceracing. I c e h o c k e y was introduced from Canada, c u r l i n g from Scotland.

B o x i n g, pursued in some crude form for centuries, was raised to a higher plane when, in 1865, the glove was adopted and wrestling tactics were abandoned. When the new code was adopted by other nations, modern international boxing began.

H o c k e y and c r o q u e t were brought from Ireland. Their great popularity however, was soon eclipsed by l a w n t e n n i s, which drew enthusiastic spectators when the first championships were started in Wimbledon in 1877. In 1900 D. F. Davis, later U.S. Secretary of War, offered a challenge cup, the *Davis Cup,* for the leading players of Britain and America. When the game was opened to all nations, it became one of the world's prominent sporting events. In 1923 Mrs. Wightman (U.S.A.) donated the *Wightman Cup* for women championships. Despite the foundation in Paris of an international controlling body, Wimbledon remained the sport's centre.

Court tennis, less popular than lawn tennis, r a c k e t s and f i v e s became increasingly the preserves of the well-to-do, particularly the Public Schools. B a d m i n t o n was brought to England by officers of the Army from India, where it was known as Poona. It was introduced in 1873 by the Duke of Beaufort at his country seat Badminton, which gave its name to clubs founded by retired officers of the Indian army.

F o o t b a l l, once the roughest game forbidden by the authorities, was now, like tennis, also played by the Public Schools. While Westminster and Charterhouse devised the safer tactics of dribbling the ball at the feet, Rugby retained the rushing tactics of street football. Moreover in 1823 a boy, W. W. Ellis, caused a sensation by catching the ball in his arms and running with it to his opponents' goal (commemorated by a granite slab on a wall of the school). This tactic, first condemned as unfair, was soon generally adopted. Thus football became two different games: s o c c e r, played by 'dribbling' clubs, which in 1863 formed themselves into the Football Association (hence also 'Association Football') and the more popular R u g b y f o o t b a l l, or rugger, which has been controlled since 1871 by the Rugby Football Union. By 1885 the popularity of football had led to professionalism with its 'transfer system', by which a player can be transferred to another club for sums which today run into many thousands of pounds.

THE 20TH CENTURY added motor and greyhound races to the sporting calendar. The first m o t o r r a c e was run in 1900 by 65 cars from Whitehall over 1000 miles of British roads as far as Edinburgh. Since the speed limit was for reasons of safety 12 miles an hour, it was really more an endurance test. In 1907 the first motor track race took place at Brooklands.

G r e y h o u n d r a c i n g, reintroduced from America, started in England in 1926 at Belle Vue, Manchester, and quickly gained popularity as the only outdoor entertainment provided even on winter evenings.

Sport Today

British sport is mainly determined by amateur enthusiasm, though the gambling element in sports, the over-rewarded professionalism and the tendency to watch rather than to play are modern elements deleterious to joyful playing in Britain. Sport is supported publicly by grants to local authorities, now especially in poorer communities of inner cities to provide playing fields, gymnasia and swimming baths.

The favourite British sports are football, cricket and lawn tennis. Football is the principal sport of the winter months. A s s o c i a t i o n f o o t b a l l or soccer has become the sport of the masses.

Nowadays football matches are sometimes connected with an alarming amount of hooliganism among football fans. In 1985 it erupted at the European Football Championship in Belgium when Liverpool fans hurled bottles and stones at the followers of the Turin team. The ensuing battle, in which a bleacher collapsed, burying many visitors, resulted in 38 deaths. For some time British teams were banned abroad.

Several million people take part in the 'betting pools' organized by the Football League, which controls professional matches.

R u g b y or 'rugger', in which the ball is handled as well as kicked, is played more by the Public Schools and the military services. It is controlled by the Rugby Union, whose headquarters are at Twickenham, London. The two annual competitions for the Challenge Cup Final of the Football Association and the Rugby League attract crowds of 100,000 spectators to Wembley Stadium.

C r i c k e t is the most characteristic national game, though it has never been popular outside the English-speaking world. The most famous matches are played at *Lord's* between Oxford and Cambridge, and Eton and Harrow. One of the 'test matches' between Commonwealth countries is played at *Lord's*. The cancellation in 1970 of a South-African cricket tour – a success for anti-apartheid campaigners – initiated the virtual elimination of sporting contacts between Britain and South Africa.

H o c k e y is now played by more women than men. Other games preferably played by women are l a c r o s s e taken over from the Indians of North America, and n e t b a l l, while b a s k e t b a l l is mainly played by men.

L a w n t e n n i s is controlled by the Lawn Tennis Association and is played in most schools and several thousand clubs. The annual championship at W i m b l e d o n takes place from the end of June to July in the presence of 30,000 spectators. The prominent international events are the competitions for the *Davis Cup* for men and for the *Wightman Cup* for women.

G o l f, 'the Royal and Ancient Game of Scotland', with its headquarters in St. Andrews, is now played in the whole of Britain. There are championships for professionals as well as amateurs.

B o w l s is played on outdoor bowling greens in the summer and on indoor greens in the winter. The Bowling Association controls the game according to the rules issued by the International Bowling Board.

P o l o, a Persian game first played by the British in India, is the preserve of the wealthier classes because of the considerable cost of purchasing and maintaining ponies. It is governed by the Hurlingham Polo Association.

A t h l e t i c s, which include running, relay racing, jumping, hurdling and throwing, is for amateurs controlled by the Amateur Athletic Association. A special attraction is the Scottish Highland games including dancing and bagpipe competitions, bagpipes being the traditional Scottish instruments.

Country sports are organized by the British Field Sports Society. H u n t i n g (now frowned upon by people who wish to prevent cruelty to animals) today means primarily fox hunting on horseback, with packs of hounds bred and trained for the purpose. It is still chiefly pursued by the landed gentry, with townspeople following the event as eager spectators. The hunting season lasts from November after the harvest is gathered till April. The traditional uniform is a scarlet coat (called pink) with a black velvet cap (cf. 18th century sporting pictures). Stag hunting is now restricted to a few shires (Somerset and Devon).

S h o o t i n g includes partridge shooting on farmland, pheasant shooting in woods, grouse shooting on grouse moors in hilly country, and wild fowling in the fens and marshes, the season lasting from August to January. In the Scottish Highlands privately owned 'deer forests' are preserved for deer stalking (from the cautious noiseless approach before shooting).

F i s h i n g is also the sport of the common man, who can easily rent a stretch of river or take part in a club's fishing rights, while coastal and deep-sea fishing, mainly for tuna and shark, is free to all. Freshwater fishing includes fishing for salmon, esp. in Scotland, trout and carp, perch, pike etc. The National Federation of Anglers, which has 450,000 members, organizes angling championships.

H o r s e   r a c i n g includes flat racing, controlled by the Jockey Club, and steeplechasing, with rules set up by the National Hunt Committee. The chief flat races are those on the *Newmarket* course, the *St. Leger* race at Doncaster in September and two races on Epsom Downs: *the Oaks* and *the Derby*. The latter takes place in early June and is one of the greatest sporting events in England. As a national entertainment which attracts about 250,000 spectators to Epsom Downs, it has often been the subject of literary and pictorial art. The most fashionable flat race is the *Royal Ascot* in mid-June, which is usually attended by the Sovereign. The outstanding steeple chase is the *Grand National* on the Aintree course near Liverpool. Another important event is the National Hunt Festival Meeting at Chelten-ham in March. In connection with the races, there is a vast amount of betting organized by licensed bookmakers who operate from their own shop premises, and whose profits are taxed under the *Betting Levy Act*, 1961 (about eleven per cent of the annual turnover). The headquarters of racing is Newmarket, which is owned by the Jockey Club.

G r e y h o u n d R a c i n g is attended by some 10 million people annually. It is controlled by the National Greyhound Racing Club. The outstanding races are held in the London area: the *Laurels* at Wimbledon, the *Derby* at the White City, the St. *Leger* at Wembley.

M o t o r r a c e s , held under the auspices of the Royal Automobile Club, enjoy great popularity. The most famous are the British *Grand Prix* at Silverstone and the RAC rally. Britain produces more racin cars and sports cars than any other country.

B o x i n g : Amateur boxing, which is also popular in boys' schools, is controlled by the Amateur Boxing Association, professional boxing by the British Boxing Board of Control.

R o w i n g and s a i l i n g provide outstanding sporting events. The chief yacht race conducted by the Royal Yachting Association is the annual *Regatta at Cowes*, in the Isle of Wight. In addition there are many yachting weeks at various sailing centres along the south coast. In 1960 British yachtsmen took part in the first single-handed race across the Atlantic. The greatest enthusiasm, however, is aroused by the two chief boat races, the *Henley-on-Thames Regatta* in July, when crews from all over the world compete in various kinds of races, especially for the Grand Challenge Cup, and the *University Boat Race* between eight-oared crews of Oxford and

Cambridge over a 4½-mile course on the Thames between Putney and Mortlake, which takes place early in spring. In the *'Head of the River Race'* from Putney to Mortlake, the largest assembly of racing boats in the world, 200 to 300 eights row in procession.

Recently snooker, equestrianism, darts and American football have become popular, and have like most other sports become professional. The Olympic Games have developed into an ever increasing megabusiness.

ARTS

English Architecture

I. Prehistoric Building

The earliest constructional efforts preserved date from the Neolithic and Bronze Ages, and are circles and burial chambers of big standing stones. The long barrows of the neolithic period and the round barrows of the Bronze Age are burial mounds covering chambers of standing stones supporting horizontal lintels. If found above ground such burial chambers are called d o l m e n s or cromlechs, some of the finest preserved being in Cornwall. S t o n e c i r c l e s , which are assumed to have served religious purposes (hence also 'sacred' or, wrongly, 'Druid circles'), are found in Keswick, Westmorland and on the Isle of Lewis in the Hebrides. The biggest, the circle at *Avebury,* Wiltshire (c. 2000 B.C.) covers a site of some 1.470 m in circumference, including the surrounding ditch and bank. The most famous stone circle is *Stonehenge,* in 'the windswept loneliness' of Salisbury Plain (until the M3 was built). It is a monumental construction of four concentric circles, two of which consist of stones standing 4 m above ground and covered by lintel stones cut to the shape of the circles. The two horseshoe formations enclosed by these two circles consist of smaller 'bluestones' brought 400 km from southwest Wales at a time when heavy weights could only be hauled on rafts and boats and pulled on sledges. Stonehenge also differs from other circles in another respect; it has a clear axis cutting through the middle, which is marked by the 'altar stone', through the open end of the horseshoe circles and ending in an avenue running across the surrounding ditch due northeast where the midsummer sun rises. This alignment suggests

1. STONEHENGE, Wiltshire, c. 1800 B. C.

2. THE ROMAN WALL near Chollerford, Northumberland; begun A. D. 122

3. EARL'S BARTON, Northamptonshire,
CHURCH TOWER: Anglo-Saxon,
10th century

4. LINCOLN CATHEDRAL, WEST FRONT:
Early English, 1220–30; Norman parts c. 1150

5. CAERNARVON CASTLE, North Wales, 1285–1301

6. DURHAM CATHEDRAL, NAVE: Norman, begun 1093

7. WELLS CATHEDRAL, NAVE, with inverted arch: Early English, 1220–39

8. WELLS CATHEDRAL, WEST FRONT: Early English, 1220–29

9. EXETER CATHEDRAL, NAVE: Decorated, late 13th century

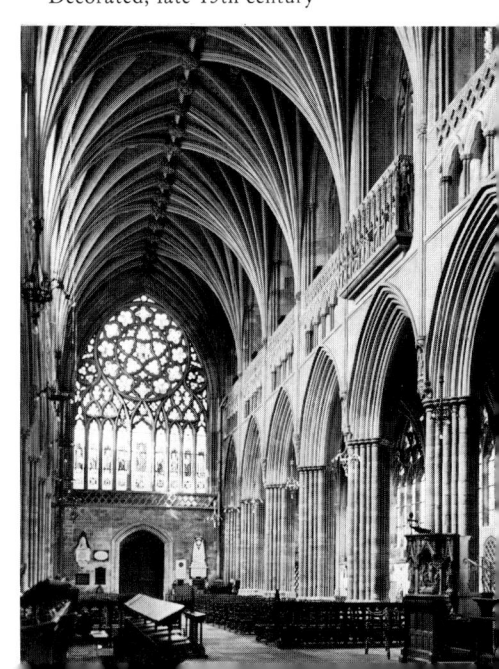

10. ELY CATHEDRAL: Late Norman, begun 1083. OCTAGON: Decorated, 1322–42

11. KING'S COLLEGE CHAPEL,
    CAMBRIDGE: Perpendicular, 1443–61

12. GLOUCESTER CATHEDRAL,
    THE CLOISTERS: Perpendicular, 1381–1412

13. HAMPTON COURT, Thames west of London: Tudor part, begun 1515

14. CHESTER, THE ROWS; centre of the city of Chester

15. BANQUETING HALL, WHITEHALL, London: Palladian, 1619–22

16. ST. PAUL'S CATHEDRAL, London: Wren's classicism, begun 1675

17. MOMPESSON HOUSE, SALISBURY: Georgian, begun 1701

18. CARLTON HOUSE TERRACE, The Mall, London: Regency

19. CRYSTAL PALACE, London: Functional Style; erected 1851, destroyed by fire, 1936

20. HOUSE OF COMMONS, NEW CHAMBER, 1950

21. COVENTRY CATHEDRAL, 1956–62
ST. MICHAEL'S PORCH;
sculpture by Sir Jacob Epstein

22. COVENTRY CATHEDRAL, NAVE,
Christ Enthroned by. G. Sutherland

that Stonehenge was connected with some form of sun worship. Dated about 1800 B.C. it may be called the most ancient temple in Europe. The many prehistoric lake villages and h i l l f o r t s found in Britain chiefly date from the Iron Age. The most impressive example of a hill fort, which consisted of a ditch and rampart protected by palisades, is *Maiden Castle* near Dorchester with an ingenious plan of defensive lines and interlocking outworks enclosing an immense mound 60ft. high, which was occupied by a considerable settlement of round huts. This earthwork remained impregnable until the Romans stormed it with superior weapons (ca. 45 B.C.). L a k e v i l l a g e s were erected over shallow water or the frequently found marshy ground on platforms of logs resting on piles of brushwood or small trees. The biggest was found in *Glastonbury,* Somerset, with 89 round huts built on a platform which was protected by a palisade of posts.

II. Roman Architecture

The urbanized Romans built c i t i e s usually protected by w a l l s , remains of which exist in several cities *(London, Chester).* The *Roman gate* in *Lincoln* still forms the northern entrance to the town. The layout of Roman cities could be reconstructed from excavations made on abandoned city sites like *Silchester* (near Reading) and *Wroxeter* (near Shrewsbury). It was symmetrical with rectangular blocks, fora and baths. Some cities, e.g. *St. Albans* (Verulamium), *Caerleon, Silchester,* had a m p h i t h e a t r e s. In *Bath,* the Roman Aquae Sulis, excavations in the 19th century unearthed the *Great Bath,* a big rectangular colonnaded basin and smaller plunge baths. Of the many Roman m o s a i c f l o o r s the finest remains have been excavated in villas at *Brading* in the Isle of Wight, at *Chedworth,* Gloucestershire, and in *Fishbourne Roman Palace* in Sussex. In the fortified parts of Britain the Romans built castles. In the north, the 120 km long *Roman Wall* running along the steep crest of a hill range from the Solway to the Tyne, was 2,7 m thick and 4 m high. It had 80 mile-castles and 320 signal-turrets at regular intervals. South of the wall ran the vallum, a steep ditch with a mound on each side.

III. Saxon Architecture

Saxon buildings were mainly wooden structures (cf. 'timbran' = to build), which have not been preserved. In contrast to earlier invaders, who had only lived in circular or oblong huts of turf or bracken on a rough framework of sticks, the Anglo-Saxons already began to build rectangular l o g h u t s. The dwelling-house of the thane was a bigger, a i s l e d h a l l (cf. Hrothgar's 'high and wide-gabled hall' Heorot in *Beowulf*). Only one example of Anglo-Saxon log structure survives in a church at *Greenstead,* Essex.

Building in stone came to England with the first Christian missionaries at the end of the 6th century. The earliest examples preserved are the 7th-century c r y p t s of *Hexham* and *Repton* with barrel vaulting supported by pillars. Anglo-Saxon c h u r c h e s are primitive, mostly single-chamber structures with rectangular, sometimes apsidal chancels, and have small, irregularly spaced windows with semicircular or triangular arches. A characteristic feature is surface patterning consisting of stone stripes and arcades on walls and towers derived from half-timbered buildings, the best examples being the church towers of *Earl's Barton,* Northamptonshire, and *Barton-on-Humber,* Lincolnshire. Other Anglo-Saxon churches are *Bradford-on-Avon,* Wilts., and *Brixworth,* Northants., originally one of the few aisled structures. All these churches were built in the 10th and early 11th centuries.

IV. **Norman (English Romanesque) Architecture,** 1066–1150, was the greatest cultural achievement of the Norman invaders, who began to build most English c a t h e d r a l s. Where these were built on the sites of Saxon churches, the latter were usually pulled down. The Norman style is characterized by the round arch, the cruciform three-aisled basilica with a short square central tower crowned by pinnacles. The nave, which has a timber ceiling, consists of three storeys: the monumental columns or piers of the nave arcade support the triforium, which is surmounted by the clerestory (clear storey) with small windows. Ornamentation on arches is simple and crude: dog-tooth, zigzag, rope. The massive, usually plain columns, the thick walls (up to 20ft. at the base) give the impression of weighty monumentality intensified by the fact that Norman cathedrals in England are lower, wider and longer than Continental churches. The length is due to the fact that English bishops used monastic churches for their cathedrals. This made it necesarry for the choir, which was occupied by the monks, to be almost as long as the nave where the congregation assembled (sometimes even longer). The choir ended in a round apse containing the bishop's throne, cathedra (hence 'cathedral'). The fact that English cathedrals were usually monastic institutions explains another characteristic feature: Unlike Continental cathedrals, which are usually tightly enclosed by houses (e.g. Chartres, Cologne), they often stand in magnificent isolation in the park-like cathedral close (e.g. Salisbury, Winchester).

The purest example of early Norman is *St. John's Chapel* in the White Tower, London, with its massive round piers and plain arches. The finest late Norman cathedral is *Durham* (begun in 1093), with incised columns and the first stone vault, completed in 1104. Other cathedrals, whose naves still have a predominantly Norman character, are

Rochester, St. Albans, Ely, Peterborough, Gloucester and *Hereford.*
The Normans built the first s t o n e c a s t l e s consisting of a square
tower or 'keep' three or four storeys high. The finest are the *White
Tower*, London, and the castle keeps of *Rochester* and *Newcastle-on-
Tyne.* The ground floor was only used for storage, the upper floors
for living accommodation. A great hall occupied the centre of the
first and second floors, smaller private rooms were built in the thickness
of the wall. The keep was surrounded by a courtyard called ward or
bailey, which was protected by a fortified wall and an outer ditch.
Later the inner ward was further strengthened by fortified outer
wards. Thus the White Tower, London, is surrounded by two
concentric walls, whose 22 towers, formerly all used as prisons, are
associated with many tragedies in English history.

V. **Gothic Architecture,** 1150–1500, introduced the pointed arch, whose
downward thrust made possible structures with bigger openings. The
pointed arch appears between columns and piers, and in the arcades
of the triforium, in ribbed vaults and 'lancet' windows, later with
intricate tracery.

1. EARLY ENGLISH 1150–1250, stressed height and verticality; towers
taper into slender spires. Thinner walls with larger windows are
supported by buttresses, while the thrust of the vault on the raised
nave is absorbed by flying buttresses. Piers consist of clusters of
columns with foliated capitals. Sometimes Purbeck marble used in
the columns forms a colour contrast to the stone arches. Churches
were usually enlarged and divided into separate places for worship,
e.g. chapter houses, presbyteries, lady chapels. The east choir was
divided from the nave by a screen and usually rebuilt in a much
longer rectangular shape, with a retro-choir behind the altar.
Secondary towers on the west front now became a common feature.
The purest example of Early English is *Salisbury* Cathedral. *Lincoln*
and *Wells* (which is also famous for its inverted arch at the central
crossing) contain some of the best Early English workmanship in
their magnificent façades (fig. 4, 7, 8).
Of the many Cistercian monasteries that were built at that time
and which were allowed to fall into decay after their dissolution
under Henry VIII, *Tintern Abbey*, Gwent, and *Fountains Abbey*,
Yorkshire, are the most beautiful.

2. DECORATED STYLE, 1250–1350, retains the structural elements of
Early English, but with richer ornamentation. Capitals and bosses
are more lavishly decorated with oak, vine and maple designs.
Tracery, esp. in windows, becomes more lively and intricate, the
earlier geometrical designs (circles, trefoil, quatrefoil) being

generally replaced by curvilinear, flamboyant ornamentation. In vaulting the number of ribs is greatly increased, a later development being the connection of weight-carrying ribs by horizontal lierne ribs. (One of the best lierne vaults is that of the choir in *Gloucester*.) The outstanding examples of Decorated Gothic are *Exeter* with its magnificent vault and west front, and the naves of *York* and *Lichfield*. The most beautiful ornamental work of the period is found in the *Angel Choir* in Lincoln, the façade of Lichfield Cathedral and the curvilinear central window of York Cathedral. The glory of Ely is its *octagon* (central tower built after the collapse of the original tower) with the star-like effect of its vault ribs.

In c a s t l e b u i l d i n g a new development was the s h e l l k e e p consisting of a fortified wall usually encircling the flat top of a hill, which enclosed an open court with the buildings of residence. Central towers, now often circular, continued to be built (frequently on an artificial mound), e.g. the *Round Tower, Windsor*. But the keep lost its importance in favour of curtain walls, which provided several concentric lines of defence all equally strengthened by a number of towers so that no part of the structure was unprotected. The best examples of this construction used by Edward I in the many Welsh and border castles he built after his invasion of Wales are *Caernavon, Conway* and *Harlech*. The inner court contained the hall, the baileys between the outer walls the garrison, stables and accommodation for peasants and cattle. Access was through a protected gateway and a drawbridge leading across a moat to the barbican (outer gatehouse). Some of the finest medieval castles to be seen in Britain are *Edinburgh Castle,* the mighty *Bamburgh Castle* and *Alnwick* in Northumberland, *Kenilworth* in Shakespeare's country, associated with Elizabethan history, *Chepstow Castle* in the Welsh borderland and *Bodiam Castle* in Sussex. One of the most original structures is *Clifford Tower*, York, whose quatrefoil plan is only found in one other place, at Étampes near Paris. *Warwick Castle* is still lived in.

After 1350 castles began to be replaced by open, spacious m a n o r h o u s e s , in which towers and gatehouses served decorative rather than military purposes. On the other hand, towns began to be fortified.

3. PERPENDICULAR GOTHIC, 1350–1500, is a version of Gothic only found in England: the upright, carved stone panel becomes the chief decorative element, being applied to walls, windows, embattled parapets, and providing a more sober effect than earlier Gothic. Arches become flat, though still with a pointed centre, and are often

set in a rectangular frame. Buildings become screen-like open structures, in which the walls are reduced to slender piers between large windows. As aisle roofs become flat, the triforium almost disappears in favour of longer clerestory windows, which are divided from the nave arcade only by a thin band of carved decoration. Ceilings become flatter but reach their decorative limits in magnificent fan-vaults (*Norwich Cathedral; Divinity School,* Oxford; *King's College Chapel,* Cambridge) and hammer-beam vaulting, esp. the famous timber roof of *Westminster Hall,* London. Cathedral building now being largely completed, the new style was applied to chapels and p a r i s h   c h u r c h e s (e.g. *St. Michael,* Coventry, the bombed shell of which now forms the precincts to the new cathedral, and *Holy Trinity Church,* Stratford-on-Avon, in the chancel of which Shakespeare lies buried). The growing wealth of the middle classes was reflected in secular buildings such as g u i l d h a l l s (e.g. London, York, Norwich) and c o l l e g e s (e.g. *Magdalen College,* Oxford, and *Eton College*). The typical college plan evolved: the quadrangle ('quad') surrounded by the dormitories, the chapel and the two-storied hall as a big meeting place and dining hall. These features of medieval college architecture, which Oxford and Cambridge have retained despite many later additions, lend the two old universities their unique charm, and much of their prestige over the new universities is founded on the beauty of their colleges. The finest Perpendicular buildings are c h a p e l s , smaller structures, in which the thin walls have no longer to support heavy weights: *King's College Chapel,* Cambridge, and the royal chapels *St. George's Chapel,* Windsor, and *Henry VII's Chapel* in Westminster Abbey. In cathedrals the finest Perpendicular work to be found is in the rebuilt naves of *Canterbury* and *Winchester,* in the five-aisled Church of *St. Giles,* Edinburgh, with its famous Crown (central tower), the west front of *Beverley Minster,* in lofty central t o w e r s *(Canterbury, Durham, Gloucester)* and the magnificent west-front towers of *York Minster. Gloucester* has the earliest example of Perpendicular in its east window (c. 1345), one of the most typical examples in its *Lady Chapel* and one of the most magnificent in its *Cloisters* (fig. 12).

VI. **Tudor Style,** 1500–1600: In accordance with the s e c u l a r   t r e n d of the Tudor Age, church building was superseded by secular structures. The transfer of monastic lands to a new gentry made necessary the building of manor houses. Endowments, now chiefly made to secular institutions, led to the erection of schools and colleges.

Anything but a pure style, Tudor architecture, which emerged in an age of national ascendancy, is considered a typically English expression in building, and has therefore remained very popular, being still used in domestic architecture, esp. in inns and restaurants.

1. TUDOR STYLE PROPER (EARLY TUDOR), 1500–60: M a n s i o n s are still Gothic, with gables, pinnacles, high chimneys and gate towers (the most typical Tudor feature), stressing the vertical character of Gothic architecture. But the gradual flattening of roofs, the flattened arch and rectangular window head, the slight classical ornament introduced by Italian craftsmen are typical of the Renaissance. At this time brick began to be used for the houses of the wealthy. The most splendid examples are Wolsey's Palace at *Hampton Court*, Henry VIII's *St. James's Palace,* of which only the *Gate House* is still extant, and *Sutton Place,* Surrey.

2. ELIZABETHAN, 1560–1600: The influence of the Italian Renaissance, which had ceased after Henry's break with the Roman Catholic Church, now entered England in a somewhat adulterated form from the Protestant Germanic countries Flanders and Germany. Flemish classicism was crude and ornate. The mansions of the newly rich were often pretentious and ill-proportioned (*Wollaton Hall,* Notts.), interiors lavishly decorated with heavily patterned plaster ceilings and oak or plaster panelling (e.g. Great Chamber in *Gilling Castle,* Yorks.). Classical ornamentation: columns, plaques, scrolls, caryatid figures, are used in fireplaces and doorways. Even chimney stacks were fluted or ornamented with spirals and zig-zags. The earlier Tudor manor houses were still built in a haphazard manner on the traditional enclosed courtyard pattern. In the later E or H-shaped houses plans became more elaborate and symmetrical. In the great hall, which was still the main feature, a staircase with an elaborately carved balustrade led up to a long gallery. The best examples of Elizabethan mansions are *Longleat House,* Wilts., and *Kirby Hall,* Northants., with its curved gables.

The finest achievement of the period was the h a l f - t i m b e r e d h o u s e s (e.g. *Moreton Old Hall,* Cheshire). They are particularly well preserved in the west, while in the east brick imported from Holland became a popular building material. Some of the finest half-timbered houses found in England are in Shakespeare's birthplace *Stratford on-Avon,* in *Shrewsbury* (Welsh borderland) and the unique *Rows* in *Chester,* where open galleries on the first floor of the close-built houses form a pedestrian walk.

VII. Classicism, 1600–ca. 1850:

1. JACOBEAN, 1600–25, was a transitional style found chiefly in university buildings (e.g. *Oriel College,* Oxford) and in great

country houses (*Hatfield House*, Hertfordshire, *Broome Park*, Denton, Kent). Still strongly under Flemish influence, Jacobean classicism was mannered and profuse in ornament (cartouches, figures, grotesques), and made much use of the Dutch curved and stepped gables.

2. PALLADIAN, 1625–60, is a refined, pure classicism introduced by the first professional English architect I n i g o J o n e s in imitation of the Italian architect Palladio, whose buildings he studied during his travels to Italy. Inigo Jones, who was appointed Surveyor General in 1615, erected the first truly classical buildings, *Queen's House*, Greenwich, and his greatest work, the *Banqueting Hall* as part of a magnificent plan for the reconstruction of Whitehall Palace. The horizontal line of the Renaissance style is stressed by straight (no longer gabled) walls crowned by a cornice and a flat roof hidden behind a parapet. There is a strict symmetry of design in the arrangement of ornamental columns and rectangular windows and doors surmounted by architraves. Wood panelling is now fully replaced by plaster panelling with gilded ornaments and painted ceilings. Other Palladian architects were Inigo Jones's disciple John W e b b , and Sir Roger P r a t t.

3. WREN'S CLASSICISM, 1660–1720: 'That miracle of a youth' (Evelyn's Diary), Christopher Wren, was a brilliant student of science at Oxford, who made some minor inventions and became Professor of Astronomy at the age of 25. After the Great Fire, which destroyed 13,000 houses and 87 churches in London, he was appointed Surveyor General and thus became principal architect for the rebuilding of the City of London. His engineering genius (cf. structure of the dome of St. Paul's Cathedral, with its famous Whispering Gallery), his fertility of invention, his mastery of composition and his ornamental use of native materials made him England's greatest architect, who developed a national classicism less ostentatious and more sober than the contemporary Continental Baroque. His plans for rebuilding the city would have made London the first modern city of Europe, had not lack of space and business interests thwarted his geometrical plan. This provided for wider streets radiating from focal points or circles, with vistas to fine classical buildings. Wren rebuilt *St. Paul's Cathedral* in a grand unostentatious classical style with a dome visible for miles around. St. Paul's is England's only classical cathedral. The outstanding features of the 53 churches he rebuilt in London are the steeples (the most beautiful being that of *St. Mary-le-Bow*), in which he achieved a Gothic effect with classical means through round colonnades built on each other tapering towards the top. Wren's

chief secular buildings are the *Sheldonian Theatre* in Oxford (with excellent acoustics!), the classical part of *Hampton Court, Chelsea Hospital* for retired soldiers, and its naval counterpart, *Greenwich*. In *Chelsea Hospital* he achieved an ornamental effect by setting off white Portland Stone against the red brick of the walls, a colour contrast which became a common feature in English house building. In *Greenwich* he incorporated Inigo Jones's *Queen's House* into a grand, spacious design of four quadrangular blocks with domes, pavilions and open colonnades framing a vista of *Queen's House*. In *Hampton Court* the severe rectangular construction is offset by the elegant stone carving and window design. Wren's foremost assistants and disciples were G r i n l i n g G i b b o n s and J a m e s G i b b s.

4. GEORGIAN, 1720–1800:

a) EARLY GEORGIAN, 1720–60, was initiated by a short era of exuberant Baroque (–1730), whose chief exponents were Sir John V a n b r u g h, officer in the army, playwright and architect, and Nicholas H a w k s m o o r. Vanbrugh was of Flemish descent. His buildings *Castle Howard,* Yorks., and *Blenheim Palace,* Oxfordshire (the latter with a frontage of 290 m) are of stupendous size, pretentious and flamboyant. They consist of a central structure connected to outlying subsidiary buildings by long arcades or colonnades. Hawksmoor, more original and inventive, built chiefly churches and colleges *(All Souls* and *Queen's Colleges,* Oxford).

The Palladian school of the 18th century was represented by Lord B u r l i n g t o n, who was equally influential as a patron and an architect, and William K e n t, the fashionable architect from 1730–50, who was also interested in interior decoration and landscape gardening as a complement to the severe, plain designs of his well-proportioned Palladian buildings *(Holkham Hall,* Norfolk; *Horse Guards,* Whitehall).

The outstanding and most brilliant architect of early Georgian, James G i b b s, was independent of both groups, but shows the influence of Wren in his churches *St. Mary-le-Strand* and *St. Martin-in-the-Fields,* London, (the latter much copied, particularly in the U.S.A.) and his college buildings *Radcliffe Camera,* Oxford, *Senate House,* Cambridge.

The typical Early Georgian house, which is also found in colonial America, is a building of noble proportions with a steep pitched roof (e.g. *Mompesson House,* Salisbury), whose chief decorative effect is often the colour contrast between red brick used in the walls and white stone architraves and doorways (fig. 17).

b) LATE GEORGIAN, 1760–1800, is characterized by the beginning of rivalry between Roman (Palladian) classicism and a neoclassical movement which regarded Greece as the cradle of classical architecture. Adherents of both schools were equally engaged in studies and excavations on Italian and Greek building sites. Of the two architects who dominated this period, Sir William C h a m b e r s was the last great representative of the Palladian school. He was widely travelled in China, India and Italy and served as architect to the King, Comptroller and finally Surveyor-General. His *pagoda* in *Kew Gardens,* which he was commissioned to lay out, initiated the 'Chinoiserie', which became one of the features of 18th-century art. His most famous work is *Somerset House,* a colossal palace of rigid classical design with a huge 270-metre frontage to the River Thames.

Robert A d a m was the most inventive genius of a Scottish family, all of whose members were architects. He has become famous particularly for his interiors which excel in variety and originality of design (*Syon House,* Middlesex; *Keddleston Hall,* Derbyshire). His free, elegant use of ornament comparable to Continental Rococo, substituted the picturesque for the heavy Palladian decoration. Plaster gave way to stucco on ceilings and walls, which were also painted with Pompeian motifs: vases, urns, garlands, draped figures. This Etruscan style was also used in Wedgwood's factory 'Etruria', whose famous pottery formed an important element of interior decoration. Colour schemes were in white and pastel shades with touches of gilt; carpets and curtains were designed to match the general style. Thus the 18th century was the great age of furnishing, the actual furniture being mostly produced according to the designs of the *Gentleman's and Cabinetmaker's Director,* by the popular cabinetmaker Thomas C h i p p e n d a l e. The Adam style of ornament was applied also to the exteriors of houses in the form of pilasters in low relief with stucco or terra-cotta decoration (e.g. *7 Adam Street,* London). In pilasters Adam preferred the Ionic order (e.g. *Stowe,* Buckinghamshire, and the *Royal Society of Arts,* the Adelphi, London).

The most original among the neo-classical architects who began their career during this period was Sir John S o a n e, whose buildings were as monumental as they were well-proportioned and free of non-essential ornament. In his principal work, the *Bank of England* (later spoilt by the 20th-century superstructures), he solved the difficult problem presented by the acute-angled corner site by his dignified, partly colonnaded triangular screen wall. Other talented architects were George Dance Senior (*Mansion House,*

London) and James Wyatt, whose *Pantheon,* a concert hall built after the Roman Pantheon but decorated in the Adam manner, created a general sensation when it was opened in 1772, and was called by Gibbon 'the wonder of the 18th century and of the British Empire'.

The 18th century also saw the beginnings of t o w n p l a n n i n g, which groups several buildings in uniform lines of terraces, circles, crescents. In B a t h, the main centre of fashionable society outside London, the first experiments were made by J o h n W o o d the Elder, who planned the *Circus* as a circle of 33 houses with identical designs (Doric for the ground floor, Ionic for the centre and Corinthian for the top stage). More impressive is the *Royal Crescent* by his son, Wood the Younger. The Adam brothers were less successful in their ambitious terrace building schemes. The *Adelphi scheme,* London, proved a financial failure though it set a pattern for later terrace planning.

The greatest architectural achievement was the E n g l i s h p a r k. In contrast to the French park with its strictly symmetrical layout it tended to cultivate the natural charms of landscape ('landscape gardening'). Meadows are interspersed with groups of trees and bushes, and traversed by streams with irregular courses. The English park cultivated the picturesque by introducing new exotic plants, small pavilions and temples and Chinese structures. The finest English parks are *St. James's* and *Regent's Parks* in London and the *English Gardens* in Munich, the work of the Bavarian minister, Count Rumford, of American birth.

5. REGENCY ARCHITECTURE, strictly speaking the short period of the later King George IV's regency (1811–20), covers the first thirty years of the 19th century until the death of George IV. It reflects the renewed enthusiasm for Greek culture inspired by Lord Byron and by Lord Elgin who brought the Parthenon frieze to England (*Elgin Marbles* in the British Museum). Despite the new endeavour to achieve Greek refinement and elegance, the Regency terraces are characterized by pretentious grandeur rather than classical proportions: gigantic colonnaded fronts rest on high pediments or carry two-storied superstructures. An outstanding example is *Carlton House Terrace* built in the white Portland stone typical of Regency architecture. Less pretentious terraces with finer proportions may be found in the watering places and seaside resorts that became fashionable during that period, esp. C h e l t e n h a m, T u n b r i d g e W e l l s and B r i g h t o n. Beside S o a n e, whose later work falls in this period (e.g. *Pitzhanger Manor* and the *Soane Museum,* London, originally his

234

own town house), the chief Regency architect was J o h n N a s h , favourite architect and town planner of George IV. Nash's far-seeing metropolitan schemes for *Regent's Park* and Trafalgar Square were ingenious conceptions. His idea was to create a whole garden city for the well-to-do in the centre of the metropolis with villas set in a park which was to have a lake and to be surrounded by crescents and terraces. Of this ambitious scheme only the park and a number of terraces were completed, the most impressive being the colonnaded row of *Cumberland Terrace*. Regent's Park was connected with the Prince's palace, Carlton House, by *Regent Street*, a royal route swerving southwest in an irregular line. Its changes of axis were marked by eye-catching buildings, the Quadrant (quarter circle) providing an uninterrupted curve of stucco façade up to Piccadilly Circus. All that remains of this scheme today is *Carlton House Terrace* in the Mall and the adjoining *St. James's Park*. On the sea front of B r i g h t o n , Nash erected the *Royal Pavilion* in an Oriental style with pierced stonework and onion domes. True Greek elegance and refinement are achieved in the *Athenaeum Club* by Decimus Burton who also built the triumphal *Wellington Arch* and screen for Hyde Park, the arch being later removed to Constitution Hill.

VIII. **Victorian Revivals** apply both the Gothic and the classical styles without regard to the special character of the building.

    1. GREEK REVIVALS: The most consistent Greek revivalists were William Wilkins, whose principal buildings are the *National Gallery* and *University College,* London, and Sir Robert Smirke, who built the *British Museum* and the *Royal Mint,* London. Other examples are *Covent Garden Theatre* by Barry, *St. George's Hall,* Liverpool, by H. Elmes, which has been praised as the outstanding classical building of the century, the *Town Hall,* Birmingham, by Hansom, inventor of the 'hansom' cab, the *Fitzwilliam Museum,* Cambridge, by G. Basevi, and the buildings in the New Town, Edinburgh, by the Scottish architects Playfair and Hamilton.

    2. GOTHIC REVIVAL was inspired by the romantic and medieval tendencies of Sir Walter Scott and the Catholic Revival of the Oxford Movement, the somewhat sombre religious sentiment of the Victorian era preferring it for ecclesiastical buildings. Its most enthusiastic advocate was the Catholic convert A. W. N. P u g i n , who wrote a book on *True Principles of Pointed or Christian Architecture* and built many Gothic churches. The movement was encouraged by the nationalistic spirit of the age which considered Gothic the truly national English style. The finest and most popular

Gothic Revival structure is found in the *Houses of Parliament*, built in Perpendicular Gothic by the notable 19th-century architect Sir Charles B a r r y. Its interior decoration and much of the exterior ornamentation was designed and supervised by Pugin. Other less inspired neo-Gothic buildings are the *Law Courts*, Strand, by G. E. Street, *St. Pancras Station* and the *Albert Memorial*, London, by Sir Gilbert Scott.

3. MORRIS MOVEMENT was a valuable stimulus to domestic architecture and interior furnishing. Under the influence of R u s k i n ' s socio-ethical theories of art, W i l l i a m M o r r i s, poet, craftsman and reformer, strove to fight the trend towards mediocre mass-production and to cultivate individual craftwork and artistic design. His *Red House* in Kent, which was built in 1860 by his friend Philipp W e b b in the rustic style of a Kentish farmhouse, is often considered as a landmark in 19th-century architecture. Its furniture, wallpaper and glass design were produced by the newly established firm *Morris and Co*. This 'vernacular' style was imitated in many manor and country houses and was also used by the most talented architect of that period, Richard Norman S h a w.

IX. Modern Architecture

1. CIVIC ENGINEERING, at first hardly recognized as architecture, nevertheless became the typical constructional expression of an industrial age with its increased need for functional buildings (bridges, factories, railway and power stations). It received an important stimulus from the new mass production of prefabricated building materials, e.g. cast-iron girders, which made possible steel-framed buildings like skyscrapers. The first great achievement of functional building was the suspension bridge over the Menai Straits between Anglesey and the Welsh mainland, which was built in 1826 by the leading engineer of his day, the Scotsman Thomas Telford. Similar structures are the *Clifton Bridge* over the Avon Gorge at Bristol, 60 m above the river, by Brunel, and the *Forth Bridge* built from 1882–90 by the architects Fowler and Baker, which spans the 2.4 km wide Firth of Forth near Edinburgh. The most spectacular achievement of functional building, however, was *Crystal Palace*, London, a gigantic construction of glass and iron girders 600 m long, which was built by J. Paxton for the Great Exhibition in 1851, but was destroyed by fire in 1936 (fig. 19).
A notable achievement of modern engineering is the *Royal Festival Hall*, London. The problem of insulating a concert hall which stands next to a big railway station was solved by the two architects

Matthew and Martin by a floating auditorium inside an isolating shell, allowing an ingenious arrangement of levels and foyers. The hall itself has remarkable acoustics.

2. NEW TOWN BUILDING: The most notable feature of post-war building is satellite towns built under the provisions of the *New Towns Act,* 1946, to take the excess population of large cities, e.g. London and Glasgow. The centres of the towns comprise civic and cultural buildings and the larger shops with parking facilities. The industrial and residential parts are adjacent but kept apart. Residential areas containing the local shops, the primary school, church, public house and community centre are separated by sports and playing fields and generally have individual houses and gardens. Where buildings are high they are spaced more widely apart for adequate ingress of light and playground facilities. The most attractive of these pleasant though rather monotonous estates (p. 168) is *Crawley New Town,* Sussex.

The principal pioneer in the field of town planning was Sir L. P. A b e r c r o m b i e , who devised replanning schemes for Dublin, Bath, Bristol, Stratford-on-Avon, and bombed cities, esp. London. The modern style of architecture, the plain cubic structure with an ample use of glass, was introduced from the Continent by Le Corbusier and emigrants from Nazi Germany, W. Gropius (director of the revolutionary Bauhaus, Dessau) and Erich Mendelssohn, though considerable influence was also exercised by the American architect Frank Lloyd Wright. The best-known British architect is the Scotsman Sir Basil S p e n c e , who won the competition for *Coventry Cathedral* (fig. 21 and 22). His work includes the *University of Sussex,* Brighton, and a number of college buildings for other new universities.

3. COVENTRY CATHEDRAL is the oustanding achievement of modern church building in England. Having been destroyed by the war's longest air raid in 1940, it was rebuilt by Sir Basil Spence with gifts and the voluntary work of Christians from many countries, who were devoted to its central idea of Reconciliation. The ruins of the former cathedral, the outer walls and the spire of which remained intact, form a precinct to the new cathedral. It is linked with it through *St. Michael's Porch* with Epstein's grandiose statue of *St. Michael Defeating the Devil.* Being a public pedestrian way this porch is contructed to give the passers-by a full view of the interior through its magnificent *Glass Screen* representing angels, prophets, apostles, and martyrs in two horizontal rows. The interior is dominated by Graham Sutherland's *Christ in Glory* behind the altar, the largest tapestry ever woven. The floating cross-ribbed

vault of the single-chamber church is supported by thin pillars. The ten cathedral windows are designed to form angled recesses, which enable both morning and afternoon sun to pour light through the coloured glass 'perhaps the loveliest made in Europe since the 15th century'. Some of the most beautiful features are the chapels: the *Chapel of Christ in Gethsemane* with a screen in the shape of a *Crown of Thorns*, the *Industrial Chapel of Christ the Servant*, the *Chapel of Unity* with a mosaic floor presented by the Church of Sweden. The *Baptistry* has a boulder from Bethlehem which serves as a font, and a gorgeous coloured window symbolizing the glory of God flooding through the world.

Pictorial Arts

I. Early Art in Britain

1. CELTIC ART IN THE BRONZE AND IRON AGES: Being very rich in metals, the British Isles made notable contributions to the excellent metal work of the Bronze Age. No country produced as many g o l d o r n a m e n t s as Ireland, then Europe's richest gold-producing country. The highly developed b r o n z e w o r k and e n a m e l o r n a m e n t s in bright colours are characterized by the Celtic genius for exquisitely devised geometrical ornamentation: bosses, scrolls, spirals often interlaced with serpent-like, long-jawed animals. Some of the finest objects found are an enamelled *bronze shield*, *Thames at Battersea*, and a *bronze mirror, Desborough, Northants.*, both in the British Museum.

In Britain the Bronze Age continued centuries longer than on the Continent, where iron began to be worked from 1000 B.C. during the first Iron Age, the Hallstatt period. The art of iron working came to Britain during the Second Iron Age, the La Tène period, and was introduced by the later Celtic immigrants, the Britons after 400 B.C. Nevertheless, bronze continued to be used for ornamental work while iron began to be worked for weapons and objects of daily use. The richest discoveries from the Iron Age were made in a pit-burial at *Aylesford, Kent*. The most famous relic of prehistoric pictorial art is the gigantic, highly impressionistic *White Horse* carved out of the flank of the Berkshire downs near Uffington. It is 125 m from nose to tail. Excavations from Roman Britain produced Roman sculptures and 'S a m i a n' p o t t e r y , red vessels with black ornaments and figures, mostly the work of native craftsmen.

2. Early Christian art in Ireland: After the introduction of Christianity, Celtic linear art was applied to the i l l u m i n a t i o n of gospels *(Books of Armagh, Durrow, Kells)* and h i g h s t o n e c r o s s e s, chiefly on monastic sites (Monasterboice, Clonmacnoise, Durrow). They are covered with abstract ornamentation as well as biblical figures and scenes.

3. Anglo-Saxon art shows strong Celtic influences beside Scandinavian and Frankish elements. Excavations, chiefly in Kent, produced primitive vessels with incised lines and stamped decoration, and gold and garnet-set brooches with remarkable mosaic-glass and gold-wire filigree ornamentation. The richest treasure dug from English soil is the *Sutton Hoo Ship Burial* excavated in Suffolk in 1939. The long ship, the form of which was indicated by the iron clench nails and bolts, contained a hut with the treasure of an East Anglian king, who died about 655. The treasure included the king's jewelled sword, his helmet with gilt ornamentation, silver bowls, buckles and a purse lid with jewelled ornaments and a gold frame.

Christian art reached an early climax (c. 700) when the *Lindisfarne Gospel* was written in the Irish mission centre in Northumbria (p. 15), and the *Bewcastle, Easby* and *Ruthwell Crosses* were carved under the inspiration of Irish high crosses. They show geometrical and foliage designs with birds perched in vines and primitively carved biblical figures, some with a pathetic humility of expression. The Winchester School of the later Wessex period (9th–11th centuries) produced fine church sculptures besides illuminations and stone and ivory crosses called roods (cf. Holyrood in Edinburgh). The finest examples of this art are the reliefs in *Chichester Cathedral* and illuminations developed in Glastonbury (centre of Dunstan's monastery reform) in close connection with the Carolingian Renaissance (cf. introduction of the classical acanthus leaf instead of Syrian vines used in Celtic art).

II. **Art in the Later Middle Ages** is chiefly connected with church architecture, and includes besides m u r a l and p a n e l p a i n t i n g s, r e l i e f s on reredos, tympana, grave stones, and rich c a r v i n g s on doorways, capitals and bosses (keystones). Norman and early Gothic carvings are usually highly naturalistic. Figures of men and animals combined with foliage, grotesque monsters interlocked in violent fights often convey the impression of intricate geometrical patterns reminiscent of Celtic abstract ornamentation. Later Gothic added s t a t u e s on porch columns or in canopied niches. Thus the whole west front of Wells Cathedral was covered with 180 statues and reliefs representing the holy story from the Creation to the Last Judgement with Christ in Majesty high up on the gable. One of the finest works of Gothic sculpture are the angel figures in the *Angel Choir* in Lincoln Cathedral. The first life-size bronze figure in English art is the effigy on the tomb of *Henry III* in Westminster Abbey.

The most remarkable paintings are the *Chichester Roundel*, Virgin and Child, (c. 1260) and the *Wilton Diptych* (c. 1390), now in the National Gallery, which was called 'one of the most remarkable embodiments of the late Gothic spirit in painting'. Both are marked by an exquisite tenderness of feeling. Under royal inspiration London became a centre of artistic activity, of which the portrait of *Richard II* in Westminster Abbey, one of the earliest known, is the finest example preserved.

III. **In the Sixteenth and Seventeenth Centuries** the i c o n o c l a s m of the Reformation doomed religious sculpture. Thousands of statues in churches were demolished, and for two centuries sculpture almost ceased to be considered an art, being left to masons rather than artists. Painting, deprived of its religious inspiration, now turned to portraiture. The rich collection of the National Portrait Gallery in London bears witness to the fact that p o r t r a i t u r e is the only English art with a permanent tradition. Though English portraiture was for two centuries overshadowed by foreign artists, some English works in the 16th century already reveal grasp of character, e.g. the portraits of *Henry VII* and of his mother *Lady Margaret Beaufort* with its singular purity and sincerity of expression. Under Elizabeth I, the most original English artist was the miniaturist Nicholas H i l l i a r d, whose *Portrait of a Gentleman* is suggestive of the Tudor court atmosphere. The greatest 16th century portraitist was Hans H o l b e i n the Younger, whose pictures of *Henry VIII* showing his royal patron's robust corpulence reveal his vigorous realism. In contrast to Holbein, the outstanding court painter of the 17th century, V a n D y c k, introduced the idealizing 'grand manner' in his distinguished portraits of *Charles I* and his courtiers, which enhance the romantic elegance of the court before the Civil War.

His English followers interpreted the character of the hostile parties in the war: William D o b s o n painted the Cavalier chivalry of the soldier courtiers, Robert W a l k e r the austere sobriety of the Puritan character *(Oliver Cromwell)*. The greatest English portraitist of the Stuart period with an admirable grasp of character was John R i l e y, who painted the portraits of the later Stuarts. His fame was, however, eclipsed by the two more successful foreign painters, Sir Peter L e l y (Pieter van der Faes), whose *Admirals* at Greenwich Hospital and *Beauties* at Hampton Court recall the colourful splendour of the court of Charles II, and the German-born Sir Godfrey K n e l l e r, whose

23. RICHARD II: late 14th century, Westminster Abbey

24. HENRY VII: early 16th century, artist unknown

25. HENRY VIII: after Holbein

26. Nicholas Hilliard: SIR WALTER RALEIGH

27. Robert Walker:
OLIVER CROMWELL

28. William Hogarth:
THE SHRIMP GIRL

29. Sir Godfrey Kneller:
SIR ISAAC NEWTON

30. Sir Joshua Reynolds:
    ANNE, COUNTESS OF ALBEMARLE

31. Thomas Gainsborough:
    MRS. SIDDONS

32. Thomas Gainsborough:
    THE MARKET CART

33. John Crome: MOONLIGHT ON THE YARE

34. John Constable: WEYMOUTH BAY

35. William Blake: SATAN SMITING JOB WITH SORE BOILS

36. Samuel Palmer:
   A HILLY SCENE

37. Dante Gabriel Rossetti:
   ECCE ANCILLA DOMINI

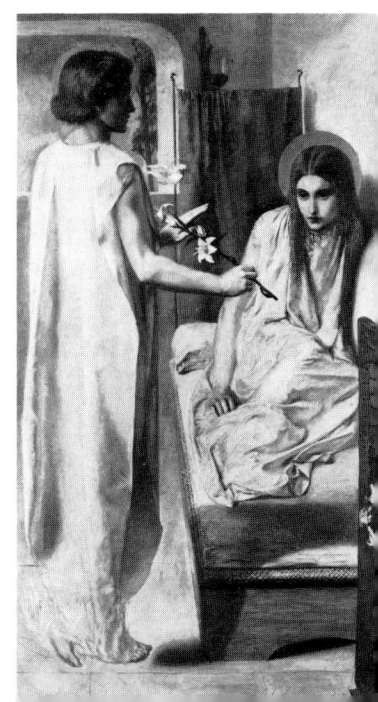

38. George Frederic Watts:
JOHN STUART MILL

39. Sir John Everett Millais:
CHRIST IN THE HOUSE
OF HIS PARENTS

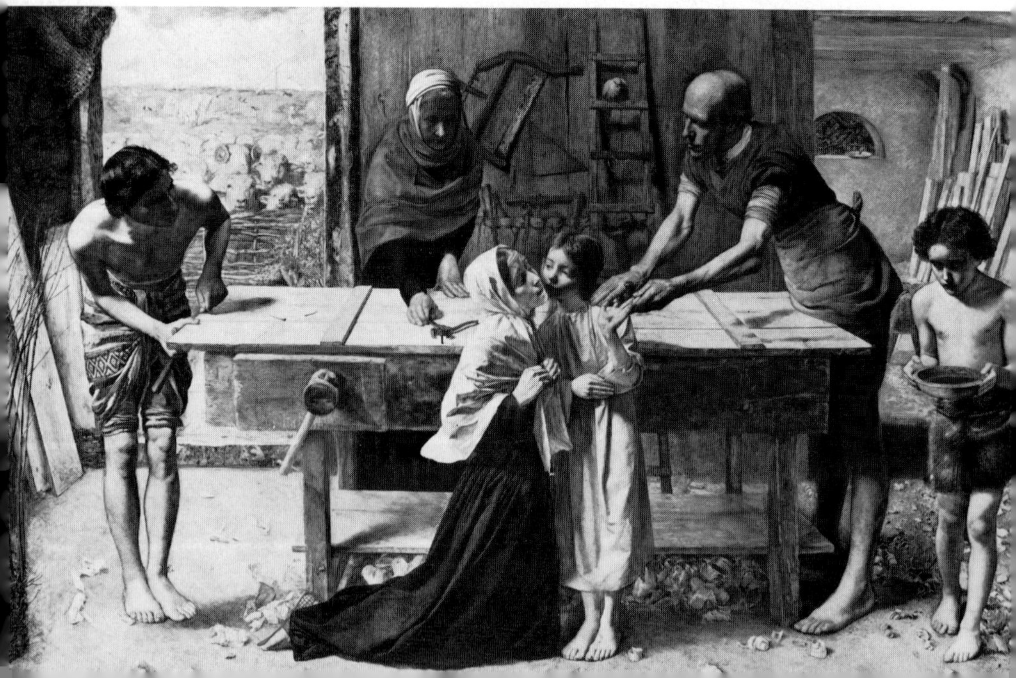

40. Sir John Everett Millais:
WILLIAM EWART
GLADSTONE
(detail)

41. Sir John Everett Millais:
BENJAMIN DISRAELI,
EARL OF
BEACONSFIELD
(detail)

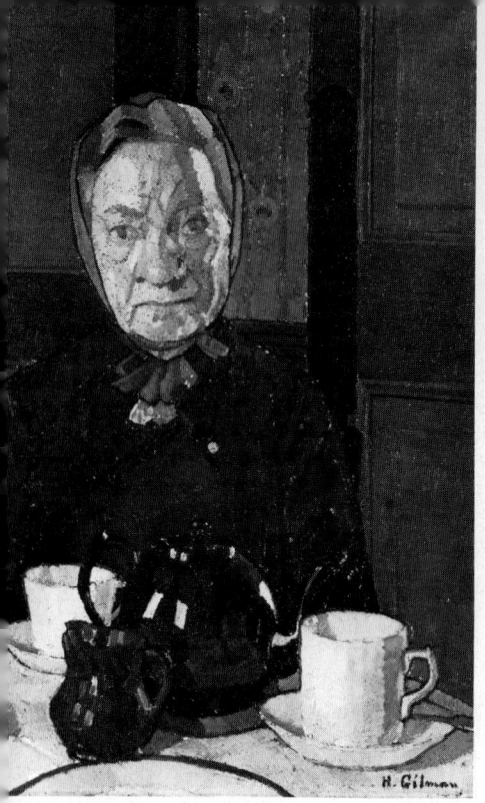

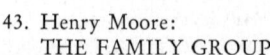

42. Harold Gilman:
    MRS. MOUNTER AT
    THE BREAKFAST
    TABLE

43. Henry Moore:
    THE FAMILY GROUP

flamboyant, somewhat superficial style dominated portraiture for almost a century.

IV. Eighteenth and Nineteenth Centuries

The 18th century saw such a blossoming of English art as never before or ever since. It produced not only most of the great English painters, but was also an age of art patronage inspired by the Grand Tour to Italy, which became the fashion among art students and men of quality. The collection of antiques, chiefly statuary, became a mania and turned many an English hall into a museum of art (cf. art collections in Windsor and Warwick Castles).

A. **Sculpture:** Inspired by Winckelmann's new interpretation of Greek art, sculpture sought to achieve classical simplicity, serenity and repose. Though the foundation of modern sculpture in England was laid by foreigners working in England, Rysbrack, Scheemakers, Nollekens and Roubillac, the art was also represented by native sculptors such as Grinling G i b b o n s , Thomas Banks, John B a c o n and, above all, John F l a x m a n , who spent seven years in Italy. As a professor at the Royal Academy he exercised an influence beyond his country (e.g. Goethe), which made him appear to later generations as the protagonist of neo-classical sculpture in England. As a 'sculptor of sentiment rather than of form' (Thomas Lawrence) he founded a tradition, which under the influence of 19th-century emotionalism eventually declined into sentimentality.

B. **Painting**

The 18th century saw the birth and climax of painting by English-born artists. Its centre was London, where the R o y a l A c a d e m y o f A r t s was founded in 1768 to set a standard for students of art. The types of art developed under its protection now became genuine expressions of the English artistic genius: painting of manners in the moralities of Hogarth, later continued in the typically English art of book illustration and caricature; portraiture reflecting the contemporary veneration of nobility; landscape painting as an expression of the English romantic appreciation of nature; animal and sporting painting representing an old tradition of the English way of life; finally the religious symbolism of William Blake rooted in Evangelical piety and later revived by the Pre-Raphaelites under the influence of the Victorian Gothic Revival.

1. PAINTING OF MANNERS: W i l l i a m H o g a r t h , 1697–1764, the first great English painter, was in his complete independence from foreign influence, in his insular outlook a wholly original autodidact, who satirized not only the current imitation of classical art but also

all fashions and follies of society in general. He began his career as a painter of small conversation pieces expressing his typically English love of the artistic treatment of human and moral subjects, 'a field not broken up in any country or in any age' (Hogarth). His progressive moralities, which he calls 'dumb shows' and p a i n t e d c o m e d i e s, *The Harlot's Progress*, *The Rake's Progress*, and *Mariage à la Mode* (his only morality depicting high life) established the descriptive and satirical school of painting. They are invaluable pictures of London life reflecting the realism and robust vitality of the rising middle classes.

2. PORTRAITURE: Hogarth's portraits (e.g. his *Self-Portrait* or that of his sister) are characterized by the same vitality, realism and contempt of aristocratic fashion apparent in his moralities. His *Shrimp Girl* was called by Whistler 'the best portrait ever painted by an Englishman'.

Sir Joshua R e y n o l d s, 1723–92, was in many ways the antithesis to Hogarth. A 'classical temperament', strongly under the influence of Italian masters, whose paintings he studied in Italy, he established 'the grand manner' of English art as court painter and first president of the Royal Academy. Through his celebrated *Discourses on Art* he became the preceptor of English art. His portraits of English aristocrats, e.g. *Lady Bingham, Countess of Albemarle*, are marked by warmth of colour derived chiefly from Venetian masters. They reveal grasp of character and natural dignity rather than spontaneity.

Thomas G a i n s b o r o u g h, 1727–88, who never went to Italy, was the more original artistic temperament, self-taught and uninfluenced by theories and foreign models. His figures, e.g. *Blue Boy, Mrs. Siddons, Perdita*, are distinguished by their unaffected grace, the delicate texture of their clothes and their harmony with the surrounding landscape.

George R o m n e y (also painter of histories), whose portraits were characterized by natural skill, taste and a somewhat superficial ease of line, painted fifty portraits of the notorious *Lady Hamilton* (mistress of Nelson).

Thomas L a w r e n c e, the most skilful technician, reached international fame at an early age. Rarely sensitive to social grace, he painted the portraits of most of the sovereigns and famous men of his time, e.g. *Pope Pius VII*, which were distinguished by richness of colour and elegance.

The chief Scottish painters were Allan R a m s a y and Sir Henry R a e b u r n (head of the Scottish school and later court painter), whose broad vigorous handling distinguished them from the London school (cf. Raeburn: *Sir John Sinclair of Ulster* and *Lady Anne Raeburn*). In the Victorian Age the grand manner was revived in George Frederick W a t t s's portraits of eminent men of his time (*Cardinal Manning, John Stuart Mill, Gladstone*).

3. ENGLISH LANDSCAPE PAINTING, the last type of painting to develop, was the western branch of the rich landscapist school on both sides of the North Sea exploiting the vast possibilities of wide horizons, iridescent skies and quickly changing transparent atmospheres, adding, however, that instinct for designing nature expressed in the English park.

Richard W i l s o n , the first English landscapist (who had studied in Rome), combined strong classical influences reflected in his earlier picturesque-classical landscapes with the gift for a realistic rendering of English scenery (e.g. *The Thames at Twickenham*).

G a i n s b o r o u g h possessed greater artistic spontaneity and vitality. His picturesque-romantic landscapes (e.g. *Crossing the Stream, The Market Cart*) are marked by a serene lightness of touch (cf. the feathery foliage of his trees). If Gainsborough differed from Wilson's generalizing manner already by introducing a local conception of landscape,

J o h n C r o m e , founder of the only school of art outside London, the Norwich Society of Artists, represented a purely local sentiment. His close observation made him a realist with a gift, however, for endowing his subjects with a calm dignified grandeur reflecting the spaciousness of the Norfolk horizon (e.g. *Moonrise on the Marshes of the Yare, Mousehold Heath*) (fig. 33).

J o h n C o n s t a b l e , 1776–1837, is often considered the first impressionist, his pictures representing immediate visions of objects at a glance rather than studied compositions. He was the first artist to see the objects of nature under the dynamic aspect of movement: piercing light *(Hampstead Heath, Rainbow)*, rolling waves *(Coast near Brighton)*, forming clouds *(Weymouth Bay)*. This tendency is symbolized in his use in later pictures of the palette knife in preference to the brush. Being the first landscapist to paint the actual green of fields and trees *(Flatford Mill)* instead of the conventional brownish tones, he achieved a new freshness and a much wider range of colours than his predecessors. Constable was the most typically English artist in his keenly empirical interest which regarded landscape painting as "a branch of natural philosophy, of which pictures are but the experiments" (cf. his preoccupation with 'skying', i.e. sketching of cloud formations). Though Constable was little recognized in England, his *Haywain* achieved a sensational success at the Salon in Paris, 1824, influencing the School of Barbizon.

William Turner, 1775–1851, was the most original landscape painter without forerunners or descendants, though impressionists like Monet, Renoir, Pissarro and Sisley acknowledged their debt to him. His career as a painter shows three distinct phases. He began in the topographic tradition as draughtsman and water-colourist with views of the English landscape. After years of travel on the Continent he painted romantic subjects done in a less sharply defined manner, imaginative and picturesque *(Gipsy Camp, Garden of Hesperides)*. In his last phase after his first visit to Italy he began to devote himself chiefly to the problems of illumination, and moved finally from the world of reality into a world of grandiose visions, 'a world of his own creation, vast, flaming and insubstantial' (J. Rothenstein). At that time he painted his pictures of the *Canale Grande* in Venice in light tones, in which forms are but vaguely defined, with incandescent skies. Golden, red and turquoise painted on white ground became his favourite colours *(Snowstorm, Fighting Temeraire)*.

WATER COLOUR, which flourished between 1775 and 1840, was particularly adapted to the English taste for intimacy, and a certain informality. It was an art enabling the painter to catch the quickly changing atmospheric effects of the English climate. Its greatest representatives were Thomas Sandby, John Robert Cozens, Thomas Girtin, John Sell Cotman, and Richard Parkes Bonington who lived mainly in France, where he exercised a notable influence on French romanticism, and, ultimately, impressionism.

4. ANIMAL AND SPORTING PAINTING gained considerable popularity in an age that indulged in the aristocratic pursuits of riding and hunting. One of the greatest horse painters was George Stubbs, who in his book *The Anatomy of the Horse* made a science of his art. His pictures show animals in subtle harmony with human figures and landscapes (cf. *Lady and Gentleman in a Carriage*). Robuster forms combined with a somewhat sombre melancholy characterize the sporting and farming subjects of George Morland.

5. HISTORY PAINTING, though advocated and practised by Reynolds, never greatly appealed to the English predilection for understatement rather than bombast and dramatic force. Of its four main exponents not one was born in England: Benjamin West and John Singleton Copley were both born in the U.S.A., James Barry in Ireland and Fuseli (Fuessli) in Zürich. They all believed in a public art in the grand manner exalting military and civic virtue. But whereas Barry was filled with the passionate desire to revive antique art, West, followed by Copley, introduced an important

innovation by painting English (rather than ancient) subjects no longer in classical but contemporary or historical costume. His *Death of General Wolfe* in this respect 'occasioned a revolution in art' (Reynolds).

6. SYMBOLISM

a) W i l l i a m B l a k e , 1757–1827, is one of the most extraordinary phenomena in the history of art. The dominant features of his works, which were mostly written, illustrated and published by himself, are loftiness of imagination and exalted pathos expressed in various emphatic ways: lurid colours, 'flaming lines', austere parallelisms. Though various elements are traceable in their form, e.g. his veneration of Gothic art and of Michelangelo, their spirit is of an originality rarely equalled. Originally based on the revelations of the Bible (e.g. *Book of Job*), they later became strongly personal reinterpretations of great works of literature (Dante's *Divine Comedy*, Milton's *Paradise Lost*), and expressions of cosmic visions all his own. Figures drawn with superb disregard of anatomic accuracy are but symbols of divine and demonic forces expressed in gestures of grandeur or violent force *(God Creating Adam, Satan Smiting Job, Procession From Calvary)*. During his lifetime Blake was almost unknown, and after his burial in a pauper's grave he was forgotten. But today his art is recognized as one of the inspirations of Surrealism.

b) Blake's most gifted direct follower was S a m u e l P a l m e r , whose exalted vision stems rather from a mystical communion with nature and whose art has thus become one of the inspirations of English neo-Romanticism. Influenced by Blake's illustration of Vergil's *Eclogues*, he created a new pastoral school in his landscapes inhabited by Arcadian figures.

This Arcadian world lives also in the work of Blake's other disciple, G e o r g e C a l v e r t , whose excellent woodcuts and engravings reveal the same lyrical sentiment, yet more serene and distinct in form.

c) A new intensely personal form of symbolism is expressed in the allegories of G. F. W a t t s (p. 242), who replaced the accepted symbols by images of his own creation and achieved a full harmony between ethical truth and nobly expressive form (fig. 38).

d) PRE-RAPHAELITES

The Pre-Raphaelite Brotherhood was formed in 1849 by young artists as a protest movement against the pomposity of conventional classicism. It tried to revive the sincere realism and medieval religious sentiment of art before Raphael. Its greatest representatives were the

245

painter-poet Dante Gabriel Rossetti, Holman Hunt and John Everett Millais. The strongly ethical and social aspect of Pre-Raphaelite art tempered by romantic sentiment was in keeping with the religious revivals, the romanticism and social tendencies of the age. 'What I sought was the power of undying appeal to the hearts of living men' (H. Hunt). Mercilessly attacked by all those critics who considered the Pre-Raphaelite ideals as a relapse from Raphael's classical beauty into the darkness of the Middle Ages, the Pre-Raphaelites found an enthusiastic advocate in the art critic John R u s k i n, who was chiefly instrumental in making their work intelligible to the public. Pre-Raphaelitism was inspired by Rossetti's teacher Ford Madox B r o w n, whose responsiveness to social life and realistic rendering made him most successful where he deals with civic subjects, e.g. his pictures *Work* and *The Last of England* depicting the embarkation of the sculptor Thomas Woolner for Australia. He helped to establish a drawing school for artisans, and taught without pay in the Working Men's College.

W i l l i a m   H o l m a n   H u n t was chiefly moved by moral and religious subjects, which he treated with an austere realism and sumptuous rendering of detail, e.g. *Awakened Conscience,* and his most popular picture *The Light of the World* representing Christ knocking at the closed door of man's conscience.

J o h n   E v e r e t t   M i l l a i s was the more spontaneous artistic talent with a vigorous sense of colour, which gave his pictures *Lorenzo and Isabella, Christ in the House of his Parents* (fig. 39), and *Blind Girl* an intensely poetical quality. For his notable portraits see fig. 40 and 41.

D a n t e   G a b r i e l   R o s s e t t i, 1828–82, son of an Italian refugee, showed extraordinary poetical and artistic gifts from childhood. He was the pupil of Madox Brown and Holman Hunt, which led to the foundation of the Pre-Raphaelite Brotherhood. His earlier paintings *The Girlhood of Mary Virgin* and *Ecce ancilla domini* show a rare intensity of religious imagination and romantic sentiment. During his marriage to the beautiful Elizabeth Siddal and after her death he drifted in his portraits of women with luscious lips and dreamy eyes into a sensuous opulence more suggestive of his Italian sense of beauty than of the original Pre-Raphaelite ideals.

e) MORRIS MOVEMENT was founded in 1853 by the Oxford students William Morris and Edward Burne-Jones under the influence of the Oxford Movement (p. 189), and took on an aesthetic-literary character under the inspiration of Burne Jones's teacher D. G. Rossetti.

E d w a r d B u r n e J o n e s took over Pre-Raphaelite romanticism and medievalism without its social and civic interests. He resembled Rossetti in that art was to him an intensely personal matter inspired by mystic dreams, which he embodied in figures rather sentimental and wistful in expression.

W i l l i a m M o r r i s, 1834–96, poet, pamphleteer and craftsman who, in contrast to his friends, had a vigorous hold on practical life, strove to realize Ruskin's socio-ethical theory in a p p l i e d a r t s. By reviving artistic design in glass-painting, carving, metal work, tapestry, weaving and embroidery, Morris hoped to give the craftsman a new sense of his responsibility in helping to overcome bad taste and industrial squalor.

7. IMPRESSIONISM: A predominantly French school of painting (which, however, had developed partly under the influence of Constable), Impressionism was introduced into England chiefly by Walter Sickert and Wilson Steer (both 1860–1942). In England it appeared as a reaction against Pre-Raphaelitism and Ruskin's theories of art, which had exalted the subject and narrative detail at the expense of the aesthetic effects of light, colour and design. From 1886 the New English Art Club sponsored the new Continental concepts of art as against the teaching of the Slade School of Fine Art (University College, London), where most contemporary English artists were trained. The School's emphasis on draughtsmanship (which has remained a characteristic of many English painters) was superseded by a new preoccupation with colour and light and by a loose handling of surface arrangement. A forerunner of impressionism in England was the aesthetic movement initiated by Whistler.

J a m e s M c N e i l l W h i s t l e r, 1834–1903, who was born in the U.S.A., went to Paris to study art and lived in England from 1859 until his death. He was a close friend of Rossetti, who was a potent influence in inspiring his colour symbolism. His White Girl, which he called *Symphony in White* was the first of a series of musical titles indicating his aim to substitute fluid colour harmonies for the former stress on personal character, a tendency also apparent in the famous portrait of his mother *Arrangement in Black and Grey*. Also in his landscapes (e.g. his series of *Nocturnes*) he sacrificed topographic and narrative detail to the subtle harmony of low tones and decorative effects, partly derived from a close study of Japanese prints. Whistler's philosophy of 'l'art pour l'art' brought him into conflict with Ruskin to whom art was a mission. Ruskin accused him of 'throwing a pot of paint in the public's face' and was subsequently sued for libel.

Whistler's greatest disciple, the German-born Walter S i c k e r t, later abjured his capricious master's influence, contending that 'taste was the death of a painter', whose function was the observation and recording of ordinary life. Sickert introduced the anecdotal manner of Degas, who inspired his earlier music-hall subjects. Later Sickert made the shabby surroundings and common-place incidents of his favourite quarter in North London, Camden Town, the subjects of his genre pictures combining realistic illustration with social comment. In contrast to Degas he was less interested in action than in repose (cf. his greatest work of the Camden Town series, *Ennui*).

Wilson S t e e r was with Sickert the principal exponent of French Impressionism in England. Influenced by Monet and Constable, he was a notable painter of English landscapes. His earlier pictures are largely beach scenes with figures against the sea, e.g. *Running Girls, Walberswick Pier* (Tate Gallery). In his mature paintings he abandoned figure subjects for mere landscapes, culminating in the sombre poetry of his masterpieces *Chepstow Castle* and *Richmond Castle*. His later paintings are loosely handled, lyrical sketches in the manner of Turner's later colour visions.

VI. Twentieth Century

A. Painting

English painting in the 20th century participates in the contemporary movements of Continental art: Post-impressionism chiefly represented by Seurat, Fauvism led by Matisse, Cubism dominated by Braque, and Surrealism inspired by Freud and sponsored by the journal *La Révolution Surrealiste*. The influence of these Parisian movements on English painters was, however, modified by the emotional and representational values of the native tradition.

1. POST-IMPRESSIONISM, which strove to substitute a more disciplined form for the dispersive effects of the Impressionist preoccupation with light and colour, was represented by Spencer G o r e and Harold G i l m a n , who received a strong impetus from the two Post-impressionist exhibitions held in London in 1910 and 1912. Spencer Gore was inspired by Matisse to bolder experiments in colour and design, while Gilman was influenced by the burning realism of van Gogh apparent in his taste for firm designs, vigorous brush strokes and brilliant colours. His greatest ambition, 'to seize the essence of a character', was achieved in the excellent portrait of his charwoman *Mrs. Mounter* (fig. 42).

2. FAUVISM, fundamentally Impressionist in the choice of its subjects, ventured on bolder colour effects. The exuberant, violent colours of Matisse and Vlaminck exerted a strong influence on M a t t h e w S m i t h , one of the most admired painters in England, who was an audacious colourist using opulent tones (esp. reds). His pictures of still-life and figures, and his Cornish landscapes express form and

space largely in terms of colour though they also reveal excellent draughtsmanship. His nudes, *Fitzroy Street No. 1 and No. 2,* are powerful drawings coloured with a harsh disciplined vigour.

Ivon H i t c h e n s is roughly comparable to Smith in the radiance of his colours, which, however, are more harmonious and refined. His manner of reducing objects of a landscape or still-life to coloured surfaces arranged behind each other reveals a studied handling of space.

Radiance of colour is characteristic also of the work of Augustus J o h n , whose portraits (e.g. *Madame Suggia, Daphne*) have a singular vitality, firmness of contour and richness of texture. Augustus John fully retained the passionate response to the visible world abandoned by Cubism and Surrealism.

3. CUBISM AND ABSTRACTION: Far more revolutionary than Fauvism, Cubism, seeking the geometric understructure of natural forms, extended its influence to all countries. It inspired the second phase of German Expressionism (Blauer Reiter), Italian Futurism and the V o r t i c i s t s in England, who tried to compromise between abstraction and representation. This movement, founded in 1914 by W y n d h a m L e w i s , who was the editor of its journal *Blast,* was, however, short-lived.

The most extreme exponent of the abstract school in England was Ben N i c h o l s o n. His paintings, in which movement and atmosphere are excluded, are well-balanced geometrical designs concentrating on a few simple shapes, mainly rectangular and circular, in which colour is reduced to a minimum. Even in his Cornish landscapes the elements of the natural scene appear as mere ornaments with no attempt at representing phenomena of nature or interpreting moods or emotions.

Victor P a s m o r e developed from an earlier realism influenced by Sickert to a totally abstract style in painting as well as in the moulding of plastic materials.

4. NEO-ROMANTICISM: From 1939 English painters began to turn away from abstraction and to follow a new line, which had its roots in English symbolism and Romanticism. Pictures became again symbols of emotional moods. Much of the change towards a renewed interest in the drama of life was inspired by the war, which placed upon those who were appointed official War Artists by the War Artists' Committee the obligation to record the horrors of destruction. The new style has affinities with Continental Surrealism, which strove to record the processes of unconscious thought (e.g. the dream), but it is more deeply rooted in representational art.

Paul N a s h is the principal exponent of this new magic realism. His war paintings record his memories of the Western Front in the First World War. His manner is most suggestive in the pictures in which he concentrates on the interplay of mysterious elemental forces (e.g. *Pillar and Moon),* or the melancholy phenomena of a seemingly desolated world: tree-trunks, stone walls, wrecked aeroplanes.

There is a similar sincerity in the more dramatic magic realism of S t a n l e y S p e n c e r. His early pictures of religious subjects, e.g. *Resurrection* which obsessed him for the greater part of his life, his war paintings and his frieze depicting work in the shipyards on the Clyde, all reveal a passionate interest in humanity in all its aspects.

John P i p e r is one of the most versatile contemporary artists with a highly personal style, who turned from abstraction to a neo-romantic interpretation of landscape. As a War Artist he painted the desolation of bombed cities in pictures which combine studied composition and accurate draughtsmanship with a dark dramatic mood. This sense of drama, engendered by the war, became the dominant feature of his work and made him a successful designer for the stage (e.g. the ballet *The Quest*). The same vigour appears in his representations of rugged English scenes, e.g. *Gordale Scar* (a gorge in Yorkshire).

G r a h a m S u t h e r l a n d, who was influenced by the imaginative tradition of Blake and Palmer, achieved a fusion of Romanticism and Surrealism. His anthropomorphic still-lifes and desolate landscapes interpreting the frightening, harsher features of nature express a gloomy, deeply emotional symbolism. His *Crucifixion* in Northampton is considered one of the most remarkable religious paintings of the 20th century. His fame as England's foremost artist at mid-20th century was acknowledged when he was commissioned to design the tapestry of *Christ Enthroned in Glory* for Coventry Cathedral and to paint the *portrait of Churchill* on his resignation at the age of 80.

The greatest contemporary English artist was H e n r y M o o r e. Born in 1898, he served in World War I and became an Official War Artist in World War II. His coloured drawings expressing the impassive resignation of exhausted sleepers in the London air raid shelters are among the most poignant visual records of the war.

B. Sculpture

H e n r y M o o r e's international fame rests on his genius as a sculptor who has exhibited with Surrealists in England and abroad. In his abstract sculptures space is given the same consideration as solid shapes which often appear only as its mantle. His figures, which he prefers to present in a few basic attitudes, standing, seated or reclining, show the

250

influence of primitive Mexican and African art. As a war artist Henry Moore developed a more humanist element in his work. While his earlier figures are primitive weight forms, his later sculptures reveal a more animated human interest, e.g. his *Family Group* (Tate Gallery), one of his best-known works (fig. 43).

S i r   J a c o b   E p s t e i n, 1880–1959, one of the most dynamic modern sculptors, was born of Polish parents in New York. He was trained in New York and the arts school in Paris, but lived for most of his life in England. He produced abstract sculptures and portraits in bronze (Einstein, Bernard Shaw, Somerset Maugham). His noble religious figures, e.g. *Madonna and Child* outside a convent in Cavendish Square, London, *Christ in Majesty* in Llandaff Cathedral, reveal a singular power of spiritual and emotional penetration. This is coupled with dynamic force in *St. Michael Defeating the Devil* (beside the entrance of Coventry Cathedral).

Music

Though England has sometimes been called 'the land without music' because it has not produced any of what are generally regarded as the world's greatest composers, musical activities have always featured large in cultural life. In its old choral tradition Britain excels most other countries.

History:

1. MIDDLE AGES: The oldest musical tradition in vocal as well as instrumental music is found in Wales. W e l s h   b a r d s, who formed a privileged hereditary guild, developed the heroic song, sung at festivities or to inspire the army in battle. The bardic song, which was accompanied by the harp, was governed by rules laid down at gatherings held under the patronage of Welsh kings, the first e i s t e d d f o d being recorded in the sixth century. An eisteddfod included one contest for poets and one for musicians (especially harpists). The greatest Welsh bards were Taliesin and Aneurin (6th century). In Anglo-Saxon England the heroic song was soon replaced by church music: to the plainsong of Roman liturgy, which was already sung by Bede in the monasteries of Wearmouth and Jarrow, the 12th century added the rhythmic p o l y p h o n i c m u s i c for metrical poems, which was most complex in Wales. The Normans introduced the C h r i s t m a s   c a r o l (cf. French refrain in one carol: 'Noel, Noel'), later sung by waits (street singers) before the houses of the rich. O r c h e s t r a l   m u s i c is recorded in the 15th-century Minstrels' Gallery in Exeter Cathedral, showing twelve angels playing many different instruments. In 1460 Henry VI granted a charter to a newly founded Musicians' Guild. One of the first great European composers was John D u n s t a b l e, a master of counterpoint, who lived in the first half of the 15th century. The universities

251

taught music as one of the Seven Liberal Arts and granted the degree of Doctor of Music.

2. RENAISSANCE: The Tudors were among the most fervent patrons of music in Europe. Most composers of this age were Gentlemen of the Chapel Royal, or served as organists or choirmasters in the cathedrals, which were still the main centres of music. The most outstanding 16th-century composers under the earlier Tudors were the polyphonists, G. Banestre, R. Fayrfax, W. Cornyshe, and the younger generation, J. Taverner, C. Tye, and Thomas Tallis, 'the father of church music'. The Reformation gave rise to A n g l i c a n c h u r c h m u s i c. In contrast to Protestant churches on the Continent, the Anglican Church developed the chant of the professional choir (anthem and psalmody) rather than the hymn sung by the congregation. Elizabethan England saw the development of secular music under Italian influence (m a d r i g a l s, airs, canzonets, dances). Its main representatives were Thomas M o r l e y, John B u l l (p. 252), and J o h n D o w l a n d, the great lutanist. The most versatile composers were William B y r d and Orlando G i b b o n s, equally great in church music (masses, motets, anthems) and madrigals, solo songs, fantasies.

3. SEVENTEENTH CENTURY: English musical prominence continued until the Puritan Revolution, when the royal musicians were disbanded and when even the organ was banned from religious services. Only the m a s q u e (mythological play with songs, dances and instrumental interludes) was allowed to continue as a mode of expressing noble ideas. It reached its climax in Milton's *Comus* set to music by Henry L a w e s, but was soon superseded by Italian opera. The first English opera was d'Avenant's *Siege of Rhodes* with music by Henry Lawes and Captain C o o k e, under whose direction the Chapel Royal was re-established after the Restoration. With the extravagant court life of the Restoration, music again came into its own and reached its highest development in England through Henry P u r c e l l, 1659–95, the most versatile European composer of his generation, 'a daring harmonist, a contrapuntist of unlimited skill, a superb inventor of tunes and an enterprising innovator in rhythm' (Blom, *Music in England).* He composed church music (vocal and instrumental), odes and songs, wrote music for masques, stage music for Dryden's *King Arthur* and *The Faerie Queen* and composed the greatest English opera *Dido and Aeneas.* His musical style gave to English music that baroque exuberance which English architecture and painting lacked.

4. EIGHTEENTH CENTURY: Until 1760 English music was dominated by Georg Friedrich H a n d e l, who came to England in 1710 and was naturalized in 1726. He controlled English opera in the Queen's Theatre, Haymarket, which was formed into a (short-lived) Academy of Music under his direction. Repeated financial failures caused him to withdraw from opera (after having written 31 operas) and to concentrate on oratorios, taking advantage of the English choral tradition to make the choir an essential part of his works. Handel's *Judas Maccabaeus* was composed to celebrate the suppression of the Jacobite Rebellion in 1745. The *Messiah,* written within three weeks, received its first performance in Dublin, which proved a triumph.

Soon musical activities began to extend to places of lighter entertainment, *Ranelagh Gardens,* the *Pantheon* and the *Vauxhall,* which became London's chief concert hall until the building of the Royal Albert Hall. Most of the notable musicians of this period were attached to these halls as singers, conductors or composers, e.g. William B o y c e , Thomas Linley and Charles Dibdin who started the tradition of shanties (sailors' songs). The chief opera composer Thomas A r n e *(Love in a Village, Artaxerxes)* was conductor at the Vauxhall. Out of this atmosphere grew the *Beggar's Opera* of John Gay with music by the German immigrant Pepusch, which dealt a blow to Italian opera. It initiated the short period of the b a l l a d o p e r a (satirical text with popular songs and a small orchestra), which was one of England's distinctive contributions to the history of music and influenced the German 'Singspiel' and comic opera.

The ancient British c h o r a l t r a d i t i o n was cultivated by innumerable choirs, glee and catch clubs. In 1724 the Three Choirs Festival was inaugurated to take place in turn in the cathedrals of the three choirs of Worcester, Hereford and Gloucester. It was soon followed by festivals in Birmingham, Norwich and Chester. The 18th century saw the birth of three celebrated patriotic songs: Arne's *Rule Britannia*, Boyce's *Hearts of Oak* and the National Anthem *God Save the King* based on a tune which is ascribed to the 17th-century composer John Bull and which was adopted by a number of other nations (e.g. *Heil dir im Siegerkranz).* By then Britain also had a wide variety of folk songs.

5. THE NINETEENTH CENTURY was a period of relative musical sterility during the greatest musical productivity on the Continent. But concert life was greatly encouraged by foreign composers: by H a y d n (who visited England in the 1790's), Beethoven, Mendelssohn, Chopin, Weber, Liszt and Wagner, who, in their turn, were inspired to some of their greatest works by their English visits. Haydn set Thomson's *Seasons* to music and composed his *Creation* to an English text translated into German, Beethoven wrote his *Ninth Symphony* for the London Philharmonic Society, which supported him generously during his last illness, Mendelssohn's overture *The Hebrides* (or *Fingal's Cave)* was inspired by a visit to Scotland. Though adaptations of Romantic literature by English composers were common, Carl Maria v o n W e b e r composed England's only great romantic opera, *Oberon,* commissioned by Covent Garden.

S y m p h o n i c m u s i c was cultivated by a number of musical institutions which were founded in the course of the century: the Philharmonic Society (1813) with Clementi as its first conductor, the Royal Academy of Music (1822), the New Philharmonic Society (1851), the Royal College of Music (1882). Orchestral concerts were held in the *Albert Hall* and the *Crystal Palace,* where oratorios of Handel were performed with choirs consisting of up to 3,000 persons before audiences of 30,000. The *Queen's Hall* (bombed in 1941) became famous through its P r o m e n a d e C o n c e r t s inaugurated in 1895 as a means to popularize classical music, and conducted by Sir Henry Wood.

The chief 19th-century composers were Sir Henry B i s h o p (operas, musicals, ballet music), the Irish composer M. W. B a l f e , who wrote the operas *The Siege of Rochelle* and *The Maid of Artois,* and Sir Arthur S u l l i v a n , one of the most successful composers of light operas since Johann Strauss. His comic operas, e.g. *The Mikado, Iolanthe,* produced in collaboration with the skilful librettist W. S. Gilbert, still flourish as minor classics today.

6. TWENTIETH CENTURY: The beginning of the century was a time of rich musical activity, which was stimulated when sound broadcasting began in 1922 (p. 214).

The year 1934 saw the death of three notable English composers: Sir Edward E l g a r, whose most famous work, *The Dream of Gerontius*, received its first performance in 1900, composed choral and orchestral works and chamber music; Frederick D e l i u s wrote impressionistic orchestral pieces *(Brigg Fair, Dance Rhapsodies)*, choral works *(Sea Drift, A Mass of Life)*, and an opera, *A Village Romeo and Juliet;* Gustav H o l s t, of Swedish descent, was a pioneer of modern music in Britain; his most outstanding orchestral work is his suite, *The Planets.* V a u g h a n W i l l i a m s, who was inspired by folk song and medieval polyphony, wrote symphonies *(Sea Symphony, A London Symphony)* and Norfolk Rhapsodies. Michael T i p p e t t, who was influenced by Schönberg, wrote operas, and text and music to his oratorio *A Child of Our Time.* William W a l t o n 's opera *Troilus and Cressida* was an international success.

England's greatest contemporary composer is Benjamin B r i t t e n (1913–77), whose song cycles, chamber music and operas, e.g. *Peter Grimes* and *The Turn of the Screw* received frequent performances in his own country as well as abroad. His *War Requiem* was first performed in 1962 at the consecration of the newly built Coventry Cathedral (p. 236).

England's most successful conductor was Sir Thomas B e e c h a m (1879–1963), a great interpreter of Mozart and Delius. He was conductor at Covent Garden and founder of the London Phiharmonic Orchestra.

Sir Adrian B o u l t, one of the leading exponents of Elgar's music, was conductor of the B.B.C. Orchestra from 1930–50, and principal conductor of the London Philharmonic Orchestra from 1950–57.

Sir Malcolm S a r g e n t was the chief conductor of the Promenade Concerts in the postwar period.

Music Today

ORCHESTRAS: The five major permanent orchestras are in London: the London Symphony (founded in 1904), the B.B.C. Symphony (founded in 1930), the London Philharmonic (founded in 1932), the Royal Philharmonic Orchestra and the New Philharmonia Orchestra (founded in 1964). The chief orchestras outside London are the Hallé in Manchester, the Royal Liverpool Philharmonic, the Scottish National Orchestra. Most orchestras are subsidized by the Arts Council and local authorities.

CONCERT HALLS: London, where the musical life of Britain is chiefly centred, has four big concert halls: The *Royal Albert Hall* built in 1871 is an immense oval amphitheatre, which can hold an audience of 8,000 and a choir and orchestra of 1,000. The annual summer season of the Promenade Concerts ('Proms') is now held in the *Albert Hall* under the direction of the BBC. Its vast repertory of orchestral classics has become one of the distinctive features of musical life in London. The *Royal Festival Hall* was opened in 1951 in connection with the Festival of Britain. Adjacent is the Queen Elizabeth Hall. *Wigmore Hall* is the principal recital centre. The *Barbican Hall* in the Barbican Centre for Arts and Conferences (opened in 1982) has become the permanent home of the London Symphony Orchestra.

OPERA HOUSES: London has two permanent opera houses. The R o y a l O p e r a known as *Covent Garden*, is the principal home of grand opera and ballet. Its ballet company has achieved an international reputation on many overseas tours. The English National Opera, which plays in the London Coliseum, is the home of popular opera. It grew out of the Sadler's Wells Theatre in the north of London (named after the medicinal wells discovered on the site by Thomas Sadler), which is now used for visiting opera companies. While Covent Garden used to perform grand opera in its original language with international star singers and conductors, Sadler's Wells possessed even before the second World War the only permanent English opera company to perform always in the English language. Operas at Covent Garden are now sung in English, which gives greater opportunities not only to English singers but also to native composers. The Royal Ballet was formed in 1957 through the merger of the ballets of Covent Garden and Sadler's Wells. There is a Scottish Opera, a Welsh National Opera Company and a Birmingham Royal Ballet.

At Glyndbourne, Sussex, an opera season, for which an international cast is annually assembled, is held every summer (May to August). The G l y n d b o u r n e o p e r a was founded in 1934 by John Christie, who built an opera house in the gardens of his ancestral Tudor home.

CHORAL SOCIETIES throughout the country cultivate the musical tradition in which Britain has always excelled. Amateur music-making is increasing.

FESTIVALS: The most attractive feature of musical life in the provinces is the festivals held in many towns throughout the U.K. and linked together by the British Federation of Music Festivals (founded in 1921). The oldest, the *Three Choirs Festival*, is still held annually in Gloucester, Worcester, and Hereford in succession, and includes both cathedral and secular concerts.

The most famous British festival is the *Edinburgh International Festival of Music and Drama* (with a film festival), held in August and September. Inaugurated in 1947, it features many artists of international reputation and attracts thousands of visitors. It includes opera and drama, symphony concerts, chamber music recitals, band concerts, the fascinating military tattoo held on the esplanade of Edinburgh Castle, and many fringe activities.

Other music festivals are: the *Cheltenham Festival* (July) mainly performing contemporary British works, the *Aldeburgh Festival of Music and Arts* (June), which includes works by Benjamin Britten, performed under his direction, the *Bath Festival of the Arts* under the direction of Yehudi Menuhin, with a repertory ranging from Bach to jazz, the *Hallé Music Festival* at Harrogate where the Hallé Orchestra, Manchester, presents classical and modern music, the *Leeds and Norwich Festivals* of choral music, the *Coventry Festival of Music*, and the *Festival of Early Music* at Haslemere founded by the Swiss A. Dolmetsch, who strove to revive interest in early musical instruments.

The *Royal National Eisteddfod* of Wales was revived in the 19th century when an upsurge of Welsh nationalism strove to revive Welsh traditions. It is a competitive festival of music, literature and arts, in which the ceremony of the Gorsedd of Bards forms a picturesque climax. Its main feature is the singing of the choirs, for which Wales is famous.

In the sixties 'pop' music became a major form of entertainment for young people in discotheques as well as concert halls, festivals and on the radio. Ever since the Beatles began their triumphant career in 1963, English groups like the Rolling Stones made their contributions to its world success. The English rock opera *Jesus Christ Superstar* became an international hit.

Theatre

Unlike Continental countries, England has not had a national theatre until recently. But the English theatre has nevertheless been a people's institution in that, throughout its history, it was the theatre-going public rather than the patronage of court or government which has largely determined the popularity of stage and actors. Accordingly, English drama took its start from the theatre (cf. Shakespeare), not from literature like German classical drama.

History:

MIDDLE AGES: V a r i e t y s h o w s with clowns, acrobats, jugglers are as old as Roman times, when beside chariot races they formed the main type of popular entertainment in the amphitheatres of garrison towns (e.g. Caerleon). Mimes toured the provinces to present short satiric plays. Later, in the Middle Ages, the mimes mixed with jugglers, bear leaders, dancers and minstrels to form a professional body with a very low social status, providing entertainments of all kinds. The actual medieval drama originated in the Church, where biblical stories came to be acted as part of the liturgical service. As Latin gave way to the vernacular, these m y s t e r y or m i r a c l e p l a y s passed into secular hands and were presented by the various town guilds. By the 14th century they had grown into cycles comprising up to 54 plays and lasting three to four days. The most important were the cycles of Chester, York, Coventry and Wakefield. The Holy Bible from the Creation to the Day of Judgement was presented on movable stages at various 'stations' in a town. Each guild would present a special scene (e.g. shipbuilders the building of Noah's ark), mingling the sacred with the profanity and humour of the burlesque. The movable platforms on which they were performed were called pageants (from the Latin word *pagina* meaning scaffold), a term later extended to shows and processions of all kinds. In the later Middle Ages, mystery plays gradually gave way to the m o r a l i t y p l a y, like *Everyman,* showing man in his relation to his material and spiritual environment as presented by allegorical figures personifying vices and virtues. Other forms of entertainment having an

important effect on the growth of drama in England were the m u m m e r ' s
p l a y s , originally processions of masked persons, who, during winter festivities,
paraded the streets and entered houses to dance in silence. These mummeries
gradually grew into real plays always containing a fight in which a champion was
killed and revived by a doctor. M o r r i s   d a n c e s , developing from the Spanish
morisco dance, which were performed by various characters, became an essential
part of village festivities under the Tudors.

THE RENAISSANCE introduced the c l a s s i c a l   d r a m a : the Senecan tragedy,
the m a s q u e treating a mythological or symbolical subject, and the erudite
comedy with its elegant witty dialogue, which was cultivated by the university
wits. The native morality play was widened in scope to include history and social
comment merging with the comic debate of the interlude (a short play originally
performed between the courses of a feast). To these types was added the romance
of adventure, which became all the more popular as the age of chivalry was
now declining. All this constituted the 'mixed' character of the Elizabethan drama,
the blending of tragedy, comedy and farce in one play so disturbing to the
scholarly neo-classicists. With Christopher M a r l o w e ' s tragedies *(Doctor
Faustus, Tamburlaine)*, the erudite drama conquered the popular stage. The world's
greatest dramatist William S h a k e s p e a r e , who was actor and leading member
of Elizabethan and Jacobean theatre companies, blended in his histories, tragedies
and romantic comedies all the styles and interests of his age.

The stage began to enjoy the patronage of the court and noblemen and was a major
form of entertainment of high and low alike. Performances usually given in inn
yards attracted large crowds, so that in London the authorities were forced to
interfere to prevent disorder and infectious diseases. This induced James Burbage,
a carpenter who had become a professional actor, to build the first playhouse *The
Theatre* (1576) outside the city walls, soon to be followed by several others, *The
Swan, The Rose* and *The Globe* (1599), to which last Shakespeare was attached. These
theatres were, in a way, replicas of the pageant cart placed against one side of an
inn yard. They were round or octagonal unroofed structures, the plays being
performed by daylight. The walls enclosing the auditorium contained three tiers
of galleries with seats for the well-to-do, while the 'groundlings' were standing
on three sides of the stage, a square high platform without scenery projecting into
the middle of the theatre ('apron-stage'). At its back was a wooden structure with
a sheltering roof supported by pillars, which protruded into the central stage. The
two stories of this back stage contained several smaller divisions, which made
possible a rapid change of scenes: inner rooms serving as tombs or hovels, the
gallery above for musicians or as battlements of a castle. Women's parts were
played by boys. Despite the existence of playhouses in London which, like *Black
Friars*, soon began to be roofed in, the majority of actors were strollers accustomed
to perform their plays wherever they found an audience, in manor houses, town-
halls or on the village green. It was these 'English comedians' who introduced
Shakespeare in an adulterated form to Germany, where he became one of the
inspirations of the Sturm und Drang and the romantic movement.

UNDER THE EARLY STUARTS the stage was enriched by the romantic comedies of
B e a u m o n t and F l e t c h e r and B e n   J o n s o n ' s 'humours' comedy, which
adapted the classical comedy to English life. The masque was revived on very
elaborate lines facilitated by the new pictorial and quickly changing scenery, which

was developed by Inigo Jones, the great architect and stage designer to the court of James I.

CROMWELL'S COMMONWEALTH dealt a deadly blow to the English theatre, closing down the playhouses and forbidding all entertainments. The nobleman's hall became the actors' refuge. The first English opera, the *Siege of Rhodes,* the text of which was written by d'Avenant, was performed at d'Avenant's own home with the first woman on the English stage.

DURING THE RESTORATION it was the court which was instrumental in reviving the theatres. Charles II authorized d'Avenant and Sir Thomas Killigrew to organize two companies of players, which led to the erection of the first Theatre Royal in *Drury Lane* (1663), whose star actor was Thomas Betterton. The other leading theatre was *Covent Garden.* Actresses like the notorious Nell Gwynne now began to play an important part (in the King's favour no less than in the theatre). The stage began to combine the features of the Shakespearean and the private indoor theatre. The large platform was extended to the side walls, while the curtained rear stage was widened to accommodate the background scenes, which were placed at the sides and pushed in grooves on the stage. If they met in the middle, they formed a background for the action or could shut off (hence 'shutters') part of the rear stage, where furniture was 'set' for a new scene while the action could continue without a break on the front stage.

The English theatre was now dominated by the comedy of manners, which was represented by the playwrights William Wycherley *(The Country Wife)* and William Congreve *(The Way of the World).* With its savoury love intrigues it reflected the extravagance of court life and the general reaction to Puritan austerity. The greatest poet of the age, Dryden, produced heroic tragedies as well as comedies.

IN THE EIGHTEENTH CENTURY the comedy of manners was brought to perfection by Richard Sheridan *(School for Scandal)* and Oliver Goldsmith *(She Stoops to Conquer).* This period produced England's greatest actresses, Mrs. Barry, Mrs. Siddons, Mrs. Cibber, and the brilliant actor-manager D. Garrick, of whom Pope wrote: 'That young man never had his equal and he will never have a rival'. The impact of the theatre was all the greater as the stage was again dominated by the public. At a trial following upon a riot in the *Haymarket Theatre,* which was caused by a visit from some French players, it was laid down 'that the public had a legal right to manifest their dislike to any play or actor, and that the judicature of the pit had been acquiesced in time immemorial'. This decision placed actor and author at the mercy of the mob, whose turbulence is evidenced by the row of iron spikes which ran along the front of the stage of *Covent Garden* and *Drury Lane.* In order to avoid grievances resulting from occasional demolition of benches and scenery, an official spokesman for the public was appointed about 1744, who was known as Mr. Town. On the other hand, political satire initiated by John Gay's *Beggar's Opera* and its sequel *Polly,* which satirized Walpole and political corruption under him, caused the government to introduce censorship. This was exercised by the Lord Chamberlain, who, as senior officer of the Royal Household, had always been responsible for the supervision of actors at court. Censorship did not touch Shakespeare since the sanction given him by Elizabeth's Lord Chamberlain still held good.

The credit of having brought Shakespeare back to the stage is due to Garrick, who fascinated the public with his brilliant interpretations of Richard III, Hamlet and King Lear. As actor manager of *Drury Lane*, he staged most of Shakespeare's plays (several of which he published in adaptations under his name). The plays were acted in contemporary costumes, even King Lear wearing a wig, lace ruffles, silk hose and high-heeled shoes. The stage was greatly improved by P. J. de L o u t e r b o u r g , a German battle painter, who came to England in 1771 and, as Garrick's scenic director, developed the imaginative use of lighting. Thus he transformed landscape from summer to autumn by filtering light through movable silk screens of various colours. His activity marked the beginning of the romantic stage.

THE NINETEENTH CENTURY saw the development of the modern stage, with gas replacing oil and candle for illumination, and plays performed in historical costumes. The *Haymarket Theatre* established its tradition of polite comedy. The classic stage was revived by the greatest 19th-century actor manager H e n r y I r v i n g , who, during his twenty years' tenancy of the *Lyceum* came to be recognized at home and abroad as the uncrowned king of the English stage. He was buried in Westminster Abbey. The decades from 1870 to the first World War witnessed an extraordinary revival of the stage. The farces of P i n e r o , the brilliant social comedies of Oscar W i l d e satirizing the sophisticated superficiality of contemporary high society *(Lady Windermere's Fan)*, the ingenious librettos of the G i l b e r t and S u l l i v a n operas, the production of Bernard S h a w s 's plays *(Plays Pleasant* and *Plays Unpleasant)* in the *Court Theatre*, the sagacious criticism of Shaw, which inspired the wish to have seen a play rather than the satisfaction of having kept away, all this reflected a passion for the stage unsurpassed in any country. It is true that the censorship not only prevented indecency but also social criticism, which kept the more daring drama of ideas (e.g. Shelley's *Cenci)* from the stage. But general dissatisfaction with such restrictions led to their relaxation after 1907.

THE TWENTIETH CENTURY brought a new revival of Shakespeare with the foundation of the Elizabethan Stage Society and the Scheme for a Shakespeare Memorial National Theatre. This materialized when the *Memorial Theatre* was built for the Stratford-on-Avon Shakespeare Festivals, which became truly international events, growing in length within twenty years from four weeks to six months. In London, the shabby variety theatre, the 'Old Vic' (Royal Victoria Hall) under the management of Miss Baylis, was refurnished and acquired a high reputation as the home of Shakespeare. During World War II the principle of state support was established through the foundation of the Council for the Encouragement of Music and the Arts, now Arts Council of Great Britain, and the Theatre Royal at Bristol, the first case of state purchase in the history of the British theatre.

The Theatre Today

Despite repeatedly voiced demands for a National Theatre, the British theatre has until 1976 been exclusively run on a commercial basis. This has made it dependent on the taste of the English public, which has always preferred comedy and romance to tragedy, expecting entertainment rather than 'the purifying and ennobling influence' which Henry Irving demanded

259

in accordance with the classic concept of the drama of Racine. This attitude may account for a similar situation in English music, which has 'naturalized' comic opera (Sullivan), while grand opera has until the '50s remained *Covent Garden's* 'outlandish fruit'. In *The British Theatre* W. Bridges-Adams observes: 'Comedy is the life-stream of English acting . . . A tragic hero who knocks his world to pieces may evoke the emotions of pity and terror, but the Englishman believes also in purgation by laughter'.

The 'fringe theatre' movement has begun to put on plays with greater emphasis on intellectual and political content.

There are about 200 professional theatres in Britain. The centre of theatrical activity is London with most of its theatres in the West End, an open air theatre being in Regent's Park. Theatres in the provinces are served by local repertory or touring companies. In 1976, the long-called-for N a t i o - n a l T h e a t r e with three separate auditoria (the *Olivier,* the *Lyttleton* and the *Cottesloe*) was opened on the South Bank in London to rehouse the Old Vic Theatre Company. The British Council* makes the British theatre known abroad by sponsoring international tours by great companies.

Music halls, which are today, like the theatres, owned by big concerns, have preserved little of their old tradition. On the other hand, the genuinely English figure of the clown was carried over into the film by its most brilliant representative, Charlie Chaplin, who began his career in London on the music-hall stage with his mother.

The musical, which enjoys a tremendous popularity similar to that of ballad opera in the 18th century, is chiefly imported from America, though it often makes use of English plays (cf. *The Threepenny Opera* based on Gay's *Beggar's Opera, My Fair Lady* based on Shaw's *Pygmalion,* and *Kiss me, Kate* based on Shakespeare's *The Taming of the Shrew*). Censorship by the Lord Chamberlain has been abolished, but the *Theatres Act* 1968 makes it a criminal offence to present an obscene performance of a play in public or private. These efforts to uphold morals in the theatre stand in marked contrast to the shows advertised in the night clubs of Soho practically adjacent to London theatres. While night clubs, like cinemas, are open the week round, theatres are still closed on Sundays.

Since 1918 the stage has been greatly enriched by the works of a number of notable dramatists: by the comedy of S o m e r s e t M a u g h a m (e.g. *The Bread-Winner, Lady Frederick*) and Noel C o w a r d *(Hay Fever,*

---

* The British Council was founded in 1934 to promote the knowledge of Britain, her language and culture overseas, and to develop closer cultural relations with other countries. It is financed almost entirely from public funds. It has staffs and maintains libraries in about 78 overseas countries. Besides arranging tours overseas by British scientists and theatrical companies, the British Council organizes study programmes in England for scholars and teachers from overseas.

Blithe Spirit), by Terence R a t t i g a n ' s *The Browning Version, The Winslow Boy, Ross* (= T. E. Lawrence), the poetic drama of T. S. E l i o t *(Murder in the Cathedral, Family Reunion)* and Christopher F r y *(The Lady's Not for Burning, Venus Observed, A Sleep of Prisoners),* the theatre of ideas by J. B. P r i e s t l e y *(An Inspector Calls, Dangerous Corner),* Graham G r e e n e ' s drama with a religious background *(The Living Room, Carving a Statue).* The social drama is represented by J. O s b o r n e *(Look Back in Anger, The Entertainer),* H. P i n t e r *(The Caretaker)* and A. W e s k e r *(The Kitchen, Roots).* The chronicle play, initiated by J. D r i n k w a t e r *(Abraham Lincoln),* owed its greatest success to Noel Coward's *Cavalcade.*

Related to this kind of drama is Tom S t o p p a r d ' s *Travesties* satirizing contemporary political and artistic movements. Influences from the Continental absurd theatre are recognizable in Samuel B e c k e t t ' s *Waiting for Godot.* The Royal Shakespeare Theatre produced the *Comedy of Errors* in modern costume as a musical farce.

The period after World War II has seen brilliant actors and actresses, whose achievements were recognized by the conferring of knighthoods, e.g. the actresses Dame Sybil Thorndike, Dame Edith Evans and Dame Peggy Ashcroft, and the actors Lord O l i v i e r, Sir John G i e l g u d and Sir Alec G u i n n e s s. Gielgud excelled in tragic roles in Shakespeare's plays. Guinness, a master of character portrayal, and Olivier, who achieved his international fame as actor-manager of St. James's Theatre, starred in many films. An outstanding actress was Vivien Leigh (Lady Olivier), who starred in *Gone with the Wind.*

Films

Film production, which goes back in Britain to 1896, soon became an important feature of entertainment. The two main trusts for the production and distribution of films are the Associated British Picture Corporation and the Rank Organization.

In 1949, when American competition was at its peak and TV was beginning to make headway, the National Film Finance Corporation was set up to lend money for film production. Nevertheless film making, stripped of financial support by the Thatcher government, has greatly declined, and attendances have fallen drastically, while TV offers a large number of films, and videos can be rented for less than the cost of a visit to the theatre.

The censorship of films is not exercised by the government but by the British Board of Film Censors founded in 1912 on the initiative of the film industry. It classifies films into four categories: 'U' (suitable for universal showing), '18' (suitable only for persons not less than 18 years of age), '15' for persons not less than 15 years, 'A' for persons not less than 5 years of age, but containing material that parents might prefer their children not to see.

The performance of good films is assured by the National Film Theatre erected on the South Bank of the Thames in London in 1957, the first permanent national film theatre in the world.

English films of international renown are those produced from Shakespeare's plays with Laurence Olivier, e.g. *Henry V, Richard III, Hamlet* and *Othello*. Characteristic of English humour are films like *Passport to Pimlico, The Man Who Loved Redheads, Hobson's Choice* with Charles Laughton, and those films which satirize English detective stories: *Ladykillers* and *Kind Hearts and Coronets*, in which Alec Guinness plays eight roles, one a woman. Many English films were produced from famous novels: e.g. Fielding's *Tom Jones*, Dickens's *Great Expectations, A Tale of Two Cities* and *Oliver Twist*, Orczy's *The Scarlet Pimpernel* and Sillitoe's *Saturday Night and Sunday Morning*.

Outstanding problem films are *The Browning Version, Fallen Idol, The Winslow Boy*. Films with a historical background treat chiefly problems created by World War II. *The Third Man* with Orson Welles shows the post-war situation in Vienna, *The Divided Heart* the conflict of a displaced Yugoslav boy reclaimed by his mother from his German foster parents. *The Young Lovers* reflects the conflict between East and West. *Simba* is set against the background of the Mau Mau revolt in Kenya. Orwell's *Animal Farm* treats the problem of the totalitarian state in the guise of an animal fable. Grierson's *Drifters* started the line of documentary films. Two remarkable films on figures of English history are *Lawrence of Arabia* and *Becket*. *Ryan's Daughter*, a film on the problem of Irish resistance to British rule, ran for two years at Leicester Square. In 1979 the film *The Death of a Princess* dealing with the execution of a Saudi princess because of an illegal love affair – which actually happened – strained British relations with Saudi Arabia. The ubiquitous secret service agent James Bond, who figures in innumerable detective films – also American – was originally the hero of a series of espionage novels by the English author Ian Fleming. Several novels by the famous English author of detective stories Agatha Christie (which were translated into many languages) have been produced as films.

Notable British films in the early 80s were Puttnam's *Chariots of Fire*, which won the Oscar, Jordan's *Angel*, Greenaway's *The Draughtsman's Contract* and Forsyth's *Local Hero* and *Gregory's Girl*. By far the most remarkable production, however, was Attenborough's *Gandhi* featuring the life of the great ascetic and liberator of India. A very popular serial film was *Brideshead Revisited* after Evelyn Waugh's novel.

ENGLISH THOUGHT

MIDDLE AGES

The early Middle Ages, from the 6th to the 10th centuries, was an era of faith, when men accepted unquestioningly the authority and dogmas of the Church. Early philosophical speculations, such as the teaching of the British monk Pelagius (5th century), were condemned by the Church.

P e l a g i u s denied original sin contending that death was not the punishment for Adam's sin but inherent in human nature, and maintained that the unassisted human will, not divine grace, was the determining factor in man's salvation.

S c o t u s E r i g e n a (the 'Irish-born Scot'), who was head of the court school in France under Charles the Bald, had to leave France when his free speculations were condemned by the Church. In a treatise on predestination he maintained the liberty of the will. In his great work *De divisione naturae* (c. 870) he developed a n e o - P l a t o n i c t h e o r y o f e m a n a t i o n based on the writings of pseudo-Dionysius Areopagita, which he translated from Greek into Latin. He maintained that neither ideas nor individual creatures have any independent existence but are only manifestations of God. From God as the source of all beings emanates the realm of ideas, according to which individual things are formed, which finally return to God. Hell is but the inner state of the sinful will. The Mosaic account of Paradise and the Fall is only allegorical.

Scholasticism

From the 11th century onwards men began to speculate about the validity of doctrines, but still with the aim of substantiating faith by reason. The new system of philosophizing about theological beliefs, which attained a measure of perfection in the monastic schools and universities of the 12th and 13th centuries and declined rapidly after the 14th century, is called Scholasticism. Since scholars were compelled to speculate only on such matters as the Church held to be orthodox and thus had to work intensively on a few subjects, the most striking characteristics of Scholasticism were the narrowness of its field of thought on the one hand and the thoroughness of its systematization on the other.

1. EARLY SCHOLASTICISM (11th and 12th centuries) is chiefly represented by A n s e l m of Canterbury (1033–1109) (p. 18), who has been called the 'father of Scholasticism'. Anselm maintained the h a r m o n y b e t w e e n r e a s o n a n d f a i t h, but believed that faith must precede reason, which can only serve to prove revelation (credo ut intellegam). His *Proslogion* contains the so-called ontological argument for the existence of God, who is defined as the perfect being, the very idea of which implies existence. If such a being can be conceived it must

also exist. His principal work *Cur Deus homo* advances a new theory of redemption, which substitutes the idea of representative atonement (Christ making amends to God for our sins through his death) for the traditional theory of Christ redeeming man from the debt he owes to Satan through his sin.

2. LATER SCHOLASTICISM: In the 13th century, Scholasticism reached its peak in the writings of T h o m a s A q u i n a s, who separated and coordinated the two realms of philosophy and theology, philosophy dealing with things in so far as they exist, theology with things in their relation to God. This gave philosophy an independent status and made possible experimenting, which was encouraged by Aristotelian thought introduced to Europe by Arab scholars in Spain. It was particularly E n g l i s h S c h o l a s t i c i s m which in contrast to the Parisian school of thought was marked by a r e a l i s t i c a n d s c i e n t i f i c t e n d e n c y. The English universities of Oxford and Cambridge soon developed an independent scientific spirit. In the 14th century the Franciscans captured Oxford and produced England's greatest medieval thinkers:

A l e x a n d e r o f H a l e s (?–1245), Franciscan and archdeacon of Coventry, taught theology in Paris. He contributed to the *Summa Theologica* (the first of frequent medieval attempts to establish a complete philosophical system), which for centuries was ascribed to him alone.

R o g e r B a c o n (c. 1220 – c. 92) who was descended from a wealthy English family, lectured in Paris before he went to Oxford, where he joined the Order of Friars Minor, and turned from the occupation with Aristotelian philosophy to the study of mathematics, optics, alchemy, astronomy, to e x p e r i m e n t a l r e s e a r c h and the building of instruments. Though he only vaguely foresaw later scientific achievements such as the use of the magnifying glass, flying, the circumnavigation of the world and the utilization of gunpowder, his real importance lies in his emphasis on the utility of positive knowledge. He spent years in prison, accused of heresy.

D u n s S c o t u s (1265–1308), the greatest British medieval philosopher, was born in Scotland and taught in Paris, Oxford and Cologne, where he died. His extensive and sagacious writings on questions of metaphysics, cosmology and psychology earned him the name of 'doctor subtilis'. He maintained that matter, with a positive entity of its own, could exist apart from form, thus anticipating Occam's later nominalism. In contrast to Thomas he held the p r i o r i t y o f t h e w i l l over reason in man as well as God, thus vindicating positive laws as against the law of nature: God does not will a thing because it is good, but we consider as good what God wills. Accordingly happiness does not consist in

264

contemplating God but in God's love to us, and the nobility of the soul not in knowing but in willing.

William of O c c a m (c. 1280–1349) joined the Franciscans and lectured in Oxford. Summoned to Avignon to answer the Pope's charges against his teaching, he became involved in the debate on evangelical poverty. According to the tenets of his order he declared papal constitutions directed against evangelical poverty to be full of heresy. He was arrested, but escaped and sided with Emperor Louis of Bavaria in his struggle against the Pope, maintaining the independence of the Emperor's authority from spiritual rule. He died in Munich. Of Occam's doctrines, which cover the fields of psychology, metaphysics and logic, the most famous are his nominalistic tenets. Whereas early scholastic 'realism' (Anselm) had upheld the Platonian idea of the reality of the spiritual world, of which singulars were only a reflection (universalia ante res), n o m i n a l i s m maintained that universal concepts were only names of visible things (universalia post res) and that the perception of singular things provided the origin of all judgements concerning reality. Suppressed since the condemnation of its early representative, Roscellinus, nominalism now became a typically English contribution towards the development of inductive, empirical thought and of the later independence of science from theology.

SIXTEENTH CENTURY

Humanism and Reformation

By the end of the 15th century, the voyages of discovery, the multiplication of books and the newly founded grammar schools had prepared man for the influx of l e a r n i n g   f r o m   I t a l y , which introduced humanism into the countries of northern Europe.

In England the 'Oxford Reformers' William L i l y , Thomas L i n a c r e and William G r o c y n , after their studies in Italy, brought classical learning to Oxford, while John C o l e t introduced it into secondary education through his newly founded school at St. Paul's. Erasmus, who taught Greek at Cambridge, described the new atmosphere in 1497 in the following way: 'The air is soft and delicious. The men are sensible and intelligent ... They know their classics so accurately that I have lost little by not going to Italy. When Colet speaks I might be listening to Plato. Linacre is as deep and acute a thinker as I have ever met with. Grocyn is a mine of knowledge, and nature never formed a sweeter or happier disposition than that of Thomas More. The number of young men who are studying ancient literature is astonishing.' But whereas Italy fully absorbed ancient thought, English humanists sought knowledge not for its own sake but for its influence on moral discipline in public and private life. Their writings are consequently concerned with religion, politics and education rather than mere philosophical speculations.

Sir Thomas E l y o t expressed the humanistic ideal of education, the harmonious development of body, mind and character, in his treatise *The Governor;* Roger A s c h a m ' s *Schoolmaster* and *Toxophilos* also emphasized the necessity of physical training.

The greatest Scottish humanist George B u c h a n a n (tutor to Mary Stuart and James I), who, in his treatise *Franciscans and Fratres,* expressed the general aversion to obscurantism and the scholastic theology of the Franciscan-dominated universities, anticipated the Scottish struggle against absolute rule in *De Iure Regni apud Scotos.*

T h o m a s M o r e's famous *Utopia,* which was inspired by Plato's *Republic,* visualizes a state based on the principles of reason and social equality, in which human worth is determined by work, not by money, in which communal life is organized collectively and the influence of the priests is limited by the dictates of political reason.

The greatest systematic English thinker of his age was Thomas H o o k e r, who gave the classical statement of Anglican thought in his *Laws of Ecclesiastical Polity*. In contrast to the scholastic theologians Duns Scotus and Occam, who maintained that the divine will was independent of reason, he conceives a rational order of the universe in which regularity and constancy express purpose (cf. the Newtonian physico-theological argument p. 271). The law of nature is the law of reason, which man's free will, despite his defects resulting from his sin, follows without the help of revelation by pursuing human perfection. In doing so men serve one another's good as well as the good of the whole.

The P u r i t a n s, concerned primarily with questions of moral discipline and ecclesiastical authority, have made important contributions to political rather than religious thought.

It was in literary and court circles that esoteric philosophies chiefly gained influence. Cabbalistic and hermetic theories were cultivated by a 'School of Night' headed by Raleigh.

While natural philosophy was greatly under the influence of astrology and Paracelsus's mystic doctrines of active principles in material things and their secret interaction, science was impeded by the conservative and religious spirit of English humanism. (Thomas More died for upholding papal supremacy!)

The first positive English contributions to science were made by the foundation of the Royal College of Physicians, and by the publication in 1600 of *De magnete* by the Queen's physician W i l l i a m G i l b e r t. The Scottish mathematician J o h n N a p i e r invented logarithms.

SEVENTEENTH CENTURY

The 17th century marks the beginning of political philosophy and e m p i r i c a l t h o u g h t initiating the age of science.

I. **The Beginnings of Empiricism** are associated with F r a n c i s B a c o n, courtier and Queen's Counsel under Elizabeth I, who became Lord Chancellor under James I. Bacon aimed at the advancement of science through substituting the i n d u c t i v e a p p r o a c h b y e x - p e r i m e n t for the deductive methods of Scholasticism. His *Novum organum scientiarum* (1620), which was to replace Aristotle's *Organum*, proposed that the supremacy of logic and a priori conceptions in Aristotelian philosophy should give way to empiric thought. 'Aristotle made his natural philosophy a mere bond servant to his logic, thereby rendering it contentious and well-nigh useless'. Bacon's *Instauratio magna* (including his earlier works *Advancement of Learning* and *Novum organum*) outlined the current state of knowledge in all fields and demanded that man should free himself from the prejudices and 'idols' inherent in his nature and advance knowledge by experiment. 'Then, and then only, may we hope well of the sciences, when in a just scale of axioms ... we rise from particulars to lesser axioms, and then to middle axioms, and last of all to the most general'. This knowledge, based on sound methods of investigation, should lead to the control of nature. 'Human knowledge and human power meet in one, for where the cause is not known the effect cannot be produced. Nature, to be commanded, must be obeyed.' Bacon's *New Atlantis* is his conception of a future state in which the results of research are applied for the benefit of human welfare. In the political field, Bacon, in keeping with the absolutism of the Tudor and Stuart Age, advocated a strong monarchy with 'a race of military men' who 'profess arms as their principal honour, study and occupation.' Holding that allegiance of the subject to the monarch, being as natural as the obedience of children to parents, takes precedence of law, he is an early representative of ' p a t e r n a l i s m '. Bacon's empiricism stimulated experimenting among amateurs as well as scientists.

II. **Beginnings of Science**

William H a r v e y, physician to James I and Charles I, initiated a new era in physiology through the discovery of blood circulation in *De motu cordis* (1628).

The year 1662 saw the foundation of the R o y a l S o c i e t y, which became a centre of s c i e n t i f i c r e s e a r c h and later the foremost authority on scientific questions as applied to public affairs (hygiene, safety in mines, geographical explorations, tropical diseases). Robert B o y l e founded scientific chemistry by refuting Aristotle's theory of the four elements. His invention of the air pump and vacuum chamber, which led to 'Boyle's law', made possible the investigation of gases.

Isaac N e w t o n, 'the greatest name in English science', created the method of modern science: the exact and generalizing mathematical description of experimental results. To this aim he developed the differential calculus, which led to his priority dispute with Leibniz. In his *Philosophiae naturalis principia mathematica,* 1687, he established theoretical mechanics (Newtonian axioms and principle of gravitation), which enabled him to calculate the motions of celestial bodies. His discovery of one simple principle of divine order (gravitation) exerted a profound influence on philosophical and theological thought in the 18th century. Newton discovered the spectrum and invented the mirror telescope (optics).

III. **Political Philosophy:** The 17th century, which was an age of intense political strife, produced most of England's political thinkers representing the contending political tenets.

Thomas H o b b e s , the most controversial English philosopher of the 17th century, who in an age of extreme religious fervour was censured as an atheist, advanced in his *Leviathan* (1651) the doctrine of absolute power. When individuals, whose natural passions would lead to a war of all against all, for their own preservation confer all their power upon one man 'this is the generation of the great Leviathan or rather of that mortal God, to which we owe under the immortal God our peace and defence'. Once elected, this mortal god is not bound by any obligation to those who elected him. In contrast to Puritan political philosophy, Hobbes held that 'covenants without the sword are but words and of no strength to secure a man at all.' The indivisibility of sovereignty implies the rejection of clerical rule, the legal status of the Church being but a gift of the Emperor.

In political life, the Anglican doctrine of the Divine Right of kings conflicted with the democratic ideas of the Puritans as advanced by Cromwell in his struggle against Charles I and by John Knox in his conflict with Mary Stuart.

John M i l t o n , who made himself the spokesman of the Puritan Revolution, is the classical exponent of the Puritan conception of government as a public trust. In *The Tenure of Kings and Magistrates* (1649) he derived government from the social contract which was formed after Adam's sin had led to the rule of violence. The monarch was accountable to the people, in whom power rested. His *Defensio pro populo anglicano* (1650) professed the people's right to punish a tyrant and rejected hereditary government as contrary to the law of nature.

The same views were advanced by the lawyer John S e l d e n and by A l g e r n o n S i d n e y , Whig leader during the Restoration, who had fought in the Civil War on the side of Parliament, and who was beheaded under Charles II. To him, tyranny would collapse if it were universally recognized that the people had the right of nature to hold the kings they chose accountable for obeying the laws they make.

More moderate views were advanced by James H a r r i n g t o n , the first political thinker to stress the importance of economics and education for the well-being of the State. His *Oceana* (1656), which advocated a 'natural aristocracy', though based on popular election by ballot, exercised a strong influence on constitutions in America (Pennsylvania and Carolina).

The position of a 'trimmer' was stated by George Savile, Lord H a l i f a x , statesman under Charles II. Despising violence and revenge, he kept aloof from the fierce party strife believing that a man tied to a party 'is very unfit to be trusted with the people's liberty after he hath given up his own'. His *Character of a Trimmer* (1684) advocated a limited monarchy and m o d e r a t i o n in politics: 'Our Church is a Trimmer between the frenzy of fanatic visions and the lethargic ignorance of Popish dreams. Our laws are Trimmers between the excesses of unbounded power and the extravagance of liberty not enough restrained. True virtue has ever been thought a Trimmer, and to have its dwelling midway between two extremes. Even God Almighty Himself is divided between His two great attributes, His mercy and His justice.'

The political philosophy of the great English philosopher John L o c k e which exercised a decisive influence on the American Revolution, is set forth in his *Two Treatises of Civil Government,* which appeared in 1690 after the overthrow of absolutism by William of Orange had ended Locke's seven years' exile on the Continent. Seeking to help 'establish the throne of our great restorer, our present King William and make good his title in the consent of the people', it advanced the c o n - s t i t u t i o n a l i d e a s of the Glorious Revolution. To Locke already the state of nature, which is a state of perfect freedom and equality 'has a l a w o f n a t u r e to govern it, which teaches all mankind that no one ought to harm another in his life, liberty or possessions'. This leads men to unite in a commonwealth, in which the individual resigns his original right to judge and punish his fellowman. Government thus being but a public trust, the individual retains his liberty of thought, worship, speech and the right to the property which he has gained by 'mixing his labour with things originally given to mankind in common'.

Locke already set forth the fundamental ideas of modern c o n - s t i t u t i o n a l i s m : the separation of the executive power from the legislative, which was to be an elected body making its decisions according to the principle of majority.

IV. **Philosophy of Cognition:** In part I of *Leviathan: Of Man,* Thomas
H o b b e s broached the problem of the nature and limits of human
understanding, which became the chief preoccupation of philosophical
thought throughout the next 200 years. Advancing a wholly
m e c h a n i s t i c t h e o r y o f c o n c e p t i o n, he maintained that
thought is but an 'accident' of a body without us, which presses on our
physical organs and, by mediation of the nerves, 'inwards to the brain
and heart'. Thus the human mind is a mere mechanism and reasoning is
the sum of sense impressions which set it in motion. By establishing
sense as the only source of knowledge, Hobbes replaced the traditional
conception of inborn ideas by a sensualistic materialism.

Hobbes' materialism was a challenge to the C a m b r i d g e P l a t o n -
i s t s. Ralph C u d w o r t h *(The True Intellectual System of the
Universe)* demonstrated that moral conceptions were communicated to
man by the spirit of God, not through sense impressions but through
innate ideas.

H e n r y M o r e represented a neo-Platonic mysticism conceiving all
entities, even physical bodies as penetrated by spirits in different phases
of development.

John L o c k e, 1632–1704, the most influential English philosopher
of the age, represented its characteristic traits. A friend of the great
champion of liberty under the later Stuarts, the Earl of Shaftesbury
(p. 46), Locke justified the Glorious Revolution, advocating the
sovereignty of the people, toleration and political reason (p. 48). A
lecturer of philosophy at Oxford in close contact with notable scientists
(Boyle, Sydenham, later Huygens), he became interested in experimental
and empirical methods and investigated the limits of human knowledge.
In his *Essay Concerning Human Understanding* (1690), which became a
standard work of 18th-century philosophy, he established psychological
empiricism by holding that the human mind has n o i n b o r n i d e a s
but is a tabula rasa until experience provides it with ideas. If ideas
were innate they would be clearest in children and savages who are not
corrupted by custom, which is not the case. All our ideas are gained
either from without, through sensation, or by reflection when the mind
'observes its own actions about those ideas', the principal operations
being willing and thinking (e.g. remembrance, discerning, reasoning,
judging).

Our ideas are by no means exact copies of physical things. Locke
distinguished between primary qualities such as solidity, extension,
motion, which the body constantly has, and secondary qualities
separable from the body, which are but powers to produce various
sensations in us, such as colours, sounds, tastes etc.

Of the simple ideas, with which sensation and reflection provide us, the
mind forms complex ideas 'with a supposition of something to which

they belong', the sun for instance being a complex of bright, hot, roundish. Locke does not believe in the certainty of such complex ideas of single substances and d e n i e s c o l l e c t i v e i d e a s altogether. Collective ideas of substances, such as army or universe are but 'the artificial draughts of the mind, bringing things very remote and independent of one another into one view'. (cf. nominalism p. 264). Indubitable knowledge can be gained only within our ideas (e.g. in mathematics), not from their archetypes without them.

V. Locke's Ideas on Religion and Education:

In his *Letter Concerning Toleration* Locke maintained that all attempts to assert the prevalence of one faith over another were 'rather marks of men striving for power and empire over one another than of the church of Christ'. He considered 'toleration to be the chief characteristic mark of the true church' and proposed that religious zeal for the salvation of souls should be directed against vice and cruelty rather than towards the establishment of opinions, for 'no man can be a Christian without charity'.

Locke's *Reasonableness of Christianity* sponsored a religion in conformity with reason, though in contrast to 18th-century deism he believed in the necessity of revelation. Christianity to him implied two essential elements: to believe in Christ as God's Messiah and to live according to his teaching.

Locke's essay *Some Thoughts Concerning Education,* which begins with the words: 'A sound mind in a sound body is a short but full description of a happy state in this world', demanded a broad type of education developing the whole man, in which learning was considered 'the last part'. 'Settle in him (your son) good habits. This is the main point and this being provided for, learning may be had into the bargain.' Thus he stressed physical and moral education enabling man to endure hardships, to subordinate his desires to reason (cf. principles of Public School education (pp. 198, 203). As an empiricist Locke maintained that 'of all men we meet with, nine parts of ten are what they are, good or evil, useful or not, by their education,' and thus believed in practice rather than the establishing of rules.

EIGHTEENTH CENTURY

The 18th century is known as the Age of E n l i g h t e n m e n t : R e a s o n became the new standard by which the traditional authority of Church and State was judged and found inadequate. With the exception of France, no European country was as prolific in philosophical theory as England.

In politics c o n s t i t u t i o n a l i s m finally substituted the idea of the social contract for the principle of absolute rule by Divine Right while

R a d i c a l i s m rejected all traditional forms of government in the name of reason.

In theology, deism divested religion of its metaphysical content, dethroning historical revelation in favour of 'n a t u r a l r e l i g i o n'.

E m p i r i c p h i l o s o p h y, which continued to test the sources and certainty of human knowledge, tended more and more towards scepticism.

I. **Deism** tried to adapt Christianity to the principles of reason inherent in human nature and thus to make it generally acceptable. It was based on ideas advanced a century earlier by H e r b e r t o f C h e r b u r y (1583–1648), who demanded a natural religion based on reason common to all men rather than on revelation or external authority. While these ideas, set forth in his main work *De veritate prout distinguitur a revelatione, a verisimile, a possibile et a falso* (1624), were premature in an age of religious fervour, 18th-century rationalism furnished free-thinking with the arguments necessary for positive criticism of revealed religion, and made deism an influential (though mainly English) movement. Its chief representatives ranged from the rational interpretation of a still orthodox Christianity to complete scepticism.

J o h n T o l a n d in his book *Christianity not Mysterious* (1696) tried to divest Christianity of all mystery and to reduce it to a philosophy. Thomas W o o l s t o n in his widely read *Discourses on Miracles*, for which he was imprisoned, explained the main facts of historical Christianity allegorically.

Matthew T i n d a l ' s *Christianity as Old as the Creation; or, the Gospel, a Republication of the Religion of Nature (1730)*, which was called the deist's bible, tried to demonstrate that Christ did not bring a new revelation but restored the pure principles of worship in the chaos of ancient religions. 'Natural' revelation has from creation been internal, i.e. deriving from the constitution of the world and nature of man rather than historical facts.

In a narrower sense, the term deism was used to describe a new interpretation of the relation of God to the world. In contrast to 'theism', which conceived of a permanent operation of God on the world in the forms of revelation, guidance and grace, deism restricted God's activity to the creation of the world. The belief in a personal God, who interferes with the laws he himself has set up, contradicts reason. He sets the clock to run by itself.

Related to deism was the cosmological or physio-theological argument advanced by Samuel C l a r k e, who conducted Newton's controversy with Leibniz, and the great philosophical critic and professor of theology Richard B e n t l e y in his *Matter and Motion Cannot Think or A Refutation of 'Atheism' from the Faculties of the Soul*. Based on Newton's *Principia*, which had established one simple principle of divine order (gravitation), it tried to refute atheism by deducing the existence of God from the divine harmony of the universal mechanism ('evidence of design'). This argument began to be used in politics by the Radical Thomas Paine (p. 62) as well as by the Tory leader Bolingbroke (p. 52) who, however, wanted to see it restricted to the higher classes because he believed that free-thinking was dangerous to the lower classes.

II. **Philosophy of Cognition,** one of the typically English contributions to philosophy, ranged from the theory of innate ideas of the S c o t t i s h S c h o o l through Berkeley's s u b j e c t i v e i d e a l i s m to Hume's conception of human knowledge as a mere association of sense impressions (a s s o c i a t i o n i s m , sensualism). The full negation of metaphysical cognition led in the 19th century to the recognition only of facts (positivism) and matter (materialism).

1. SUBJECTIVISM

George B e r k e l e y , 1685–1753, Anglican Bishop of Cloyne, Ireland, who encouraged higher education in the American colonies, tried to uphold religion against scepticism increasing with the development of natural science. In his philosophical *Treatise Concerning the Principles of Human Knowledge* he went beyond Locke's empiricism, which had distinguished between primary sensations (solidity, extension) corresponding to real objects, and secondary qualities (colour, taste), which were projections of our own senses, by denying the objective existence even of primary qualities. Corporeal substance does not exist. There is no other substance than Spirit or that which perceives. Berkeley's doctrine: 'esse est percipi' maintains that the corporeal world consists in its being perceived, being but the product of the immaterial spirit (immaterialism) and its ideas (idealism). Our ideas, however, are communicated to us by a cosmic mind, which is the origin of all consciousness. What we conceive as natural laws is the sequence in which God realizes his ideas in our minds. Although conceived as a refutation of atheism and materialism, Berkeley's philosophy was on the contrary charged with leading to scepticism, and prepared the subjectivism of Hume's sensualistic materialism.

David H u m e 1711–76, Scottish philosopher, was the most versatile British thinker, who discussed all the problems of his time. He made considerable contributions to the philosophy of cognition, ethics (p. 275), religion (in a study of 'the natural history of religion' in *Four Dissertations*), politics *(Political Discourses)* and national economy, all of which he comprised in a uniform philosophical system based on strictly psychological principles. He was the first thinker who combined the philosophical with the historical sense (he wrote the first *History of England*), and discussed even religion from historical and psychological rather than theological points of view. In his *Treatise on Human Nature,* later rewritten as *Enquiry Concerning Human Understanding,* he followed Locke and Berkeley by asserting that no question of importance could be solved without an understanding of the working of the human mind. In his psychology of cognition he went beyond Berkeley, however, by denying spiritual as well as material substance and beyond Locke by denying the capacity of the human mind to form complex ideas, leaving but a train of single impressions. The conceptions of substance, existence and causality are a mechanical process comparable to gravitation in the physical world, our ideas being derived from the association of a set of impressions by the mechanical processes of compounding, augmenting and diminishing. What appears to us as causal connection is but the habitual association of certain impressions. There is no proof of our ideas corresponding to reality. Demonstrative knowledge is possible only in mathematics, which deals with conceptions of our mind without claiming to say anything about their relation to reality. Hume's remarkable interest in the practical questions of morality, politics and national economy, despite his scepticism with regard to objective knowledge, is accounted for by his theory of a 'natural belief' derived from the habitualness of phenomena strong enough to rule man's practical conduct.

Hume's philosophy had an important influence on Kant and through him on European Enlightenment. On the other hand it marks the end of Enlightenment by dethroning reason as the ultimate criterion of cognition and judgement.

The chief representative of associationism after Hume was David H a r t l e y who, as a physician, was primarily interested in the correspondence of physical and mental impressions. In his *De motu sensus et idearum generatione* and *Observations on Man* he introduced a completely physiological psychology by explaining mental impressions as vibrations produced by sensory stimuli which are propagated to the brain through the nerves. A frequent recurrence of such vibrations in a certain order produces the memory and a disposition to expect similar sequences of vibrations (imagination, reasoning).

While Hartley upheld a qualitative difference between physiological and psychological impressions, thereby trying to avoid complete materialism, J o s e p h P r i e s t l e y in his *Disquisition of Matter and Spirit* completely identified the experience of the body and soul, thereby substituting physiology for psychology. As Hobbes's materialism had been fought in the 17th century by the Cambridge

Platonists, opposition to associationism in the 18th century came from a group of philosophers in Scotland, whose aim was to uphold the human soul as a spiritual entity.

2. THE SCOTTISH SCHOOL: If the natural instinct of taste and benevolence are criteria of our aesthetic and moral judgement (p. 275), then our reasoning about truth and falsity must also have its root in our original instinct, a c o m m o n s e n s e, whose reliability is proved by the very fact that it is common to all mankind. Main representative of the Scottish School was Thomas R e i d, who succeeded Adam Smith as Professor of Moral Philosophy at the University of Glasgow. His life-long aim was to refute the scepticism to which Hume's philosophy was bound to lead. In his *Inquiry into the Human Mind, on the Principle of Common Sense* he constituted certain axioms, self-evident truths which form our knowledge. It is not the philosopher's task to question pieces of knowledge such as the existence of the material object, of our own identity, etc., but to understand more fully what our common sense tells us about them. Reid's followers were James B e a t t i e, Dugald S t e w a r t and Thomas B r o w n, who were all professors of Moral Philosophy in Edinburgh. James Beattie in his Essay on the *Nature and Immutability of Truth in Opposition to Sophistry and Scepticism* used the consensus omnium as an argument to prove the reliability of cognition as well as of our moral instinct. The doctrine of common sense exercised considerable influence in England and America and on German popular philosophy, especially on Moses Mendelssohn and Nicolai, who held that extremist views were fallacies.

III. **Moral Philosophy:** Ethics gained in importance as man ceased to look to revelation as a guide to moral conduct (deism), and as man, rather than God, became the main preoccupation of philosophic thought. Anthony Ashley Cooper, third Earl of S h a f t e s b u r y, in early youth strongly under the influence of his grandfather, the first Earl of Shaftesbury (leader of the Whigs) and his tutor John Locke, pursued as M.P. an independent liberal policy. He was greatly influenced by the classics during his Grand Tour of France and Italy and later developed his m o r a l a e s t h e t i c i s m in a number of essays and his main work *Characteristics of Men, Manners, Opinions and Times.* He was the first English moral philosopher to examine the structure of the human self and the interplay of its impulses. In contrast to Hobbes, however, he did not derive human action from purely egoistic impulses. To Shaftesbury, man's personal morality consisted in his instinctive desire to be in harmony with his environment by pursuing the good of the whole species. Morality thus appears as the undisturbed development of man's natural disposition, the harmony between his self-love and his benevolent instincts. Pope, who popularized Shaftesbury's ideas in his *Essay on Man* compared this relation with the double movement of the planets round the sun and their own axis. To Shaftesbury, the source of our knowledge of what is moral is not reasoning or an empiric approval of what is useful or agreeable (Hume), but an inner sense, which approves those instincts that work for the good of the individual and the whole.

Shaftesbury's identification of ethical and aesthetic instincts has dominated the literature of the 18th century, particularly in Germany, where his conception of the indivisibility of the psychic organism formed a parallel to Leibniz's doctrine of the monad, and where his demand for the harmonious development of man's whole personality formed an integral part of classical humanism, the ideal of 'die schöne Seele'.

Francis H u t c h e s o n, moral philosopher in Glasgow, largely followed Shaftesbury's ideas in his *Inquiry into the Original of Our Ideas of Beauty and Virtue,* his *System of Moral Philosophy* and his *Essay on the Nature and Conduct of the Passions and Affections.* Like Shaftesbury he believed in the analogy of beauty and virtue, and in the impulse to promote the common good as the criterion of virtuous action, thus anticipating Bentham's utilitarianism. To Hutcheson, however, the moral sense consisted not so much in the principle of universal sympathy as in an infallible instinct approving even of an enemy's virtue.

H u m e in his *Enquiry Concerning the Principle of Morals* defines morality as qualities that are approved either for their utility or agreeableness.

The gradual shift from mere intellectualism to an investigation of instincts and of the relation of ethical and aesthetic values, which was thus initiated by Shaftesbury and Hutcheson, found a new expression in Edmund B u r k e ' s *Philosophical Inquiry into the Origin of our Ideas on the Sublime and Beautiful,* in which he examined the relation between aesthetic and ethical values. To him everything is beautiful that produces love, thus transforming the egoistic instinct of benevolence into a social faculty. Burke's passion for order and integrity, his horror of corruption and violence, became the leading motives also of his political career (impeachment of Warren Hastings, agitation in speeches and writings against England's American War and the French Revolution). In Germany Burke's aesthetic theories exerted a considerable influence on Moses Mendelssohn and Lessing.

Jeremy B e n t h a m, 1748–1832, lawyer and writer, was the philosopher who exercised the strongest influence on English life, his utilitarian ideal of 'the greatest happiness of the greatest number' being a precept of social conduct capable of realization in private and public life. In his *Introduction to the Principles of Morals and Legislation* he pointed to the close relation between the two, legislation being to him but the application of moral standards to the whole community. He defined his philosophy of utility as 'that principle which states the greatest happiness of those whose interest is in question as being the . . . only, right and proper and universally desirable end of human action'. Thus the criterion of the goodness of law is the measure in which it contributes to the general happiness.

Despite the logical impossibility of measuring quantitatively mere sensations (greatest happiness), the principle of utility, a typical product of English 'common sense' was realized in the political, social and judicial reforms it inspired and thus became the philosophical predecessor of English socialism. Bentham's *Fragment on Government* marked the beginning of philosophical Radicalism. His *Catechism of Parliamentary Reform* sought to realize full democracy, visualizing the abolition of class privileges on the principle that 'everybody is to count for one and no one for more'. It voiced the Radical demands of annual Parliaments, secret ballot, male suffrage, the abolition of monarchy and the House of Lords.

Bentham's greatest ambition to codify English law did not materialize, but his proposals for legal reforms were widely read in America and on the Continent, and his *Draught of a Code for the Organization of the Judicial Establishment in France* secured him French citizenship.

IV. **Political Philosophy:** English political thought in the 18th century ranged from constitutionalism to radicalism. Through Voltaire's *Lettres sur les Anglais* English constitutional ideas reached the Continent and helped to inspire the French Revolution through Rousseau's *Contrat Social* (constitution) and Montesquieu's *Esprit des Lois* (division of powers), while English Radicalism had great influence in America.

Thomas P a i n e (1737–1809), political and philosophical writer, was one of the chief inspirers of the American Revolution. The principal ideas of his publications were formed by the influences of his youth. The suppressed conditions of the lower classes from which he descended, and the humanitarian ideas of the Quakers made him a fervent champion of liberty and social reform, his autodidactic studies of the Newtonian philosophy a deist and defender of the physio-theological argument (p. 271). After his emigration to America he published his pamphlet *Common Sense* and the series of tracts *The Crisis*, with which he rallied all those who still hesitated to take up arms for the cause of liberty. His fight against the monarchy: 'Government by kings . . . was the most prosperous invention the Devil ever set on foot for the promotion of idolatry' was continued after his return to England in his *Rights of Man,* which was inspired by Burke's hostile *Reflections on the Revolution in France.* Indicted for treason, he fled to France where he took an active part in the French Revolution but was soon imprisoned under Robespierre for his moderate principles. On his return to America he was suspected of atheism on account of the publication of his *Age of Reason*, in which he deprecated orthodox Christianity and advanced a religion based on reason and the physio-theological argument: 'What more does man want to know than that the hand or power that made these things (cosmos) is divine, is omnipotent?' In the second part he developed a liberal programme for social and humanitarian reforms which accounted for his influence on the 19th-century reformers.

William G o d w i n (1756–1836) started as a Nonconformist minister, but under the influence of the French philosophy of Enlightenment became the most radical of philosophical Radicals. The best-known of his miscellaneous writings (biography, history, dramas, novels) is his political work *An Inquiry concerning Political Justice, and its Influence on General Virtue and Happiness* (1793), in which he rejected not only the monarchy as 'unavoidably corrupt' but government altogether as 'counteracting the improvement of the original mind'. Rejecting compulsion of any kind, he believed that society could be based on absolute freedom when man had learned to act according to reason. On the other hand Godwin's inveterate belief in the power of reason to solve all problems made him an enemy also of any violent overthrow: by learning to act according to the principles of reason alone could man create perfect society.

His revolutionary ideas exercised a profound influence on the younger generation, esp. on Shelley, who married his daughter. His wife, Mary Wollstonecraft, was the first advocate of equality of education for women, whose *Vindication of the Rights of Woman* caused a considerable outcry owing to its unconventional tenets. Himself rooted in 18th-century rationalism, Godwin anticipated two influential ideas of the 19th century: the belief in the perfection of mankind and the doctrine 'that our virtues and our vices may be traced to the incidents which make the history of our lives', which influenced Robert Owen (p. 70).

V. Political Economy

1. ECONOMIC THEORIES BEFORE ADAM SMITH: M e r c a n t i l i s m, which had reigned in Europe long before the system reached its perfection through Louis XIV's minister of finance, Colbert, was, in effect, economic nationalism based on an elaborate system of import tariffs, preferences and other forms of State control over economic activities. In England it was symbolized by *Navigation Acts* to restrict colonial and Irish trade. Its theory that a nation's prosperity rested on its monetary wealth had led to an emphasis on mining of gold and silver, on colonization as a source of cheap raw materials, and on industry for the export of manufactures rather than domestic

agriculture. The French p h y s i o c r a t s , Turgot and Quesnay, introduced the 'agricultural system' by asserting that only nature (hence 'physiocrats') was really productive, being able to supply agricultural surpluses while manufacture only processed existing materials.

2. ECONOMIC LIBERALISM: The physiocrats exercised some influence on A d a m S m i t h , 1723–90, Scottish political economist and philosopher, who was Professor of Logic and Moral Philosophy at Glasgow University. His famous *Wealth of Nations* (1776) is the most influential book on economics ever written. In contrast to mercantilism and physiocracy it established labour, not money or agricultural produce, as the main source of national prosperity. Thus the chief criterion for the wealth of a nation is the question how the greatest volume of work can be achieved. This is effected on the one hand by division of labour which establishes cooperation, with its economic advantages of time-saving inventions through specialization, and on the other hand by self-interest. Man's natural instinct to improve his conditions is established as the most productive force in economic life, the root of all progress. Through this instinct the individual also promotes the interest of society, the wealth of the nation being the wealth of the sum of its individuals. Determined by these principles and influenced by his intercourse with Glasgow tobacco merchants who suffered from the restrictions of British colonial policy, Smith was against any state interference, restrictive regulations and monopolistic institutions. He wanted to see free trade established internally and with the colonies because, to him, only the natural relation between supply and demand could be the basis of a healthy economy. The *Wealth of Nations*, beside providing a first great survey of economic life, revolutionized economic and political thinking, and became a potent force for the development of 19th-century liberalism and free trade. Moreover through its emphasis on the interdependence of the human and economic factors (labour and production) it initiated 19th-century sociology.

VI. **Science:** J o s e p h B l a c k , Professor of Medicine in Glasgow and of Chemistry in Edinburgh, started quantitative chemical analysis and discovered carbon dioxide. His investigations into the quantities of heat needed to turn water into steam led to the invention of the steam engine by his assistant James Watt, which brought on the Industrial Revolution. The investigation of gases was continued by J o s e p h P r i e s t l e y , who isolated oxygen, and Henry C a v e n d i s h , who destroyed the theory of water being an element by discovering its composition, namely hydrogen and oxygen.

279

One of the outstanding features of the 18th century was the development of medicine. Thomas S y d e n h a m and the Scottish physicians W i l l i a m and J o h n H u n t e r introduced scientific surgery and obstetrics. Edward J e n n e r started vaccination. All these improvements and the development of public hygiene led to the first 'explosive phase' of population growth.

NINETEENTH CENTURY

19th-century thought was determined by two conflicting tendencies: materialism resulting from the negation of metaphysical cognition by the associationist thinkers of the 18th century, and a new faith in spiritual life, in the powers of imagination and emotion. This revolt found its expression in the literature of romanticism, the religious revivals (pp. 189, 191), and in the German idealistic philosophy of Fichte and Hegel, which also helped the theologians to vindicate Christian doctrine in the face of positivism which only believed in facts. English philosophers such as Stirling, Green and Caird defended the religious doctrines in Hegelian terms, and Martineau, after studying the empiricists Locke and James Mill, described the effect of German philosophy on him as a new intellectual birth.

The typically English contributions to modern thought, however, were still made in the more practical fields of science, political economy and social ethics.

I. **Political Economy:** T. R. M a l t h u s is 'the pioneer in the fundamental treatment of demographic problems' (Encyclopedia Britannica). In his *Essay on the Principle of Population as It Affects the Future Improvement of Society* he advanced the view that the population growth proceeds in geometrical ratio, while subsistence increases only in arithmetical ratio. This means that population tends to outrun the means of existence unless it is checked by war, famine or pestilence. From this theory Malthus drew the conclusion that the progress of mankind would always be hindered by the miseries operating as checks to the natural population growth and that consequently the existing poor-law system was to be condemned as encouraging large families. As his Essay roused a storm of criticism, Malthus, in the second edition, substantiated his theory with abundant statistical material and allowed, in addition to the positive checks of famine and misery, the preventive check of moral restraint (late marriages and sexual continence).

David R i c a r d o, who, as MP and publicist, helped to bring about a change of opinion in favour fo free trade, gave economic liberalism ist classical formulation in his *Principles of Political Economy and Taxation* (1817), which investigated the laws regulating the distribution of the produce of the earth under free competition. Ricardo considerably influenced the economic theories of James and John Stuart Mill.

II. **Utilitarianism:** J a m e s   M i l l , philosopher and economist, was the chief follower of Jeremy Bentham (p. 275) and the most prominent representative of philosophical radicalism. His political writings were influential in bringing about governmental reforms in India and at home (*Reform Bill* of 1832). His utilitarian moral philosophy made the utility of intention the criterion of moral action, the moral man being 'the greatest calculator'. In his philosophical work *Analysis of the Human Mind* he embraced Hartley's associationism (p. 273), which was also followed by the Scottish philosopher, Alexander B a i n , in his *The Senses and the Intellect.*

J o h n   S t u a r t   M i l l (1806–73), the son of James Mill, was one of the most universal 19th-century publicists writing on all questions of human activity as a philosopher, political economist, logician and ethical theorist. John Stuart Mill was carefully educated by his father to carry on the utilitarian tradition, which he formulated in his essay *Utilitarianism.* His *System of Logic, Ratiocinative and Inductive* (1843), which reduced the inductive process of empirical thought to strict logical rules, his *Principles of Political Economy* (1848), *Thoughts on Parliamentary Reform* (1859) and *Considerations on Representative Government* (1860) systematized most important trends of 19th-century thought and made him one of the most influential English thinkers of his age.

A fervent disciple of philosophical Radicalism, John Stuart Mill demanded in his famous *Essay on Liberty* that the individual should have the utmost freedom for development, freedom of thought, speech and action, and that government should be based on laissez-faire: 'Every departure from it, unless required by some great good, is a certain evil'. He therefore had no sympathy with extreme socialist tenets, such as the nationalization of land, and regarded a capitalist society based on free competition as a safeguard against the evils of monopoly. But his growing awareness of the hardships of the labouring classes caused him to plead for their education as the only means of emancipation. His qualified approval of socialist principles made him the chief inspirer of the moderate English form of socialism based on evolution rather than revolution, which was also advocated by the Fabians (p. 83). This attitude also accounts for his plea for the emancipation of women expounded in his *Subjection of Women.* Under the influence of Comte's positivism, Mill applied the empirical method to social science, rejecting Continental a priori philosophy as intellectual support of false doctrines and bad institutions and upholding the sounder tradition of English empiricism as the principle of progress and freedom.

III. **Social Ethics:** John R u s k i n , publicist and later Professor of Art at Oxford, who had acquired a profound aesthetic education through wide travels and studies of European works of art, exercised considerable influence through his writings on art. The *Seven Lamps of Architecture* and *Stones of Venice,* which expressed his conviction that the art of a people reflected their whole national, social and religious attitude, already condemned the social evils of modern industrial society and the degradation of its labouring classes. 'To feel their souls withering within them . . . to be counted off into a heap of mechanism, numbered with its wheels and weighed with its hammer strokes – this nature bade not, this God blesses not.' In his essay *Unto this Last* Ruskin denounced the doctrines of political economy, opposing its materialistic interpretation of the terms value and wealth. 'The real science of political economy . . . is that which teaches nations to desire and labour for the things that lead to life.' Wealth is interpreted as the possession of the valuable by the valiant. 'We need examples of people who, leaving Heaven to decide whether they are to rise in the world, decide for themselves that they will be happy in it and have resolved to seek – not greater wealth, but simpler pleasure; not higher fortune but deeper felicity making the first of possessions, self-possession.'

IV. **Science and Evolutionary Naturalism:** English philosophy in the late 19th century was determined by the great discoveries in physical theory and biology to which the typical English tradition of experimental naturalism, stimulated by the foundation in 1800 of the R o y a l   I n s t i t u t i o n , had in its turn made considerable contributions.

1. PHYSICS: Thomas   Y o u n g , mathematician, Egyptologist and physician, established the wave theory of light and the principle of interference. He found the key to Egyptian hieroglyphics in the Rosetta Stone.

Humphrey   D a v y   founded physical chemistry by applying electrolysis to chemical experiments, which made possible the discovery of many new elements. He invented the miner's safety lamp.

Michael   F a r a d a y   elaborated the principles of electrolysis and, by discovering the law of induction, established electromagnetism, which founded electrical engineering.

J. P. J o u l e investigated the relationship between electrical currents, mechanical force and heat. He developed the doctrine of the conservation and changeability of force (established by Helmholtz) and showed that energy produced by a mechanical or electrical engine is transformed into an equivalent amount of heat.

W. Thomson, Lord K e l v i n , applied the principle of the conservation of force to the system of the universe showing that the sum total of all the energy in the universe remains constant. He developed thermodynamics and invented a tide predictor and instruments essential to underwater telegraphy. He took an active part in laying the Atlantic cable.

J. C. M a x w e l l discovered electromagnetic waves and their relation to light, leading to 20th-century wireless telegraphy, radio and wave mechanics.

2. ORGANIC CHEMISTRY was initiated by Wiliam P e r k i n ' s discovery, at the age of 18, of the first coal-tar dye, which foreshadowed the later development of the synthetic dye and drug industry.

3. MODERN GEOLOGY was founded by two Scotsmen, James H u t t o n and Charles L y e l l , who showed that the earth developed by natural processes such as occur today (erosion etc.). By establishing the great antiquity of the earth, they dethroned the biblical account of creation, and paved the way for the acceptance of Darwin's theory of evolution. The pioneer work of British geologists is reflected in the names of geological periods which are derived from British areas where ancient formations occur (e.g. Cambrian being an ancient name for Wales, Silurian for a Celtic tribe).

4. BIOLOGY: The theory of organic evolution had been advanced in the 18th century by the physician E r a s m u s D a r w i n. But it was left to his grandson C h a r l e s D a r w i n (1809–82) to substantiate it with a mechanical law to account for it, namely the theory of natural selection. Two circumstances contributed to the development of his theory. From 1831–36 he sailed on H.M.S. *Beagle* as a naturalist for a surveying expedition round the world observing in his studies of animal life in South America and the Galapagos Islands that species varied on opposite sides of mountain barriers and on separate islands. In 1838 he read Malthus' *Essay on the Principle of Population,* which not only confirmed his theory of the struggle for existence, but also suggested to him 'that under these circumstances favourable variations would tend to be preserved and unfavourable ones to be destroyed'. This discovery of natural selection was made in the same year by Henry Russell W a l l a c e (after whom the 'Wallace Line', separating the species of Australian and Asian origin, is called). Darwin applied the principle of natural selection even to ethics, believing that the development of morals depended on the question which habits made social units best fit to survive.

Darwin's great work *On the Origin of Species by Means of Natural Selection or the Preservation of Favoured Races in the Struggle for*

Life (1859), which sold out on the day of issue, roused a storm of controversy between Darwin's followers and the upholders of revealed religion, who maintained the special creation of species. The brilliant young biologist, T h o m a s H u x l e y , won a victory for science at Oxford in a heated debate with Bishop Wilberforce, who tried to ridicule Darwin's theory by alluding to his opponent's alleged descent from monkeys. Proving man's affinities with the ape (which was facilitated by the discovery of the Neandertal man), Huxley further developed Darwin's theory in the field of anthropology. He was convinced, however, that Darwin's 'cosmic process' must be checked by 'the ethical process, the end of which is not the survival of those who may happen to be the fittest . . . but of those who are ethically the best.' *(Evolution and Ethics).*

5. PHILOSOPHY: Darwin's principle of evolution inaugurated a new era of thought. The principle of natural selection was applied to political, economic and social phenomena, from competition in private enterprise to class war, and in biology it was integrated with Mendel's genetics to form neo-Darwinism. Together with Newtonian classical physics, evolution constituted the unifying element in Herbert S p e n c e r ' s *Synthetic Philosophy* which sought to systematize the knowledge of the age by co-ordinating all sciences into a uniform system of thought. Spencer held that philosophy could not deal with the absolute, which is beyond the powers of human comprehension, but only with its manifestations. 'The domain left is that occupied by science'. Spencer believed in a rhythm of concentration and dissolution, which is illustrated in every respect from the consolidation of a planet out of a nebulous ring to the organization of modern states. His social works *The Proper Sphere of Government* and *The Principles of Sociology* represent evolution in the social sphere as a process of individuation, which sees the possibility of progress only in complete liberalism.

TWENTIETH CENTURY

Bertrand R u s s e l l ' s philosophical thought ranges from mathematical philosophy to sociological theories comprising ethics, religion, politics and education. The grandson of Lord John Russell (one of the great champions of liberal reforms in the 19th century), Bertrand Russell has become famous chiefly for his championship of individual liberty. In his wireless talks *Authority and the Individual* (1948) he pointed to the importance of preserving personal freedom and initiative in a society ruled by the modern authoritarian state. All ethical ideals, art and science have their roots in the individual.

A fervent pacifist, who was imprisoned during World War I, Russell (who died in 1970) came to the fore as an uncompromising enemy of atomic warfare. The imminent nuclear war can only be averted by a world state, which puts an end to national rivalries. Russell's sceptical pessimism (cf. *Sceptical Essays*) is tempered by his strong belief in ethical values, tolerance and humanitarianism.

His philosophy, decribed by him as 'logical atomism', is based on logical analysis as a method to elaborate ultimate 'atomic facts' logically independent of each other. Similarly, his mathematical philosophy first published in *The Principles of Mathematics* (1903) and demonstrated in detail in the voluminous *Principia Mathematica* written with his friend A. N. Whitehead deduces the whole of pure mathematics from a small number of logical axioms.

In the 20th century Britain has a number of important scientific achievements to its credit.

1. PHYSICS: G. L. Baird developed t e l e v i s i o n (1923), Sir Robert Watson-Watt, r a d a r. Making possible the location of objects, radar was first used by Britain in World War II as an important weapon in naval and aerial warfare.

2. NUCLEAR SCIENCE: Electronics was established by J. J. Thomson's discovery of the e l e c t r o n and by C. T. R. Wilson's invention of the c l o u d c h a m b e r to visualize paths of charged atomic and elementary particles. W. H. Bragg investigated the atomic structure of solid matter by X-ray diffraction. Nuclear science proper was founded by Ernest Rutherford (born in New Zealand), who established the e l e c t r i c a l s t r u c t u r e o f m a t t e r at the Cavendish Laboratory, Cambridge, by explaining the atom as a system of electrons revolving round a charged nucleus analogous to the solar system. The knowledge of the atom build led to the first attempts at a t o m s m a s h i n g by Rutherford. The use of i s o t o p e s was developed at the Energy Research Establishment, Harwell. In 1991 nuclear fusion was developed at Culham (Oxford).

3. BIOLOGY received new impulses from studies fo v i t a m i n s by Sir Frederick Hopkins, of the h e a r t ' s a c t i o n and hormones by E. H. Starling, of the n e r v o u s s y s t e m by Sir Charles Sherrington, and from discoveries of the structure of complex biological molecules.

4. MEDICINE was revolutionized by Sir Alexander Fleming's discovery of p e n i c i l l i n. Fleming received the Nobel prize in medicine in 1945. In 1978 the physicians Patrick Steptoe and Robert Edwards produced the world's first test tube baby conceived outside the mother's womb.

5. ASTRONOMY: A. Eddington's investigation of s p i r a l n e b u l a e and the internal constitution of stars was a great success of astro-physics.

6. ECONOMICS: John Maynard K e y n e s revolutionized economic theories with his work *The General Theory of Employment, Interest and Money* (1936) in which he set forth his theory that depressions and unemployment could only be fought by public investment in public works and a cheap-money policy. His theories divided economists throughout the world into two opposing camps. In the U.S.A. they influenced President F. D. Roosevelt's policies for economic recovery. In the course of time, however, state borrowing and cheap money increased inflation and public indebtedness, giving rise to Milton Friedman's monetarism. Thus, in the 80s, Reagan and Mrs. Thatcher began to pursue a tight-money policy reducing inflation, but keeping unemployment figures high.

7. APPLIED SCIENCES: The need to revitalize industry has encouraged innovative research in many fields. In order to advance information technology, the government allocated millions to fibre-optics and opto-electronics. The technology of transmitting telephone calls through optic fibres, which, in contrast to the conventional copper cables, makes it possible to carry thousands of calls simultaneously, was invented in Britain.
The foundation of genetic engineering was laid by the British Nobel prize winner F. Sanger through his research in molecular biology. The National Research Development Corporation now funds projects on genetic engineering, antibiotics and vaccines, and the potential industrial applications of micro-organisms and enzymes. Thus Britain is making important contributions to biotechnology.
Britain has pioneered laser technology and the technique of fluidized bed combustion claimed to be the most important advance in large-scale coal combustion in the 20th century. The government instituted a programme of work on combined heat and power district heating, which uses the heat discharged to the atmosphere as a by-product of electricity generation.
In a speech at the opening of the Information Technology '82 Conference in London, Mrs Thatcher claimed that British research centres in biochemistry and telecommunications are the envy of the world, that the British are world leaders in fibre optics and in medical scanning with nuclear magnetic resonance, and that Britain's teletext software has been accepted as effectively the world standard. She mentioned that sixty Nobel prize winners have been British.

THE BRITISH COMMONWEALTH

England built up the largest empire in history. Its influence as a colonial power has been stronger and more extended than that of any other colonizing nation. Two continents (North America and Australia/New Zealand) are white and speak the English language. Though the former British colonies are now independent, most of them have not severed the ties that bound them to the mother country and have remained members of the British Commonwealth of Nations. A number of African countries have retained English as their official language. Even in those territories which have left the Commonwealth the economic, political and educational systems still show the influence of English traditions. The British Commonwealth including the dependent territories comprises nearly a quarter of the world's surface and population (over 1,000 million).

Historical Survey

A. FOUNDING OF THE EMPIRE proceeded in three major stages:

I. **Private Initiative** partly backed by the government for economic reasons.

1. EXPLORATION, ADVENTURE, PIRACY (chiefly 16th century): John Cabot discovered Newfoundland in 1498. In the 16th century Raleigh, Hudson, Baffin, Davis, Frobisher explored American waters (p. 36). Drake sank Spanish ships and sailed round the world. Richard Chancellor reached Moscow, sailing northeast via the White Sea. Ralph Fitch reached the Far East overland. John Hawkins carried on slave trade in West Africa.
James Cook discovered Australia and New Zealand in 1770.

2. TRADE, ECONOMIC EXPLOITATION by chartered trading companies:
   a) Eastern countries: Muscovy Company, 1554, Levant Company, 1581, East India Company, 1600.
   b) America: London Company (after settlement of Virginia called Virginia Company), 1606, Massachusetts Bay Company, 1628.
   c) Africa (19th century): Royal Niger Company (1886), East Africa Association (1886), Chartered Company of South Africa (1889).

3. SETTLEMENT (since the 17th century): The British colonies in North America were first settled chiefly by persecuted sects under land grants given either to companies (e.g. Massachusetts Bay Company)

or to individual proprietors (e.g. William Penn). The New England colonies were founded by Puritans, Pennsylvania by Quakers, Maryland by Roman Catholics. Nova Scotia and western Canada (the Great Lakes region) were first settled by British Empire Loyalists immigrating from the rebel colonies at the close of the American Revolution. Large-scale emigration from Britain to Canada, Australia and New Zealand began in the 19th century. North America and Australia/New Zealand are predominantly British-settled.

II. **Conquests and Acquisitions in Wars against European Rivals** (18th century):

1. Jamaica in the war with Spain under Cromwell (1658).

2. New York in the first Dutch war under Charles II (1664).

3. Newfoundland, Nova Scotia, Hudson Bay, Gibraltar in the War of Spanish Succession (1713).

4. Bengal (India), Canada, and the territory between Appalachians and Mississippi in the great Colonial War with France (1763).

5. Dutch and French colonies in the Napoleonic Wars: Cape Colony (1795), Ceylon and Guiana (1796).

III. **Imperialism** in the 19th century pursued a policy of systematically linking the hitherto scattered possessions.

1. ACQUISITION OF STRATEGIC BASES AND TRADING POSTS: Malta (1800), Singapore (1824), Gulf of Aden (1839), Hongkong (1842), purchase of Suez Canal shares (1875), Cyprus (1878).

2. ESTABLISHING OF NEW COLONIES (pp. 78–81):

a) S o u t h   S e a : New Zealand was colonized from 1840 by the New Zealand Company, British Malaya was founded in 1824 as Straits Settlement (chief supplier of rubber and tin). Later acquisitions were British Borneo (1846), Fiji Isles (1874), British New Guinea (1884).

b) A f r i c a :
N i l e   c o u n t r i e s : Egypt was occupied in 1882 to protect the Suez Canal. Sudan, which was first occupied as an Egyptian condominium but was lost as a consequence of a revolt, was finally conquered in 1898. The British administration did much for the economic development of both countries. Cotton culture was made possible by great Nile barrages bringing more land under cultivation.
B r i t i s h   E a s t   A f r i c a : British Somaliland and Socotra were occupied in 1884 and 1886 respectively, to strengthen the route to India. Kenya and Uganda were colonized by the East Africa Association in 1886 and 1890 respectively. Zanzibar

became a British protectorate in 1890. Chief products of the East African colonies were cotton, coffee, sisal.

British West Africa: Sierra Leone was founded in 1787 by humanitarians for liberated slaves. The Gold Coast (now Ghana) was purchased from the Dutch in 1874. Nigeria was colonized from 1886 by the Royal Niger Company. The colony of Gambia was formed in 1888. Products of the West African colonies were cocoa, palm oil and gold (cf. 'Gold Coast').

Central Africa: Rhodesia was acquired in 1888 and colonized by the South Africa Company. Basutoland and Bechuanaland became protectorates in 1884 and 1885 respectively. Nyasaland became the British Central Africa Protectorate in 1893.

South Africa: The Cape, settled by Dutch Boers, had been annexed in 1795. After the trek of discontented Boers to the territories north of the Cape, Natal was annexed by the British in 1843. The Boer republics Transvaal and Orange Free State were conquered in the South African War, 1899–1902 (p. 81).

c) India : Numerous wars brought further Indian territories under British control: Central Provinces (1818), Assam (1826), Sind (1843), Punjab and Kashmir (1846), Burma after three wars in 1885.

IV. **Acquisitions in World War I:** Britain took over conquered territory under mandate from the League of Nations: in Asia Minor the former Turkish dependencies Palestine, Iraq and Trans-Jordan, in Africa German territories: Tanganyika (larger part of German East Africa), and parts of Togoland and the Cameroons.

B. DEVELOPMENT OF COMMONWEALTH through granting of autonomy and equal status.

I. **Original Colonial Governments** (still existing in crown colonies containing subject races):

1. GOVERNOR, representing the Crown, was appointed by and responsible to the Crown (which caused friction with colonial legislative assemblies).

2. EXECUTIVE COUNCIL consisted of nominated officials responsible to the governor, not to the legislative assembly.

3. LEGISLATIVE ASSEMBLY was wholly or partly elected in colonies with European settlers. Colonies with non-white inhabitants had legislative councils mainly nominated by the governor.

II. **Representative Responsible Governments,** advocated by Lord Durham, who had investigated the causes of revolts in Canada, were established in colonies with large white populations. The executive council was no longer appointed in England, but chosen from the prevailing party in the colonial assembly and responsible to the assembly.

III. **Dominion Status** gave the colonies with large white populations full internal sovereignty. Dominions took over defence, taxation, and imposed tariffs even on British imports to protect their young industries. The Governor-General was still appointed from London, but had to sign all bills of the Dominion Parliament provided they did not conflict with treaties between Britain and foreign powers. Dominion status was granted to Canada (1867), Australia (1900), New Zealand (1907), the South African Union (1910), Ireland (1922). Most non-white dependencies gained dominion status after World War II.

IV. **Equal Status** chiefly following military support of the motherland in World War I:

1. Since 1887 colonies were represented at Imperial Conferences, today Commonwealth Conferences, meeting at regular intervals.

2. Dominions had their own diplomatic representations at the Peace Conference of Versailles, 1919. They signed the peace treaty separately and received mandates (Union of South Africa: German South-West Africa; Australia: German New Guinea). They became independent voting members of the League of Nations, thus able to outvote the mother country.

3. Independent foreign policy through diplomatic representation in foreign countries and power to conclude separate agreements determined by regional interests, e.g. economic and defence treaties between Canada and the U.S.A. and ANZUS (treaty between Australia, New Zealand and the U.S.A. 1951).

4. Imperial Conference, 1926, established unity without centralization: Dominions were defined as 'autonomous communities within the British Empire, equal in status, in no way subordinate one to another in any respect of their domestic and external affairs, though united by a common allegiance to the Crown and freely associated as members of the British Commonwealth of Nations'.

5. *The Statute of Westminster,* 1931, confirmed the sovereignty of dominions and established the Crown as the only remaining constitutional link between Commonwealth countries.

6. Imperial preference adopted at the Ottawa Conference, 1932: In commerce, Commonwealth countries instituted mutual preference against foreign competitors (later one of the important handicaps against British association with the European Economic Community).

7. Voluntary cooperation in World War II: The overseas Empire contributed fifty per cent of the total British armed forces and ten per cent of all munitions.

C. DISINTEGRATION OF EMPIRE

1. IRELAND became a republic in 1937 and severed her last links with Britain and the Commonwealth in 1949.

2. MIDDLE EAST: I r a q and Trans-Jordan (now J o r d a n) were soon granted virtual independence under native sovereigns with British advisers headed by a British High Commissioner and Resident.
In P a l e s t i n e increasing Jewish immigration under the Balfour Declaration, 1917, which had promised the Zionists Palestine as a national home, caused friction with the native Arabs. After World War II Britain, trying to stop Jewish immigration, was forced by riots on both sides to submit the issue to the U.N. When the U.N. had approved a partition plan, troops of the Arab League attacked the Jews, but were defeated. In 1948 the Jews proclaimed the state of Israel. A smaller part of Palestine, which remained Arab, was united with Jordan. A d e n and the S o u t h A r a b i a n F e d e r a t i o n of South Arabian sheikdoms became independent in 1967 and 1971 respectively.

3. ASIA: B u r m a , separated from British India in 1937, became independent in 1947. P a k i s t a n left the Commonwealth in 1972.

4. AFRICA: E g y p t , nominally independent since 1922, remained under partial military occupation and was an important strategic base of British forces in World War II. After 1945, vigorous agitation for evacuation of the Suez Canal led to occasional revolts. Upon the withdrawal of British troops in 1956, Egypt nationalized the Suez Canal.
S u d a n obtained self-government in 1953 with the right to determine its political status after three years. In 1956 Sudan left the Commonwealth.
S o m a l i l a n d became the Republic of Somalia and left the Commonwealth in 1961.
The U n i o n o f S o u t h A f r i c a left the Commonwealth in 1961 upon censure of the South African apartheid policy (racial segregation) by other Commonwealth countries.

5. For colonies gaining independence but remaining members of the Commonwealth see p. 292.

The British Commonwealth
and Dependent Territories Today

A. THE BRITISH COMMONWEALTH OF NATIONS

The British Commonwealth of Nations is a voluntary community of 50 independent nations with a combined population of over 1,000 million. The

Commonwealth Relations Office in London has no jurisdiction in Commonwealth countries but acts mainly as a liaison agency. The original link between the member countries was common allegiance to the Crown. The major white Commonwealth countries – Canada, Australia and New Zealand – are still parliamentary monarchies under the British Crown, which is represented by the Governor-General, who is appointed on the advice of the government concerned. In most Asian and African member countries, however, the monarchy and the British parliamentary system have gradually been replaced by presidential democracies tending towards dictatorship. Today the majority of these nations are republics. The Community of the Commonwealth countries is partly based on historical tradition (most members being former British colonies) and partly on racial and cultural ties. The white English-speaking countries, Canada, Australia and New Zealand, still regarding themselves as belonging to a larger family of nations, gave voluntary support to the motherland in World War II with troops and supplies. In most cases political and economic interests are at issue – defence treaties, preferential tariffs and aid for economic development, which was liberally granted in the postwar period.

In all Commonwealth countries English is still a language understood and spoken by all educated people and generally used in commercial transaction. Some African countries have retained it as the official language. The judicial systems of most Commonwealth countries are based on English Common Law, and the final court of appeal is the Judicial Committee of the Privy Council, in which decisions may depend on precedents evolved in Commonwealth countries. The Commonwealth Conference usually held in London, which meets approximately every two years, unites all Commonwealth prime ministers but cannot make decisions binding any of its members to a common policy. There are still British forces stationed at some Commonwealth bases, and Britain has officer training facilities for Commonwealth personnel. Thus Africans and Asians have come to adopt the rituals of the British military, just as their elites like to adopt the habits of their former rulers. Thousands of British teachers teach in Commonwealth countries, which account for almost 50% of all overseas students in Britain. But restrictions on the immigration of Commonwealth citizens into Britain and abolition of aid to foreign students have begun to strain relations with the countries concerned. Moreover, accession of Britain to the EEC affects trade relations with the Commonwealth countries, which had enjoyed preferential treatment since 1932.

The nations forming the British Commonwealth are listed below with their former names and dates of independence.

1. White countries: B r i t a i n, C a n a d a 1867, A u s t r a l i a 1900, N e w Z e a l a n d 1907, C y p r u s 1961, M a l t a 1964.

2. Asian countries: India 1947, Sri Lanka (Ceylon) 1948, Malaysia (Malaya, North Borneo, Sarawak) 1963, Singapore 1965, Bangladesh 1972, Brunei 1984.
3. Western Pacific: Nauru 1968, Western Samoa, Tonga and Fiji Isles 1970, Papua New Guinea 1975, Solomon Islands 1978, Tuvula (Ellice Islands) 1978, Kiribati (Gilbert Islands) 1979, Vanuatu (New Hebrides) 1980.
4. Indian Ocean: Mauritius 1968, Seychelles 1976.
5. Caribbean Isles: Jamaica and Trinidad-Tobago 1962, Barbados 1966, Bahamas 1973, Grenada 1974, Dominica 1978, St. Lucia 1979, St. Vincent 1979, Antigua and Barbuda 1981, St. Christopher-Nevis 1983.
6. Central America: Belize (British Honduras) 1981.
7. South America: Guyana (British Guiana) 1966.
8. Africa: Ghana 1957, Nigeria 1961, Sierra-Leone 1961, Uganda 1962, Kenya 1963, Malawi (Nyasaland) 1964, Zambia (Northern Rhodesia) 1964, Tanzania (Tanganyika, independent since 1961, united with Zanzibar in 1964), Gambia 1965, Botswana (Basutoland) and Lesotho (Bechuanaland) 1966, Ngwane (Swaziland) 1968, Zimbabwe 1980.

The CW countries have had their share of the problems of developing countries. In Asia, Bangladesh, which emerged as an independent country after a bloody rebellion against Pakistan, is, apart from disostrous floods, beset by the same problems that haunt its neighbour, India: mismanagement and appalling poverty among the masses.

In Africa, Nigeria was torn by a murderous civil war between the rebellious province of Biafra and the central government, in which thousands died as a result of violence and starvation. In Uganda, the terror regime of Idi Amin drove thousands of Ugandan Asians to Britain, increasing racial problems there. Amin's fall through military intervention from Tanzania did not solve Uganda's economic and social problems.

Rhodesia, which had declared unilateral independence from Britain and delayed giving the large black majority a share in the government, was long haunted by guerilla warfare. In regions where most of the clashes occurred, the black population was confined in villages behind barbed wire. In 1969 the prime minister, Ian Smith, even asked South Africa to send police troops to fight the 'terrorists'. When finally, in 1980, the independent state of Zimbabwe emerged, internal strife flared up again, this time between warring black groups.

The Caribbean island of Grenada was stirred in 1983 by a communist coup, which was suppressed by US troops under President Reagan.

B. DEPENDENT TERRITORIES

The few remaining dependencies (crown colonies and protectorates) are ruled from London by the Colonial Office. Their inhabitants have the status of British subjects but are not members of the United Kingdom.

The chief remaining dependencies are:

1. Mediterranean: Gibraltar.
2. Atlantic: St. Helena, Ascension, Bermuda, Falkland Islands
3. Carribbean dependencies: British Virgin Islands, Anguilla, Montserrat; Turks and Caicos Islands; Cayman Islands.
4. Western Pacific: Pitcairn
5. China: Hong Kong
6. British Antarctic Territory and British Indian Ocean Territory

The survival of parts of an empire may seem an anachronism in an age of anti-colonialism. Britain still has dependencies with a total population of 5.2 million, ranging from c.5 million in Hong Kong to 61 descendants of the mutinous crew of the Bounty on the Pitcairn Islands. Although responsibility for these territories, many of which are small islands offering no economic advantages, has become a burden to a country itself beset by economic problems, many of them resent becoming independent because they fear absorption by stronger neighbours.

Thus, in 1977, the Falkland Islands, a group of two hundred islands near the southern tip of South America, which were claimed by Argentina, demonstrated in favour of British rule, being apprehensive of the régime of terror in Argentina, and the possible introduction of Spanish as a national language. In 1982 the Falklands were occupied by Argentine troops, but were reconquered by a British fleet within 50 days (p. 113).

In Gibraltar (British colony since 1714) a referendum in 1967 brought 12,138 votes in favour of British rule as against 44 in favour of Spain.

Hong Kong will return to China in 1997. The Sino-British Treaty of 1984 contains safeguards for fifty years, which, it is hoped, will prevent the subjection of the Hong Kong people to a very different regime and allow their dynamic economy to continue. The islands in the Pacific (where Chines ships cruise in ever increasing numbers) would enjoy a precarious state of freedom.

In British Honduras (now independent Belize) Britain doubled its garrison to ward off the threat of on invasion from Guatemala. But a Foreign Office spokesman remarked: 'We can't go on doing that. Gunboat diplomacy days are over.' It is an irony of history that even the descendants of the Bounty crew, which rebelled against a cruel English commander, feel that their freedom is best guaranteed under British rule, although Britain would be prepared to cede the Pitcairn Islands to Australia.

All this indicates that freedom, readily granted according to modern political principles, may again be threatened by the national ambitions of larger countries – thought by the postwar generation to be a thing of the past.

English-speaking Commonwealth Countries

CANADA

Size: Canada is the world's s e c o n d l a r g e s t c o u n t r y : its east-west extension is 5,780 miles, the north-south extension 2,850 miles.

Provinces: Canada is divided into t e n p r o v i n c e s (with self-government) and t w o t e r r i t o r i e s (ruled by the federal government).

1. NEWFOUNDLAND including the island of Newfoundland and the coast of Labrador.
2. MARITIME PROVINCES: Prince Edward Island, Nova Scotia, New-Brunswick.
3. CENTRAL PROVINCES: Quebec (earliest French colony, with a large minority in favour of independence), Ontario (the richest province with the largest population and chief mineral and industrial production).
4. PRAIRIE PROVINCES: Manitoba, Saskatchewan, Alberta.
5. PACIFIC PROVINCE: British Columbia.
6. TERRITORIES: North West Territory, Yukon.

Climate: The South is temperate, the North is arctic. The east coast is cold because of the Labrador current, the Pacific coast is moderated by a warm Japanese current. The prairies have a continental climate with extreme temperatures.

Physical Geography and Land Use: Chief physical regions from east to west are: the level *Canadian Shield,* which is rich in forests and minerals; the *Great Lakes-St. Lawrence lowlands;* the *prairies,* rich, level wheat land, and the *Cordilleran Belt* consisting of two parallel ranges, the Rockies and Coast Ranges with the Interior Upland in between. The east provinces have thin glacial soil with fertile loam pockets used for diversified farming. Newfoundland has poor soil but large forests and rich fishing grounds. The *Canadian North,* practically uninhabited, is now being opened up by railroads and airlines only for mining without permanent settlement because agriculture on marginal land is no longer competitive. Fur production sustains almost the whole population.

Economy: Canada is beside Britain the leading industrial country of the Commonwealth, though only one third of its total area has hitherto been brought under development.

AGRICULTURE: Farmland occupies 8 per cent of Canada's total land area; 4 per cent are under cultivation. *Wheat* is grown in the prairie provinces, which, however, are not as productive as the U.S. Wheat Belt because of a shorter growing season. Commercial centre is Winnipeg. *Dairying* is carried on in Newfoundland and Nova Scotia, *beef cattle* are reared in southern Alberta and Saskatchewan, where frosts endanger crops. *Fruit* is grown on the Great Lakes. Intensive mixed farming (oats, hay, dairy farming) is found in the St. Lawrence lowlands and the maritime provinces (especially the fertile Prince Edward Island).

FORESTS occupying one third of the land area are the chief reserves of *softwood timber* of the British Commonwealth though only 65 per cent of the productive forested land is accessible. The tallest and most valuable stands are on the west coast. Much of Canadian wood is turned into paper and wood pulp. Forest products account for 28 per cent of the total export.

FISHERIES are very extensive along the Pacific coast (chiefly *salmon*) and the Newfoundland Bank, the world's most important *cod* fishing ground. *Lobster* fisheries of the maritime provinces are the largest in the world.

WATER POWER: Canada is the world's second largest producer of hydro-electricity after the U.S.A. Innumerable lakes and streams with rapids and waterfalls (esp. Niagara Falls) facilitate the generation of water power. Major resources are the St. Lawrence River system and the mountains of British Columbia. Gigantic model power plants in the Cordilleras (e.g. Kitimat) and on the St. Lawrence have made Canada the leading country for aluminium production.

MINERALS are very rich and varied. Canada is the world's biggest producer of *nickel, zinc* and *asbestos*. The St. Lawrence Valley produces 70 per cent of the world's asbestos; the nickel mine at Sudbury, Ontario, still supplies 50 per cent of the world production, formerly 90 per cent (now finds in Manitoba). Canada ranks second in *silver* and *uranium*, third in gold and platinum. The Hollinger mine in Ontario is the world's third largest gold mine. New beds of *uranium* discovered on Blind River, Lake Huron, promise to become the world's richest uranium source. *Radium* on Great Bear Lake depends on air transport. Production of great industrial minerals has considerably increased in recent years, Canada being so far the leading *oil* producer of the Commonwealth. A big *iron ore* mine in Labrador already supplements the decreasing supply of Mesabi Range, U.S.A. Prospecting and production are difficult because of the inaccessibility of vast regions (huge forests, no transport).

INDUSTRY, favoured by water power, mineral wealth, and the proximity to U.S. coal, ranks first among Commonwealth countries. Ontario and Quebec account for 80 per cent of all manufactures, but British Columbia and the Prairie Provinces are developing rapidly. Chief manufactures are wood pulp and paper, meat packing, metal smelting and refining, petroleum products, motor vehicles. The U.S.A. has large interests in Canadian industry, esp. in aluminium production.

TRADE: Canada ranks fifth in world trade after the U.S.A., the U.K., West Germany and France. By far the most important trading partner is Canada's continental neighbour, the U.S.A., followed by Japan, Britain and Venezuela.

a) *Exports* are machines, vehicles, oil, wheat (ranking second after the U.S.A.), minerals (aluminium, nickel, zinc, copper, asbestos), and forest products (including wood pulp and newsprint). Canada is the world's biggest exporter of timber.

b) *Imports*, chiefly from the U.S.A., include machinery, raw materials for textile production, coal, sugar, coffee.

TRANSPORT is made difficult by the uneven distribution of the population: chief traffic is in the Southeast; 72 per cent of the North is scarcely reached by railways. The two continental railroads are the Canadian Pacific (private) and Canadian National (government-owned). The two airlines are Air Canada (government-owned) and the Canadian Pacific. The *Alaska Highway* built during World War II, helps to open the North. Water transport is hampered by ice in winter. The main water route is the 2,300-mile *St. Lawrence Seaway* (completed in 1959) made navigable for ocean-going ships. River transport is carried on also on the Mackenzie and Yukon Rivers. Coastal shipping is favoured by deeply indented coasts and good harbours.

Population: Canada has 26,9 million inhabitants according to the estimate of 1982. The 1966 census showed 20 million. The population is unevenly distributed: the southern parts of Ontario and Quebec contain 65 per cent of the population, the Prairie Provinces are expanding rapidly, Yukon is almost uninhabited (0.2 per cent). The two chief nationalities, the B r i t i s h (44.6 per cent) und the F r e n c h (28.7 per cent, but with a higher birthrate) form two distinct groups, separated by religion and language. The French, chiefly rural, are concentrated in the province of Quebec (80 per cent), which has preserved its French colonial tradition and separate institutions (e.g. schools). Industrialization, however, attracts the younger people to British urban and industrial centres, where they are assimilated. I n d i a n s

(367,810) live in reservations, E s k i m o s (25,390) are mostly fishermen and hunters living north of the tree line. While their numbers are steadily decreasing, the C h i n e s e and B l a c k s are on the increase.

Religion: C a t h o l i c s, chiefly French, constitute 47 per cent of the population. They are usually educated in denominational schools separated from Protestants. P r o t e s t a n t s (chiefly British) split into several denominations.

Government: Canada is a parliamentary monarchy with a federal constitution. Parliament consists of the House of Commons, elected for five years, and the Senate. In 1982 a new constitution established the government's full independence of Britain.

Cities: In the east Montreal, Toronto, Quebec, Ottawa (the capital); in the west Winnipeg (export centre for wheat), Calgary (business centre of the oil province Alberta), Vancouver (the main Pacific port).

AUSTRALIA

Political Organization: The Commonwealth of Australia is a parliamentary monarchy with a federal constitution. It consists of six states – Queensland, New South Wales, Victoria, Tasmania, South Australia, Western Australia – and the Northern Territory, and has a number of dependencies in the Indian and Pacific Oceans.
Its legislature is modelled on the American pattern. Parliament consists of a House of Representatives, which is elected every three years from the population as a whole, and a Senate, which represents the six states. The 60 senators (10 from each state) are elected for a term of six years, one half of the Senate being reconstituted every three years.

Situation: Australia is the most i s o l a t e d c o n t i n e n t. It was therefore the last to be settled by whites (at first only convicts).

Morphology: The continent is a c o m p a c t l a n d m a s s with a moderately high plateau in the West and, in the East, the folded mountains of the Great Dividing Range with lowlands between.

Climate is Australia's greatest handicap. The interior, 'the dead heart of the continent' is mainly desert because of the eastern mountain barrier. The North is t r o p i c a l, the South s u b t r o p i c a l. The Southeast has the most favourable climate owing to sufficient rainfall through trade winds ('the roaring forties'). The north coast is swept by hot and unhealthy monsoons.

Population: The country's total population is 17 million. *Europeans* constitute 98%, *Aborigines* 1.6%, *Orientals*, mostly Chinese, 0,07%. But immigration from the Orient has increased since immigration laws were liberalized in 1973.

1. E m p t y   c o n t i n e n t : Until 1973 immigration of Orientals was prevented by rigorous exclusion laws caused by the fear of competitive labour coming from densely populated Asia. In 1973 Australia abandoned its racially discriminatory policies.

2. U r b a n i z a t i o n : 50 per cent of the population lives in the six biggest cities.

Livestock: Australia is the l e a d i n g   w o o l   c o u n t r y.

Sheep: Australia has 154 million sheep, 80 per cent merinos (only for wool), 20 per cent cross-breeds for meat and wool. The very dry land only supports e x t e n s i v e   g r a z i n g. An average 'station' has c. ten thousand sheep managed by three to four men and itinerant seasonal shearers.

Cattle (33 million) are reared in the moist sections: dairy cows in the Southeast near the chief markets, beef cattle in the Northeast.

Arable farming occupies only 1 per cent of the land.

Wheat is the dominant crop. It is grown chiefly in the Southeast, west of the Great Dividing Range (moderate rainfall). Other crops are *oats* and *barley* in South Australia and Western Australia, *maize* in New South Wales, *cotton* in the subtropical and cane *sugar* in the tropical climate of the northeast coast, *citrus fruits* in South Australia.

Minerals are not abundant but varied. Most important is gold, followed by coal and uranium (about one fifth of the world's known deposits). The chief gold mines are in the desert (Coolgardie and Kalgoorlie). One of the world's most valuable silverlead-zinc deposits is the Broken Hill mine, New South Wales. *Iron ore* in South and Western Australia has become the basis of an efficient steel industry. *Uranium* is found in Radium Hill, New South Wales, and Rum Jungle near the north coast.

Industries: iron, steel, textiles, chemicals, aircraft, ships, machinery.

Exports: Australia is a leading exporter of wheat, meat and wool. Other exports are sugar, iron ore, lead, zinc, uranium, machinery and vehicles.

Economic problems:

P e s t s : Rabbits and kangaroos eat the sparse grass.

Great d i s t a n c e s increase transport costs and prices.

Exclusion of competition by highly organized labour impairs efficiency (Australia was the earliest welfare state).

Cities lie chiefly in the earliest settled and most populated East and South. The federal capital C a n b e r r a (191,900 inhabitants) is a 'planned', beautifully laid-out city in a separate federal district. The state capitals are Sydney (3.3 million) in New South Wales with a capacious harbour; Melbourne (2.8 million) in Victoria, Brisbane, Queensland; Adelaide, South Australia; Perth, Western Australia; Hobart, Tasmania; Darwin, Northern Territory. Important steel cities are Newcastle and Port Kembla, New South Wales.

NEW ZEALAND

Situation: 1,200 miles southeast of Australia.

Physical Features: Two islands, stretching southwest to northeast, are occupied by high mountain ranges (called Alps in the South Island). Great scenic beauty: the North Island has volcanoes and and hot sulphur springs, the South Island glaciers and fjords.

Climate: New Zealand has one of the world's most favourable and temperate island climes with abundant rainfall.

Population: Europeans (3.4 million) constitute 90 per cent of the population, Maoris, an intelligent, brave native population with a high birthrate, 8.9%. The Maoris are the only native population in the British Commonwealth with equality of status, at least in theory. Orientals are largely excluded (0.5 per cent). New Zealand has one of the world's highest living standards.

Economy is predominantly pastoral. The warm temperature allows outdoor grazing throughout the year. Two thirds of the surface are suitable for agriculture. One third is forested and provides timber.
Cattle (9.6 million) are reared chiefly in the North Island.
Sheep (57 million) are kept to supply meat as well as wool. New Zealand is the world's third producer of wool.
Wheat is grown only for home consumption. It has a higher yield per acre than anywhere in the southern hemisphere, but is increasingly superseded by sheep farming, wool and lamb being more profitable for long-distance export.
MINERALS: oil, gas, gold, iron, coal.
EXPORTS: Pastoral products constitute the greater part of exports. New Zealand's chief exports are meat and meat preparations followed by wool, butter and wood products.

Cities: Wellington (393,982) is the capital because of its central position on the Cook Straits between the two islands. Auckland, with 829,519 inhabitants the biggest city, has a busy overseas trade.

Political Organization: New Zealand is a parliamentary monarchy. The General Assembly has one chamber – the House of Representatives – where the Maoris hold 4 out of 97 seats. New Zealand's dependency, the Cook Islands, has home rule.

INDEX

Please note the following for the use of the index:
1. All acts, cathedrals, churches (chapels), rebellions, treaties and wars are listed under one reference respectively.
2. Acts, rebellions, treaties, wars are to be found in chronological order.
3. In the case of a chart, the number of the page is printed in italics.

303

310

311

313

320

322

323